Sustainable Development in a Globalized World

Also edited by Björn Hettne

HUMAN VALUES AND GLOBAL GOVERNANCE

Sustainable Development in a Globalized World

Studies in Development, Security and Culture

Volume 1

Edited by

Björn Hettne

First published in 2008 by
PALGRAVE MACMILLAN
Houndmills, Basingstoke, Hampshire RG21 6XS and
175 Fifth Avenue, New York, N.Y. 10010
Companies and representatives throughout the world.

PALGRAVE MACMILLAN is the global academic imprint of the Palgrave
Macmillan division of St. Martin's Press, LLC and of Palgrave Macmillan Ltd.
Macmillan® is a registered trademark in the United States, United Kingdom
and other countries. Palgrave is a registered trademark in the European
Union and other countries.

ISBN-13: 978–0–230–55127–5 hardback
ISBN-10: 0–230–55127–0 hardback

This book is printed on paper suitable for recycling and made from fully
managed and sustained forest sources. Logging, pulping and manufacturing
processes are expected to conform to the environmental regulations of
the country of origin.

A catalogue record for this book is available from the British Library.

A catalog record for this book is available from the Library of Congress.

10   9   8   7   6   5   4   3   2   1
17 16 15 14 13 12 11 10 09 08

Printed and bound in Great Britain by
CPI Antony Rowe, Chippenham and Eastbourne

In memory of Karl Eric Knutsson

Contents

Editor's Preface: Development, Security and Culture

Björn Hettne

This book, focussing on *sustainable development in a globalized world*, together with a companion volume on *human values and global govern-ance*, is the final outcome of six years' work of the 'Sector Committee on Culture, Security and Sustainable Social Development' within Riksbankens Jubileumsfond. This preface, providing an overall frame-work for the work, elaborates on the original programmatic text devel-oped as a platform for the committee.[1] The purpose of that text was to present the genesis and scientific context of 'culture, security and devel-opment' and to discuss how the current meaning of these concepts has been influenced by what has become known as 'globalization'. Our point of departure was that the concepts should constitute an interre-lated, albeit complex, research area with a focus on development and security in a cultural perspective. In the course of our work since the group was constituted in the year 2000, certain additional themes have imposed themselves through global events, in particular September 11th and the subsequent theme of terrorism, as well as intellectual encoun-ters experienced by the group on visits in South Africa, Egypt and Brazil, actualizing issues such as reconciliation, dialogue among cultures and democratization as particular foci within the general theme. All this together, constituting the learning process of the group, forms the framework of the two books.

The ambition was thus to see how the three concepts could relate to one another, after each of them had been individually examined in the perspective of globalization. They are all good examples of 'essentially contested concepts' in the sense that there are a number of different and not always mutually consistent definitions of them, plus the fact that their meanings necessarily change over time, particularly at times of transformation.[2] This is what justifies historical specification and sensitivity to contextual discourses.[3] It is fascinating to study changes in the meaning of such contested definitions, since they reflect an under-lying transformation of society about which we have but partial know-ledge. That applies in particular in the case when the transformation is

of a qualitative nature, that is to say, a perceived change in the fundamental social structure and the social rationality which lies behind it.

How can one know that a structural change with such dramatic ontological consequences is taking place? A reasonable method is to study
what happens to the constituent principles of the system which is
undergoing change. As regards the Westphalian states system and its
basic unit, the nation-state, these principles comprise territorialism,
sovereignty and centralized authority (based on different forms of
legitimacy).[4] If these principles, albeit being social constructions, are
undergoing change, we can reasonably subscribe to the view that a
more fundamental structural change is actually taking place. The fact
that the institutional forms of the nation-state remain in place does not
imply any high degree of continuity in a situation in which the transnational context is changing and the cohesion of the nation-state is
breaking up. This particular institution's historic role has changed irreversibly, but some of its functions may nevertheless remain and be
taken over by other types of structures.

In the case of the nation-state, its historical efficiency has above all
rested on its military capacity which was largely forgotten during the
Cold War and the bilateral world order, stabilized by balance of terror
(mutually assured destruction). After September 11th and the global
war against terrorism the coercive and military role of nation-states in
general, and the US in particular, has again become more visible, coun-
tering previous post-sovereign tendencies linked to human rights and
'human' or 'liberal' intervention undertaken in correspondence with
changing praxis of international law.[5] Whether this imperialist trend
contradicts globalization or should be seen as a new, more coercive,
militarized form of globalization is a matter of definition.[6]

The analysis that follows is divided into three parts: metatheoretical
reflections, discursive analysis of the three concepts, and a discussion of
some crucial themes and research areas suggested by the framework. To
propose new research areas and facilitate organizational ways of doing
interdisciplinary research were the main purposes of the committee.[7]

Metatheoretical reflections

The renaissance which has taken place over the last two decades in the
theory of culture has a definite link with the equally strong interest in
'globalization'. It is thus the consequences of globalization, or what we
here call 'the globalized condition', which have given the concepts a
partly new meaning, which in turn justifies new research into the post-

national, post-sovereign or post-Westphalian society. Therefore it is impossible to avoid a discussion also of the ontological dimension of globalization.[8]

Ontology of globalization

There is still a lack of clarity about the concept of globalization, even a debate about whether globalization really exists. This discussion does not seem very relevant however. Something has certainly happened, and then the debate is about whether this is to be called globalization or not, which in turn has to do with how the concept is defined. Communications between certain places throughout the world are virtually instantaneous (compression of the world in terms of space and time), with no significant barriers between societies previously considered as more or less separately demarcated national and local arenas. The world at large is felt to have shrunk and to be omnipresent. The world economy is integrated and the autonomy of national economies is diminished. Common ecological conditions have created a planetary existential problem for mankind. From a cultural perspective globalization is more complex giving birth to hybrid forms. Cultural phenomena which previously were more geographically limited are now to be found throughout the world, often in new and very innovative hybrid combinations.

The question whether globalization is something new or old is also basically a matter of definition.[9] It is widely held that globalization means something more profound than internationalization, by which is meant merely an increase in the contacts between national societies, whereas globalization defines a growing transnational arena in which limited nation-state control operates and where players other than state players assert themselves. It further binds together a large number of players at different levels of society, including various sub-national levels, for example, micro-regions and local communities. It can perhaps be said that the criterion for the fact that we are faced with globalization rather than internationalization is precisely the impact on local society, as well as that local society in itself thereby comes to form part of globalization ('glocalization').

A third major debate concerns whether globalization, seen from a normative point of view, is a good or bad thing. This depends on how different individuals and groups are affected, and we can with great certainty maintain that they are affected differently. Globalization reduces the space for action by the nation-state. In consequence the state functions less and less as a protector of its 'own' population, and instead more and more as a medium for signals from the world market: structural adaptation and cutbacks on welfare.[10] This perceived 'betrayal' alienates the state from society, diminishes its legitimacy in the eyes of segments of its own population. In collapsing states the nation-state order is replaced by all kinds of local leaders, including warlords, a situation which recalls the Middle Ages. There is nothing determined by nature in a process of globalization which also unleashes anti-modern counter-movements, for example, in the form of neo-nationalism and religious fundamentalism. This, finally, implies that globalization must be thought of in the plural.[11]

Epistemological observations

This ontological transformation – the globalization of the world – suggests certain epistemological observations. The scope of the question of understanding goes wider than methodology. It is also a matter of the epistemological consequences of the globalized condition.[12] Many theorists of globalization have dwelt on the question of the compression of the world in terms of time and space. Contemporaneity in social relations and liberation from the limitations of space obviously affect identity formation and the experience of belonging, in ways which as yet can scarcely be glimpsed.[13] Epistemologically, globalization has been linked with various anti-rationalistic tendencies, which can be as dissimilar to one another as fundamentalism and post-modernism, at the same time as globalization has been seen as a consequence of modernity.[14]

In the first place, the time is now ripe to take globalization as a given point of departure, rather than to dwell on the question of what globalization actually is, as if it were a newly discovered botanical species. Globalization can instead be regarded as the new 'condition' in which all social science research must be formulated, which implies qualitatively new premises in the theory of knowledge, roughly what was earlier discussed as 'paradigm shifts'.[15] In this perspective 'normal science' no longer functions as an organizing principle for the formation of knowledge. There is a natural link between stability in a social structure, and the researcher's ability to make forecasts and to construct stringent models. If representations of society in the form of theories and models do not satisfactorily explain the course of events, it is time to strive for observing reality without preconceptions, that is to say, to try to determine its historical specificity. The focus should be on the new reality per se, rather than the relatively abstract problem of the meaning of globalization. The problem is that reality is changing faster than the scientific tools to which we have for a long time been accustomed.

That applies to all three areas of research in point. There has been an upsurge in *cultural research*, directly linked with the equally rapidly increasing interest in globalization, the more complex manifestations of which are concerned precisely with the cultural sphere. In *security research* it is a question of the changed role of the nation-state and the emergence of both new identities and new threat images, that is to say, a broader concept of security and risk. In the field of *development research*, globalization implies that the traditional arena of the development expert, the national arena and the 'national development strategy' which is connected to it, is disappearing. Together these fields form part of what is often referred to as 'global studies'.

Secondly, the holistic ideal of research implied by this, the whole as something more than its parts (and parts understood in relation to the whole), deserves a revival.[16] It can, however, also be asked whether holism is really an adequate concept in the globalized social condition, characterized by networks, interaction, flows and 'hybridity'. Nowadays, the concept *complexity* is more often used in connection with analysis of globalization, but with a partly different meaning than the older concept of holism, which usually referred to territorially based and defined cultural systems, in which an analysis of the whole was considered theoretically meaningful and empirically feasible.[17] Can complexity perhaps be seen as the globalized, supra-territorial condition's counterpart to holism?[18]

Thirdly, it appears desirable, indeed necessary, that the relevant research tasks should be organized on an interdisciplinary basis, a point which is closely connected with the holistic ideal of research (or, if you wish, the ambition to take complexity seriously). It should, however, be the research problem which governs what combination of scientific specialities is appropriate. A truly interdisciplinary approach presupposes a combination of specialist and generalist competences which take a long time to acquire. Therefore it is important to give priority to cooperation between subject areas and facilitate more profound cooperation between different scientific specialities. At the same time, the increasing prevalence of collapsing societies in different parts of the world justifies greater interest in the fundamental matters of political philosophy and classical sociology (what makes society possible?), questions that were posed long before the present disciplinary specialization.

We should also, *fourthly*, encourage research at a metatheoretical level, in order better to understand the new ontology created by globalization. It is a matter not only of making the research landscape more

complete, but also of being able (with the aid of appropriate methodological tools) to comprehend fundamental changes in the economic,
social, political, and cultural landscapes. In addition to these two ambitions, there is the need for the analysis of society to reflect a new global
reality, for which we still lack an adequate scientific language, since
ontological changes have epistemological consequences. The social science language is at present far too related to a nation-state reality (methodological nationalism) and to what happens in a national arena (the
container theory). The point is to change perspectives from society as
contained in the nation-state to society as an emerging transnational
phenomenon, which is hard to describe with the tools that current
social science, confined by methodological nationalism, provides.[19]

Pluralism in research has come to stay. Postmodern theory has shown
with some success how reality can be represented by symbols and models
that are not immediately inter-subjective, but instead carry matters
forward by means of an exchange of opinions or dialogue between
observers, in which greater insight emerges in the form of a growing
consensus, or at least mutual understanding. In a situation of metatheoretical uncertainty an open dialogue oriented standpoint methodology
is important. In certain respects this can perhaps be compared with a
multicultural dialogue between different social groups in society. The
perception that disagreement on the definitions of fundamental concepts in the field of human or cultural studies is an obstacle to research
and progress, rather than a natural state of affairs, builds on a false view
of the formation of concepts and of their role (Åhlberg 1995). Despite
this legitimate programmatic openness we cannot avoid discussions
about definitions of the three concepts, but it must be made quite clear
that we regard the different definitions as alternative angles of approach
and not as something which is intended to lock future research into an
altogether too fixed framework.

According to the postmodern view there is no given 'out there', at
least, nothing that we can for certain (scientifically) know anything
about. That makes it even more difficult to assert the existence of distinct researchable relations between the three concepts. We must therefore somehow relate to this dilemma. A reasonable approach has been
suggested by Fredrik Barth (1987: 87):

> I assume that there is a real world out there, but that our representa-
> tions of that world are constructions. People create and apply these
> cultural constructions in a struggle to grasp the world, relate to it,
> and manipulate it through concepts, knowledge, and acts. In the

process, reality impinges, and the events that occur consequently are not predicated by the cultural system of representations employed by the people, though they may largely be interpretable within it [...] The real [...] is composed of this widest compass: natural world, a human population with all its collective and statistical social features, and a set of cultural ideas in terms of which [...] people try to understand and cope with themselves and their habitat.[20]

It is important to acknowledge the simultaneous existence of different cultural concepts and a pluralistic understanding of the need for different approaches to different research requirements, which also includes normative theory as a legitimate form of knowledge-formation. On the other hand, one cannot study reality on the basis solely of normative definitions. Holism and the study of complexity presuppose pluralism, as regards both values and methodology. The conclusion is that we must take relativism seriously without allowing ourselves to become subservient to it. Scientific pluralism presupposes a programmatically open and experimental attitude to methodological alternatives.

The conceptual troika

Let us now tackle the task of delimiting and defining the field to be investigated, a field defined by the three concepts: development, security, and culture. As regards development and security it is interesting to note that the intra-disciplinary discussion of these two fields has followed separate tracks that seldom did intersect. They constituted separate academic sub-cultures institutionalized in radically different ways (but equally closely linked to the modern project). Development theory was built on contributions from development economics, gradually extended through sociology, social anthropology, political science, geography, and several other disciplines. After it had been paired with ecology, the theory of sustainable development arose. Security theory emanates from political science, international relations, and the more specialized discipline of strategic studies and has, as mentioned above, later also been enlarged in a fashion which has assigned an ever more subordinate role to conventional security. That has to do with the diminished likelihood of inter-state confrontations in the new geopolitical global environment.

Culture is of course of a different nature, in our approach providing the frame within which issue areas such as development and security are, consciously or unconsciously, understood. They are not only theory-dependent but also context-dependent. Each of the terms has its own complex intellectual history but will here be related to one another, as if they were a more or less coherent research area.

What difference does it make if development and security are more systematically related to culture? Security conventionally means absence from the threat of physical violence. Bring in culture, and security would also imply identity. Development could mean development of infrastructure and increased production, but with a more conscious application of the cultural dimension focus will be on human development.

Development

Development is one of the most tricky concepts to define, even in the company of security and culture. *Development studies* is generally described as an interdisciplinary field, and as such influenced by several different intra-disciplinary approaches: development economics, geography, modernization sociology, political development theory, development anthropology, etc. *Development theory* takes up elements from different theories specific to the various disciplines, but its ambition is to comprehend the totality, whether that is termed 'holistic' or 'complex'.[21]

Sustainable development takes us into the environmental sector, which makes particularly heavy demands on the interdisciplinary approach, since we are here moving between faculty boundaries.[22] We can also note a paradigm shift from nationally demarcated environmental problems, over which states were considered to have control (the Stockholm Conference 1972), to the idea of a global ecology, the problems of which can be managed only by global measures (often it is in practice a matter of local measures with global consequences) implemented by transnational players. The concept 'sustainable societal development' further broadens the sustainability dimension, from ecology to social structure, political institutions, and culture (compare with societal security). In fact, the environment can no longer be seen as an external context of human action.[23]

The concept 'sustainable development' derives from principles within the international movement for nature conservation, in which the idea was launched of a sustainable exploitation of natural resources (and later also of the environment in general).[24] It made its great breakthrough as a result of the Brundtland Commission's report entitled 'Our Common Future' in 1987 (WCDE 1987). Here sustainable development was described as 'development that meets the needs of the present generation without jeopardizing the ability of future generations to meet their own needs'. This definition, which has come to permeate debate and continued work in the United Nations, puts the concept of 'need' at the centre, and in particular the fundamental needs of the world's poor. Attention has also been drawn to the limitations that the state must impose, faced with the capacity of the environment and natural resources to satisfy human needs.[25]

Sustainable development thus deals with combining protection of the environment with global growth in which justice is applied as between the South and the North, and in a long-term perspective also for future generations. The earlier polarization between growth and environment in the debate of the 1970s could thereby be partly bridged over through the acceptance of sustainable development as a matter common to both the industrialized countries and the poor countries of the Third World. Principles of common responsibility, solidarity, and differentiated obligations have developed as important parts of the concept of sustainable development.[26]

Sustainable development, or its opposite, is strongly bound up with culturally-based patterns of behaviour ('the American way of life is not negotiable') which must first be understood if it is to be possible to change them. One of the fundamental dimensions of this concept is thus inter-generational justice, that is to say that one generation must not have the right, for the sake of its own advantage, to impair the conditions of life for future generations. The problem is that what constitutes such a development can only be determined by coming generations. A reverse problem is the dilemma involved in giving guarantees for future generations, in a situation in which human beings now living are so far from reasonable satisfaction of their needs. The definition is therefore better understood as a moral principle than as a definition of development. As argued by several contributions to this book, this principle ought also to include a children's perspective on the future.

The concept *societal* sustainable development is problematic, since the question as to which society is, in fact, meant by it is left open or, rather, is taken for granted. It is normally the 'national society' that is referred to, a society which no longer exists in its 'pure', that is to say, territorially demarcated, form. That raises intricate questions about the boundaries between societies in a globalized, deterritorialized world. These questions which affect the problem of multi-level analysis, as well as what was discussed above as the 'complexity problem', are not altogether new, but have become more and more acute as a problem of method. Is it a matter of the local society, the national society – the nation-state – a regional formation (such as the EU), or is it the world society? A decisive point when defining the meaning of 'sustainability' is thus which territorial entity does one intend to be sustainable? The ecological imperative, the absence of borders in the global condition, makes it natural to consider sustainable social development as a global process which must be governed by the insights of natural science, that is to say a continuation of the modern project on the global scale (Eriksson 1997).

Within the subject of international relations most attention has been paid to the question of responsibility and implementation, in the case that some form of transnational measure is regarded as necessary (global governance).

Criticism of the established theory of development has come from many quarters. Latterly it has chiefly applied to 'interventionism', that is to say, the view of the state as an omnipotent director of the development process (Toye 1987). It has also been a matter of a more fundamental criticism of the 'actually existing development', which more and more violates ecological systems, or violence against the cultural pluralism which expresses itself in a growing number of politicized ethnic groups, partly as a reaction against 'development', taking violent steps against one another or against the government (Stavenhagen 1990). This fundamental critical position forms part of what is usually called 'alternative' development.[27] The alternative development theory aims to subordinate development to ecological principles, i.e. sustainable development. It is thus at root a question of an ecologically appropriate development, even if the concept has, as we have seen, been broadened to include culture and security. Feminist perspectives have further underlined the potential importance of the alternative theory (e.g. Sen and Grown 1987).

Today it has become common to talk about global development, as different from although part of, globalization. Since development problems are globalized, and 'national development' has lost much of its meaning, development theory is necessarily merging with International Political Economy into global social theory and the new interdisciplinary field of 'Global Studies' (drawing on IR, IPE, development studies, cultural studies, the new security paradigm etc.) (Björn Hettne, volume 1). Global development necessitates a further strengthening of the societal (welfare) dimension of world order – the provision of global public goods. Global development, so defined, would mean that standards applied in most (non-failed) domestic systems are increasingly taken as norms in the international system as well (Gun-Britt

Andersson, volume 2). It may be said simply to refer to the quality of international relations.

Security

The conventional realist view of security emanates from the position of the individual nation-state in an anarchic international system and basically concerns the survival of the state as such, that is to say, the preservation of its sovereignty. Security policy consists, within the framework of this discourse, in warding off, above all, military threats against national sovereignty.

The perspective is historically grounded in the Westphalian era and the Westphalian political rationality. The conventional security concept therefore contains a built-in conservatism which goes together with its historical connection to balance of power, the load-bearing security principle in the Westphalian structure. The balance of power policy aims at preserving the relative strength between states, or groups of states, if necessary, by means of war. Neutrality is in practice subordinate to the balance of power policy in that it (often explicitly) pays regard to the reigning geopolitical balance.

The end of the Cold War, the collapse of the communist system, and the wave of ethno-nationalism and collapsing state formations, that is to say, internally generated security problems, plunged the world of international relations in its conventional form into a deep crisis of confidence and opened the door to culture analysis and normative theory (Lapid and Kratochwil 1996; see also Smith 1992). None the less, militarily defined security retains a special position in the security discourse, even though threats in this area are not regarded as imminent or are overshadowed by other threat images in the global 'risk society', including terrorist threats which after September 11th reached an unprecedented scale (mega-terrorism) with the purpose of transforming world order (Falk 2004). Globalization has changed man's basic perception of security, whether that is now explicitly linked with the globalized condition or not. Such a link is made by Ulrich Beck, in his concept of the 'risk society', which is also a global society (Beck 1992; 1999).[28]

Once again, it is globalization that has changed the context, preceded by processes that were earlier described as internationalization and interdependence. The new security problem arises from internally generated disintegration within society, manifested inter alia by the decline in the power and capacity, and hence in the legitimacy of the state; by sub-national economic strategies aimed at linking parts of a country more directly with a transnational economic structure; by the disintegration of the pluralistic and inclusive community created by civil society; by a corresponding reinforcement of ethnocentric loyalties with consequent social conflicts; and by the emergence of sub-groups and subcultures, protecting what they regard as their own legitimate security interests and the right to be 'respected'.

The broader security concept is often linked with various environmental problems, but since this dimension is already covered by the concept of 'sustainability', in this connection the concept of societal security can constitute a relevant point of departure for the discussion about security (Waever et al. 1993; Buzan et al. 1998). That does not mean underrating the ecological dimension of the security problem, which would be extremely foolish: a country threatened by rising sea levels cannot defend itself by force of arms.[29] Peace (and conflict), on the one hand, and development (and underdevelopment), on the other hand, are on the concrete plane de facto very strongly related to each other, as can clearly be noted in current aid policy and the new awareness of the need to integrate aid policy and security policy. This has already gone so far that there are grounds to post a warning about the 'securitization' of the development and aid discourse.

The enlargement of the approach known as 'societal security' is thus concerned with a shift from sovereignty to identity and from state to society. But what is 'society'? The concept 'society' must not be inseparably bound to any specific historic societal entity. One may also speak of a European society, as of a world society, and nor does nation need to be the same as nation-state. There is a Kurdish nation in Turkey-Iran-Iraq and a Mohawk nation in Canada-the US. Once again we must note that globalization has made the idea of a delimited 'society' anachronistic.

A different critical line of argumentation maintains that security must be sought at the level of the individual, which likewise presupposes a break with the fixation on the state (Walker 1988). Taking it as a whole, one can evidently speak of a democratization of the concept of security, since more and more sections of society lay claim to this value. Making a question a matter of security policy is a way of putting it on the agenda. Securitization also means a risk from the point of view of democracy, since a security issue, automatically defined as 'high politics', is detached from normal democratic management (Eriksson 2001).

The UNDP's Human Development Report 1994 took up the question of *human security*, defined as 'safety from hunger, disease, and repression'.

It is also of interest here to note the stark contrast between the people's and the state's need for security:

> For too long, the concept of security has been shaped by the potential for conflict between states. For too long, security has been equated with threats to a country's borders. For too long, nations have sought arms to protect their security. For most people today, a feeling of insecurity arises more from worries about daily life than from the dread of a cataclysmic world event. Job security, income security, health security, environmental security, security from crime, these are the emerging concerns of human security all over the world. (UNDP 1994: 3)

In later UNDP reports the concept was linked to 'human development', and ultimately to the whole complex of human rights.[30] Other relevant links are 'humanitarian emergency' and 'humanitarian intervention'. One can see this contemporary focus on 'human' as part of the paradigm shift which goes together with globalization giving rise to a post-national logic. The frequent use of the concept 'human' gives associations with a transnational assumption of responsibility (the responsibility to protect), as if one could no longer rely on states to fulfil their responsibility for their citizens. It was implicit in the old state-centred paradigm that it was the task of the state to protect its citizens not only against military threat but also against other security and risk factors, as was most clearly expressed in the welfare state in which the citizen was taken care of from the cradle to the grave.

The International Commission for Global Governance spoke of 'the security of people and the planet'.[31] This line, which from the conceptual point of view is expansionist, is also supported by feminist perspectives on global security as being less directed towards dominance and sovereignty, and more towards cooperation and the construction of society (Tickner 1992).[32] All this can be summarized under the concept 'comprehensive security', expressing the complex societal connections in the globalized condition.

Culture

'Culture' is probably the most complex (according to some, 'hypercomplex') of the three concepts under discussion here. There is therefore nothing odd about the fact that there are many definitions. In this context it is obligatory to point to the classic study by Kroeber and

Kluckhohn (1952), in which no less than 164 different definitions of culture were enumerated. Many definitions in this list are, of course, more or less overlapping, and can readily be reduced to a few basic perspectives on culture and society.[33] Still there remain some basic distinctions which seem to be hard to bridge.

It is customary to distinguish between an aesthetic and an anthropological/ethnological concept of culture. The former, which among other things comprises music, literature, and pictorial art, also normally includes, particularly in earlier formulations of it, a value-judgment dimension. The latter is exemplified by phenomena such as 'Swedish culture', 'immigrant culture', and 'the multicultural society'. A concept such as 'cultural landscape' falls somewhere between nature and culture. In this context it is of course highly relevant that there exist intellectual, academic cultures, such as C. P. Snow's 'two cultures' (humanities versus science), which never meet.

Culture is to do with cultivation, and 'the prerequisite for cultivation – the process – is always man as an active and thinking being' (Ek 1989). This definition in no way implies that man lives with a 'ready-made' identity.[34] From this it follows that it is complicated to choose definitions of culture. The classic definition, more than 100 years old, is probably that by E. B. Tylor: 'Culture or Civilization, taken in its wide ethnographic sense, is that complex whole which includes knowledge, belief, art, morality, law, custom, and any other capabilities and habits acquired by man as a member of society' (Tylor 1871). By virtue of its range and breadth this definition has often been taken as the point of departure for discussion of the phenomenon 'culture'. Culture is in this definition identified with civilization, which is not compatible with current usage in which the concept of civilization, based on the idea of levels of cultural aggregation, is reserved for the most aggregated cultural level, namely macro-culture. This definition emphasizes further that culture is something that the individual acquires in his/her capacity as a member of society, a perspective which, on the contrary, still seems to hold good. The result is that the cultural phenomenon is social, and vice versa.

Within the social anthropology tradition, which is less homogeneous than the above-mentioned distinctions may appear to suggest, there are according to Ulf Hannerz three ways of looking at culture, mutually quite compatible, but given different degrees of emphasis in different contexts: (1) culture is something that men learn, (2) culture is an integrated pattern of thought, (3) cultures are distinct, territorially-bound, social collectives. Of these it is the first view that in principle is valid, but the two others (that culture exists in packaged form and that there are several such packages) need to be thoroughly re-examined (something which, by the way, has largely already happened). By culture we here primarily mean the production of meaning, thus providing the prism through which the other concepts are interpreted.[35] The postmodern turn has put culture as a coherent phenomenon in question.

In this connection we are primarily interested in the relevance of the concept of culture in relation to the globalized condition of society, where culture is manifested in 'de-territorialized' form, which in principle makes impossible a view of culture in which cultures are perceived as integrated and localized.

Globalization of culture does not imply homogenization. In fact there is no such thing as a homogenous culture in the first place. This is what creates 'the problem of culture'. 'Culture is everywhere', as shifting as social reality itself. Culture is a way of understanding social reality. Culture can be seen as instrumental for economic growth, or as the very purpose of development, meaning ability to choose the 'good life', often culturally defined. It can be the foundation for peace as well as providing the mobilizing symbols for struggle, conflict and violence.

Civilizational dialogue is a research area experiencing a renaissance as a consequence of the increasing importance of culture on the macroplane in the globalized condition. The concept of civilization has a long and controversial history. As far back as the eighteenth century Herder formulated the insight that the world consisted of many cultures, rather than of one civilization and many barbarians.[36] The concept of civilization in the singular was complemented by the plural understanding. Thus was laid the foundation for ethnography (and social anthropology) which took upon itself the task of describing all these cultures, a task which subsequently was made significantly more difficult by the 'Creolization' of the world (Hannerz 1996).

Totalizing tendencies

Each of the three concepts dealt with here has a built-in 'totalizing' tendency towards hegemony, in the sense that they all expand and through extension come to include each other. This is an expression of the inherent urge for holism in the subject areas covered by the concepts. The definition of *culture* in particular has become more and more inclusive. In 'Our Creative Diversity' by the World Commission for Culture and Development, a distinction is made between two ways of looking at the relationship between culture and development. In one view, culture can have an instrumental value for the achievement of economic growth.[37] In another view, with which the Commission was obviously in sympathy, it is economic growth that is the instrument for attaining what human beings attach value to, which obviously has to do with culture (Knutsson 2000). In accordance with the UNDP, *development* is seen as *human* development and defined as a process which increases mankind's opportunities to devote themselves to what they value in life. The definition was chosen on the basis of the Commission's special preoccupation that culture is a dimension of development, if not something even more comprehensive. It is asserted, for example, that culture is the basis of all development (World Commission on Culture and Development 1996: 233). It is also asserted there that culture is decisive as regards mankind's relationship with nature and the socially constructed environment, the earth, and the universe. That can be said to illustrate a totalizing culture view. As used in our framework culture is total in the sense that nothing can be conceived and understood outside a cultural prism.

The concept of *security* has also become highly expansive. To the old meaning of military security at the nation-state level have been added environmental, cultural, ethnic, economic, social, societal, individual, and other kinds of security at different levels of society. If one adds all the hitherto proposed security dimensions, one obtains a more or less complete model of society, focussed on everything that can go wrong, that is to say, which reduces security and increases uncertainty and 'risk' in a society. To define a problem as a security problem moreover implies, as discussed above, that it acquires a higher priority, thus adding to the motivation of seeing almost everything through the security prism.

Cultural identity is in itself often seen as a security issue. The importance of the culture factor in 'the new conflicts' is clear, but how is it to be understood? The new conflicts are often described as 'ethnic'. The concept 'ethnic conflicts' refers to the form and expression of the conflict, not to its inherent nature. Ethnic difference is in itself rarely or never a cause for conflict. Every ethnic conflict has its own unique features and cannot be explained by inter-civilizational division. Both the management and the solution of a conflict must therefore take its point of departure both in the underlying socio-economic problem and in the specifically ethnic way in which the distributional conflict has evolved. The state is often part of the problem – but must as a rule also be a part of the solution. In a multi-ethnic society the state is primarily an institution for conflict-resolution – or ought to be so. In a 'failed state' the protective function falls back on the primary group, defined as the smallest group bound together by a collective consciousness.

Sustainable development has gradually also come to include concerns about everything that can 'get broken' (thus being unsustainable) in the societal construction, not only the ecological balance which constituted the original problem when the concept was formulated. This extension finds expression in the concept 'sustainable societal development'. For the sake of simplicity we have used the development concept in a broad sense covering different kinds of sustainability as well, assuming that nobody wants unsustainable development. Ecology, 'ecocentrism' or 'deep ecology', has a totalizing tendency in the sense that the anthropocentric (or cultural) perspective is subordinated to broader biological contexts.

So much for the totalizing tendency of the three concepts. If instead one wishes them to be, in a meaningful way, related to each other and to constitute a common research area, they must in some way be analytically delineated in order to avoid too great an overlap. An alternative idea might be to focus on just one of the three concepts, which thus becomes the main problem, in order later to allow the other two to constitute dimensions of the problem chosen. The environmental question has, for example, completely decisive importance both for the development discussion (i.e. sustainable social development) and the security discussion (comprehensive security).

Notes

1. For a more detailed description, see *Culture, Security and Social Sustainable Development* (Gidlund 2003) from the sector committee, authored by Björn Hettne in dialogue with the rest of the group.
2. Gudrun Dahl discusses the concept of 'essentially contested concepts' (volume 1).
3. The contribution by Björn Hettne (volume 1) thus presents the development of development thinking in terms of historically contextualized discourses. Similarly Urban Jonsson (volume 1) describes changing paradigms in the field of nutrition, and Yudhishthir Raj Isar (volume 2) provides a discourse analysis of 'culture and development' in the UNESCO context.
4. This world order, the European dominated post-1648 world order, is often referred to as Westphalia. The post-Westphalian world order being created by globalization has certain structural similarities (the multilevel structure) with the pre-Westphalian order and sometimes therefore referred to as 'neo-medieval'.
5. In the publication *Culture, Security, and Sustainable Social Development after September 11* (Lundmark 2004) members of the group reflect over the implications of September 11th. The views differed with respect to how new the post-September 11th situation actually is. It is argued by Peter Wallensteen

(volume 2) that the debate now has come to circulate around certain key conceptions: the unipolar world (in practice Pax Americana), the order of the international society (what could be called the Pax Omnium Inter Omnes) and possible people-based alternatives (such as the democratic, Kantian, or enlightened peace).

6. James Mittelman (2004: 43) argues that multilateral globalization after September 11th changed into militarized globalization: from consent to coercion.

7. This contributed among other things to establishing the School of Global Studies at Göteborg University.

8. Critical central works are Ulrich Beck (1997) and Zygmunt Bauman (1998). For a systematic introduction, see Jan Art Scholte (2005), James Mittelman (2000) and David Held et al. (1999). As regards the globalization myth, see Paul Hirst and Grahame Thompson (1999). On the positive and negative effects of globalization, see Richard Falk (1999).

9. Immanuel Wallerstein (2000) says: 'Globalization is a misleading concept, since what is described as globalization has been happening for 500 years'. On the other hand, the recent dramatic spread of the concept would indicate a new underlying 'reality' (assuming that 'reality' can be known). Once upon a time (the 1780s) 'international' was also a new word (Scholte 2005: 51).

10. See Robert W. Cox and Timothy J. Sinclair (1996) *Approaches to World Order*, especially chapter 15.

11. Compare the Routledge Journal *Globalizations*.

12. Jan Art Scholte (2005: chapter 8) has made a preliminary attempt to judge what globalization means for the fundamental premises of the formation of knowledge. A similar concern may be found in James Mittelman (2004).

13. Roland Robertson (1992: 183) has defined globalization as a growth in 'the scope and depth of consciousness of the world as a single place'.

14. Anthony Giddens (1990) argues that modernity has an inherent tendency to globalization. See also Stephen Toulmin (1990) and further Ulrich Beck et al. (1995).

15. For arguments that social science must go in the direction of 'global social theory', see Björn Hettne and Frederik Söderbaum (1999).

16. Karl Erik Knutsson used the concept 'reality room': 'people live and act, not in any social, cultural, political, economic or religious sector or in any analytically constructed compartment but in a total "reality room" which has all these aspects'. In this connection one should also reiterate that, quoting Karl Eric Knutsson, synthesizing research, 'knowing what is known', is itself an important form of research.

17. This is not to say that all anthropologists were only concerned with such locally situated studies. The isolated village was never the norm but nevertheless serves as a (albeit constructed) metaphorical opposite to the globalized condition, which today is studied by what is known as global anthropology. Enrique Rodriguez Larreta (taking his departure in Karl Eric Knutsson's inaugural lecture on the 'anthropological perspective') discusses the problem of the local and the global (volume 1).

18. See Ulf Hannerz (1992 and 1996). Complexity theory is referred to by Urban Jonsson (volume 1).

19. In this context Ulrich Beck's critique of 'methodological nationalism' is highly relevant (volume 1). A similar idea lies behind methodological territorialism (Scholte 2005).
20. The quotation is taken, as abbreviated, from 'Culture and Human Development. Report on a Conference on Culture, Cultural Research and Cultural Policy', held in Stockholm, August 1977, compiled and edited by Karl Eric Knutsson, Royal Academy of Letters, History and Antiquities.
21. Here too, it is the case that all the recent literature includes a discussion of sustainable development. See Björn Hettne (1995). The culture dimension has also received more and more attention, see Vincent Tucker (1996) and Peter Worsley (1999).
22. 'Sustainable development is so challenging, morally and intellectually, and so demanding that it will require us to organize scientific knowledge and to ask scientific questions in new ways', it is stated in the report of the Friibergh seminar (Culture and Human Development, p. 13).
23. What is 'natural' is now so thoroughly entangled with what is 'social' that there can be nothing taken for granted about it any more, see Beck et al. (1995: vii).
24. The following text dealing with the emergence of the concept of sustainability is by Katarina Eckerberg. For a background description of the evolution of the idea of sustainable development, see Michael Redclift (1987), S. Lélé (1991) and W. Adams (1990).
25. Alf Hornborg has significantly pointed out that the technology which brings about the 'time-space compression' in the centre of the world system does so at the expense of (human) time and (natural) space at the periphery, which once again brings to the fore environmental justice and risk. 'Time-space compression' is made possible by an unequal global exchange, which Hornborg has inventively called 'time-space appropriation' (volume 1).
26. Specifically, justice and the North-South problem within the concept of sustainability are discussed in detail in Adams (1990), James Meadowcroft (1997) and William Lafferty and Oluf Langhelle (1999).
27. The development concept has in the post-modernist spirit also been called an 'intellectual ruin'. Wolfgang Sachs (1992) thus speaks of an 'age of development', which begins on 20 January 1949. On that day, the American President Harry Truman attached the label 'underdeveloped areas' to a large part of the world outside Europe and the US. The lack of development appeared as a global security policy problem which must be put right in order to guarantee the stability of the new world order, and of American hegemony. Karl Eric Knutsson has described the concept of development as a 'logical invalid'.
28. Anthony Giddens talks of 'manufactured uncertainty'.
29. There is a hardly a recent textbook on international relations that does not have a chapter about the environment and sustainable development. See e.g. Dickson (1997), Booth and Smith (1995), Brown (1997) and Nicholson (1998).
30. Thorleif Pettersson provides a definition of human development (volume 2) and Urban Jonsson discusses children's human right to nutrition (volume 1).

31. See also the discussion on cultural security by Raj Isar, (volume 2).
32. See also Tickner's (1988) attempt to formulate a feminist epistemology in this field, with her reformulation of Hans Morgenthau's principles of political realism.
33. 'The mere fact that there have been so many definitions of culture [...] suggests that there is a need to discuss "the problem of culture" rather than culture "itself"' (Robertson 1992: 33).
34. 'When culture is characterized as *complex* my reading of it is that it must be understood as both *composed* of material conditions, social structures and thought patterns, and that the interplay between them is *complicated*' (Frykman 1999). See also Åhlberg (1998). In another context, Åhlberg distinguishes between the traditional (corresponding with the aesthetic) concept of culture and the anthropological-sociological concept (Åhlberg 1995).
35. This is consistent with the definition given by Raj Isar: 'Culture is the social construction, articulation and reception of meaning' (volume 2).
36. The use of the term civilization in the singular often has an ethno(euro) centric meaning, which under imperialism was described as 'the white man's burden' or 'la mission civilisatrice'.
37. From this it also follows that culture can have the opposite effect. The earlier discourse on development, which is usually summarized as the modernization paradigm, dwelt heavily on 'traditional' culture as a barrier to development that must be removed to make development possible.

References

Abiri, E. (2000) *The Securitization of Migration. Towards an Understanding of Migration Policy Changes in the 1990s. The Case of Sweden*, PhD thesis, Göteborg: Göteborg University.

Adams, W. (1990) *Green Development: Environment and Sustainability in the Third World*, London: Routledge.

Åhlberg, L-O. (1995) 'Om kulturbegreppet' [On the Concept of Culture], in Liss, P-E. and Petersson, B. (eds) (1995) *Hälsosamma tankar. 11 filosofiska uppsatser tillägnade Lennart Nordenfelt*, Nora: Nya Doxa.

Åhlberg, L-O (1998) 'Universalism, pluralism and relativism', in *Our Creative Diversity* and 'In from the Margins', *Tidskrift för kulturstudier*, no. 4.

Barth, F. (1987) *Cosmologies in the Making, A Generative Approach to Cultural Variation in Inner New Guinea*, Cambridge: Cambridge University Press.

Bauman, Z. (1998) *Globalization: The Human Consequences*, Cambridge: Polity Press.

Beck, U. (1992) *Risk Society: Towards a New Modernity*, London: Sage.

Beck, U. (1997) *Was ist Globalisierung?*, Frankfurt am Main: Suhrkamp.

Beck, U. (1999) *World Risk Society*, Cambridge: Polity Press.

Beck, U., Giddens, A. and Lash, S. (1995) *Reflexive Modernization: Politics, Tradition and Aesthetics in the Modern Social Order*, Cambridge: Polity Press.

Booth, K. and Smith, S. (eds) (1995) *International Relations Theory Today*, Cambridge: Polity Press.

Brown, C. (1997) *Understanding International Relations*, London: Macmillan.

Buzan, B., Waever, O. and de Wilde, J. (1998) *Security: a new framework for analysis*, London: Lynne Rienner.

Cox, R. W. and Sinclair, T. J. (1996) *Approaches to World Order*, Cambridge: Cambridge University Press.

Dickson, A. K. (1997) *Development and International Relations*, Cambridge: Polity Press.

Ek, S. B. (1989) *Kultur som problem*, Göteborg: Robek-Konsult.

Eriksson, J. (ed) (2001) *Threat Politics. New Perspectives on Security, Risk and Crisis Management*, Aldershot: Ashgate Publishing.

Eriksson, K-E. (1997) 'On the Roles of Science and Culture in Sustainable Development', Proceedings of the 47th Pugwash Conference on Science and World Affairs, Lillehammer, Norway, 1–7 August, 1997.

Falk, R. (1999) *Predatory Globalization. A critique*, Cambridge: Polity Press.

Falk, R. (2004) *Declining World Order. America's Imperial Geopolitics*, New York and London: Routledge.

Fornäs, J. (2001) *Advancing Cultural Studies in Sweden: An infrastructural initiative*, Norrköping: Arbetslivsinstitutet (Arbetslivsrapport 2001:1).

Frykman, B. Skarin (1999) 'Demokrati, kultur och kunskap' [Democracy, culture and knowledge], contribution to *Demokratins estetik* (Demokratiutredningens forskarvolym IV), SOU 1999:129.

Giddens, A. (1990) *The Consequences of Modernity*, Cambridge: Polity Press.

Hannerz, U. (1992) *Cultural Complexity*, New York: Columbia University Press.

Hannerz, U. (1996) *Transnational Connections. Culture, People, Places*, London and New York: Routledge.

Held, D., McGrew, A., Goldblatt, D. and Perraton, J. (1999) *Global Transformations: Politics, Economics and Culture*, Cambridge: Polity Press.

Hettne, B. (1995) *Development Theory and the Three Worlds*, London: Longman.

Hettne, B. (2003) *Culture, Security and Social Sustainable Development*, Stockholm: Gidlund.

Hettne, B. and Odén, B. (eds) (2002) *Global Governance in the 21st Century: Alternative Perspectives on World Order* (Expert Group on Development Issues, Ministry of Foreign Affairs, Sweden).

Hettne, B. and Söderbaum, F. (1999) 'Towards Global Social Theory', *Journal of International Relations and Development*, vol. 2 no. 4.

Hirst, P. and Thompson, G. (1999) *Globalization in Question*, Cambridge: Polity Press.

Huntington, S. (1993) 'The Clash of Civilizations', *Foreign Affairs*, 72:. 22.

Knutsson, K. E. (2000) 'Without Culture No Sustainable Development: Some reflections on the topic for the Stjernsund Seminar', September 2000.

Kroeber, A. L. and Kluckhohn, C. (1952) *Culture: A Critical Review of Concepts and Definitions*, New York: Vintage Books.

Lafferty, W. and Langhelle, O. (eds) (1999) *Towards Sustainable Development*, London: Macmillan.

Lapid, Y. and Kratochwil, F. (1996) *The Return of Culture and Identity in IR Theory*, London: Lynne Rienner.

Lélé, S. (1991) 'Sustainable Development: A Critical Review', *World Development*: 607–621.

Lundmark, F. (ed) (2004) *Culture, Security and Sustainable Social Development after September 11*, Stockholm: Gidlund.

Meadowcroft, J. (1997) 'Planning, Democracy and the Challenge of Sustainable Development', *International Political Science Review*, 20:. 167–90.

Mittelman, J. (2000) *The Globalization Syndrome: Transformation and Resistance*, Princeton: Princeton University Press.

Mittelman, J. H. (2004) *Whither Globalization. The Vortex of Knowledge and Ideology*, London and New York: Routledge.

Nicholson, M. (1998) *International Relations. A Concise Introduction*, London: Macmillan.

Redclift, M. (1987) *Sustainable Development: Exploring the Contradictions*, London: Routledge.

Robertson, R. (1992) *Globalization. Social Theory and Global Culture*, London: Sage.

Sachs, W. (1992) *The Development Dictionary: A Guide to Knowledge and Power*, London: Zed Books.

Scholte, J. A. (2005) *Globalization. A Critical Introduction*, London: Palgrave.

Sen, G. and Grown, C. (1987) *Development, Crises and Alternative Visions: Third World Women's Perspectives*, New York: Monthly Review Press.

Skelton, T. and Allen, T. (eds) (1999) *Culture and Global Change*, London and New York: Routledge.

Smith, S. (1992) 'The Forty Years Retour: The Resurgence of Normative Theory in International Relations', *Millennium*, 1992, 21: 489–506.

Söderbaum, F. and Shaw, T. M. (eds) (2003) *Theories of New Regionalism. A Palgrave Reader*, Basingstoke: Palgrave.

Stavenhagen, R. (1990) *The Ethnic Question. Conflict, Development, and Human Rights*, Tokyo: United Nations University Press.

Tickner, J. A. (1992) *Gender in International Relations. Feminist Perspectives on Achieving Global Security*, New York: Columbia University Press.

Tickner, J. A. (1988) 'Hans Morgenthau's Principles of Political Realism: A Feminist Reformulation', *Millenium: Journal of International Studies*, 17(3): 429–440.

Toulmin, S. (1990) *Cosmopolis. The Hidden Agenda of Modernity*, New York: Free Press.

Toye, J. (1987) *Dilemma of Development. Reflections on the Counterrevolution in development theory*, Oxford: Basil Blackwell.

Tucker, V. (1996) 'Introduction: A Cultural Perspective on Development', *European Journal of Development Research*, 8 (2): 1–21.

Tylor, E. B. (1871) Primitive Culture, 2 vols., London: John Murray; quoted from Frykman (1999).

UNDP (1994) *Human Development Report*, New York: UNDP.

Waever, O., Buzan, B., Kesitrup, M. and Lemaitre, P. (1993) *Identity, Migration and the New Security Agenda in Europe*, London: Pinter.

Walker, R. B .J. (1988) *One World, Many Worlds: Struggles for a Just World Peace*, Colorado: Lynne Rienner.

Wallerstein, I. (2000) 'Globalization or the Age of Transition. A Long-Term View of the Trajectory of the World System', *International Sociology*, June 2000, vol. 15 (2): 249–285.

World Commission on Culture and Development (1996) *Our Creative Diversity*, Paris: UNESCO.

Worsley, P. (1999) 'Culture and Development Theory', in Skelton, T. and Allen, T. (eds) (1999) *Culture and Global Change*, London and New York: Routledge.

Foreword

Over a period of some years the Swedish research foundation Riksbankens Jubileumsfond has become ever more engaged in questions concerned with links between culture and societal development. Cultural affiliation, values, identity, and traditions have been seen to play a decisive role in many both acute and long-term problems faced by individual nations and by the world as a whole. The research community has a double task: it must analyse and understand the role of culture, but also faces a challenge to try to influence cultures in the direction of reinforcing human rights, equality and democracy, and tackling poverty, thereby encouraging development towards peace and security. In many cases the task entails creating the foundations for the translation of morally defensible actions into norms for social, cultural and political practice. In all these contexts, cultural research has great responsibility and important tasks to perform.

In the second half of the 1990s the foundation played an active part in this field. In 1995 the World Commission on Culture and Development published its final report, 'Our Creative Diversity'. The following year the foundation decided – together with the Swedish Council for Research in the Humanities and Social Sciences and with the Royal Academy of Letters, History and Antiquities – to take part in the follow-up work on the report, by arranging a Nordic interdisciplinary conference in August 1997. A paper on the tasks and responsibilities of cultural research was published under the title 'Culture and Human Development' and given both national and international circulation during the preparations for the conference of Ministers of Culture in Stockholm in 1998.

In connection with the conference, the foundation organized three international seminars under the headings, 'The Need for a New Agenda for Research', 'Shared Values in Global Governance', and 'The Role of Foundations in Cultural Research'. A report drawn up by these seminars, entitled 'Promoting Cultural Research for Human Development' has been given wide international circulation.

In cooperation with Professor Göran Bexell, Department of Theology at Lund University, and UNESCO, the foundation also arranged a Nordic conference 3–5 June 1999, on the theme 'Universal Ethics; from the Nordic Perspectives', where the relation between human rights and global ethics was examined in detail. Moreover, the foundation took the initiative in the field of research policy to reinforce, among other things, research cooperation. This work has been carried out both in Sweden and abroad in cooperation with UNESCO along with a number of European foundations. A comparative research project, entitled 'Creative Europe', about the conditions for creativity and its role in a changing Europe is in progress. The foundation has also decided to create a firmer framework for Swedish involvement in the major international project, 'World Value Survey' (WVS), which has received support both for an international secretariat in Sweden and for work at Uppsala University. This project is a long-term comparative research programme on the subject of human values, which has been in progress for 20 years and embraces more than 60 countries.

During this period we also began cooperating with the Swedish Institute of International Affairs and with STINT (The Swedish Foundation for International Cooperation in Research and Higher Education), with a view to analysing the role of the Swedish Institute of International Affairs as a strategic resource and meeting place for research and for the discussion of ideas regarding human rights, national crisis management and security policy.

The immediate background for the formal initiation of this project was a conference on research cooperation into culture and sustainable social development, arranged together with the Royal Academy of Letters, History and Antiquities and the Swedish Council for Research in the Humanities and Social Sciences. This conference was held at Stjernsund Castle in Askersund in September 2000. The background document for the conference, written by Karl Eric Knutsson, the founding father of the project, was particularly important.

To coordinate these efforts and to promote future research efforts within the field, the management of the foundation decided in 2000 to establish a new sector committee, with responsibility for research into culture, security and sustainable development. By tradition the foundation establishes sector committees within scientific areas that are deemed important, but still not fully developed or insufficiently noticed. Their task has been to map out areas where research is needed, to initiate new research and to stimulate the dissemination of knowledge and dialogue on specific subjects. This committee held a first constituent meeting in November 2000 at which its working methods, tasks, and fields of responsibility were discussed.

At an early stage of discussion in the sector committee, the need arose to relate this research area to the societal changes inherent in what is now generally described as globalization, the consequences of which hereby will be termed 'the globalized condition'. This condition imparts to the chosen concepts a partly new content, and it is expected likewise to change the ontological, epistemological and methodological premises for the project of studying culture, security, and sustainable social development within a reasonably coordinated conceptual framework. Professor Björn Hettne was invited to provide the sector committee with a basis for discussion, presenting the three concepts ('culture', 'security', 'sustainable social development') and their genesis in the context of the history of ideas, as well as analysing the internal relations between these concepts with a view to identifying a coherent area for research.

Three unexpected shocks have affected the work of the committee. On September 11th 2001, the twin towers of the World Trade Center in New York City collapsed after being rammed by two airplanes hijacked by Islamic terrorists. A third plane crashed into the American defence headquarters, the Pentagon, in Washington D.C., while a fourth plane, which in all probability had the White House or the US Capitol building in Washington D.C. as its target, crashed in Pennsylvania. The actual meaning of these events has been interpreted in various ways, but it is plain that world political events have taken a new course since they occurred. The previously more generalized discussion about new security threats has become much more serious and concrete. In the United States there has been talk about a 'war against terrorism' since the events took place, yet without a clearly defined enemy, explicit goal, or definable end. After having been attacked on its own territory for the first time in the modern era, the world's sole superpower no longer appeared primarily to be the force behind an economic and political globalization process, but instead mainly manifested itself as a military power. This change involved the United States simultaneously turning inwards upon itself, and outwards through its external involvement in considerable military enterprises, both in Afghanistan, which was generally accepted by the world community, and in Iraq, which provoked, and continues to provoke, considerable opposition around the world.

As a result of this, the link between culture and values on the one hand, and stringent security measures on the other, became all too clear in the general world political debate. The focus in the debate on cultural values shifted from 'Asian values' to 'militant Islam'. 'The clash of civilizations' determined much of the agenda, even if the concept itself was usually treated with scepticism. After September 11th 2001 the whole context changed, and the committee was asked to reflect on how this event impacted on its work. This resulted in a collective work: 'Culture, Security and Sustainable Social Development after September 11', edited by Fredrik Lundmark (2003).

In autumn 2002, Karl Eric Knutsson passed away after a brief period of illness. Apart from the personal loss of a friend, initiator, and inspiration, Knutsson's death had a direct impact on much of the work of the group. There had long been a plan to summarize the committee's work with a broad anthology which would incorporate Knutsson's global network of contacts, and those of other group members, and which would encompass the issues dealt with by the committee itself. Once again developmental issues became the central focus of the committee's work, and it was these issues which persuaded the group to participate in an international working meeting in Brazil in January 2006. At this time many members of the group found themselves reminded of the Latin American perspective which so strongly influenced the developmental debate during the 1970s.

The eleventh of September once again had a tragic resonance when, on 11 September 2003, Sweden's Foreign Minister, Anna Lindh died of her injuries after having been stabbed in an attack the previous day. Her work as Foreign Minister was greatly influenced by her strong commitment to providing Sweden with an active role in the EU partnership. This was particularly the case in the area of foreign and security policy issues, but she was also highly active in emphasizing the importance of conflict prevention, and of the EU possessing the ability to handle crises. In honour of Anna Lindh, Riksbankens Jubileumsfond and the sector committee have undertaken a series of initiatives. These involve new projects dealing with conflict prevention, and European foreign and security policy issues. These projects are being sponsored together with partners in the European foundation sphere.

The present work in two volumes, produced in memory of the late Karl Eric Knutsson, is thus a result of this long work, which hereby is reaching its end. It is to be seen as a challenge to the global research community to tackle, in collaborative forms, research problems in which the focus is on global questions. The work is an outgrowth of the many discussions within the committee, first based on the original framework or platform, and later on intellectual encounters in both Swedish and international academic environments, as well as parallel dramatic changes in the world context, most importantly the September 11th horror, the subsequent war against terrorism, and the rise of inter-civilizational tensions which place the issue of culture and the need for dialogue in focus as never before.

These two volumes reflect this learning process but also, being memorial volumes, the life-work of Karl Eric Knutsson – anthropologist, international civil servant and initiator of the committee. Necessarily, this special purpose means lack of coherence in a strict academic sense. However, we nevertheless hope that it is consistent in the sense of reflecting the work of one intellectual mind struggling to make sense of the world 'out there' – but also trying to make this world a better world in very concrete terms.

Karl Eric, an anthropologist who combined field research with development work, was instrumental in establishing social anthropology as a social science in Sweden. This also meant that social anthropology became a crucial part of the development discourse. Through the Swedish Agency for Research Cooperation with Developing Countries (SAREC), Karl Eric created the institutional framework for development research in Sweden, although the main function of the organization was to strengthen research capacity in developing countries. In 1977 he organized, as the first director of SAREC, an international seminar on development theory which initiated a broader development discourse in Sweden. Participants in that historic seminar which also appear in these volumes are from Sweden, Peter Wallensteen and Björn Hettne, and from other parts of the world, Osvaldo Sunkel from Chile and Ponna Wignaraja from Sri Lanka, both concerned as much with development theory as with development strategy. Peter Wallensteen discusses the future of the UN and Björn Hettne provides a retrospective overview of development thinking, similar to the one he did 35 years ago in the context of the creation of SAREC. This is followed up by another student of Karl Eric, Gudrun Dahl, who explores contemporary development discourses. Penina Mlama, an old friend and colleague of Karl Eric, discusses gender and development in an African context. Gun-Britt Andersson who worked with Karl Eric in SAREC from the start in 1975 deals with global development in the form of production and distribution of global public goods.

After SAREC, Karl Eric became involved in international development concerning the welfare of children, serving for many years in UNICEF where he worked together with Urban Jonsson who succeeded him in the South Asia office (Kathmandu). Much of their joint experience is reflected in the contribution by Urban Jonsson. Other international contacts of Karl Eric within the UN family are Raj Isar (UNESCO) and Thoraya Obaid (UNFPA) who write about the cultural dimension of development.

After his retirement from UNICEF and his position as Assistant Secretary General of the UN, Karl Eric returned to Sweden and continued to work on his original vision for holistic social and cultural science in the framework of the Royal Academy of Letters and finally in the sector committee on Culture, Security and Sustainable Development, which was his brainchild. The rest of the contributions relate to the subsequent work of this group, some chapters written by members, others by researchers working in the same spirit and in close contact with the group.

Focussing on the key concept sustainable development, Alf Hornborg shows how unsustainability has been implied in the ecologically unequal change that has taken place over millennia. The work of the committee has been linked to the World Value Survey through Thorleif Pettersson, who contributed the chapter on 'Adolescent Education for Good Citizenship'. This project is also discussed in Hans-Dieter Klingemann's and Christian Welzel's chapter on democracy. Close to this theme and also based on the same body of data is Göran Bexell's analysis of global ethics. Gita Sen explores the role of solidarity in creating sustainable institutions for human well-being. A distinctly European perspective is provided by Ulrich Beck who also expresses the methodological basis for both the books: the need to analyse the globalized condition in an approach liberated from what he terms methodological nationalism.

In connection with visits abroad, the group participated in crucial debates on reconciliation, cultural dialogue and democratization, for instance in Stellenbosch, Cairo, Alexandria, Egypt, and Rio de Janeiro. Ursula van Beek, who organized the South African visit, analyses the issue of reconciliation in South Africa. Saad Eddin Ibrahim, who heads the Ibn Khaldun Centre of Development in Cairo, writes about the emerging civil society and its importance for democracy and development in the Arab world. Nadia Mostafa (also from Egypt) and Assia BenSalah Alaoui (Morocco) write about civilizational dialogue with a focus on Europe and Islam, an issue that became very central during the last year of the group. Jan Niederveen Pietersee discusses cosmopolitanism in Islam.

Many of the contributors in these two volumes participated in a workshop in Rio in January 2006, generously hosted by the Candido Mendes University. The workshop which came to focus on democratization and elite-people relations, included two Brazilian contributions: by Enrique Rodriguez Larreta and Candido Mendes, both dealing with cultural identity and globalization. They illuminate the globalized condition from the point of view of cultural studies.

In the broad sense, the papers produced within the project constitute two interrelated categories, the first dealing with Sustainable Development and Globalization, and the second with Values and Global Governance, forming the two complementary volumes of the book project, with culture as the overarching perspective. The essays are different in size, reflecting the double purpose of the project to provide state-of-the-art reports on themes which were of crucial concern to Karl Eric, and smaller pieces, reflecting on various issues which belong to his field of interests. However, in essence, the books reflect the necessarily unfinished work of the Sector Committee for Culture, Security and Sustainable Social Development to come to grips with this complex but fascinating field. Hopefully others will take over from here.

* * *

Finally, the foundation would like to express its great gratitude to the members of the committee for their work during the past six years and to the smaller publishing group including Birgitta Skarin Frykman and Anders Mellbourn. But, above all, our thanks go to Björn Hettne, for his tremendous efforts in editing these two volumes and his invaluable contributions which have been central to the committee's work from the start, and without which we would have accomplished much less. Thanks also to Malin Hasselskog for being such an efficient assistant editor.

DAN BRÄNDSTRÖM
Chairman of the Sector Committee

FREDRIK LUNDMARK
Secretary of the Sector
Committee

List of Members of the Sector Committee for Culture, Security and Sustainable Social Development

Managing Director Dan Brändström, Riksbankens Jubileumsfond, Chairperson.

Professor Göran Bexell, the Centre for Theology and Religious Studies, Lund University.

Professor Katarina Eckerberg, the Department of Political Science, Umeå University (up to and including 2002).

Ms Viola Furubjelke, MP for the Swedish Social Democratic Party, and Member of the Riksdag Committee for Foreign Affairs (as of 2002).

Mr Berndt Ekholm, MP for the Swedish Social Democratic Party.

Professor Björn Hettne, the School of Global Studies, Göteborg University.

Professor Alf Hornborg, the Department of Human Ecology, Lund University.

Professor Magnus Jerneck, the Department of Political Science, Lund University.

Professor Karl Eric Knutsson, the Royal Academy of Letters, History, and Antiquities (deceased, October 2002).

Mr Göran Lennmarker, MP for Moderaterna, and Member of the Riksdag Committee for Foreign Affairs.

Dr Jan Lundius, Ph.D., the Department for Research Co-Operation (Sarec), at the Swedish International Development Co-Operation Agency (Sida) (as of 2003); Ms. Lena Johansson, Section Head at the Division for Culture and Media, at Sida.

Director and Consulting Professor Anders Mellbourn (as of 2005 independent consultant to Riksbankens Jubileumsfond, among others).

Professor Thorleif Pettersson, the Department of Theology, Uppsala University.

Professor Birgitta Skarin Frykman, the Department of Ethnology, Göteborg University.

Professor Peter Wallensteen, the Department of Peace and Conflict Research, Uppsala University (as of 2003).

Professor Mats Widgren, the Department of Human Geography, Stockholm University.

Notes on Contributors

Ulrich Beck, Professor of Sociology, München.

Dan Brändström, Professor; former Director of the Bank of Sweden Tercentenary Foundation; Chairman of the Riksbankens Jubileumsfond's Sector Committee for Culture, Security and Sustainable Social Development.

Gudrun Dahl, Professor of Social Anthropology; Dean of the Social Faculty, Stockholm University.

Björn Hettne, Emeritus Professor of Peace and Development Research, School of Global Studies, Göteborg University.

Alf Hornborg, Professor of Human Ecology, Lund University.

Saad Eddin Ibrahim, Professor and Director of Ibn Khaldun Centre of Development, Cairo.

Urban Jonsson, former Regional Director, the United Nations Children's Fund.

Enrique Rodriguez Larreta, Director of Centre for Cultural Studies, Sergio Mendes University, Rio de Janeiro.

Fredrik Lundmark, Ph D in Sociology; Secretary of the Riksbankens Jubileumsfond's Sector Committee for Culture, Security and Sustainable Social Development.

Penina Mlama, Professor and Executive Director of the Forum for African Women Educationalists (FAWE), Nairobi.

Jan Nederveen Pieterse, Professor of Sociology, University of Illinois.

Thoraya Obaid, Executive Director, the United Nations Population Fund.

Osvaldo Sunkel, Emeritus Professor of Economics, Santiago de Chile.

Ponna Wignaraja, Chairman of South Asian Perspectives Network Association, Colombo.

Introduction

Björn Hettne

This book situates the problem of development in the context of the globalized condition which raises ontological and epistemological problems constitutive for global studies moving from methodological nationalism to more 'cosmopolitan' views. It also recognizes the importance of distinct regional perspectives and explores some central issues such as unequal exchange in the environmental field over time, the problem of child malnutrition, and theories of democracy. The historical dimension is very central, thus the changing paradigms and the contextual dimensions are emphasized.

The first set of chapters focusses on development in regional perspectives and changing paradigms over time. Björn Hettne provides a retrospective and prospective overview of development thinking which originated in the West. Development theory is analysed as a succession of discourses rather than as an evolutionary process of theoretical improvement, which has been the most common approach in development theory. The discourses are historically contextualized but linked through the ongoing process of globalization transforming the very meaning of development. Six different discourses are identified, from the discourse in the eighteenth century focussed on the causes and meanings of *progress*, to the current concern with *global development* defined as an improvement in the quality of international relations by the means of new supranational political institutions.

A distinct European perspective is provided by the German sociologist Ulrich Beck who also expresses the methodological basis for the book: the need to analyse the globalized condition in an approach radically liberated from what he terms methodological nationalism. From this perspective he sees the regionalization of Europe as a response to globalization. When the citizens of Europe in a paradoxical show of self-confidence reject the European constitution, the time has come to listen to them and to open the door to a democratization of Europe from below. To achieve this purpose, Europe needs to be reinvented. The trouble is that there is no political script running through the heads of all Europeans. There is no continuously updated narrative that could help them grasp events in the same way or feel part of a common enterprise. This, rather than geographical distance, is the real reason why the EU institutions strike ordinary people as intangible, unreal, and irrelevant. Europe should not be thought of in national terms as an unfinished nation or as an incomplete federal state. A cosmopolitan Europe is first and foremost a Europe based on difference, on actually practised, recognized national particularities. To a cosmopolitan outlook, this diversity (be it of languages, forms of economic or democratic organization or political cultures) appears to be a source of Europe's self-awareness, and not as it appears in the national (rather than cosmopolitan) outlook, as an obstacle to integration. Methodological nationalism is blind to the new realities of Europe – and therefore makes us blind to them as well.

The next chapter turns to Latin America and is written by one who actually has formed the regional development debate to a very large degree, both inside and outside ECLA (Economic Commission for Latin America). Osvaldo Sunkel from Chile was a prominent contributor to the Latin American structuralist approach to inflation, development, dependency, and transnationalization debates in the 1960s and 1970s, and has more recently formulated a development strategy addressing the failures of neo-liberalism in Latin America. In this chapter Sunkel argues for a neo-structural approach to development, that recognizes the contemporary capitalist reality of globalized finance and markets but rejects the crude government-hands-off ideology, proposing instead a critical role for the state as regards technological innovation, diversification of production and exports, regulation of markets, upgrading of small scale and regional productive activities, and effective social policies.

Ponna Wignaraja from Sri Lanka, with a similarly long record of reflective thinking on development. reports from a series of critical reports and books on South Asia published over the years, focussing on poverty, rural development, and empowerment. These reports form part of an intellectual project for providing a new development strategy for South Asia, organized by the South Asian Perspectives Network Organization (SAPNA). The holistic methodology used by SAPNA to probe the South Asian reality in moving towards good governance through a transitional strategy, involved interdisciplinary action research, collective creativity, and social praxis. Compared to Latin America the South Asian region has been more introverted. A fundamental and substantive difference in the SAPNA approach to poverty eradication is that it does not consider the poor as the problem, but as part of the solution. The strategy rests on notions of restraint and simplicity inherent in the regional culture rather than on unlimited progress, i.e. the western paradigm.

Focussing on the key concept 'sustainable development', Alf Hornborg, drawing on human ecology, shows how non-sustainability has been implied in the ecologically unequal change that has taken place over millennia. Globalization is not a new phenomenon in world history. Processes leading to greater societal connectedness over vast areas of the world can be traced far back in time. A commonly neglected aspect of such processes is the inclination of more highly 'developed' regions – centres of 'civilization' – to establish asymmetric relations of exchange with their local or global hinterlands, leading to accumulation of resources in the centres and often to environmental deterioration in their peripheries. Hornborg reviews some of the evidence for various kinds of such 'environmental load displacement' in different societies and cultures over the past few millennia. Rewriting global environmental history in these terms allows us to conceptualize contemporary concerns with 'sustainable development' and 'environmental security' in analytically more precise ways, integrating social and natural science and illuminating continuities and discontinuities between successive cultural patterns of resource use and their accompanying cosmologies.

Urban Jonsson gives a broad and comprehensive overview of changing paradigms in nutritional research connected with the child in poor areas of the world. His experience reflects a lifelong career in UNICEF. The problem of young child malnutrition in developing countries provides an excellent example of how the changes in theory have resulted in dramatic changes in approaches to solve the problem. The problem of child malnutrition has been redefined several times, with each new approach or paradigm reflecting broader and increasingly more normative content. The author argues that a human rights-based approach to development will be the next logical step in the process of moving development theory and practice forward.

A socio-cultural perspective is, according to Thoraya Obaid from UNFPA (United Nations Population Fund), particularly important when dealing with the sensitive issues of gender equity and the right to sexual and reproductive health. We can minimize the tension between culture and human rights when promoting universal human rights, therefore it is necessary to gain local ownership , which requires investing time in knowing the culture in which you are operating. Understanding how values, practices, and beliefs affect human behaviour is fundamental to the design of effective programmes. Nowhere is this more important than in the area of power relations between men and women and reproductive health and rights.

Next we turn to the sometimes confusing language of development and its moral connotations. Social movements, international aid organizations, social science, and neo-liberal reform programmes have in the last decade turned out to use more or less the same vocabulary of 'essentially contested terms' or 'buzzwords'. Terms such as 'empowerment', 'participation', 'mobilization', 'civil society', 'capacity building', 'local knowledge', 'community-based', 'ownership' etc. are often in different ways conveying emancipatory ambitions to involve citizens in more actively taking part in policy- and decision-making and sharing 'power' and responsibility. Gudrun Dahl discusses such words in their use as cultural capital and emotional mobilizers, and problematizes the way in which seeming political opponents share the same discursive tools. The examples are drawn from Swedish development aid cooperation.

One of the 'buzzwords' is 'civil society'. Saad Eddin Ibrahim writes about the emerging civil society and its importance for democracy and development in the Arab world. After half a century of failed development paradigms, it has now been accepted that participatory strategies are the way to move forward if development is to be sustainable. This chapter critically assesses the comparative advantage of civil society as a vehicle of development in the Third World with special emphasis given to community and faith-based organizations (FBOs) in the Arab and Muslim world. The development field has begun to acknowledge the role which faith-based organizations can play at the community level. Indeed, organizations bound by the glue of common faith and endowed with an innate stock of social capital, may have a comparative advantage over secular formations within civil society. The author concludes that both the Muslim Brothers and Hamas, and before them the Justice and Development Party in Turkey (AKP), and the Partie de Justice et Democratie in Morocco have travelled similar routes. They nearly all started as faith-based organizations, and now that they have ended up in power it looks as if this gradual transition will be the prevailing wave in the next decade at least.

In the process of addressing the overall cultural dimension of development, the gender factor in development has become even more glaring. Deeply entrenched cultural values, attitudes and practices make it extremely difficult to bring about change in gender relations in the African societies. Penina Mlama discusses gender and development with the focus on the cultural factor. She does so drawing on concrete experiences of FAWE – Forum for African Women Educationalists. FAWE is a non-governmental organization with the objective to improve the participation of girls in education in Sub-Sahara Africa. With its headquarters in Nairobi, Kenya, FAWE has chapters in 32 countries which undertake many interventions to influence policy in favour of girls as well as to increase girls' access and improve their retention and performance. The challenge facing Africa today is how to transform its formal education system in a way that it can be an effective socialization tool for eliminating the cultural impediments to development emerging out of its deeply entrenched gender-biased traditional socialization of its people. Success in transforming the education system however, has to go hand in hand with addressing the broader gender construction of the society at large.

Jan Nederveen Pieterse focusses on Islamic cosmopolitanism and the historical role and self-perception of the Islamic world as a 'middle nation', a bridging civilization. A further question is whether and how this applies to contemporary radical political Islam, which in the West is often viewed as an anti-modern and anti-western bunker mentality. In discussing Islamic cosmopolitanism the author suggests a triple movement of recentring, decentring, and again recentring the Islamic world – in a broad geopolitical, geo-economic and geo-cultural sense. In each round Islam makes different contributions to cosmopolitanism. This reorientation of history suggests that we must decentre and provincialize Eurocentric social theory and develop instead a historicist theory of modernities. As the emphasis shifts to examining how Asia and the Islamic world shape and inform European development and modernity, the Eurocentric view of modernity comes across as ethnocentric.

Enrique Rodriguez Larreta, after having problematized the concepts 'local' and 'global' in the light of recent social anthropological theorizing, gives interesting examples of how the Latin American region is affected by the complex relationship between the local and the global. Locality is seen as relational and contextual rather than scalar or spatial, whereas neighbourhoods are actually existing social forms. To fully understand the local, it is necessary to analyse the global processes that contribute to their formation. The Latin American identity came with imperialism to the continent later to be called Latin America; this identity crystallized as anti-imperialism (against North America), and is now influencing parts of the US, creating a discourse on North American identity.

Finally, the editor wants to acknowledge the important help from the assistant editor Malin Hasselskog.

1
Development Discourses in History

Björn Hettne

Introduction

Theorizing about development constitutes an exceptionally rich tradition in social science, encompassing important theoretical debates on the dynamics of social change and strategies to achieve 'development' as well as a heroic ambition to represent a global experience of empirical societal conditions in different local corners of the world.[1] This rather healthy baby must therefore, in spite of all criticism against the 'modern project', not be thrown away with the bathwater. To my mind it should grow up to become what I have termed 'global social theory'.

How should development then be understood? Either we give development a very general and abstract meaning valid for all situations, or we look for contextual meanings that change over time.[2] The latter approach is chosen here. My emphasis on the European experience is due to its importance for the early development of development theory (Senghaas 1985) and the hegemonic position of the western discourse, covering a very long historical period, but shifting over time. Therefore I shall distinguish between six consecutive discourses within the larger western development discourse. This can also be conceived of as historical and geographical (situational) contextualization of the western discourse, coinciding with what is called 'the modern project' and the belief in the critical role of human agency (rather than providence) in the pursuit of 'progress' (an older word for development). Progress can be seen as an *immanent* historical process accessible to rational, scientific analysis, in contrast to the religious view that providence determined outcomes. Development in the modern sense implies intentional social change in accordance with societal objectives. This chapter describes these three phases: *from providence over progress to development* (Cowen and Shenton 1996).

Western development thinking can as a whole be analysed as a belief system. The link between the cult of progress and religion (or rather western religion) is paradoxical but significant, due to the Judaeo–Christian tradition of seeing history as a moral drama whose last act is salvation, repeated in secular religions such as Marxism and neo-liberalism (Gray 2003).[3] By 'western' is here meant primarily European, but since the European world order, from the beginning, in different ways included extra European territories, the 'non-European' figures as 'the other' in the various historical phases of western development thinking. Thus the 'western' is to be understood in relation to 'the other', both identities shifting over time. The American approach, the second leg of the western paradigm, differs from the European in being more geopolitically motivated, 'development' usually seen as some sort of social work.[4] Development Studies as it is known in Europe hardly exists in the US.

The notion of 'modernity' is thus often associated with ethnocentric arrogance. In the eighteenth century the non-European areas were looked upon with respect and admiration. Admiration later changed into contempt as Europe grew more powerful and 'civilized'. The 'non-West' was instead conceived as 'non-historical', representing an earlier 'stage' in development. Karl Marx thought that these areas were stagnant societies which had to be 'dragged into history' by colonization, which therefore was supposed to be fortunate for them. This particular configuration of thought lies behind much of later theorizing on the 'Third World', albeit dressed in a more diplomatic language.

The dialectical tension between market solutions and political regulation takes place within what I call the 'mainstream'. By that concept I refer to the predominant, hegemonic, and 'politically correct' part of the discourse on the goals and means of development, the former expressed in concepts such as industrialization, modernization and, more recently, globalization, the latter stressing the relative effectiveness of using the market mechanism in comparison with state intervention in achieving the goals. By 'counterpoint', in contrast, I refer to a fundamental questioning of the prevailing development goals, and consequently also the means to achieve the goals, whether by regulation or market exchange. The contradiction between the mainstream and the counterpoint manifests itself throughout the western development discourse. The counter-discourse must be seen as an integral part of the discourse – a reaction to, and a force for, changing mainstream thinking and practice.

The critique of the *mainstream* paradigm has recently been addressed in terms of post-structuralism, post-modernism, and post-colonialism. Much of this contemporary criticism, valid as it may be, seems to be unaware of the fact that the hegemonic discourse has all the time been accompanied with anti-modernist or alternative (or even 'extra-discursive') perspectives, trying to give voice to those excluded from, opposing, or not even being part of mainstream development. This takes the meanings of development into a pluralist framework, bringing in the culture factor (the cultural turn). The lack of success in this alter-nativist endeavour does not minimize the intellectual attraction and strength of the anti-modernist tradition, or 'the counterpoint', in devel-opment thinking. It constitutes an interesting continuity between the discourses discussed below, in spite of their different contexts. The con-tinuities are explained by the fact that all of them formed part of the modern project, which they wanted to modify. This is a difference as compared to the notion of 'post-development', which actually lacks the will and even fails to see the need to enter the discourse in trying to change the hegemonic paradigm of development, or *mainstream*.

It is difficult to summarize the development debate in terms of clear-cut results, theoretical achievements, or a blueprint for 'development'. No progression is evident in spite of the historical connection between the concepts of development and progress. The common approach has therefore been to see older schools as precursors for those coming after, which tends to maker earlier thinking 'outdated', less relevant, and less interesting. This overview instead rests on the assumption that, in order to make sense, successive schools of development thinking, or dis-courses, should be historically contextualized, rather than understood as a linear cumulative evolution of ideas towards a universal theory. They all have a message, if understood in the context in which they were born, and they tell the story about how different generations tried to improve the human condition in line with their interests, values, and understanding of the situation. The time periods indicated are, of course, only tentative. Ideas do not disappear overnight and if they do, they may return in new shapes merging with more recent counterpoint perspectives and also being absorbed by the mainstream.

The idea of progress (1750–1815)

The modern project was closely associated with the new emphasis on the role of scientific knowledge. The 'scientific approach' (associated with Francis Bacon, 1561–1621) was generally applied in the field of the natural sciences but later on to society as well, first in the mercantilist discourse.[5] Since societal development thinking forms the perhaps most characteristic part of the European modernization project, I take my departure in the paradigm of modernity which emerged in the second part of the eighteenth century Europe in the form of Enlightenment and politically manifested in the French and American revolutions/ constitutions. This was a time when several 'development ideologies' clashed and the foundations of political economy, or classical economics, were laid, most importantly by Adam Smith (1723–1790).

Mercantilism, which was the oldest tradition with roots in the seventeenth century, was linked to state-formation and therefore marked by distinct national and class-based interests, whereas the Enlightenment idea of progress was a broader European discourse with wider universalist ambitions.[6] Physiocratism and classical liberalism saw the economy as an autonomous system and suggested different pathways to 'the wealth of nations', wealth becoming increasingly associated with society at large, rather than with the monarch. This was a significant change. The end of the Ancient Regime was near. This era saw the birth of economic science in the sense that the economy was understood as a system with laws of its own, possible to manipulate. Mercantilism in the narrow sense had been concerned with the trade balance. The Physiocrats favoured free trade but saw agriculture, understood as a national resource, as the only source of wealth. Liberals saw the productive system as a self-regulating system (the market system), not to be interfered with by national regimes. Immanence rather than intention largely characterized this thinking, but to the extent that mercantilism was understood as nation-building, there was necessarily increasingly an element of intention. The mercantilist discourse is often described as the negative backdrop to the liberal creed, but the contradiction between the two lines of thought is exaggerated.[7]

One of the founders of Physiocratism was Anne Robert Turgot (1727–1781), for whom freedom was the essential aspect of progress. As Nisbet (1969) points out, there was a successive secularization in his thinking as the identification of progress with divine providence disappears. Turgot was also an early economist, predating much of what Adam Smith later was to preach about the 'natural liberty' of economic life. Turgot saw economic progress pass through stages: hunting-gathering, agriculture, and manufacturing. Thus we can already here see the core features of the evolutionist modernization paradigm.

Adam Smith, strongly influenced by Turgot, belonged to eighteenth century Enlightenment, even though he is often mentioned in the company of Malthus and Ricardo – both belonging to a vastly different era. Smith in fact built on the earlier mercantilist discourse but described it as 'the mercantile system' based on mistakes, misunderstandings, and narrow interests. Free competition and expanding markets leading to division of labour was, according to Smith, the key to progress. The ideal (but also natural) economic system was in principal self-regulating and capable of finding its equilibrium without intervention. Smith and Turgot both argued for deregulation (trade, the guild system etc). Smith also declared that each society went through stages: hunting, pasturage, farming, and commerce (Smith 1776). However, for Smith it was possible that some societies remained in a 'barbarous and uncivilized state'.

Turgot also had a major impact on Marquis de Condorcet (1743–1794), seen by many as the father of the modern project, as well as the subsequent discourses on progress, involving most thinkers that we today consider as social scientists. Condorcet, politically involved in the French Revolution, wrote his major work on progress and freedom (the key concept) while hiding from the Jacobin regime (Condorcet 1795). He asserted that although progress may differ in speed, it will never be reversed and it concerns the whole human race.

In its rationalist zeal modernity rejected religion but nevertheless ended up as secular religion, or 'Catholicism minus Christianity' (Gray 2003: 33). I am referring to positivist religion, the Religion of Humanity, created by Auguste Comte (1798–1857). The 'teachings' of this religion were the encyclopaedic sciences. Modernity was articulated by a new intelligentsia mostly coming from the enlightened nobility and challenging the clergy, transmitter of traditional knowledge (Power 2002). The authority of this paradigm came from Science, the absolute Force, inherent in mankind, that could not be challenged.

The most prominent thinkers behind the 'scientific' doctrine of positivism, which was a rationalist and 'scientific' elaboration of the Enlightenment tradition, were Henri de Saint Simon (1760–1825) and August Comte. They are, together with Marquis de Condorcet (their great master), the foremost representatives of the modern project in its original European form, the semi-religious belief in progress. They represent the idealism of the modern age. This worldview can be seen as the foundation of European development thinking.

The counterpoint (opposing the mainstream discourse) in the era of rationalist thought rejected reason. In his *Reflections on the Revolution in France* (1790), Edmund Burke (1729–1797) argued in favour of pre-modern rural society built on tradition, religion, and paternalism. Johann Gottfried von Herder (1744–1803) rejected the Enlightenment idea of universal civilization, believing that there were many unique cultures. Herder cherished localism, decentralization, and multiplicity of loyalties. For him Germany was constituted by small national communities, and he detested centralized, militarized Prussia. Johann Gottlieb Fichte saw specific cultures as manifestations of humanity, all of them unique and therefore to be preserved as such. Thus Germany was a reservoir of pre-modern-anti/modern ideas and counterpoint values, which re-emerged in the Nazi movement.

The industrialization imperative (1815–1914)

A convenient starting-point for analysing the European development experience, on which modern development theory was founded, is the consolidation of nation-states and the international system constituted by them. The classical approach to security and world order, i.e. to consider the international system as a form of 'anarchy', took shape during the 'modern' phase in European history, which started with the peace of Westphalia (1648), following a 30 years' war. Thus began the 'Westphalian era' of territorial, sovereign states. It was an era of state-formation and nation-building, during which 'development' became a 'national interest', even an imperative for state survival. The major threat was that of peripheralization, i.e. to fall behind in the industrialization race (Senghaas 1985). The international system, marked by inter-state competition, created a 'modernization imperative' or, more precisely, an industrialization imperative, i.e. in order to survive, development (or rather industrialization) was necessary for security reasons.

Throughout European modern history there have been several efforts to create geopolitical hegemony or dominion, provoking 'anti-hegemonic' wars. These attempts at continental control have come from the dominant nations: France and Germany (Prussia), whereas England and Holland have been 'guardians' of the principle of balance of power (Watson 1992). Progress in that context was for military reasons identified with economic development, which in the nineteenth century meant industrialization. The state ultimately became responsible for what came to be called 'development', and the nation-state territory became the privileged space (container) in which development was to take place, security to be guaranteed and welfare to be created. The world order was a regional European system (with non-European colonial satellites), stabilized by what became known as the European Concert. The 'anarchy' thereby became an 'anarchical society' (Bull 1977).

This durable improvement of political order in the European region facilitated the breakthrough of market society.

The roots of the belief in the market can, as was discussed above, be found in the doctrine of harmony of interests, expressed in its classical form by Adam Smith. David Ricardo (1772–1823) later built the systematic classical economic theory on Smith's observations, adding among other things the comparative (or relative) advantage argument for trade to Smith's argument for absolute advantage. Classical economics as an approach was on the whole taken over by Karl Marx (1818–1883), but for him (in turning Hegel on his head) classes were the main agents in history. However, classes played their role according to material conditions in different historical stages: primitive communism, the ancient system, feudalism, capitalism, communism. Development was first of all the development of capitalism. New higher relations of production (e.g. socialism paving way for the communist 'utopia') could not appear 'before the material conditions of their existence have matured in the womb of the old society'. Here the immanence from the first discourse lingers on.

The European development experience is, nevertheless, largely 'mercantilistic' (in the broad sense of the word), which implies the involvement of the state in creating the conditions for development. In nineteenth century Europe this was general practice. The degree of 'backwardness' determined the degree of state intervention that was needed to catch up. Few European countries actually developed in accordance with the way the World Bank and the International Monetary Fund (IMF) now recommend the underdeveloped countries to develop. Rather, there was a change in the content of progress and a change from immanence associated with progress and belief in the market to a stronger component of intention as manifested in efforts to industrialize.

In the nineteenth century, there emerged a sharp development differential due to the industrial revolution in England, which made this particular country 'the workshop of the world'. The 'development problem' was then 'industrialize or perish', a dilemma most authoritatively formulated by the German economist Friedrich List, who therefore can be called the father of development economics (Senghaas 1985), in opposition to the British (Ricardian) theory of comparative advantage and free trade (Ricardo 1841). List was influenced by the debate in America – involving among others Alexander Hamilton and Henry Carey. In order to challenge the dominant industrial power, protectionism and support to 'infant industries' was needed, according to the

Listian theory of how to 'catch up' with the strong powers. 'Catching up' was a typical expression of the modernization imperative, the metaphor being some sort of 'race', even a deadly race, since the losers may also lose their statehood. In spite of defending protectionism (the infant industry argument) List was essentially liberal, loyal to the predominant paradigm and acknowledging the benefits of competition as soon as the structure of comparative advantages had been transformed in favour of one's own state. He contrasted this national political economy to a 'cosmopolitan economy'.

Development in an anarchical system implied a strengthening of the material base of the state through industrialization, a process remarkably similar from one (successful) country to another, and reinforced by the security interests of the ruling elite (Sen 1984). In the mainstream model, there is consequently a potential conflict, primarily between competing states within the inter-state system, and, secondly, between state power, on the one hand, and restive, unassimilated social and ethnic groups challenging the legitimacy of the state, on the other. The concept of the nation-building project is a key to understanding what mainstream development (the industrialization imperative) essentially came to be about. Similarities in the pattern of economic development did not reveal inherent or immanent tendencies in history towards 'modernity' but rather security imperatives for the emerging states, making industrialization necessary simply for military reasons. The state-building process in Europe was violent; therefore people gradually learned to conceive 'their' state as a protector, and the rest of the world as a threat. The realist logic was born. Similarly, the Soviet state after 1917 was consolidated by war against both internal and external enemies. This was the modernization imperative as it appeared to the Russian revolutionaries and it led to an extreme variant of the modern project.

To this should be added that the 'expansion of Europe', which also became an 'expansion of international society' (Bull and Watson 1984) was a competitive process, involving a number of core-states struggling for hegemony, with crucial repercussions in the rest of the world, subsequently divided into colonial empires. The world order was an imperialist order. In a global perspective the second discourse thus coincided with the era of colonialism in Asia and Africa and neo-colonialism in Latin America.

Modernization was not necessarily linked to optimism. The transition from *Gemeinschaft* to *Gesellschaft* was taken by the classical sociologists to be painful for the individual. Many mainstream thinkers thus expressed doubts about the benefits of development even if they saw the process as irreversible. Max Weber pointed out that the irreversible rationalization of modern society made it dull and unbearable because it lost its 'charm' (*Entzauberung*), but he saw no alternative options. To Karl Marx alienation was a necessary consequence of the capitalist mode of production. This stress on 'necessity' makes Marx part of mainstream, whereas the so called 'utopian socialists' gave expression to counterpoint values as a voluntary escape from the iron cage of Weber. There was thus also a conscious anti-modern debate on *not* to 'catch up' or imitate, since industrialization implied the sacrifice of values inherent in pre-modern or 'traditional society'. Claude Henri de Saint Simon (1760–1825), Charles Fourier (1772–1837), and Robert Owen (1771–1858) looked for more or less radical solutions to the anomie created by the emerging industrial order, which threatened the pre-industrial world of handicraft and small manufacturing. The key word in their thinking was 'harmony', which in a sense replaced progress. They did not consider themselves as utopians (this was the name given by Marx because they did not understand the necessity of going through the capitalist ordeal). Saint-Simon can be seen as more mainstream because of his association with Comte's ideas and his worship of '*le système industriel*'. Owen's commitment to small-scale organization makes him a more typical representative for the counterpoint, while Fourier who criticized the dullness of industrial society and stressed the importance of 'passions' also comes closer to the counterpoint.

The most articulate counterpoint position was represented by the Narodniks, or Russian populists (Walicki 1969; Kitching, 1982) representing the counterpoint in the debate on development in Russia. The Narodniks argued against industrialism as a large-scale and centralized form of production and were for similar reasons also against the state as a centralized political institution. Of particular interest in this context is their engagement with the concept of progress, which they dismissed in the typical objectivist form it had received in the western discourse, stressing instead its subjectivist dimension and the focus on the individual.[8]

Progress as planning (1914–1945)

After 'the long peace' in the nineteenth century came war and depression, characterizing much of the first half of the twentieth century, probably the worst period in European history. Peace, understood as 'absence of war', was synonymous with balance of power, focusing on military security at the level of the state. The relative stability based on the European Concert came to an end with the coming of the twentieth century when the Concert was replaced by an unstable alliance system. External conflicts in this era therefore became increasingly dangerous and the intellectual mood turned into pessimism (fin de siècle), related to a loss of faith in the modern project. But there was also a (temporary) feeling of rejuvenation based on war and heroism, facilitating political extremism as well as anti-liberal interventionism. But the political breakthrough of fascism had to wait until the Crash in 1929 and the Great Depression.

Internal conflicts were related to the process of nation-building, which implied the imposition of a uniform order upon heterogeneous local communities. This led to ethno-national unrest (particularly after First World War). Other internal conflicts, for instance food and tax riots, were related to the deepening of the market system to include all factors of production, thus reducing social security embedded in the 'traditional' social structure. This signalled a second movement in a Polanyian great transformation and the end of what Polanyi called '19th century civilization', based on the four foundations: the balance of power system, the international gold standard, the self-regulating market, and the liberal state (Polanyi 2001: 3). An important factor in development thinking was the crisis in capitalist development manifested in the Great Depression, which provoked the ideological radicalism implied in the second movement of the double movement. According to Polanyi (2001: 248), 'Fascism, like socialism, was rooted in a market society that refused to function'. Fascist economics rejected economics, liberal as well as socialist. It implied the imposition of politics over the economy, stressing the importance of human will. Ruralism (a return to peasant values) was a populist part of fascist ideology. In reality, fascist economic policy compromised with the traditionalist values and adapted to the real world of capitalism simply in order to stay in power.

Interventionism (re-regulating or re-embedding the national economy) therefore also became part of the mainstream. Planning can be seen as the ultimate expression of the modern project and progress as human purpose. The main theorist behind this mainstream in Europe was John Maynard Keynes (1883–1946) with his magnum opus 'General Theory' from 1936 (Keynes 1936). The neo-liberal position represented by Friedrich Hayek (building on Ludvig von Mises) was still marginal. But Hayek's time would come.

Keynesianism, in contrast to the Listian state capitalist strategy discussed earlier, was a manifestation of mature if not stable capitalism

(Hettne 1995: 33). Its departure from the basic liberal model consisted of denying that the market possessed the capacity for self-regulation and in granting the state a responsibility for the stability and continuous growth of capitalist systems. It provided the rationale behind much of post-war interventionism.

The Soviet model was to a large extent a continuation of the state capitalist strategy of pre-revolutionary Russia, although the ideological inspiration and political context differed. In the famous policy debate in the 1920s several options were discussed (Erlich 1960). Ultimately Stalin responded with his five-year-plans which completely transformed the Soviet economy. In the Soviet Union planning became a high prestige economic science admired also in the capitalist world where state intervention, due to depression as well as the war experience, was still something normal. This was before the Cold War.

The counterpoint, at the same time anti-liberal and anti-communist, was on the streets during the crisis, and ironically led to authoritarian, modernist governments exposing the worst features of capitalism and modernism. There were antirational movements both to the right and to the left. The 'dark times' led to a growing disbelief in modernity among intellectuals. A typical example was Max Horkheimer's and Theodor Adorno's *Dialektik der Aufklärung* (1947). They made the distinction between modern science and technology, on the one hand, and ethics, morality, religion, on the other, arguing that there was a contradiction between the two. The modern project was in doubt.

The geopolitics of poverty (1945–1980)

The Great Depression and its political consequences was obviously a deep crisis for the modern project, but during the dynamic decades after the Second World War belief in continued modernization, reminding about the first discourse, returned. It is amazing that the old optimism associated with the progress paradigm could be so quickly restored. Economic planning for reconstruction and thereafter welfare politics in the lucky states under the umbrella of US hegemony consolidated the nation-state and the international, in fact globalized, order. The fourth 'discourse', the geopolitics of poverty, starting soon after the Second World War, concerned global poverty and 'underdevelopment', then understood as a threat to the post-war world order ('the free world') in the context of the emerging Cold War. The development issue was now subsumed under altogether different security concerns: a struggle for power between the superpowers and at the same time a worldwide competition between two different socio-economic systems: the geopolitical structure of bipolarity. This tension facilitated a 'great compromise' between national regulation and international free trade and paved way for the 'golden years', the 1950s and the 1960s. Modernization and progress were back, at least in the 'first' and 'second' worlds. Socialism was still a model for many developing countries.

The fourth development discourse emerged within a global security complex characterized not only by a competition between two political and socio-economic systems, but also a nuclear 'terror balance' which ruled out war between major powers, at the same time as it imposed a straightjacket on the other regions of the world, very different from the post-First World War situation. The emergence of the Soviet system implied the division of the world into two hostile blocs, two socio-economic systems, and two development ideologies, albeit similar in their belief in modernity (competing forms of modernity). All regions were artificially divided according to this bipolar logic (East–West), and all conflicts were interpreted in Cold War terms. This new, truly global conflict pattern also shaped the post-colonial world, described by president Truman in 'point four' of his often quoted 1949 inauguration speech, as the 'underdeveloped areas' of 'hunger, misery, and despair'; constituting a potential threat to what in Cold War terms was to be called the 'free world' (Rist 1997: appendix 1). For great powers, involved in power politics and strategic action (as they had to be), this was the main rationale behind development aid, whereas the smaller and more neutral ('like-minded') countries could afford to develop a more extravagant 'Third Worldist', non-securitized position.

Also on the economic front conflicts were avoided through what Ruggie (1998: 72), has termed the 'compromise of embedded liberalism'. Most importantly, it was a compromise between economic liberty and free trade outside the nation-state, and economic regulation for the purpose of full employment, welfare, and social peace inside it. The result in terms of economic growth was dramatic. Growth was seen as built into the system. The belief in social engineering was best symbolized in Keynesianism.

The security strategy (balance of terror) guaranteed a fairly high degree of predictability, except in the (improbable) case that the 'impossible' nuclear war actually was to take place. In the Cold War both superpowers defined security in terms of bloc stability, which drastically limited the principle of sovereignty, particularly for the decolonized poor world or 'developing countries', which responded with their little appreciated Non-Aligned Movement (NAM) and, subsequently, equally futile demands for a New International Economic Order (NIEO). However, these radical initiatives, in general applauded by academic development studies, maintained the radical spirit throughout the 1970s, until the showdown in Cancún 1981 which can be said to mark the symbolic end of this discourse.

In the post-colonial era, state-building became a global process, and the nation-state a universal political phenomenon. In this particular respect the fourth discourse was a generalization of the second, which had been confined to the consolidation of states in the European region. The anti-systemic guerrilla struggle labelled 'communist insurgency' by the West, was the typical war during this period, particularly in Africa, Southeast Asia, and Latin America. But there were also inter-state tensions, for instance in East Asia, South Asia and the Middle East. Here we find more conventional rivalries and occasional wars which can be related to balance of power politics, regional security complexes, reminiscent of the nineteenth century European states system. Also, the development strategy was similar, which can be explained by the similarities in context. These military tensions had a clear impact on the development discourse, pushing the countries towards mainstream approaches, by focussing on modernization and industrialization, and therefore marginalizing counterpoint positions in development thinking which might have benefited, for instance, rural areas and marginalized minorities. Gandhiism in India, as well as Maoism in China are cases in point.

The reconstruction of Europe after the Second World War provided the model for state-directed *modernization* of the 'new nations'. Development economics of an interventionist kind, inspired by Keynesian theory and the experiences from the Great Depression of the 1930s, were the core of this paradigm, which had its counterpart in the so called 'non-capitalist development' or 'socialist-oriented' strategy in the rival bloc. This development strategy from above played down the need for revolutions and gave heavy industry the role of the leading sector in a development strategy from above. The socialist experience, supported by the other block, can be seen as another mainstream strategy, informed by the Soviet development model.

Development was seen in an evolutionary perspective, and the state of underdevelopment defined in terms of observable economic, political, social, and cultural differences between rich and poor nations. What was called 'tradition' was seen as an obstacle to development in the spirit of Enlightenment. Development implied the bridging of these gaps by means of an imitative process, in which the less developed countries gradually assumed the qualities of the industrialized nations through an active interventionist state. This was the art of nation-building inherent in the modernization paradigm.

The neo-colonial implications of this Eurocentric model led to the rise of the *dependency paradigm,* first emerging in Latin America and reflecting the subordinate economic position of the non-European areas in the world system as well as the limited political sovereignty implied in bipolar domination (Blomström and Hettne 1984). In this theoretical perspective there were within a given structure certain positions which regularly and more or less automatically accumulated material and non-material resources, whereas other positions were deprived of these resources. Development for one unit could therefore lead to underdevelopment for another, depending on how the two units were structurally linked. Poverty was seen as a structure rather than as a particular stage (backwardness) as in the second discourse. The conclusion drawn was that real development implied self-reliance and even de-linking from the capitalist system.

Interdependence was the reformist variety of the North–South dichotomy. The Brandt Report (1980) was an ambitious but stillborn (Cancún meeting 1981) attempt to apply the interventionist development strategy from the second discourse to the emerging globalized condition. What now became 'the North' and 'the South' were said to be 'interdependent', the conclusion being that a massive transfer of resources from the North to South also would stimulate the northern economies by increasing demand, providing a Keynesian instrument for economic cycles management in a globalizing world (Global Keynesianism).

These rival mainstream approaches, which dominated the debate in the 1970s, were in turn challenged by the counterpoint, or 'alternative' theoretical positions, grounded in environmentalism, endogenous and indigenous development, eco-development, ethno-development, human development, feminist theorizing and the like. Its main concern was the many problems created by mainstream development, and the social groups and classes that were excluded from development. Mainstream development was a painful process. *Another Development* was defined as need-oriented, endogenous, self-reliant, ecologically sound, and based on structural transformation (Nerfin 1977). The ideas can be summed up and reformulated in the three principles of *territorial development, ecological sustainability,* and *cultural pluralism* (Hettne 1995). They can also generally be described as 'the voices of the excluded' (including future generations). The 'green' ideology (as it was termed in the North) can be seen as a modern synthesis of neo-populist and neo-anarchist ideas, revived in the 1960s and forming part of the New Left movement in the US and in Europe, inspired by the Frankfurt school. Later they merged with ecology, peace, and feminist movements both in the North and in the South. These ideas bear a certain resemblance to the classical populism and anarchism in urging for community (*Gemeinschaft*) and in their distaste of industrial civilization (*Gesellschaft*).

Globalization and disorder (1980–2000)

The shift from the fourth to the fifth development discourse came during the 1980s and as important markers one could mention the rise of the New Right and the New Cold War, the so-called impasse in radical development studies, the counter-revolution in development economics, and the escape from the impasse into postmodernism, all in the context of globalization. In the course of the 1980s the communist system broke down which also contributed to the liberal triumphalism.

As a significant mark of the changing intellectual climate in the 1980s, one can take note of the rather quick demise of the global Keynesian development paradigm outlined in the Brandt Report. Through what was called a 'counter-revolution' in development economics (Toye 1987), which took up momentum in the 1980s, the non-interventionist, anti-Keynesian, neoclassical, unidimensional (economistic) approach, at first politically associated with 'Thatcherism' and 'Reaganomics', became predominant, paving way for structural adjustment programmes (with or without a human face) and privatization, orchestrated by the Bretton Woods institutions, now pressing for a more consequent liberal policy. In this way the domestic bases for continued globalization were created and secured. This marked the end of the Great Compromise and the Golden Age and the beginning of the Washington consensus. Globalism entered the development discourse as immanent and inevitable progress: the modernization paradigm globalized and simplified. Other central issues were democracy and human rights. The development problems and their solutions were thus looked for inside the developing countries rather than in their unequal international relations.

Globalism or 'global adjustment' as experienced by the poor countries implied as its ideological core the growth of a world market, increasingly penetrating and dominating the 'national' economies. Since this process is seen as synonymous to increased efficiency and a higher 'world product', globalists consider 'too much government' as a systemic fault. Good governance was consequently often defined as less government. Thus, the ideology of globalism argued in favour of a particular form of globalization, namely neo-liberal economic globalization: the institutionalization of the market on a global scale. The purpose of political order, according to the globalist vision, was to facilitate the free movement of economic factors. This is seen not only as a 'natural' (in the modernist sense) but also as the most beneficial condition for development and welfare. Any attempt to isolate oneself from market forces (as had been suggested by radical dependency theory) was, according to the liberal view, a sentence to stagnation for a country or even a region. The optimum size of an economy (and therefore its ultimate form) was the world market as once was asserted by Adam Smith. All other arrangements, for instance, regional trade agreements, were only second best, but acceptable to the extent that they were stepping stones rather than stumbling blocks to the world market.

'Contemporary globalization' (there are different historical phases of globalization (Held et al. 1999) can be seen as a further deepening of the market system, which (including its disturbing social repercussions) now is taking place in a truly global scale. We should not expect a uniform response to this 'second great transformation', but, as history shows, many forms of adaptation and resistance. So far the globalist (neo-liberal) hegemony has been powerful. Highly contrasting political forces converged on the same neo-liberal economic policies ('there is no alternative').

In accepting the neo-liberal ideology of globalism the state became the disciplining spokesman of external economic forces, rather than the protector of society against these forces, which was the classical task of nation-building, culminating in the modern welfare state. The retreat of the state from these historical functions also implied a changed relationship between the state and *civil society* (Tester 1992; Chandhoke 1995) and, in particular, a tendency for the state to become alienated from civil society. Inclusion as well as exclusion is inherent in the networking process implied in globalization, and benefits occurring somewhere are negatively balanced by misery and violence elsewhere. Particularly in the South, there is an ongoing informalization of economy and fragmentation of society. The fundamental problem with globalization is the selectiveness of the process. Not everybody is invited to join. The exclusivist implications lead to 'politics of identity', as loyalties are being transferred from civil society to 'primary groups' (defined as the smallest 'we-group' in a particular social context), competing for scarce resources in growing development crises.

Development, as a crucial part of modernity, was traditionally seen as a rational progressive process organized by the state (nation-building). The idea that the world is instead moving into global chaos (Sadowski 1998) has been forcefully presented by a school of thought represented by Robert Kaplan (1994) and Samuel Huntington (1993). Others apply a more sophisticated theory of chaos borrowed from science, which seems to imply that the social system can be made to move in unforeseeable directions though minor changes occurring anywhere in the system. A related postmodern line of reasoning acknowledges the fact that globalization has undermined the nation-state order, but tries to identify some sort of logic in this seemingly turbulent situation in which domestic chaos or durable disorder can go on for decades, thus no longer being abnormal, but rather the birth of a new order very different from modernist assumptions. Conventional view has it that disintegration of the state implies non-development, but some studies of 'real' substantive economies suggest a more complex picture of emerging 'local' (or rather 'glocalized') economies, de-linked from state control, run by a new type of entrepreneur, supported by private military protection, and drawing on international connections (cf. Chabal and Daloz 1999). All this was possible, since the state is becoming unable to legally define and protect various assets and resources situated within the 'national' territory (Duffield 1998; 2001). Those who cannot control the state turn to 'warlord politics' (Reno 1998).

Even if 'new wars' are usually defined as 'internal', the new situation is actually characterized by the erosion of the external–internal distinction. As a state is dissolved, it can no longer be territorially defined, and occasionally neighbouring states are drawn into clashes among themselves (regionalization of conflict), underlining the increasingly irrelevant distinction between 'internal' and 'external'. The phenomenon may, as noted, not only be a simple passing crisis for the state, but a 'durable disorder' or, in metaphorical terms, 'a new medievalism' (Cerny 1998). In terms of 'development' *durable disorder* can mean a generalized war-lord economy with limited influence of external forms of authority on the local power-holders and social forces. The mode of development possible in such a context may at best be some sort of 'primitive accumulation'. Obviously the standard definitions of development were hard to apply in this situation.

In the globalized world there emerged during the 1990s, as a result of the spread of disorder, a qualitatively new discourse on intervention called 'humanitarian intervention', which implied a coercive involvement by external powers in a domestic crises with the purpose of preventing anarchy, punishing human rights abuses, and promoting democracy and 'good governance'. It can be seen as an extension of international development assistance into a more coercive form challenging established principles of territorial sovereignty. The recent focus upon human security rather than state security is significant for understanding the change of the security and development discourse and the fundamental challenge to sovereignty. Implied in concepts such as 'human security', 'human development', 'humanitarian emergency', and 'humanitarian intervention' was the idea of a transnational responsibility for human welfare (the responsibility to protect).

More recently the discourse has again changed from 'humanitarian intervention' to pre-emptive intervention or 'war against terrorism'. The full implications of this, as far as the future world order is concerned, are yet to be seen. The war against Iraq was not compatible with international law and may be a turning point as far as liberal interventionism is concerned, further undermining the Westphalian foundations of world order.

Globalization constitutes processes of both inclusion and exclusion; thus the alternative tradition in development theory can still be defined as incorporating demands from 'the excluded' but it is, in the era of 'post-development', no longer so clear into what they are supposed to be included. An additional alternative development dimension in a context of societal disintegration is the role model of remaining 'islands of civility' in a sea of civil war (Kaldor 1999). Development was in collapsing states reduced to what development workers had to do in situations of crisis and conflict. Development aid was in this context reduced to a civil form of humanitarian intervention, and the major reason for intervention was violent conflict; to prevent it, to manage it, or to reconstruct societies in post-conflict situations (Munslow 2002). The complex rebuilding (or rather the creation of a new equilibrium) cannot be done by outside players alone, but normally not without them either. Local players have become paralysed by mutual hostility and fear, apart from lacking necessary resources, destroyed by the war. There is thus no alternative but to build on the combined efforts of external interveners and remaining 'islands of civility' to combat hate, suspicion, corruption, and criminality.

Towards global development? (2000–)

Global development, the emerging discourse which so far is lacking in terms of social practice, can be defined as an improvement in the quality of international relations, which traditionally have been described as 'anarchic', or at the most as 'anarchical society' (Bull 1977), i.e. more than anarchy but less than community. The purpose of global development would thus be to create a global community for all human beings. Humanity does not yet, however, constitute a political community, much less a political player. Nevertheless, the qualitative dimension of global governance, encompassing a number of basic human values, is, I suggest, what global development is all about. The definition is therefore a normative one. To make it as politically relevant and operational as possible, one can depart from the September 2000 Millennium Declaration, which was based on the following fundamental values: freedom, equality, solidarity, tolerance, respect for nature, and shared responsibility.[9] This declaration was a high point in respect for international law, and multilateralism. It was also a loyalty declaration to the UN – and the principle of multilateralism. The World Bank Development Reports from 2001 and onwards showed a change in tone and approach towards a more complex involvement of markets, states, and civil society After September 11th a new world order context emerged in which the US hegemony, rooted in multilateralism, was transformed into dominance, expressed in unilateralism, 'the unipolar movement', and the security doctrine of pre-emption. Development thinking reappeared in a rude, caricatured form of 'nation-building' under conditions that remind about colonialism and 'the white man's burden'.

The unilateralist trend in the US and the consequent conflict with Europe meant the end of western consensus. The US was preoccupied with security, but gradually the Washington consensus was transformed into a post-Washington consensus, implying a greater degree of flexibility in the approach to development (Stiglitz 2006). In Europe the preferred ideology was the Third Way. At the same time attempts were made to revive the UN through reforms. In spite of failed states and horrific conflicts, as well as the return of imperialism, development thinking forms part of the 'modern project', retaining its normative approach and its belief in the rational human being. The discouraging elements in the fifth discourse have paved way for a more constructive approach, focussed on the normative project of global development. Globalization and its problems raise the issue of a new theoretical approach as well as a new content of development.

Global development necessitates a further strengthening of the societal (welfare) dimension of world order – the provision of global public goods (see volume 2, by Gun-Britt Andersson). Global development, so defined, would mean that standards applied in most (non-failed) domestic systems are increasingly taken as norms in the international system as well. In the present context, the historical process of market expansion is a worldwide process, which is likely to make the social and political counter-movements even more varying in the different regions of the world, and therefore even harder to predict. This new double movement, of which its second movement has hardly begun, has been interpreted as a 'second great transformation' (Hettne 1997). It can be argued that the European regional integration model, due to its strong focus on the role of institutions in Europe's own integration process as well as on the importance of institutionalized interregional relations, represents a potential world order. The European Union is in the process of building interregional relations with all regions of the world. The overall purpose of interregionalism is to make the external environment of Europe, that is the rest of the world, more stable and more predictable. The significance of this experience is that transregional institutions have the potentiality of shaping, through intersubjectivity and mutual learning, the outlook of regional civilizations towards compatible patterns of coexistence, ultimately through multiculturalism and multiregionalism.

From a global development perspective, there is, however, still a striking governance gap. The concept of global governance is by itself a recognition of the possibility of a rules-bound order, a refutation of the anarchy model of international relations as well as the utopia of the self-regulating market. What can be put in their place? The need is for a new great compromise. Such a compromise should provide the framework for *global development*, which in a globalized world is the relevant form of development. The disrupting social consequences of deterritorialization implied in the process of market-led globalization generate political forces to halt and modify the process of globalization in order to guarantee territorial control, cultural diversity, and human security. In order to promote global development there must, instead of cultural homogenization and structural polarization, be an inter-civilizational dialogue on the level of the macro-regions/macro-cultures; such a dialogue would necessitate a reasonably symmetric power base for regionally based civilizations; instead of asymmetry and polarization, the structural gap between regions must be bridged, and the vertical structure of the world order horizontalized through the strengthening of weak and incoherent regions in the periphery. Of importance is also that weaker/intermediate regions are capable of advancing their interest in changing the structure of comparative advantages rather than simply adapting to the received pattern of comparative advantages. For this the building of transnational and interregional institutions are needed. Interregionalism is also a way of institutionalizing the much needed 'dialogue among civilizations'. If this is to be seen as progress it has to be *negotiated progress,* in contrast with immanent progress, or intentional imposed progress from the earlier discourses reviewed here. For an intercultural dialogue to be possible some kind of commonality, or even cosmopolitan elements, would be needed. There are no inherent reasons why this would not exist in all cultures, in contrast to cultural trends which due to specific historical contextual reasons take a hardened, introvert, fundamentalist form (politics of identity; see volume 1, by Jan Nederveen Pieterse). There is in other words no such thing as a fundamentalist culture or religion, only fundamentalist interpretations emerging from specific social and political situations in specific historical situations.

Global development appears in the shape of mainstream as well as counterpoint. The mainstream can be illustrated by the Millennium Development Goals and the new Swedish policy for global development, while the counterpoint can be illustrated by the World Social Forums since 2004. All of these documents, however, put a strong emphasis on *justice.* Justice is by many theorists and political philosophers seen as applicable on the national level only. For justice to become a core value in global development there is thus a need for a dramatic expansion of global consciousness and solidarity (see volume 2, by Gita Sen). Obviously this cannot happen without struggle. The new global solidarity movements are more realistic than the 'international community' as manifest in development diplomacy. But it is significant that solidarity is one of the fundamental values in the Millennium Declaration.

Conclusion: Global social theory

This overview of development thinking has focused on the western or rather European development thinking from the birth of the idea of human progress shaped by human agency in the optimistic eighteenth century, the idea of development (industrialization) as essential for state survival in the nineteenth century, the economic crises and emergence of welfarism and international aid in the twentieth century, which also saw the discourse on globalization and disorder, and, finally, the universal goal of global development in the beginning of the twenty-first century. Can the western development discourse be relevant for a universal global theory?

This overview has not provided a consistent and permanent definition of development. This was never my intention. If I may quote myself from an earlier work: 'There can be no fixed and final definition of development; only suggestions of what it should imply in particular contexts' (Hettne 1995: 15). Development has meant different things in different discourses. Development is still, to my mind, part of the unfulfilled modern project, defined as critical, reflexive, and potentially universal. But the universalization of theory can only be seen as a pluralist goal of increasing richness and relevance; it is nothing that can be taken for granted as an inherent property revealing itself over time. Rather it can be defined as acknowledgement of 'the other' and readiness to become involved in dialogue with an open mind. Immanent progress became intentional and thereby imposed. It now has to become negotiated.

It is easy to agree with the post-development position, if development as part of the modern project is simply defined as imperialism or intellectual dependency with destructive consequences. A global social theory should be global (covering the globe), which must be distinguished from universal (meaning the same everywhere). Global implies that a variety of societal experiences from around the world are taken into account, as well as a pluralist understanding of development goals. The great achievement of development studies has perhaps been to create such a worldwide empirical base for building a global social theory by providing so much concrete knowledge of local development and underdevelopment situations from the world, together with varying perspectives on the meaning of development. No other social science specialization can match this wealth of empirical data from a multitude of cultures. These various situations, which have to be contextually understood, are coexisting worlds, not stages in a 'natural history' of development as modernization and progress. Since development problems are globalized, and 'national development' has lost much of its meaning, development theory is necessarily merging with International Political Economy into global social theory and the new interdisciplinary field of 'Global Studies' (drawing on IR, IPE, development studies, cultural studies, the new security paradigm etc.). Global social theory does not yet exist as such, it will be created by the theoretical discourse focusing on the causes and consequences, as well as improvement, of the globalized condition in all parts – more or less and differently globalized – of the world. Thus the discourse on global development is not concluded, it has just begun.

Notes

1. This essay is a retrospective (and of course 'rethinking') overview of development thinking by an author who in his early university years (in the turbulent 1960s) was, like so many other of that generation, carried away by the problem of 'development', being politically relevant as well as theoretically rewarding. Professor Karl Eric Knutsson gave me the first chance to work seriously on this issue for the report that ultimately (not without political controversy) gave birth to the Swedish Agency for Research Cooperation with Developing Countries (SAREC). I was, in line with the current Zeitgeist, both attracted by the Grand Theory tradition which hade emerged in connection to grappling with the development issue (Gunnar Myrdal was the giant in the Swedish context), and mystified by the scepticism against the predominant western modernization paradigm (well represented by Myrdal) from unorthodox cultural studies such as Social Anthropology, articulated elegantly by the young and dynamic professor in Gothenburg, later Stockholm. The resulting ambivalence has stayed on, but in spite of the more recent postmodernist onslaught, I retain an unreformed, if somewhat shaken, belief in the modern project. In spite of that bias, development theory is here tentatively analysed as a succession of discourses rather than as an evolutionary process, which was the format of the earlier overview, dating from the early 1970s (Hettne 1978).
2. Nederveen Pieterse, (2001: 7) in a similar vein suggests that '"Development" serves as a mirror of changing economic and social capacities, priorities and choices'.
3. The goal of salvation was in 'scientific' elaborations typically preceded by a number of stages, sometimes three, sometimes five. In positivist theory, human thinking evolved from religious, over metaphysical to positive. Marx's theory of human development went from primitive communism to modern communism, which ironically was to restore basic values from the first stage, but at a higher level of technology and production. W.W. Rostow's liberal stages ended up in an 'era of mass consumerism', which to Fukuyama was 'the end of history'. The neo-liberal view of economic history of the emergence of the market system was an evolutionary emancipatory (disembedding) process.
4. Francis Fukuyama (2006: 114) regrets that American policy approaches to development have been heavily driven by the needs of American foreign policy and wants an upgrading of development policy in the post-Bush era.
5. At this early stage rationalism and belief in science could be seen as a counterpoint to a Christian mainstream.
6. There were, however, differences, for instance between the British, French, and American Enlightenments (Himmelfarb 2005).
7. Lars Magnusson (1993) has shown that also mercantilists (not a very homogeneous category) thought of the economy as a law-bound system which could be manipulated in different directions depending on different interests.
8. Progress was given a new meaning in Mikhailovski's law of progress, far from the mainstream conceptions of division of labour: 'Progress is the gradual approach to the integral individual, to the fullest possible and the most

diversified division of labour among man's organs and the least possible division of labour among men. Everything that diminishes the heterogeneity of society and there by increases the heterogeneity of its members is moral, just, reasonable and beneficial' (Walicki 1969: 53).

9. It is interesting to note that the first mentioned basic value also was a key concept in the eighteenth century discourse on progress, for instance in the case of Condorcet. Based on the fundamental values, there are eight goals and 18 targets.

References

Blomström, M. and Hettne, B. (1984) *Development Theory in Transition: The Dependency* Debate *and Beyond: Third World Responses*, London: Zed Books.

Bull, H. (1977) *The Anarchical Society. A Study of Order in World Politics*, London: Macmillan.

Bull, H. and Watson, A. (eds) (1984) *The Expansion of International Society*, Oxford: Clarendon Press.

Cerny, P. G. (1998) 'Neomediavalism, Civil War and the New Security Dilemma: Globalization as Durable Disorder', *Civil Wars*, 1(1): 36–64.

Chabal, P. and Daloz, J-P. (1999) *Africa Works. Disorder as Political Instrument*, Oxford: James Currey.

Chandhoke, N. (1995) *State and Civil Society. Explorations in Political Theory*, New Delhi: Sage.

Condorcet, M. (1795) Esquisse d'un tableau historique des progrès de l'esprit humain (Sketch of the Progress of the Human Mind).

Cowen, M. P. and Shenton, R. W. (1996) *Doctrines of Development*, London and New York: Routledge.

Cox, R. W. (ed) (1997) *The New Realism. Perspectives on Multilateralism and World Order*, Tokyo: United Nations University Press.

Desai, V. and Potter, R. B. (eds) (2002) *The Companion to Development Studies*, London: Arnold Publications.

Duffield, M. (1998) 'Post-modern conflict: Warlords, Post-adjustment States and Private Protection', *Civil Wars*, 1(1): 65–102.

Duffield, M. (2001) *Global Governance and the New Wars*, London and New York: Zed Books.

Fukuyama, F. (2006) *After the Necons*, London: Profile Books.

Gray, J. (2003) *Al Qaeda and What It Means to be Modern*, London: Faber and Faber.

Held, D. et al. (1999) *Global Transformations*, Oxford: Polity Press.

Hettne, B. (1978) *Current Issues in Development Theory*, SAREC Report , R5.

Hettne, B. (1995) *Development Theory and the Three Worlds. Towards an International Political Economy of Development*, London: Longman.

Hettne, Björn (1997) 'The Double Movement: global market versus regionalism', in Cox, R. W. (ed) (1997) *The New Realism. Perspectives on Multilateralism and World Order*, Tokyo: United Nations University Press.

Himmelfarb, G. (1996) *The Roads to Modernity: The British, French, and American Enlightenments*, New York: Knopf, distributed by Random House.

Hobsbawm, Eric (1994), *The Age of Extremes. The Short Twentieth Century 1914–1991*, London: Abacus.

Horkheimer, M. and Adorno, T. (1947) Dialektik der Aufklärung, Philosophische Fragmente, Frankfurt am Main: S. Fischer Verlag.

Huntington, S. P. (1993) 'The Clash of Civilizations', *Foreign Affairs*, 72(3): 22–42.

Kaldor, M. (1999) *New & Old Wars. Organized Violence in a Global Era*, Cambridge: Polity Press.

Kaplan, R. (1994) 'The Coming Anarchy', *Atlantic Monthly*, February: 44–76.

Keynes, J. M. (1936) *The General Theory of Employment, Interest and Money*, London: Macmillan.

Kitching, G. (1982) *Development and Underdevelopment in Historical Perspective*, London: Methuen.

Magnusson, L. (1993) *Mercantilism. The Shaping of Economic Language*, London: Routledge.

Munslow, B. (2002) 'Complex emergencies and development', in Desai, V. and Potter, R. B. (eds) *The Companion to Development Studies*, London: Arnold Publications.

Nederveen Pieterse, J. (2001) *Development Theory. Deconstructions/Reconstructions*, London, Thousand Oaks, New Delhi: Sage Publications.

Nerfin, M. (ed) (1977) *Another Development: Approaches and Strategies*, Uppsala: Dag Hammarsköld Foundation.

Nisbet, R. A. (1969) *Social Change and History*, New York: Oxford University Press.

Polanyi, K. (1957/2001) *The Great Transformation*, Boston: Beacon Press.

Power, M. (2002) 'Enlightenment and the era of modernity', in Desai, V. and Potter, R. B. (eds) (2002) *The Companion to Development Studies*, London: Arnold Publications.

Reno, W. (1998) *Warlord Politics and African States*, London: Lynne Rienner.

Rist, G. (1997) *The History of Development*, London: Zed Books.

Ruggie, J. (1998) *Constructing the World Polity*. Essays on International Institutionalization, London and New York: Routledge.

Sadowski, Y. (1998) *The Myth of Global Chaos*, Washington: Brookings Institution Press.

Sen, G. (1984) *The Military Origins of Industrialization and International Trade Rivalry*, London: Frances Pinter.

Senghaas, D. (1985) *The European Experience*, Oxford: Berg Publishers.

Stiglitz, J. (2006) *Making Globalization Work. The Next Steps to Global Justice*, London: Allen Lane.

Tester, K. (1992) *Civil Society*, London and New York: Routledge.

Toye, J. (1987) *Dilemmas of Development. Reflections on the Counter-revolution in Development Theory and Policy*, Oxford: Basil Blackwell.

Walicki, A. (1969) *The Controversy Over Capitalism. Studies in the Social philosophy of the Russian Populists*, Oxford: Clarendon Press.

Watson, A. (1992) *The Evolution of International Society*, London: Routledge.

2
Reinventing Europe.
A Cosmopolitan Vision

Ulrich Beck

The European Union is in a small-minded soul searching for a purpose. When the citizens of Europe flex their political muscles and, in a paradoxical show of self-confidence, reject the European constitution, the time has come to listen to them and to open the door to a democratization of Europe from below. To achieve this purpose, Europe needs to be reinvented. The trouble is that there is no political script running through the heads of all Europeans. There is no continuously updated narrative that could help them grasp events in the same way or feel part of a common enterprise. This, rather than geographical distance, is the real reason why EU institutions strike ordinary people as intangible, unreal, and irrelevant.

In this chapter I want to offer and outline a 'cosmopolitan narrative for Europe' as an answer to the rejection of the EU constitution in referenda in France and the Netherlands (Beck and Grande 2004). I will do this in five steps. I start, first, with a few reflections on what the vote means. Second, I will argue that one of the most important blockings in European politics is its national misunderstanding. Third, I will argue that another basic element of a 'narrative of Europeanization' is the European positive sum game: common solutions serve the national interest. Fourth, I will argue that a strong part of the European narrative is to understand Europeanization in transnational culture of remembrance. The fifth and final part is to reflect upon a new cosmopolitan concept of integration.

What does the 'no' mean?

To be sure, the 'no' against the constitution was a revolt. But this raises the question: who revolted against what or whom? The vote can be a terribly blunt instrument. On the ballot paper there were only the simplest of choices: either for the constitution (500 pages with all its complexities and ambivalences) or against it. Let us consider for a moment three options:

1. *for* the constitution and *for* Europe
2. *against* the constitution and *for* Europe
3. *against* the constitution and *against* Europe.

The trouble is that none of these options were on the ballot paper.

It is not very difficult to argue that the majority of those who voted against the constitution in France and the Netherlands would have put their cross by the second option: against the constitution but for Europe.

There are surprisingly many on the neo-national left and on the neo-national right, who would have voted against *both* – the constitution and Europe – and this mixing of left and right anti-European sentiments is one of the most spectacular outcome of this vote. Still, we have to realize that there are strong *European* motifs to reject the European constitution. It was a paradoxical vote of Europeans against a Europe without Europeans. Here the 'non' and 'nee' spell: 'Help, we don't understand Europe. What does it stand for? Has the enlargement of Europe transformed it into an unknown, undefinable object? How can we make sense of Europe?'. To be sure, with the French and Dutch rejection the constitution is pretty much a dead letter. But this does not have to be a fiasco. The implication is: Europe has to be reinvented. What does that mean?

The national self-misunderstanding is blocking European politics

To think of Europe in nation-based terms is to awaken Europeans' deepest nation-based fears – this is the paradox we need to grasp. Thinking in national terms elicits the conclusion that one can either have Europe *or* European nations – a third possibility is ruled out. This nation-based misconception ultimately turns Europe and its member states into arch rivals who threaten one another's existence. Misconstrued in this way, Europeanization becomes a diabolical zero-sum game, in which both Europe and its nations are the losers in the end.

The other side of the paradox is: if the European Union's member states are to be rid of their fear that by acceding to EU expansion they are, as it were, committing cultural suicide, then it is necessary to reject nation-based concepts of society and politics and to think of Europe in cosmopolitan terms. Thus, a cosmopolitan Europe is first and foremost a *Europe based on difference*, on actually practised, recognized national particularities. To a cosmopolitan outlook, this diversity (be it of languages, forms of economic or democratic organization or political cultures) appears first and foremost to be a source of Europe's self-awareness, and not, as it appears in the national outlook, as an obstacle to integration. The European dream then, is being equal and different at the same time.

However, Europe continues to be thought of in national terms as an 'unfinished nation', as an 'incomplete federal state', and treated as though it had to become both – a nation *and* a state. This inability to understand the historically new reality of Europeanization forms a considerable part of Europe's real plight. And it is also one crucial reason why the institutions of the European Union appear unapproachable, unreal, and often even threatening to the citizens they are supposed to serve. Even sophisticated research on Europe has thus far hardly dared go beyond the basic conventional patterns of nation-state thinking. The European Union itself is also viewed in the light of nation-state patterns of territoriality, sovereignty, division of competences, and national isolation. Even when it speaks in more complex terms of 'governance' or of a 'multi-level system', research on Europe – heavily influenced as it is by political science and law – remains caught up in ordering systems aimed at comprehending the European Union on the basis of nation-state patterns.

Something that is particularly striking is the failure of sociology with regard to Europe. Sociology acquired its conceptual tools through analysis of national societies towards the end of the nineteenth and the beginning of the twentieth century, and since these tools are poorly suited for analysing European society, it draws the conclusion that there is obviously no European society worth speaking about. There are a number of explanations for this, but there is also a reason for it that is especially vulnerable to critique, and that is that the concept of society constitutes the focal point of sociology's methodological nationalism (Beck 2006; Beck and Sznaider 2006). According to the latter, Europe has to be conceived of in the plural, as a collection of socie*ties*, in other words, in an additive manner. To put it another way: European society coincides with Europe's national societies. By setting the conceptual stage in this way, it is small wonder that sociology brings the lack of understanding to the topic of Europe that it does. The methodological nationalism of the social sciences is historically wrongheaded, because it blocks out Europe's complex realities and arenas of interaction. To put it in a nutshell: methodological nationalism is blind to the realities of Europe – and therefore makes us blind to them as well.

A similar pattern of thinking gives rise to the political science formula 'a European demos does not exist'. In response to this it bears asking: what kind of demos is being referred to – the demos of the Greek polis, that of the Swiss cantons or that of nation-states? And what about the real societies of our interconnected countries? Do nation-states themselves still have a homogeneous demos of state citizens?

Running through all this (and yet unspoken) is the nation-state in the form of a conceptual benchmark, in relation to which the realities of Europeanization seem to be lacking: no demos, no nation, no state, no democracy, no public sphere. What *does* exist, however, besides disinterest and a plain lack of understanding for the debates going on in other member states, is an ever growing volume of transnational processes of communication about the challenges facing every member state including, most recently, reactions to the Iraq war, to the democratic uprisings in the Ukraine and to European anti-Semitism. Thus, rather than doggedly continuing to assert that there is no such thing as a European public sphere, perhaps the nation-state-fixated understanding of the 'public sphere' ought to be opened up to cosmopolitan meanings in order to take in the real dynamics that give rise to cross-boundary forms of a European public sphere.

Thus, Europeanization needs to be thought about not only in terms of the usual vertical dimension (national societies implementing European law, for example), but also in terms of a *horizontal* dimension. Here, Europeanization refers to the manner in which national societies, national education systems, national families, scientific institutions, economies, and so forth, form networks and merge with one another. In this respect, horizontal Europeanization means opening up the nation-state containers *at their sides*.

What counts as 'European' in this scheme are the 'co-national' forms of identity, ways of life, and modes of production that reach through and across the barriers of individual states. Effectively, these are forms and movements based on incessant boundary transgression. New parallel realities emerge in the wake of horizontal Europeanization and are lived out 'behind the scenes' in immigration offices, becoming widespread and taken for granted to the next generation: multi-linguilism, multi-national networks, bi-national marriages, 'multi-locatedness', educational mobility, transnational careers, scientific and economic integration.

The data available on these key indicators are devastatingly poor, which just goes to show once again that the weightiness and significance of these new forms of transnational Europeanization cannot be perceived because state statistics – as well as empirical social research – are caught up in methodological nationalism.

The European positive sum game: Common solutions serve the national interest

Let us start with the dilemma of nation-state politics in times of economic globalization. There is only one thing worse than being bulldozed by national corporations: *not* being bulldozed by national corporations! What frightens people is that, in the middle of the democratic society in which they live, they suddenly find themselves faced with a cruel gaping hole in the fabric of political power: the people they have elected sit powerlessly in the spectator stands, while those they have not elected make all the decisions that affect their lives. Actually, I think the vote against the constitution was a vote against the dragon of globalization.

In fact, it was Helmut Kohl, the former German Chancellor, who understood that it is wrong to see everything through national spectacles – because collective EU agreements often serve the national interest better. It was this attitude that produced the internal market and the euro, projects which entail letting go of some degree of sovereignty – but which also bring enormous benefits for national companies and employees. And this is where the European Union shows its political additional value: common solutions bear more fruit than the solo efforts of individual nations.

Look around: all over Europe national governments struggle in the national context with what are seemingly national problems; they attempt to solve them by going it alone, and generally fail. This can be demonstrated by looking at the export of jobs and at controls on company taxation as examples. Businesses that are mobile and have operations throughout the world are in a position to weaken individual states by playing them off against one another. The more the national point of view is ingrained in the thoughts and actions of people and governments alike, the better such businesses are able to consolidate their power. This is the paradox we need to grasp: the national point of view is *harmful* to national interests because national interests can be better realized in a context of European – and possibly even global – interaction!

Population decline, for example, is neither a national problem affecting specific societies, nor can it be adequately tackled by any nation alone. No matter where one looks, the same situation appears throughout Europe. We will soon have an increase in older people in all societies, pension systems are breaking down, and yet the reforms needed to counter these trends are being blocked by organized resistance from the groups affected by them. One important way of finding a positive way out of this trap could be to define the complex of problems facing our societies – declining populations, ageing societies, the difficult but necessary reforms of social welfare and targeted migration policy, along with the problem of job exports and, not least, the taxation of company profits – as a *European issue* to be addressed in a cooperative way. All those governments that are stuck in a national rut, content to accept pseudo solutions, can benefit from this.

The national outlook sees only the end of politics; the cosmopolitan outlook, by contrast, can see the end of the end of politics.

Let us assume that, in the face of a shrinking population, an EU plan could be developed and approved for dealing with the problems of migration and offering people a measure of security in old age. Such a project would ease the burden on national governments, as people would begin to realize that the situation they are in is not the result of any one nation's failure, but is rather an issue that every European country and government is forced to answer one way or the other. Moreover, it would enable national governments to strengthen their own hand by putting forward European arguments. For example, experiences gleaned from neighbouring countries can be utilized when it comes to the issue of labour market reforms. Denmark has radically pared down its laws on protection against wrongful dismissal. As a consequence, Danish companies are highly flexible. Conversely, unemployed people in Denmark receive up to 89 per cent of their most recent net income, so they do not become charity cases one year later. Instead, they have the right to pay, training, and job centre assistance until they are in work again. This is why Danish labour market policy is nearly 40 per cent more expensive than German policy, and yet has only half as many unemployed people to deal with. It is worth noting, too, that the Danish model was redesigned completely in cooperation with the workers, rather than in opposition to them.

What the success of Europeanization teaches us, generally speaking, is simply the new logic of cosmopolitan realism: pressing national problems can best be solved through transnational cooperation. In other words, permanent cooperation between states does not hinder state capacity, it *increases* it. To put it in the form of a paradox: when you relinquish sovereignty, you *extend* it. And *that* is the secret of the European Union's success. By contrast, those who attempt the impossible task of isolating themselves nationally will only endanger their own prosperity and democratic freedoms. This is because wealth and economic growth, as well as managing unemployment and maintaining the stability of democracy, all presuppose a cosmopolitan approach.

Europeanization as a transnational culture of remembrance

'Oh, Europe', says Thomas Mann, referring to the calamitous history of the West. Two and a half thousand years filled with war and bloodshed. Go to any village in Europe, and there, in the middle, you will find a large monument engraved with the names of those who have fallen – 1915, 1917. And over there, mounted on the wall in the church, is a stone tablet commemorating the dead from the Second World War. It bears the names of three men from the same family: fallen in 1942, fallen in 1944, missing in 1945. The concentration camp memorials remind us of the Europeanization of race hatred. That is how Europe *used to be*.

How long ago did it all happen? Not very long at all – even up until the end of the 1980s, the people of this belligerent Europe faced one another in a nuclear stalemate. The policy of rapprochement between East and West only seemed possible by accepting that Europe would apparently remain divided for ever. Yet look at where we are today! A European miracle has occurred: enemies have turned into neighbours! This is something that is historically unique – in fact, it is more or less inconceivable. It is incredible to think that at the very moment when the history of states is at its most volatile, a political invention should have succeeded that makes something almost inconceivable into a possibility: that states themselves might transform their monopoly on violence into a taboo *against* violence. The threat of force as a political option – whether between member states or towards supranational institutions – has been banished absolutely, once and for all, from the European horizon.

This possibility has come about because something new has arisen in Europe's historical space: the horror of the extermination of the Jews, the pain of war and forced migration – these things are no longer remembered solely as events affecting individual nations. Instead, the national space of remembrance is being forced to open itself up – albeit painfully – to the European space of remembrance, breaking through the parochialisms of methodological nationalism in the process. This means that we are seeing at least the beginnings of a Europeanization of perspectives.

This change to a European perspective is no substitute for different national histories, but it does enrich them by adding new external perspectives and constant border crossings, thereby opening them up and extending them further. It was Hannah Arendt who drew attention to the connection between remembrance and political action. For her, too, no punishment is adequate or appropriate in the face of concentration camp crimes. But she gives the 'senselessness' of the Holocaust a political meaning. Every course of action becomes entangled in the irreversibility of its consequences. Not only must God offer forgiveness, so too must people forgive other people – publicly, because this is the only way to regain the capacity to act. If this is true in general, then it is especially true in the face of the monstrous crime of Jewish genocide. For Hannah Arendt, the important thing is that people should be able to start anew and not have to remain captive to the past. This is what forgiveness is all about. Only through the ability to forgive, something that cannot be forced on anybody, can the kind of action that is more urgent than ever renew its creativity as a political force.

In this respect, the Europeanization of remembrance contains a genuinely European contradiction in itself – morally, legally, and politically. If the traditions out of which the horror of the Holocaust – as well as that of colonialism, nationalism, and genocide – emerged are European, then so too are the values and legal categories that enable these deeds to be adjudicated for what they are in the global public sphere: crimes against humanity. Both nation-based modernity and postmodernity make us blind to Europe. Europeanization means struggling to formulate institutional answers to the barbarity of European modernity – and, as such, entails departing from postmodernity, which fails to recognize it at all. In this sense, a cosmopolitan Europe is the institutionalized self-critique of the 'European way'.

This sort of cosmopolitanism is different from multiculturalism or postmodern vagueness. It involves opening up lines of communication and incorporating what is foreign and strange, while focussing on common interests and accepting the inevitable interdependencies this brings with it; it also involves incorporating the historical exchange of perspectives between perpetrators and victims in a post-war Europe. Even though this cosmopolitanism is supposed to be based on a framework of binding norms aimed at preventing us from sliding towards postmodern particularism, nonetheless it is not merely universalistic. For an entity such as Europe, active engagement with diverse cultures, traditions, and interests in the course of integrating national societies is crucial to survival. Only forgiveness based on such engagement can create the trust required to define a common European interest across borders.

In a cosmopolitan perspective cultural tolerance becomes constitutional tolerance. National particularities are not erased, they are acknowledged – indeed, they are what give rise to a European identity. However, this principle of tolerance and mutual recognition of national particularities assumes that agreement has been reached on a shared set of procedural and substantive norms, in order to ensure that these national particularities are compatible with European values.

So what does 'cosmopolitanism' mean in all this? Nationalism, we can assume, is the typical means of dealing with otherness in the first modernity. Cosmopolitanism differs from all the other previously mentioned forms, however, in that the principle of recognizing and accepting otherness becomes ingrained in people's thinking, acting and coexistence – both domestically and in our external relations.

A new cosmopolitan mode of integration

The process of EU expansion and its active policy of neighbourliness can and must be understood in the sense of *integration through expansion*. The introduction of a new cosmopolitan integrationist approach that no longer depends upon the 'harmonization' of rules and the elimination of (national) differences, but on their recognition, opens up new arenas of cooperation and institutional power for Europeanization.

For a long time, the European process of integration took place primarily by means of *eliminating difference*, that is, national and local differences. This 'policy of harmonization' confuses unity with uniformity; it assumes that uniformity is the precondition for achieving unity. In this respect, unity became the most important regulatory principle of modern Europe – rather like applying the principles of classic constitutional law to European institutions. The more successful EU policy became within this primary principle of uniformity, the greater resistance it met with and the more clearly its counter-productive effects came to the fore.

Cosmopolitan integration, by contrast, is based on a paradigm change that says: *diversity is not a problem, it is the solution.* In this way of thinking, the ongoing process of European integration should not be oriented towards traditional notions of uniformity associated with a European 'federal state', but must take the unalterable diversity of Europe as its starting point. Only in this way is it possible to link together two requirements in the process of Europeanization that at first sight seem to be mutually exclusive, namely, the recognition of difference on the one hand and the integration of difference on the other.

This is exactly what cosmopolitan integration is about. Any further integration of Europe must be guided not by the traditional ideas of uniformity in a European federal state, but must take the unalterable diversity of Europe as its starting point. It must view difference not as the problem, as a restriction to economic transactions that has to be exterminated, but as a potential to be preserved and exploited. Only if this is done will it be possible to reconcile two fundamental requirements of the European project that at first sight seem mutually exclusive: to recognize difference and to integrate it. Basically, what is at stake is maintaining a certain degree of uniformity, especially legal uniformity, in an integrated Europe, without damaging the autonomy of its member states on the one hand, and the prospects of the European project on the other hand.

The key point is that the potential of the concept of differentiated integration can be completely exploited only when it is spelled out completely in both of its dimensions, namely, differentiation *and* integration. Consequently, one can distinguish two principal varieties of differentiated integration:

First, forms of *difference-friendly integration* (for example, the principle of mutual recognition). Here the claim to complete integration is maintained but it is put into effect in ways hospitable to difference; hence, it is more tolerant towards national, regional, and local peculiarities than the usual harmonization approach.

Second, forms of *integration-friendly differentiation* (for example, functional differentiation, geographical differentiation). Here the claim that all member states must accomplish everything simultaneously is abandoned. Integration is restricted accordingly and the claim to complete integration is subject to spatial, temporal, and material limitations.

Europeanization needs to be understood in the sense of an historically tried and tested political model for a post-imperial empire based on law and democracy. As such, it holds great fascination not least for Americans who are critical of their own polity, as an alternative to the 'American way'. It is, as Jeremy Rifkin has said, 'the European dream' of a gentle world power (Rifkin 2004).

To summarize my argument: What does the French and Dutch 'no' to the European constitution mean? And what are its consequences?

First, the national idea is not capable of uniting Europe. A large super-state made up of an expanded Europe makes people afraid. I do not believe that Europe can rise up from the ruins of nation-states. If there is one idea, though, that could unite Europeans today, it is the idea of a cosmopolitan Europe, because it takes away Europeans' fears about losing their identity, elevates constitutional tolerance in relations among the many European nations to a goal, and at the same time opens up new political arenas for action in a globalized world. The more sure Europeans feel of themselves, the more acknowledged they feel in their national dignity, the less they will need the nation-state, and the more determinedly they will openly argue for European values in the world and make the destiny of others their own. What does this idea include? It includes, second, forms and practices of direct democracy. The European Union cannot survive without offering voters real choices. It is essential that future presidents of the commission have a direct demo-cratic mandate of their own. Unless this happens, people and state leaders will regard the commission and its president as mere civil servants without the common European interest against singular national state leaders.

There should be the option for a *European referendum on European affairs*, binding European politics. This opens up doors for European politics transnationally, creating a European public and civil society from below. Creating a European society is important because of its absence: it is the missing piece of the integration.

Thus the European Union must demonstrate that its main institu-tions can secure a better future for Europeans, conceived as individuals with personal goals and aspirations rather than as bearers of particular ethnic identities, than can national governments acting alone. In a glo-balized world, such a hope is not unrealistic. In commerce monetary policy, immigration, the environment law and order, foreign policy and defence, the European Union is better placed to advance people's inter-ests, regardless of their language or location, than are its constitution states. Reason, not raw emotion, will be the cement that holds the European Union together.

Third, there is, of course, a danger that the crisis will block entry to new members. It is inevitable that the failure of the constitution will lead to a period of introspection, but Europe is simply too important, too big, and too rich – and the world is moving too fast – for the

European Union to succumb to a self-indulgent paralysis. In particular, it would be a terrible mistake to close the doors to countries like Turkey that are already on the take-off ramp for membership. The European Union represents a powerful incentive for countries emerging from dictatorship or war to bring their governance and civil rights up to the highest global standards. Succumbing to Turkophobia in particular would be an enormous and potentially dangerous blow to the most modern of Muslim countries.

The referenda revealed many errors and weaknesses in the European Union. But the greatest mistake would be to overreact, and undermine the many things that are right about the Union. In fact, the many crises could be run up to a chance, redefining Europe as a cosmopolitan project, that is: something completely new in human history, namely a vision of the future involving a state structure that has as its foundation stone the recognition of those who are culturally different.

References

Beck, U. (2006) *The Cosmopolitan Vision*, Cambridge: Polity Press.

Beck, U. and Grande, E. (2004) *Das kosmopolitische Europa*, Frankfurt a. M.: Suhrkamp (forthcoming in English translation (2007) Cambridge: Polity Press).

Beck, U. and Sznaider, N. (eds) (2006) 'Cosmopolitan Sociology', special issue of *The British Journal of Sociology*, 1, 2006.

Rifkin, J. (2004) *The European Dream*, Cambridge: Polity Press.

3
The Precarious Sustainability of Democracy in Latin America

Osvaldo Sunkel

Introduction

Since the 1980s, for the first time in history, all Latin American countries except Cuba have achieved the political status of democracies, at least in the sense that their political authorities have been elected in relatively free and more or less fair elections (UNDP 2005). Moreover, in contrast to what was a frequent occurrence in previous history, no military coup has overthrown a government in the last decades. Until recently, the common expectation was that democracy would take hold and flourish, reinforced by the simultaneous processes of globalization and the adoption of neo-liberal policy measures to reduce the role of the state and expand that of the market. Democratization, globalization, and neo-liberalism were supposed to come hand-in-hand.

Unfortunately the trend has been in the opposite direction. Democracy seems to have become weaker and more precarious in several countries in recent years, as shown most obviously by the frequent and severe governability crises caused by massive popular mobilizations. This is attested by the fact that since 1990 nine presidents have been ousted or had to resign before the end of their official terms of office: Alberto Fujimori (Peru 1992), Jorge Serrano (Guatemala 1993), Abdala Bucaram (Ecuador 1997), Luis María Argaña (Paraguay 1999), Jamil Mahuad (Ecuador 2000), Fernando de la Rua (Argentina 2001), Gonzalo Sanchez de Losada (Bolivia 2002), followed most recently in 2005 by Carlos Meza (Bolivia), and Lucio Gutierrez (Ecuador). Furthermore, most recent presidential elections have been won by candidates who are critical of neo-liberal policies and the globalization process: Hugo Chávez (Venezuela, re-elected in 2004 and 2006), Daniel Ortega (Nicaragua 2006), Rafael Correa (Ecuador 2006), Néstor Kirchner (Argentina 2004),

Tabaré Vázquez (Uruguay 2005), Evo Morales (Bolivia 2006), and the strong challenges of Ollanta Humala and Andres Manuel Lopez Obrador in the recent presidential elections in Peru and Mexico.

In order to better comprehend this situation, it is necessary to understand the positive and negative effects of the profound socio-economic transformations that Latin American countries have undergone in the last three decades, as a consequence of the wholesale adoption of the neo-liberal policies of the so-called 'Washington Consensus'. But this is far from enough. It is also indispensable to go further back in history, because the socio-political consequences of contemporary neo-liberal policies play themselves out in the midst of social, cultural, economic, and political legacies, going as far back as Latin America's colonial and nineteenth century backgrounds, which have left indelible marks in these countries.

The roots of some of the more formidable obstacles to democracy in this region and, paradoxically, to the strong and unwavering longing and support for more democratic societies, at least among the elites, go back to colonial times at the end of the eighteenth century. The persistence of some of these characteristics throughout the nineteenth and twentieth centuries, in spite of significant, although only partial, socio-economic, cultural and political modernization and development processes, have contributed seriously to hinder the advancement of democracy in Latin America until today.

Consequently, this essay will begin with some basic references to the socio-political, institutional, and cultural background inherited from colonial Latin America at the time of independence in the late eighteenth and early nineteenth centuries, and to the significance of the independence movement, particularly from the point of view of its commitment to democratic ideals. It will then refer briefly to the development and modernization processes that took place in Latin America during the second half of the nineteenth century, at the time of the worldwide expansion of the British Empire, later joined and then replaced by the United States of America, which left an indelible imprint in the economic, social, and political structures of most Latin American countries, particularly as a result of the development of specialized primary export activities.

Reference will then be made to the profound transformations that set in after the two World Wars, and particularly to the more lasting consequences of the Great Depression of the early 1930s, which through a widened and more active role of the state in the economic, social, and international realms changed the worldwide as well as the Latin

American development and modernization scenarios from the 1940s to the 1970s. This is a period characterized, to different degrees in the various countries, by rapid industrialization, and the development of the infrastructure of transportation, communications, and energy, basic public social services and public enterprises, all of which stimulated a fast urbanization process. Among other consequences, this generated a further and socio-politically stronger and more widespread demand for democracy.

This will be followed by a reference to the consequences of the onset of the globalization process in the 1970s, the debt and development crises of the early 1980s, and the dramatic change from state-centric to market-centric economic policies, leading to the coincidence of the adoption of free market economics on the one hand and the establishment of electoral democracies on the other.

The following sections will examine the contrast between the expectations aroused by the establishment of democratic regimes and the poor results of neo-liberal economic policies, the consequent disillusionment and loss of faith in democracy and neo-liberal economic policies, and the reactions and responses that are taking place. Particular attention will be paid to the surfacing of long repressed and/or dormant sectors of the population, in countries with large sectors of poor indigenous and/ or black populations, which is a remainder of social structures and conditions originating far back in history, and which most Latin American countries have up to now been unable and/or unwilling to overcome. Their increasing political restlessness, shared also by important segments of the working and middle classes, has not only generated new social movements and left-leaning presidential elections. It has also brought to the fore, in the realm of development thinking and acting, the neo-structuralist approach, a critical reaction to the disappointing neo-liberal economic policies of the last decades. The last section of the chapter will refer to this most interesting revival of the structuralist approach to development of the 1950s to the 1970s, renewed and updated in the light of a critique of its earlier shortcomings and of the new circumstances of the globalization process.

Socio-political and cultural colonial background

Latin America was under the colonial rule of Spain and Portugal for three centuries, from the sixteenth to the eighteenth century, longer than the colonial experience of any other region of the world. The Iberian colonizers thoroughly destroyed and disarticulated pre-existing

Aztec and Inca empires and civilizations. Building new social systems, they created an ad hoc culture, institutions, and formal and informal sets of rules, thus facilitating the exploitation of the extant abundant indigenous population, in order to produce what was needed for the sustenance of the colonial population, particularly the elite of colonizers, but above all for the large work force that was shifted to the mining and tropical export activities.

It is essential to recall that the culture and the formal as well as informal institutions that were imposed by Spain and Portugal, came from the part of Europe that was pre-liberal, pre-modern, pre-scientific, and pre-industrial, and that met the North European religious Reformation movements with the Counter-Reformation, including its infamous Inquisition, in a close alliance of the Catholic church and the state. These empires were furthermore highly centralized, authoritarian, corporative, mercantilistic, scholastic, patrimonial, seigniorial, and warlike. The idea of liberty did not arise as a natural citizenship right, but from the granting of a juridical privilege from above (Wiarda 1998).

The pre-existing indigenous societies were largely concentrated in the Aztec and Inca empires, while other regions were scarcely populated by pre-agricultural societies, or largely unpopulated. An important differentiation therefore arose during the colonial period and the nineteenth century among different regions of Latin America (Sunkel y Paz 1970). The reorganization of pre-existing indigenous empires and cultures to export precious metals took place mostly in Mexico, Central America (except Costa Rica), and the Andean countries, especially Peru, Bolivia, and Ecuador, where the Crown established Viceroyalties. The capitals Mexico City, Quito, and Lima became the centres of power, wealth, and prestige, to which their magnificent colonial architecture still attests. The other side of the coin is the large masses of underprivileged, culturally and racially discriminated, and economically exploited people of indigenous origin, mostly in rural, but also increasingly in urban areas, who make up the vast majority of the poorer population until today.

In contrast to these areas, provided with an abundant labour force and mineral riches, a large part of the Americas – the Caribbean islands and Brazil – consisted of sparsely populated rich tropical lands. Here, the labour force was brought in from Africa and the economy was organized on the basis of the plantation system, giving rise to another kind of highly hierarchical societies based on slavery, and ruled by a small white minority. As a consequence, poor, and culturally as well as racially discriminated black and mulatto people still make up the vast majority in the rural and increasingly urban areas of the Caribbean countries and Brazil, as well as in some of the tropical coastal areas of other countries like Colombia and Venezuela.

In these countries, new agricultural and mining export activities developed on a large scale in the latter part of the nineteenth and the early twentieth centuries, as a consequence first of the worldwide expansion of the British Empire and later of the growing economic and political interests of the United States in Central and South America (Cortés Conde and Hunt 1985). This brought about an early era of a very partial capitalist modernization, with heavy foreign investments in the export sector and related transportation, communication, commercial and financial activities, concentrated in urban areas and ports. The socio-political structures in the hinterlands, where most of the new and expanded agricultural and mining export activities took place, remained more or less unchanged, with economic and political power concentrated by large traditional landowners and new big foreign firms, which continued to exploit the great masses of pre-existing rural populations as in colonial times.

The countries of the Southern Cone of Latin America, including Argentina, Uruguay, the southern part of Brazil, and to some extent Chile, as well as Costa Rica in Central America, had been sparsely populated by pre-agricultural tribes, that did not allow for the same scale of colonial exploitation, but forced the scarce colonial conquerors to engage themselves to some extent in productive survival activities.

During the second half of the nineteenth century, a large wave of European migration overseas took place, caused among other factors by the great expansion of the British Empire in the wake of the Industrial Revolution, which brought about the development of specialized export activities in these countries.

Many of the migrants landed in the Southern Cone of Latin America and in Costa Rica, where they came to make up a significant proportion of the population. In contrast to the Spanish and Portuguese conquerors and colonizers, they brought with them elements of the modern agricultural and industrial culture of Europe, including entrepreneurial experience, technical skills, familiarity with social organizations, and progressive religious and political ideas. Furthermore, due to the scarcity of servile or slave labour in the regions where they settled, they had to rely more extensively on their own and family work in their efforts to survive and prosper.

The most important consequence of this, from the point of view here, was the development of urban working class movements and parties, and of larger urban middle classes than in the other two groups of countries, providing some middle ground between the upper and lower classes. Nevertheless, the powerful landowning classes of colonial and nineteenth century origins, some of the latter related to foreign investments, managed to concentrate land ownership to a few hands, and to organize a dominating rural social structure based on the latifundia-minifundia complex, that has to some extent remained until recently or even today.

Initial steps in the long march to democracy

From the end of the eighteenth century, in the last decades before independence from the Spanish colonial empire in the 1810s, democracy became the inspiration and aspiration of Latin American elites seeking to organize the newly born republics. The leaders of the independence movement, like Francisco de Miranda, Simón Bolívar, Simón Rodriguez, and José de San Martin, were heavily influenced by the ideals of the Enlightenment, liberalism, the French Revolution, and North American independence. In these latter processes many of them actually participated in both Europe and the United States.

Their ideals of the Enlightenment – independence, freedom, and the North American example – made them want to establish a republican form of government in Latin America. However, they had to face the harsh reality of oligarchical social structures inherited from colonial times and of fragmentation and disintegration tendencies inherent in the collapse of the Spanish colonial system. The pragmatic solutions adopted were to concentrate all power to the executive branch of government, to the detriment of the judiciary and the legislative branches, to restrict democratic representation to landowners, to grant special corporative privileges to the army and the church, and to establish mechanisms to keep the lower classes under control (Prats 2005).

The Spanish colonial system was a gigantic hierarchical network of corporative and individual privileges that depended in the final analysis directly on the authority of the monarch and his delegates. This network of clientelism, patrimonialism, and interconnected corporate bodies disintegrated with the wars of independence and the breakdown of the Spanish Viceroyalties of Mexico, Quito, and Lima into several independent states. This led to internal political strife and conflicts in many of the new states for over a century, and to the prevalence of military dictatorships and strong-men regimes, with few interludes of highly elitist democratic governments.

Brazil, almost half the territory of South America, did not break into several independent states thanks to the fact that the Portuguese monarchy fled there in 1808 before Napoleon's troupes invaded Portugal, and by establishing itself there, held the different regions together. After its demise in 1889, Brazil also had its share of strong-men and military dictatorships. Important, but only partial, exceptions were Chile, Costa Rica, and Uruguay.

Meanwhile, from the 1920s onwards, with important differences among the larger and smaller countries, and their different colonial backgrounds, increasing urbanization and continued expansion of the export sectors and foreign investments took place, as well as an incipient process of industrialization, leading to expanding working and middle classes, socio-political movements, and demands for democracy. But they were systematically confronted and put down in most cases by traditional conservative alliances of big landowners, foreign capital, and related financial and commercial interests. These alliances broke down in many countries in the aftermath of the financial crash in 1929 and the Great Depression that followed in the early 1930s in the industrialized countries, notably in Great Britain and the United States, which were the dominant powers vis-à-vis Latin America.

As a consequence, in all Latin American countries exports collapsed, foreign investments and finance disappeared, unemployment grew huge, foreign reserves dwindled, and fiscal deficits mounted, in brief, a catastrophic economic and socio-political crisis. This weakened the prevailing traditional rural oligarchical power structure and brought to an end the dynamic primary product export cycle and model that had prevailed since around the 1870s, and with it the late nineteenth century liberal era was closed.

State-centred industrialization and development

In order to extricate themselves from this deep crisis, in Latin American, as in most countries in the world, the state was brought into action. The state enacted fiscal, monetary, financial, tariff, employment, foreign exchange, and international trade policies that favoured an increase in domestic production, employment, and investments, while limiting and controlling imports. It was the beginning of the period of so-called import substitution, not only in Latin America but throughout the world, including the industrialized countries.

In Latin American and other underdeveloped countries, the reduction and control of the importation of manufactured goods created conditions for the development of a national industrial sector. Meanwhile, in industrial countries the importation of agricultural goods was limited, which led eventually to the protection, support, and subsidization of their agricultural sectors, a situation which still remains – witness the recent renewed breakdown of the Doha Round of trade negotiations.

The problem that most affected and worried the industrial countries was the immense mass of urban unemployment generated by the Great Depression, and the corresponding idle productive capacity in the manufacturing sector. This situation gave rise to large increases in government spending in programmes like President Roosevelt's New Deal in the United States, the social policies that led to the welfare state in several European countries, and the public works and armament programmes of Nazi Germany and fascist Italy.

The worldwide economic crisis which gave rise to these emergency policies also eventually led to a revolution in economic thinking with the publication of Keynes's 'General Theory'. Here, the increase in government deficit spending in situations characterized by insufficient effective demand was theoretically justified, full employment was made the central aim of economic policy, and the state was thereby given a central role in economic growth.

The issue of economic development and modernization was also brought to the top of the international agenda, as the result of a complex historical process, including crucial elements such as the socialist revolution in the Soviet Union, the Second World War, the creation of the United Nations, the emergence of socialist regimes in central European countries and China, the decolonization process in Africa and Asia, the Cold War, the practice of economic planning in the socialist countries, and the new Keynesian full employment economic growth thinking and policies in the capitalist world.

In Latin America, a new attitude was generated in favour of deliberate policies for the promotion of economic development, industrialization and social improvements. This change of attitude was caused mainly by factors such as the breakdown and final collapse of the nineteenth century primary product export model in the 1930s, the new conditions created thereby for the development and/or expansion of a national manufacturing sector, the economic difficulties experienced during the Second World War, the fundamental changes in the international economic and socio-political environment just referred to, and a rapidly growing urban population.

This led to an increasing role of the state in economic development, an expanding public sector with new state agencies in charge of social services and public enterprises, an increase in the professional middle classes, and the rise of labour unions and populist and leftwing parties. This was accompanied by strong international political and cultural influences in favour of economic progress, democracy, and human rights. The significance of this process was obviously quite diverse among the different Latin American countries, depending on their size, degree of industrialization and urbanization, ethnic composition of the population, and so on.

A crucial component of this fundamental change and reorientation in the economic and social policies of Latin America, as was the case of the Keynesian and socialist revolutions abroad, was the important ideological, theoretical, and advisory role performed by a group of economists brought together under the umbrella of the United Nations Economic Commission for Latin America (ECLAC), created in 1948 and located in Santiago, Chile. The leader of this group was Raul Prebisch, an Argentinean economist who had headed the Central Bank of Argentina during the time of the Great Depression, implementing highly unorthodox counter-cyclical monetary policies. He had also experienced the dependent historical economic relationship of Argentina vis-à-vis Britain, particularly the negotiations which took place between the countries in the 1920s and 1930s. Moreover, he was familiar with the experience of other Latin American countries like Uruguay, Brazil, Mexico, and Venezuela.

Prebisch was not only a practitioner and participant observer, but also a powerful theoretician of great originality. He is best known internationally for his (and Hans Singer's) famous and polemical thesis of the secularly declining terms of trade of primary products in international trade, but this is only the corollary of his analysis of development and underdevelopment in the world capitalist system. In fact, he formulated the first full fledged theoretical statement originating outside the academic circles of Europe and the United States, aimed at explaining the nature of the world economy.

Prebisch conceived the international economic system as constituted by a centre, i.e. the industrial powers of Europe and North America, and a periphery, including the Latin American and other non-industrial economies. The dynamism of this system was determined by the productivity increases brought about by the technological progress which took place in the manufacturing sector of the more advanced industrial economies, leading to substantial increases in income and wealth in those countries. These increases were to some extent shared by the working classes due to their organizational capacity and to the relative scarcity of labour.

The development of the industrialized countries required the importation of mineral and agricultural materials, which were provided by the countries of the periphery, in exchange for their importation of manufactures. In this historical process, the centre had acquired comparative advantages in the production and exchange of industrial goods, where technological progress and productivity increases took place, while the periphery specialized in the production and export of raw materials and agricultural products. Technological progress and productivity increases did not spread significantly to these activities as labour was abundant and cheap, keeping wages at subsistence levels. Therefore, income and wealth in these countries increased relatively slower than in the industrial countries of the centre, and accrued mostly to the land and mine owners and commercial interests, determining a very uneven distribution of income.

Furthermore, as mentioned above, the international exchange of products tended in the long term to benefit the industrial countries, since the terms of trade of primary product exports decreased in relation to those of manufactured imports. This was the consequence of two factors. First, the elasticity of demand for the manufactured products that underdeveloped countries imported was much higher than that of the primary products imported by industrial countries. Second, the technological progress in the industrial countries led to the replacement and/or a more effective utilization of the primary products obtained from the peripheral countries, determining a declining coefficient of primary imports per unit of output. To this had to be added a further disadvantage of these countries: the severe short term instability which had historically characterized primary export production, exports, and prices in the international economy.

Therefore, the characteristics of the centre-periphery system, while contributing positively to the development of the industrial countries, had also contributed to determining the heterogeneous structure and historical evolution of the economies of Latin America, characterized by a relatively modernized tradable sector specialized in the supply of primary products for exports, and a rural hinterland kept in a condition of colonial backwardness and underdevelopment.

Two main strategic conclusions of this analysis followed. First, it was obvious that the modernization and development of these countries required industrialization, as the industrial sector was the bearer of technological progress, and as the eventual exportation of manufactures would redress the disadvantage experienced by primary product exporters in international trade. Second, agrarian reform and rural modernization were also essential in order to overcome the historical backwardness and exploitation prevalent in the agricultural hinterlands. The main public policy conclusion was that, as in the contemporary experience of the developed and socialist countries, the state had to play a central role in bringing about both processes: industrialization and rural transformation and modernization.

The collapse of the nineteenth century liberal international economic and financial order, as a consequence of the Great Depression of the 1930s and the Second World War provided the national and international economic, political, and ideological conditions for a shift in policy, from the primary product export model to a strategy of import substituting industrialization, adopted almost everywhere in the developing and socialist world from the end of the 1940s.

Manufacturing industry was not altogether absent from Latin American countries. Some manufactured goods were already produced in those countries that had developed significant export sectors. This had generated, directly or indirectly, an internal market for such products in Argentina, Brazil, Mexico, and Chile, and to a lesser extent in other countries. Additionally, the foreign trade and exchange crises of the 1930s, and later the Second World War, created further opportunities to locally produce manufactured goods that used to be imported. This also led to the gradual creation of a social class of entrepreneurs and business men, as well as urban working and middle classes, which became sources of political power interested in backing the industrialization effort.

The availability of a theory that justified industrialization as the means to overcome underdevelopment, and the existence of entrepreneurial and related classes to back it, provided the definitive cornerstone for the adoption of development, industrialization and modernization as a political programme and ideology. The other leg of the modernization programme, agrarian reform and rural transformation was, of course, postponed, in many cases until today, as this continued to be the stronghold of the traditional ruling classes.

The industrialization policies were supported, as already mentioned, by the new practice of economic and social policies and planning to achieve growth and full employment in industrial countries, and of industrialization and modernization in socialist nations. To this must be added the new foreign assistance policies of the United States to support Europe, i.e. the Marshall Plan, and the development of underdeveloped countries (President Truman's Point IV foreign aid programme) in the face of the beginning of the Cold War. As a consequence, in many underdeveloped countries, what used to be more or less ad hoc responses to importation bottlenecks and foreign exchange difficulties, became henceforward deliberate development policy, with the state as the main player and promoter of economic and social development.

The main new functions which the state had to undertake were: intervention through taxation, subsidies, and foreign exchange and price controls in the goods and factors markets to shift resources to industrialization and modernization; creation of specialized development corporations and banks for the financing of long-term projects and programmes to overcome the lack of a private financial market; redistribution of income through the creation and expansion of the public social services sectors (health, education, culture, housing, urban development, social security); public investments to provide the necessary physical support for the creation of an integrated internal market of national scope by means of building up transportation and communications networks; the creation of public enterprises in basic activities that did not interest or were beyond the capacities of the private sector (iron and steel, basic chemicals, energy, etc.); special programmes to modernize at least partially the agricultural sector; etc.

In order to fulfil these tasks, the state apparatus had to widen and modernize its activities, creating new institutions and adopting new methods of administration, organization, planning, budgeting, project analysis, statistical information, and so on. All of this generated increased employment opportunities, which contributed substantially to the development and diversification of universities and technical schools for the training of the qualified personnel needed in all these new activities. This, in turn, contributed to the widening of new middle and organized working classes.

The period from the late 1940s to the 1970s was exceptionally successful worldwide in terms of growth, employment, industrialization, modernization, social improvements, accumulation of economic and social capital, and development. But in Latin America the process of import substituting industrialization, which was one of the main driving forces, ran into increasing difficulties due to excessively high and prolonged protection, insufficient emphasis on increasing exports, lack of modernization of the agricultural sector, and restricted internal markets. Furthermore, the resistance to an increase in taxation, that was required to finance the much greater activities of the state, led to inflation and increasing foreign debt. There was also increasing social unrest as the benefits of development failed to reach the rural population and the increasing numbers of urban poor.

At the same time the Cold War was felt in Latin America in the form of the Cuban revolution, which stimulated revolutionary movements, particularly in the rural areas, also in the context of the Vietnam War. President Kennedy, followed, after his assassination, by Lyndon Johnson, launched the Alliance for Progress in 1961 as a reformist response. However, reactionary conservative governments, in most countries still controlled by landowning elites, remained reluctant to progressive reforms, such as a long overdue land reform. Social and political upheavals increased and several revolutionary or semi-revolutionary governments were established in Guatemala, Argentina, Brazil, Bolivia, Chile, and other countries. They were followed by repressive military dictatorships, promoted by national oligarchies and conservative political forces and strongly supported by the United States, under the doctrine of National Security in the face of what was considered an 'internal enemy', a Latin American sequel to the Vietnam War. Only four electoral democracies, of the restrictive kind instituted long ago, survived in the late 1970s in Colombia, Mexico, Costa Rica, and Venezuela.

Globalization in the 1980s: facts and expectations

In the 1980s, the development and debt crises, growing internal popular pressures and an international movement in favour of human rights and democracy contributed to the end of the repressive and corrupt military regimes of the 1970s. Since then, the globalization of human rights and democratic values, the collapse of socialism in the Soviet Union and Eastern Europe, the end of the Cold War, international support for democratic regimes, and widespread popular demand for political participation led to the generation of electoral democracies. For the first time in independent history, all Latin American countries, with the exception of Cuba, had established electoral democratic regimes.

I use the expressions 'electoral democracies' and 'electoral democratic regimes' advisedly. All Latin American countries, except Cuba, have elected their governments in the last two and a half decades in more or less fair elections. Many of the requirements of a full-blown democracy are however still partially or totally absent in most countries. In general, but with important differences among countries, and some partial exceptions like Costa Rica, Chile, and Uruguay, political participation is low, particularly among the younger generations; political parties are weak, lack clear ideological definitions, and are inclined to opportunistic populist positions; the mass media is overwhelmingly controlled by the largest economic groups; massive poverty and high inequality prevent real social and political participation of the majority of the population; parliaments, as well as regional and local governments, are weak; and justice is inefficient and corrupt, another inheritance from the colonial past.

The generation of democratically elected governments since the 1980s represented a promise of an improvement in these conditions and raised strong expectations of widening socio-political participation, freedom of expression, better paid and secure jobs, poverty alleviation, more equal opportunities and outcomes, access to fair and prompt justice, a future for one's children, social protection, an end to corruption, and the overcoming of privilege. The achievement of these goals, or at least recognizable progress towards them, became therefore a condition for the legitimacy of democracy.

The advent of democratically elected governments in the political field coincided with a dramatic shift in the economic field: the earlier development model of a state-led or state-centred closed economy, which prevailed from the 1940s to the 1980s, was replaced by neo-liberalism and a market-centred open economy model, following the policies of what came to be known as the 'Washington consensus': a reduction of the role of the government in the economy through limitations in public spending and investments, privatization of public enterprises, partial privatization of public social services, elimination of subsidies and controls, deregulation and liberalization of markets, in particular the opening up of highly protected economies to international competition and foreign capital. The hope was, paraphrasing the famous title and catchphrase of Francis Fukuyama, that free market economics and political democracy would reinforce each other and bring about 'the end of history'.

The economic performance of neo-liberalism

In contrast to these high socio-economic expectations, which had been accumulating for decades, the social and economic performance of neo-liberal policies since the 1980s has been disappointing. It is true that they have brought the end of the scourge of high and persistent inflation and a recovery from the debt crisis. Increased external openness has also generated fast export growth. But the overall growth of the economy has been very slow, only half of what it used to be in the previous period, so income per capita has remained practically stagnant for over two decades. Furthermore, the economy has become highly volatile, bringing about increased cyclical instability in exports, foreign finance, and investment, and therefore in GDP and employment. The effects of this volatility are lasting and cumulative, since recovery after a crisis does not compensate for time lost, nor does it restore the pre-crisis levels of employment (histeresis) nor, for several years, private investments (ECLAC 2003).

As a consequence of the opening of the economy to international competition, which required drastic reductions in tariffs and other forms of protection, and of export subsidies and promotion, there has been increased growth in productivity and competitiveness in exports and surviving import substitution activities. This has gone hand in hand with the increase and spread of foreign capital and different kinds of associations and mergers of local and foreign firms.

The growth of exports has taken two main forms in accordance with the idea of comparative advantages: concentration on natural resources exports in South America and on labour-intensive exports in Mexico, Central America, and the Caribbean. Exports based on natural resources (mining, forestry, fisheries, agribusiness) are capital intensive and generate little employment. Moreover, these expanding export sectors frequently disrupt pre-existing labour-intensive activities, thus displacing labour. On the other hand, labour-intensive exports generate employment, but based on low wages in competition with the lowest wage levels around the world, meaning China. As a matter of fact, many of these activities are relocating there.

Furthermore, given the policies of export orientation and the competition from cheap imports, import replacing industries have also had to become efficient and competitive, through technological innovation, mergers, conglomeration, 'rationalization' (meaning reductions in the labour force), subcontracting (meaning lower wages, intensification of work, and avoidance of the costs of social legislation), and 'flexibility' (meaning lower minimum wages and lower hiring and firing costs). This process has also had to spread to the related service activities required by the tradable sector: banking, financial services, telecommunications, energy, consulting, engineering, health, education, public relations, publicity, the media, personal services, etc.

In all these cases – import substitution activities, services and the export sector – an important vehicle for opening up to the world economy has been the incorporation of technical progress and the growing presence of foreign firms and different forms of local associations with foreign capital. This accelerated modernization process, and its disruptive effects on pre-existing labour intensive activities, have given rise to a process that I many years ago labelled 'transnational integration and national disintegration', long before globalization became the talk of the town (Sunkel 1973).

Social consequences of neo-liberalism

In the process of integration into the world market, there has therefore operated a generalized downward pressure on employment and wages, stemming from three main sources: (a) the increased productivity and competitiveness of the capital and skill intensive transnationalized tradeable sectors and related service activities, carriers of the recent technological revolutions, (b) the scores of medium and smaller labour intensive firms, which have gone out of business as they have not been able to cope with intensified competition, and (c) the decline in public employment as a consequence of the reduction in government activities and services, subcontracting and the privatization of public enterprises, one of the main objectives of neo-liberal policies.

As a consequence, formal unemployment has remained very high and wages low, while there has been a steep increase in the numbers of marginalized medium and small entrepreneurs, self-employed, underemployed and informal workers, and a generalized situation of insecurity. All this has meant a serious worsening in working conditions: increase in temporary work, longer working hours, intensification of work and lack of contracts and social protection. If we add to this the consequences of urbanization and bad public transportation services, and the consequent increasing length of transportation time, workers hardly have time left for rest and the family (Tokman 2004).

Furthermore, the privatization of social services has generated a growing gap between world class private and very poor public education, health, housing, and social security. Social protection has also diminished for the majority of the population in terms of health insurance, unemployment benefits, pensions, subsidies, etc. This is another manifestation of the growing apartheid between the privileged transnationalized minority of the population and the large domestic majority of underprivileged, with the traditionally small middle classes withering away, contributing to social polarization. Consequently, poverty of a large proportion of the population has persisted in spite of increased and better focalized public social expenditures. Moreover, since increases in income and wealth have largely been flowing to the social sectors associated with the transnational economy and society, the very unequal income distribution, which has characterized the region throughout history, has persisted or become even worse in most countries.

Market-centred reforms have reduced the role of the state, privatized public goods, enterprises, and services, lowered tariffs and opened the economy to the world market, liberalized and deregulated internal markets, eliminated subsidies, and promoted competition and private enterprise. All of this has led to a widening and deepening of a culture of individualism and competitiveness, and to the disruption of the pre-existing culture of state-protected or tradition-related socio-economic arrangements. This has generated feelings of great personal insecurity and, as a response, anti-systemic forms of individual behaviour as well as reactive socio-political protest movements, leading to political instability.

Given the profound structural transformations that the pursuit of neo-liberal market- oriented economic policies has brought about in countries whose social formations used to be state and/or tradition bound, the kind of analysis pursued here falls clearly in line with the approaches proposed by Karl Polanyi. In his classic book 'The Great Transformation', he analyses the disruption of traditional social relations brought about by the extension of market relations, which is then followed by attempts to resist and react to the consequences: the 'double movement'. Albert Hirschman in 'Exit, Voice and Loyalty' suggests a similar process, as is the case even of Marx's dialectics of replacement of modes of production, as well as Schumpeter's 'creative destruction'.

According to a more recent analysis in this line of thought (Portes and Hoffman 2003), the reactions to the disruptive forces of transnationalization have been 'enthusiastic adaptation' by a privileged few and 'reluctant adaptation' or 'forced entrepreneurialism' by most, some of whom have been successful and most of them unsuccessful. This process, in addition to high levels of unemployment and underemployment, which is particularly serious among the younger and poorer sectors of society, has at the individual level led to emigration and anti-systemic behaviour: crime, drugs, and violence. At the collective level it has generated protest movements of all kinds: political, regional, ethnic, youth, gender, and environmental. At the international level these protest movements have been brought together under the anti-globalization banners.

A special mention must here be made regarding the case of Chile, which is quite out of line with the previous analysis. The negative economic and social consequences of neo-liberalism in Latin America described in the previous two sections do not seem to apply in this case.

The Chilean economy has grown at an exceptional average rate of growth of 5.7 per cent between 1990 and 2005, almost doubling income per capita, with a substantial reduction in absolute poverty from 39 to 19 per cent. This is generally attributed to having been more competent, comprehensive, and systematic in the application of the neo-liberal policy package. In the last section of the chapter, which describes the emergence of a neo-structuralist approach to development, I will argue that this view is largely mistaken. Quite the contrary, the successful Chilean experience since 1990 owes a lot to the systematic application on the part of a smaller but expanding and very active state of deliberate public policies aimed at improving social conditions, developing new and innovative productive activities, promoting exports, inducing private investments in infrastructure, establishing several strong regulatory agencies, and so on.

Environmental consequences of neo-liberalism

The adoption of neo-liberal policies in the 1980s coincided not only with the establishment of democratic regimes, but also with the incorporation and adoption of environmental policies and institutions. Environmental problems had been gaining momentum during the earlier decades of state-centred development policies. Industrialization, the modernization of agriculture, urbanization, the building up of transportation infrastructure, telecommunications and energy, and so on, had well known deleterious effects in terms of pollution of air, water, and soil, while also impinging on renewable natural resources such as forests, fisheries, agricultural land, etc. Nevertheless, they were minimized and tolerated because they were perceived as an inevitable price to be paid for modernization, progress, and development.

But these developments were accompanied by an increasing international awareness of the importance of preserving the environment, particularly following the 1972 Stockholm Conference and its follow-up. This eventually led to an increase in the national awareness of environmental problems caused by rapid and disorganized urbanization, industrialization, modernization of agriculture, depletion of natural resources, disruption of ecosystems, and so on.

As a consequence, during the 1980s and early 1990s environmental legislation was enacted in most Latin American countries. Processes of environmental institution building and education, training, and research were also started, leading to the eventual adoption and implementation of environmental policies. This was greatly helped by international pressures coming from NGOs, developed country governments, international organizations, and increasingly from business itself, as good environmental business behaviour became a condition for access to international markets. Nevertheless, environmental policies have not been able to harness market forces: deforestation, pressure on rain and native forests and biodiversity, energy intensity, and urban sprawl continue mostly unabated, while some progress has been made regarding CO_2 emissions and urban, river, and coastal pollution.

Urban concentration, environmental pollution and congestion, and the depletion of renewable natural resources have been accentuated due to neo-liberal policies, with the opening up of the economy and the promotion of natural resources export activities, due to increased imports of consumer durables, especially automobiles, and to technologically advanced chemical inputs such as fertilizers and pesticides.

Political consequences of neo-liberalism

The stark contrast between the promise brought about by the establishment of electoral democratic regimes in the 1980s, and the disappointing results recorded over the last two decades of the simultaneously adopted set of neo-liberal economic policies, has prevented the newly established electoral democracies from attaining political legitimacy. On the contrary, it has led to acute governability crises and an increasing loss of faith in democratic politics. The degree to which countries are affected by this situation varies of course within Latin America.

One initial disappointment in most countries was the fact that many presidents were elected on the basis of progressive platforms, only to turn to highly unpopular stabilization policies and neo-liberal structural reforms as soon as they took office. There is also a perception that political participation is irrelevant, as policies are largely decided by technocrats, big business elites (mostly transnational) and international financial organizations. In addition, there is disappointment with the fact that procedural electoral democracies have not promoted sociopolitical participation and have had little to show in terms of economic improvements, reduction of poverty, social justice, and equity. Meanwhile, corruption has persisted or even increased, much of it linked to the privatization of public enterprises. There is also a crisis of representation, particularly regarding younger generations, as politicians and parties do not perform their function of perceiving, understanding, and articulating society's old and new demands.

It is remarkable that this disastrous recent political history has not been the consequence of military coups and/or foreign interventions, as used to be the case due to the historical conditions reviewed earlier, and more recently to the repercussions of the Cold War. On the contrary, it is now the result of increased popular dissatisfaction, unrest and political mobilizations which have built up to a point where presidents have had no choice but to resign, in an international context where democracy is favoured and political pressure used to achieve negotiated civilian transitions.

At present, several governments are still, or again, in deep trouble, and many of them let off political pressure through massive emigration, as in Mexico, most countries of Central America and the Caribbean, and also, to a lesser extent, Ecuador, Bolivia, and Peru. Recent elections in several countries, as mentioned earlier, also show signs that politics leans towards the left. Although Chile has also moved somewhat to the left, it continues to constitute, with Uruguay and Costa Rica, the group of countries where democracy is not threatened, basically because the societies are not so segregated and the democratic political systems have stronger historical roots and are more consolidated. In the case of Chile, as mentioned above, this is also due to rather exceptionally successful policies of economic growth and social improvement since 1990, in the post-Pinochet era of the coalition governments of the Concertación de Partidos por la Democracia.

In other cases, political systems are historically weaker, and populist and messianic strong-men traditions persist, leading time and again to a plebiscitarian conception of democracy. Guillermo O'Donnell has coined the concept of 'delegative regimes', where the president, having been elected by a popular majority, is thereafter supposed to have the right to do as he pleases. Difficult political times, as now prevail in many Latin American countries, promote delegative regimes that strengthen the president, but weaken the other institutions of democracy: the legislative and judicial powers, the controller, regional, and local governments, and other accountability agencies. The recent political trend in the region seems to favour these kinds of regimes rather than the institutionalization of representative democracies (*Diario Financiero* 2006).

Many of the political problems of several Latin American countries have to do with increasing insecurity, restlessness, unfulfilled demands, mobilization, and organization of the large masses of permanently marginalized and segregated indigenous populations, that have for centuries been governed by small white elites. This is particularly the case of countries like Bolivia, Peru, Ecuador, Paraguay, and Guatemala. Indigenous popular mobilization has produced a new kind of leader in Venezuela with Hugo Chavez. Making a proud case of being of indigenous origin, he promotes a nationalistic 'twenty-first century socialism' ideology, pretended to have its historical roots in Bolivar, Rodriguez, and other heroes of the wars of independence from Spain, from where the Bolivarian revolution stems. Other emerging leaders of a similar kind, but without the overabundant petrodollar support of Chavez, are Morales in Bolivia and Humala in Peru, who have run for presidential office with the support mainly from the indigenous populations.

These movements are largely reactions to the democratic and economic promises of the 1980s, and to the frustrating incapacity of neo-liberal economic policies to deliver the expected benefits of economic progress to the masses. They are also the results of the lack of a sense of democratic citizenship and belongingness to the new market-centred institutional and cultural framework of the nation-state. The opening of the economy, the expansion of new export sectors, and the competition of cheap imports have undermined traditional agricultural and artisan activities and uprooted masses of rural population. These people flock to urban areas, already ripe with unemployment and informal activities, lack of decent living conditions, environmental deterioration, crime, and drugs (ECLAC 2001, 2002b, 2004). These people resent officialdom – judges, the police, parliamentarians, ministers, bureaucracy in general – and traditional politicians, as well as the affluent white transnational elite of businessmen, economists, lawyers, and other professionals and technocrats. They are therefore easy pray to neo-populist leaders of their ethnic background.

In conclusion, neo-liberal economic policies, which are the ideological expression of globalization, have generated great opportunities for economic progress in the tradeable sectors and general expectations of economic development and social improvement. But the process of transnationalization has also generated heavy economic, social, environmental, cultural, and political costs, with the consequent frustration of those expectations. The media transmits a virtual or symbolic globalization message, in stark contrast to the miserable living conditions of the majority.

There are selected economic sectors, social segments, and geographical areas that have been able to develop activities and/or obtain jobs that allow them to join the globalization process at both the level of expectations and that of reality. These are the winners. But there are also much more considerable economic sectors, social groups and geographical areas that are being displaced, rejected, and marginalized. These are the losers, once again the traditional losers. Under the historical circumstances of most Latin American countries, the balance of this dialectical process of profound social change tends unfortunately to be quite negative: few winners and too many losers. This is not a very wholesome climate for democracy and development to thrive.

Development from within: a neo-structuralist response?

The crises of the state-centred development strategy of 1950–1970, together with the generalization of the globalization process and the overwhelming predominance of financial markets and institutions since the 1980s, brought with it the ideology and the policies of neo-liberalism. The debt crisis of the early 1980s provided the international financial institutions with the golden opportunity to impose the 'Washington consensus' policies on the debt-ridden countries.

There was undoubtedly a need for profound revisions of these countries' development strategies and policies. The state had been overburdened with an excessive number of planning, regulatory, redistributive, and production tasks. This interfered with a reasonable working of the market mechanisms and, together with deficient taxation systems, generated serious fiscal disequilibria. Economies were excessively and irrationally protected from international competition. The import substitution process had come to a dead end, and exports failed to expand, creating balance of payments crises and excessive foreign indebtedness. Inflation was out of control. Financial institutions and policies had to be aligned with the novel globalizing reality of powerful international conglomerates, exploding private finance and investments markets, the digital and transportation revolutions and so on.

In order to engage in the corresponding corrections and improvements of public policies, however, from the 1980s the neo-liberal economic recipe was frequently applied in a blind and drastic manner. This stripped governments of most of the instruments for engaging in the planning and promotion of innovative and more diversified production capabilities, and for providing badly needed social services. From then on, almost everything was supposed to be provided by the market and private enterprise. The baby was thrown out with the bathwater.

While recognizing the need for considerable changes in development policies, and going along with the fundamental transformation that had taken place in the international environment with the onset of globalization, from as early as the late 1980s many experienced observers began criticizing the extreme simplism and ideologism of neo-liberal policies, and foreseeing their probable negative consequences (Griffith-Jones and Sunkel 1986; Bitar 1988; French-Davis 1988; Rosales 1988; Sunkel and Zuleta 1990; ECLAC 1990; Lustig 1991; Sunkel 1991, 1993).[1] Basically, they strongly denied the naïve belief that, in countries characterized by profound heterogeneity and divisions in their economic, social, cultural, and political structures and institutions, less government, more markets and private enterprise, and the opening up to the international economy, would bring about economic growth, social improvement, and democracy, without the purposeful strategic orientation, coordination, and direct participation of the state.

Thus arose neo-structuralism, a response to neo-liberalism. Neo-structuralism recognizes the insufficiencies of the structuralism of the 1950s regarding short term macro-economic balances, overemphasis on import substitution over interaction with the international economy, overburdened government intervention, etc., while defending the need for strong and deliberate long-term state policies to deal with the problems of overcoming structural heterogeneity and creating, complementing, and regulating markets in the frequent cases of market absence, imperfections and failures, characteristic of the underdevelopment syndrome; ensuring, not necessarily by public enterprises, the provision of public goods such as transportation, energy, communications, and other long-term investments; promoting the diversification of production and exports into higher value added and technologically more advanced and competitive productive activities; actively supporting their penetration into foreign markets; widening the coverage and upgrading the quality of education and social services in health, housing, and social protection, particularly for the poor and less well off; as well as implementing policies to ensure environmental sustainability and the achievement of a better regional balance. In other words, rather than letting the increasingly internationalized global market be the only or main determining factor of the long-term development orientation of the country, 'from abroad' as it were, there is an irreplaceable need for an explicit development strategy 'from within'.

It is not demand and markets that are critical. The heart of development lies in the supply side: quality, flexibility, the efficient combination and utilization of productive resources, the adoption of technological developments, an innovative spirit, creativity, the capacity for organization and social discipline, private and public austerity, and emphasis on savings and the development of skills to compete internationally; in short, independent efforts *from within* to achieve self-sustained development. (Ramos and Sunkel 1993: 8f)

This view is not only based on an analysis of the economic realities and needs of these countries, but on the new national and international political requirements of the need to strengthen democracy.

The relatively successful economic, social, and political performance of the Chilean 'growth with equity' model, adopted by the democratic government since the 1990s, to which reference has been made earlier, far from being a show piece of neo-liberalism, as is being heralded by the international financial press and mainstream economists, owes a lot precisely to the implementation of several of these kind of neo-structuralist policies (Sunkel 2006).

While recognizing the new realities of globalization, and within the inevitable new global framework, countries can and should negotiate national development goals and pursue them through public policies adopted and decided democratically by their societies at the national level and implemented by their governments (Ocampo 2002; Sunkel and Zuleta 1990; Sunkel 1993). The relative compromise on several general policy orientations, such as the need of a dynamic integration into the world economy, the importance of macro-economic balances, greater reliance on the market mechanism, reducing the number and role of state enterprises, etc., is to some extent a recognition of earlier policy failures, frequently the consequence of unavoidable historical circumstances, but more fundamentally the result of completely changed internal and international conditions. Furthermore, the concrete policy measures employed to implement those policy orientations are frequently of a quite different nature, neo-liberals relying more on markets, neo-structuralists more on government interventions.

Finally, there is a fundamental difference in the axiomatic and philosophical premises underlying the two approaches. This is not the place to delve into this question, but it should at least be recalled that liberalism and structuralism and their corresponding 'neo' versions, conceive of and explain in very different ways the behaviour of the individual in society. The liberals, as the heirs of individualism and utilitarianism, presuppose the existence of the abstract categories of freedom of choice and the rational calculations of the individual economic agent in a more or less perfect market, be she/he consumer or producer. The underlying assumptions result logically in the most efficient forms of individual action and economic performance. Therefore, any interferences that limit people's freedom of choice, especially those coming from the state, are considered to be the originators and ultimate guarantors of the inefficient functioning of the economic system.

The structuralists, in turn, at least in Latin America, interpret the economic behaviour of individuals according to historical contexts, especially of a socio-economic, cultural, and institutional character, in which such agents formulate their limited options and develop their conduct. They consider that individuals form themselves into organized social groups in a multitude of public and private institutions, which develop over time a series of values and rules of behaviour. These forms of social organization constitute, in turn, veritable cultures which limit and orient individual conduct. Thus, because of their different national historical experience and international relations, Latin American societies and economies have their own distinctive structural and institutional characteristics, which development policies need to take into account. Hence, to underline it one last time, even though some general lines of development policy may look similar, considerable differences can persist in the concrete spheres of action and in the choice of policy instruments, especially, of course, regarding the role of the state (Sunkel and Zuleta 1990).

Note

1. A very important contributor to this debate and to the crucial ECLAC 1990 publication *Changing production patterns with social equity*, was Fernando Fajnsylber, who unfortunately died in 1991. A recent book analyses and collects his main writings (Torres Olivos 2006).

References

Bitar, S. (1988) 'Neoliberalism versus neostructuralism in Latin America', *CEPAL Review*, 34: 45–62.

Cortés Conde, R. and Hunt, S. (1985) *The Latin American Economies: Growth and the Export Sector 1880–1930*, New York and London: Holmes and Meier.

Diario Financiero (2006) Interview with Guillermo O'Donnel, Santiago, 10 March.

ECLAC (1990) *Changing Production Patterns with Social Equity*, Santiago: ECLAC.

ECLAC (2001) *Equity, Development and Citizenship*, Santiago: ECLAC.

ECLAC (2002a) *The Equity Gap*, Santiago: ECLAC.

ECLAC (2002b) *Social Panorama of Latin America 2001–2002*, Santiago: ECLAC.

ECLAC (2003) *A Decade of Light and Shadow; Latin America and the Caribbean in the 1990s*, Santiago: ECLAC.

ECLAC (2004) *Social Panorama of Latin America 2002–2003*, Santiago: ECLAC.

French-Davis, R. (1988) 'An outline of a neo-structuralist approach', *CEPAL Review*, 34: 37–44.

Griffith-Jones, S. and Sunkel, O. (1986) *Debt and Development Crises in Latin America: The End of an Illusion*, Oxford: Oxford University Press.

Gwynne R. N. and Kay, C. (2004) *Latin America Transformed; Globalization and Modernity* (second edition), London: Hodder Arnold.

Lustig, N. (1991) 'From structuralism to neo-structuralism: the search for a heterodox paradigm', pp. 27–42 in Meller, P. (ed) (1991) *The Latin American Development Debate : Neostructuralism, Neomonetarism and Adjustment Processes*, Boulder, CO: Westview Press.

Meller, P. (ed) (1991) *The Latin American development debate : neostructuralism, neomonetarism and adjustment processes*, Boulder, CO: Westview Press.

Ocampo, J. A. (2002) 'Rethinking the Development Agenda', *Cambridge Journal of Economics*, 26(3).

Portes, A. and Hoffman, K. (2003) 'Latin American Class Structures: Their Composition and Change During the Neo-liberal Era', *Latin American Research Review*, 38(1).

Prats, J. (2005) 'Quién bloquea a Latinoamérica?', *Revista Cuarto Intermedio*, Bolivia noviembre.

Ramos, J and Sunkel, O (1993), 'Toward a neostructuralist synthesis' in Sunkel (ed.) (1993).

Rosales, O. (1988) 'An assessment of the structuralist paradigm for Latin American development and the prospects for its development' *CEPAL Review*, 34: 19–36.

Solimano, A., Sunkel O. and Blejer, M. (eds) (1994) *Rebuilding Capitalism; Alternative Roads after Socialism and Dirigisme*, Ann Arbor: University of Michigan Press.

Sunkel, O. y Paz, P. (1970) 'El subdesarrollo latinoamericano y la teoría del desarrollo', *Siglo XXI*, México.

Sunkel, O. (1973) 'Transnational Integration and National Disintegration in Latin America', *Social and Economic Studies*, Institute of Social and Economic Research, University of the West Indies, 22(1).

Sunkel, O. (ed) (1991) *El desarrollo desde dentro; un enfoque neoestructuralista para América Latina*, México: Fondo de Cultura Económica.

Sunkel, O. (ed) (1993) *Development from Within; toward a Neostructuralist Approach for Latin America*, London: Lynne Rienner.

Sunkel, O. (1993) 'From Inward-looking Development to Development from Within', in Sunkel, O. (ed) (1993) *Development from Within; Toward a Neostructuralist Approach for Latin America*, London: Lynne Rienner.

Sunkel, O. (1994) 'Contemporary Economic Reform in Historical Perspective', in Solimano, A., Sunkel, O. and Blejer, M., (eds) (1994) *Rebuilding Capitalism; Alternative Roads after Socialism and Dirigisme*, Ann Arbor: University of Michigan Press.

Sunkel, O. (2005) 'The unbearable lightness of neo-liberalism', in Wood, Ch. H. and Roberts, B. (eds) (2005) *Rethinking Development in Latin America*, Philadelphia: Pennsylvania University Press.

Sunkel, O. (2006) 'Un ensayo sobre los grandes giros de la política económica chilena y sus principales legados', in Bielschovsky, R. et al. (eds) (2006) *Una mirada hacia América Latina*, Santiago: Instituto de Estudios Internacionales/ Embajada de Brasil.

Sunkel, O. and Zuleta, G. (1990) 'Neo-liberalism versus neostructuralism in the 90s', *CEPAL Review*.

Tokman, V. (2004) *Una voz en el camino. Empleo y equidad en América Latina: 40 años de búsqueda*, Santiago: Fondo de Cultura Económica.

Torres Olivos, M. (2006) *Fernando Fajnsylber. Una visión renovadora del desarrollo en América Latina*, Santiago: CEPAL.

UNDP (2005) *Democracy in Latin America: Toward a Citizens Democracy*, Buenos Aires: Aguilar.

Vellinga, M. (ed) (1998) *The Changing of the State in Latin America*, Boulder: Westview Press.

Wiarda, H. J. (1998) 'Historical Determinants of the Latin American State', in Vellinga, M. (ed) (1998) *The Changing of the State in Latin America*, Boulder: Westview Press.

Wood, Ch. H. and Roberts, B. (eds) (2005) *Rethinking Development in Latin America*, Philadelphia: Pennsylvania University Press.

4
Towards a New School of Thought on Development in South Asia

Ponna Wignaraja

The critical governance and development challenge

The response to the wider development challenge being faced in South Asia, as the region moves into the new millennium, is inextricably linked to the inadequacy of mainstream development thinking and action to deal simultaneously with problems of globalization, multifaceted crises posed by poverty, youth unemployment, and violence resulting from sharpening contradictions in the polity. The manner in which globalization is impacting on the political economies of South Asia after liberalizing their economies, raises new implications for governance, security, and fundamental human rights.

In South Asia, a group of social scientists (SAPNA)[1] had in the 1970s already initiated an intellectual quest for systematically probing the South Asian reality. Through social praxis and interdisciplinary participatory action research lessons from the ground have been learned, and in an undogmatic and constructive dissent from received wisdom, macro-micro policy options have been identified. This has provided an 'entry point' for the emergence of an unreformist school of thought on a pro-poor growth-oriented development strategy, linking economic and political democracy.

Three decades later, the report of the high-level UN panel on threats, challenges, and change, together with the Secretary-General's proposal for restructuring the UN, provide the 'space' for revisiting and further mainstreaming the thinking and action on the links between the development with equity, security, and human rights defined in broad terms.

The rigorous pursuit of new directions can be placed in a more coherent analytical framework, emerging from earlier work in South Asia and helping to deepen the discourses on freedom and good governance.

It is now possible to introduce a new rationality in the global discourse, going beyond the limited options provided by neo-classical liberalism and Marxism and the false debates that projected these orthodoxies as the only real options. It is also possible to assert that the debt-led growth of the 1970s, the Keynesian consensus, and the conventional frameworks of development thinking and action were inadequate to mediate between the contradictions and to meet the challenges of governance and sustainable development with equity. A priori theorizing did not permit a holistic understanding of the multifaceted crises, not only in economic but also in political, cultural, and wider human terms. Now a material basis on the ground is available to support critical elements of a new holistic framework, based on analytical methodology relevant to the study of social change and transformative processes.

The SAPNA network did not take the form of a mere critique of global and national policies and recommending marginal reformist policies. Through a holistic interdisciplinary action research process, it drew lessons from the ground and attempted to identify undogmatic critical elements, which could be a basis for an alternative school of thought and a value-led culturally rooted pattern of development and democracy in South Asia. There was no a priori theorizing, and the methodology used involved social praxis for managing transition. The results of three decades of pioneering intellectual quest and experiential collective learning are reflected in eight published studies, which will be discussed in the following section.

Experiential learning on political democracy and economic democracy through pro-poor growth

The first study (De Silva et al. 1988) attempted to analyse the problem of rural mass poverty with a view to identifying critical elements in a conceptual framework for an alternative approach to rural development and the operational guidelines that went with it. The broad construct of the theory that emerged, albeit rudimentary, sought to explain the long-run direction and goals of a holistic development effort and the social mobilization process involved, with the poor as subjects in the process. A new social movement in India provided the material basis for refining some of the theoretical insights. 'Bhoomi Sena', which means land army, is a movement for liberation from feudal and elite oppression and the establishment of countervailing power for more self-reliant development by the poor and marginalized in rural areas. This was different from the capture of dominant power in other situations.

The methodology used by the South Asian team was based on 'collective creativity'. An interdisciplinary group of researchers and the Bhoomi Sena cadres together investigated reality and engaged in a constant interplay between theory and practice. Every resulting hypothesis was tested in the field and the result was fed back into reflection to enrich the theory, i.e. *the methodology of praxis*. This underlies what is now called the methodology of participatory action research (PAR),[2] a new departure in relevant social science methodology, organizing the poor to receive delivered inputs, very different from 'tool kit' approaches and pseudo participatory processes like PRA and RRA.

The study highlighted emerging dangers such as (1) polarization between the rich and the poor, (2) resource waste and environmental degradation, and (3) youth alienation and the dead end which would result if the development strategies of the past were uncritically followed. This study showed that redistributive justice, based on a two-sector (public and private) growth model, 'trickle down', 'top down' or 'delivery of services' to the poor, along with a conventional accumulation process, was not a sustainable option for the large number of poor.

The second study (Wignaraja and Hussain 1989) highlighted three interrelated dimensions of a deepening crisis that threatened, not only some of the existing state structures, but the very fabric of society. The first dimension is the growing polarization along ethnic, linguistic, and religious lines and, associated with this, the undermining of fundamental social values, through which diverse communities have lived together in tolerance and accommodation in a pluralistic society. The second dimension is the perceived failure of highly centralized political structures to give effective representation to all strata of society, and the growing militarization associated with the use of coercive state power to quell resurgent sub-nationalism. The third dimension is the collapse of the kind of capital-intensive development, adopted in post-colonial South Asia, which has generated endemic poverty, growing interpersonal and interregional disparities, erosion of the ecological environment, and growing dependence on foreign aid. The study pointed towards the potential of reconstructing both the consciousness and political and economic institutions, through which stable supportive state structures and viable regional cooperation, based on 'unity in diversity', could be achieved.[3]

The new reality of globalization was also analysed. As state structures in a number of South Asian countries were threatened by internal upheavals, elites were forming alliances with superpowers and economic forces outside the region as a means of acquiring political and economic support. They were thereby incorporated into an iniquitous global system and supplied with economic aid, arms, and the technology and tactics of crowd control and counter-insurgency from powerful countries outside the region. It was clear that as the superpowers got drawn into the national crises, the momentum of violence and fragmentation within was accentuated, resulting in 'soft' societies and 'failed' states. The ruling regimes tended to show a knee-jerk reaction to the crises and emerging challenges, as they were unable to find a fundamentally different solution to the problem of poverty and inequality, as well as to provide a political framework and a value-based intellectual vision, within which the diversities of culture, language, and religion could enrich rather than undermine society.

The study concluded that no South Asian country can solve these problems by itself. Sustainable regional cooperation is required and must be based on restructuring of national ideological, political, and economic systems. At the level of ideology, the deep-rooted civilizational and cultural consciousness of tolerance, humanism, and freedom of belief must be tapped. At the level of politics, what is needed is decentralization, devolution of power, and the emergence of local institutions, through which the individual and groups, whatever their social status, can participate in decisions that affect their immediate economic, cultural, and ecological environment.[4] This was the beginning of the thinking which links political and economic democracy in the search for sustainable approaches. The study also clearly stated that, at the level of economics, a wider holistic development strategy and an accumulation process are required, combining self-reliance, equity, and a balance between people, nature, and growth.

In the third study (Wigaraja 1990) another dimension was identified, i.e. eradication of women's poverty. Poor women have a double burden of being poor and being women, but even in the global discourse at that time, the gender equity issue was not addressed in depth.

Lessons from case studies, as far back as in the early 1980s, showed that the solutions to women's double burden can only come from actions by women's groups and by better organization of poor women. The problem of powerlessness can only be addressed through collective action. The organization of women around issues of common concern is thus a prerequisite for effective and sustainable economic and social development. Mere provision of credit in the absence of empowerment through awareness creation and organization is not developmental or sustainable. Rather, the study highlighted that credit alone results in deepening the debt trap, and further erodes self-respect and dignity of poor women. Women-led micro-level 'success cases' also showed that in South Asian cultural fundamentals, women respond holistically to issues of patriarchy and feminism, and reasserted the complementarity between men and women.

In the fourth study (Wignaraja et al. 1991), the 1980s in South Asia were further probed. Following upon the golden years of the 1950s and 1960s, and the illusionary debt-led growth of the 1970s, the 1980s have been called a 'lost decade' for development. For many poor countries, development went into reverse (with some exceptions where the Keynesian welfare system has worked temporarily) and conventional development thinking then moved away from the Keynesian consensus to an even more sharply monetarist and neo-classical approach.

Given the present crisis of development, increasing doubts were felt by important segments of the global academic community and parts of the UN system about the validity of this dominant neo-classical paradigm. While the critique began to place emphasis on human and social bases for sustainable development, broader based growth and the importance of participation, action was still 'marginal tinkering'.

Lessons from this study, while further highlighting the multifaceted crises, in economic as well as political and human terms, also pointed to the need for new forms of accumulation. Through case studies, it indicated that participatory development at the micro-level reflects a new approach to resource mobilization, resource use, and growth as well as to economic democracy. A third growth sector at the base of the political economy can also be an economically viable and cost-effective approach to poverty eradication, as well as contributing to political stability. This sector is based on a factor in surplus, i.e. the creativity and knowledge of the poor. A development strategy, focussed on the strengths of the poor, can help reverse costs effectively to much of the past imbalances and contradictions created by the conventional development pathway and marginal tinkering with it. By elaborating on the methodology of participatory development, the study made a deeper contribution to an understanding of the new approach and the key instrumentalities, where the poor themselves are not the problem but can be part of the solution.

In the fifth study (Wignaraja 1993), a new element was introduced, i.e. how to multiply and sustain successful experiments and 'seeds of change'. It also highlighted the dangers of an over-centralized bureaucratic state becoming militarized, even if it has a welfare orientation. Moreover, the study made a distinction between the new social movements such as ecological and women's movements, and older social movements such as the trade union and peasant movements. The former reflect collective strategic efforts to bring about transformative social change, while the latter are more system-maintaining.

There were several additional lessons from the new social movements to reinforce an emerging school of thought. First, the social transformative movements and experiments are, in effect, part of a people's response to the reality of the contemporary global crisis. The myriad new social movements do not fight to assume state power, but constitute an integral part of the present crisis and response aimed at building countervailing power. Secondly, the social movements are regarded as new players, performing multiple functions – political, economic, social, and cultural. These new players, while fighting to counter state power, represent a new breed of actors, interested not narrowly in state power but rather in creating a free space from where a truly democratic society can emerge. Thirdly, in these social movements, there are 'seeds' preparing a desirable future society. The movements' potential role goes beyond that of existing fragmented NGOs in civil society, many with built-in inequality and non-authenticity, often money-led and hidden behind the window-dressing of 'democracy' or 'development' (ibid.).

The analysis concludes that the national liberation movements represent a lost historical opportunity and leave an unfinished agenda. The new social movements are the carriers of the message of an alternative modernity, projecting more endogenous, more participatory, and more authentic processes. Such new thinking and practices provide a point of departure for a new school of thought and a new social contract yet to be forged, for which the material basis has emerged on the ground. The coherence in knitting together new thinking and practice is hampered by the fragmentation in practice, which has become a new orthodoxy permitting intellectuals and civil society to continue their conventional modes of thinking and action. Unravelling this reality is also part of the intellectual quest and challenge.

In the sixth study (Wignaraja and Sirivardana 1998), the thinking within SAPNA so far was knitted together. South Asia, with more that 1.1 billion people, accounts for more than one fifth of the world population, and has the highest concentration in the world of poverty, hunger, malnutrition, child mortality, and illiteracy. Two aspects of the recent development experience of South Asia are further analysed.

Firstly, in South Asia, as elsewhere, reforms are undertaken comprising of trade and foreign exchange liberalization, reduction of government budgetary deficits, lifting of administrative controls on domestic economic activity, and encouragement of foreign investment, resulting in a greater role for markets and the private sector. If fully implemented, the reforms could contribute to a significant acceleration of the growth rate in the medium-term. But as experience indicates, they are also likely to accentuate economic inequalities. Furthermore, unless the process of economic expansion is broad-based, there is no reason to believe that it will necessarily lead to poverty reduction and sustainable human development. South Asian states have no real power over the global forces and financial markets that direct and perpetuate the iniquitous global system. The countervailing forces need to be better organized within a rational intellectual framework.

The second distinctive aspect of the South Asian experience relates to the origins and processes by which social movements and grassroots and micro-initiatives emerged, either spontaneously or through catalytic action. Of the developing regions of the world, South Asia has in the past three decades generated the most impressive and diverse range of new holistic social movements. Many of them are recognized to be extremely effective in poverty reduction and promotion of human development. The key to their success is the building of participatory organizations of homogeneous groups that are being strengthened through awareness raising, education, learning by doing, and capacity building.

The study emphasized that the pace and pattern of development in the region in the coming years need coherence. While recognizing that the contribution of the new social movements to this end has been significant, it concluded that their impact has fallen short of the needed response to the challenge.

In the seventh study (Wignaraja and Sirivardana 2004), the pursuit of good governance was accepted as a widely shared goal among various development players since the early 1990s. However, in the conventional intellectual discourse, organized in a Cartesian mould of knowledge management, for some good governance is a means of ensuring effective macro-economic management by down-sizing the state and reducing the scope of bureaucratic interference. Others emphasize the opportunities presented for increasing participation in decision-making and resource allocations, especially for the poor. There is yet no consensus or synthesis.

Apart from this, another two agendas have become increasingly important in recent years, though not always in tandem with good governance, namely those of poverty reduction and decentralization. Poverty reduction is rightly considered the primary purpose of development, and the UN millennium declaration for 2015 represents a clear commitment from among governments and donors to this end. Decentralization is another focal point for donor policy, and many governments around the world are making efforts to devolve powers and resources to lower tiers.

Despite their high visibility and scope for complementarity, these three agendas centring on governance, poverty reduction, and devolution are rarely brought together in a coherent framework of thinking and action. The study recognized that the governance agenda, with an emphasis on participatory development, can be combined with systematic devolution of power and resources to the grassroots, in order to lay the basis for sustained poverty reduction. The key to this process is community mobilization through social movements that can catalyse change through partnerships with sensitive state organizations, and by advocating for deeper reforms in governance that bring about systemic changes in the conditions of the poor. When combined with decentralization and devolution, there are opportunities for poverty reduction. But neither poverty reduction nor filling the democratic deficit results automatically from decentralization reforms alone. Without social mobilization and empowerment, decentralization creates scope for vested local interests to monopolize power and resources to their advantage. Various experiments in Bangladesh, India, Nepal, Pakistan, and Sri Lanka illustrate how social movements and local organizations are mobilizing the poor to take advantage of the decentralization reforms to mobilize resources and influence to bring about pro-poor development, starting from the base of political economies of South Asia. To mature, such successful pro-poor efforts hinge on other, complementary reforms in governance that foster participation, accountability and transparency, without which decentralization may concentrate power and resources in the hands of the few at the local level. What is critical is the capacity of the new social movements to rigorously mobilize, conscientize and organize the poor to articulate their rights as citizens and elected representatives in local governments, to channel the creative potential of democratic decentralization, and to initiate sustainable development in a manner that empowers and enhances pro-poor growth. This would crystallize the forces of establishing real participatory and economic democracy and lead to new partnerships, reinforcing civil society protest movements and successful developmental experiments to provide a complementary strategic thrust to more conventional financial sector and administrative reforms.

The eighth study (Wignaraja and Sirivardana forthcoming) deals with the role of facilitators/animators, and how they are to be sensitized and trained. Their role is to catalyse and generate a massive transformative process, thus completing the unfinished agenda of decolonization in South Asia, on the assumption that a 'spontaneous process' is insufficient to cope with the magnitude of challenges. A major social mobilization process is called for, in which the elites need to be remoulded and a new sense of social responsibility introduced among all stakeholders.

Revising the agenda for action: Beyond critique and reformism

SAARC moving towards core areas of cooperation

In 1990 SAPNA's constructive dissent and coherent macro-micro policy options were brought squarely into the mainstream of policy and debate on governance, highlighting the need for an alternative modernity, greater self-reliant, pro-poor growth in development, a participatory democratic approach, and linking economic and political democracy.

In the Maldives Summit in 1990, the heads of states of SAARC began to sense the sharpening contradictions and polarization between rich and poor in South Asia, the link between poverty and violence, and the inadequacy of conventional thinking and action to respond to the realities within and outside the region. By then the multifaceted crisis was increasingly visible and the compulsion for a shift in strategic thinking was strong.

Until then, insufficient attention had been given to emerging national, regional, and global changes, with a view to developing a rigorous and comprehensive strategic response to them. The intellectual underpinnings of vigorous South Asian regional cooperation were weak. At the Maldives Summit, however, it was recognized that SAARC, as it was evolving, was unprepared for the globalization scenario, for the new challenges posed by 'Europe 1992' and other regional groupings, and for the emerging multifaceted crisis of governance and development in South Asia.

It was decided that SAARC should focus on core areas of economic cooperation, and that scholars, professionals, NGOs, and the media should help reinforce the official SAARC process in moving into these core areas. Recognizing the need for a new partnership between the official process and independent players, reflected concern among the heads of state that SAARC could not move forward purely as an official intergovernmental process. There was political awareness of the potential for a South Asian economic community, but also that it required intellectual stimulus. To achieve this, a real process of learning from the ground had to be initiated, and the lessons had to be translated into a coherent agenda for action.

The SAPNA network responded immediately to the call upon SAARC to move into core areas of regional cooperation. It was recognized that this required recognition of the cultural diversity in South Asia, within which a framework of 'unity in diversity' could be identified. A vision was formulated of a South Asian community and common future, based on shared fundamental values, a common ecosystem, common history and culture, subordination and fragmentation of the economies, and the common ordeal of decolonization. It was recognized that South Asia was being pushed to the margins of the world economy and the international political arena due to external trends together with multifaceted crises, including poverty, slow economic growth, uneven development, population pressure, natural resource erosion, high defence expenditure, internal arms race, social polarization, religious fundamentalism, youth alienation, and ethnic and other conflicts. It was argued that a development strategy, including decentralization, social mobilization, and empowerment, could respond to the region's immediate needs and mediate the sharp contradictions in the political economy (SAPNA Center 1991).

Five core areas for immediate action were also identified: poverty eradication, food security, trade cooperation, a payments union, and external resource mobilization. The areas are closely interrelated, and all necessary prerequisites for achieving the vision of a South Asian economic community with sustainable human development, real democratic political formations, good governance, and poverty eradication. Without the eradication of the worst forms of poverty, however, SAARC could not establish the one-billion-strong South Asian market. Food security is the other side of the poverty coin in a region, which has a food surplus and further potential for food production and food-for-work programmes in the transition. Poverty eradication and the right to food go hand-in-hand, and could be combined with the right to work. For trade cooperation, payments arrangements are essential. In Europe, the payments union preceded economic cooperation. Mobilization of external resources is necessary both for poverty eradication and for industrialization and building South Asia's technological capabilities.

In 1994, a follow-up enquiry looked deeper into the monetary and financial aspects of trade cooperation, decentralized industrialization, and food security, and of moving towards a South Asian economic community. Representatives of central banks of the region and some leading South Asian economists collaborated in this enquiry. Their report, entitled 'Towards a Regional Monetary and Financial System in South Asia', urged that the SAARC look at a coherent vision for trade, payments, monetary and financial cooperation and then proceed to implement the strategy in a step-by-step well-researched manner. The report made it clear that financial cooperation and payment arrangements do not require anything like a common currency. However, they require going much further than the pure bookkeeping arrangements of the Asian clearing union.

The official SAARC process was followed up at subsequent summits on the recommendations on poverty and trade. The poverty issue has yet to be linked to the South Asian development fund, and the trade issue to appropriate payment arrangements. Also, the implementation processes of the recommendations have yet to transcend bureaucratic and technocratic approaches and transform into a real political process and real commitment.

Report of the Independent South Asian commission on poverty alleviation

Of the five interrelated core areas for action, it was the establishment of the Independent South Asian commission for poverty alleviation (ISACPA) in 1991 that provided a common ground for stimulating regional cooperation on the basis of 'unity in diversity' and 'development with equity'. In effect, it was a commission not merely on poverty, but also on larger governance and development issues, to sort out the contradictions between the reality and conventional development thinking and action, and to provide practical solutions which could be implemented within a given time frame.

ISACPA was an innovative collaborative partnership between SAARC governments and an independent group of southern scholars and civil society activists. The report of the commission (SAARC 1992) emerged from an enquiry and wide-ranging dialogues with a range of stakeholders, exploring the complementarities between measures of economic reform and participatory development by the poor themselves. It helped to mainstream ideas that were at the margins, and to reinforce the debate towards practice of decentralized participatory democracy and development with equity, and towards macro-micro policy options and institution building for cost-effective sustainable eradication of the worst forms of poverty within a given time frame. It was stated that the magnitude and complexity of poverty in South Asia puts democracy at risk and poses a threat to the very fabric of South Asian societies. The number of people living below the conventional 'poverty line' was estimated to be 440 million, and the structural adjustment policies which accompany the open-economy industrialization strategy adopted by most SAARC countries, are likely to put further strains on the poor. It was argued that the past 50 years of development interventions, based on 'trickle down' and administrative redistribution, had been inadequate, and that the role of the state therefore must change from that of a highly centralized doer to that of an enabler and supporter of growth in a three-sector growth model. Further, it was argued that eradicating poverty in South Asia would require a political approach, including social mobilization and empowerment of the poor. With the poor as subjects in the development process, they would be able to generate growth, and human development and increasing equity would be complementary elements in the same process. A pro-poor development strategy, based on a three-sector growth-oriented approach, was recommended, along with a pro-poor plan ensuring a net transfer of resources to the poor. A cautious open-economy industrialization with pro-poor reforms should be combined with poverty eradication measures of social mobilization and participation, and the two processes could be harmonized as they provide transitional responses to the poverty as well as the global problem.

At the seventh SAARC summit in 1993, the heads of state unanimously endorsed the 1992 Poverty Commission recommendations and reiterated this in the SAARC summits of 1995 and 1997. In an era of inequalities and globalization, this consensus within the SAARC constituted a major coherent response to critical elements in the multifaceted crisis in South Asia, and reflected the strong compulsion to bring poverty to the centre stage of national and regional concern with innovative action.

A critical mass of South Asian policymakers, scholars, and civil society leaders yet have to fully internalize the contents of the report and the coherent macro-micro options available. They continue to underestimate the magnitude and complexity of the problem, to marginally reform centralized decision-making processes, mesmerized by generalities on human development and equating it with poverty eradication, and to provide reformist options in terms of two-sector growth models and fragmented safety nets, welfare, and charity, with a view to tranquillizing the poor. The international development community for all its rhetoric, with few exceptions, is still locked into a priori theorizing, narrow fragmented ideologically oriented solutions, and 'tool kit' approaches to development and poverty, which at best help the ten per cent less poor.

Other dialogues to change the terms of the discourse

A first dialogue was organized with the World Bank in 1993 (The World Bank and SAARC 1993). The members of the SAARC Standing Committee officially approved the World Bank's invitation to discuss the Poverty Commission report at a high-level workshop on poverty reduction in South Asia, with the participation of the Secretary-General of the SAARC and members of the Poverty Commission. Representatives of the World Bank, IMF, ADB, UNDP, Ifad, and UNICEF participated. The World Bank is currently talking of pro-poor growth and going beyond mere 'delivery of services' to the poor.

The process was repeated in 1995 in a second dialogue with the government of Germany, which is a leading advocate of the Millenium Development Goal of poverty reduction by 50 per cent by 2015 (The German Foundation for International Development and the Federal Ministry of Economic Cooperation and Development 1995).

Apart from these two formal dialogues, the SAPNA Network advocates its strategic thrust in several national, regional, and international fora, engaging in policy dialogues with governments, civil society organizations, and scholars, as well as with the poor (Wignaraja and Sirivardana 2004). The aim is to reorient and build capacities and raise awareness to meet the challenge of development with equity, and to establish new partnerships with stakeholders to move the holistic process towards a new paradigm.

A new school of thought

Through policy dialogues and publications, SAPNA warning signals were sent to South Asian governments, scholars, and civil society organizations that the mainstream development strategies and decision-making instrumentalities, that had followed after independence in the late 1940s, were sharpening the contradictions. Also, institutions and highly centralized decision-making processes of the state and the private sector were inadequate in dealing with them, including the polarization that was taking place in South Asia between rich and poor. These lessons helped identify emerging options and alternatives, which were formulated into a school of thought for a transitional time frame.

The emerging school of thought was crystallized at a time when the interrelated governance issues, linking development to equity, security, and human rights in wider terms, were becoming the main concerns in the political discourse in South Asia as well as internationally.

The new thinking went beyond critique and dissent of mainstream development/democracy thinking and action to articulating, in a rudimentary but focussed manner, constructive alternatives, in which the processes of development and democracy were intertwined. The links between political and economic democracy were consistent with a growth-oriented strategy and a new accumulation process, all of which are prerequisites for good governance.

The material bases for the new school of thought and for a new social contract are provided by the new social movements, which have been emerging from the ground in every South Asian country in the past 25 years (Wignaraja 1993).

The new social movements differ from the old social movements which were engaged in anti-colonial struggles, from the trade union action and from party politics. They represent a new group of players interested not in state power as such, but in creating people's power where a participatory democratic society is the persistent quest. Larger and larger numbers of people are no longer willing to accept fatalistic, exploitative, alienating, or repressive regimes and state structures, or a development paradigm that excludes them and deprives them of dignity. These movements represent a form of countervailing power, demonstrating ways to humanize the larger macro-processes and assert that the terms of incorporation into the mainstream can be changed at all levels.

This intellectual quest led to probing the way in which state and non-state institutions exercise power. It was clear that, while the role of the state was important, it was not the only governance player in society. Nor was it possible for market forces alone to lead the way. Civil society also needed to grow, move and exercise countervailing power. Organizations of the poor have a cutting edge role in institutional restructuring, growth-generating, and polity mediations, and therefore need to develop more coherent strategic approaches and practices. The international community, too, has a role to play and can provide sensitive support.

Fundamentals for strengthening the links between economic and political democracy

This paper shows how SAPNA has attempted to advocate the new school of thought, and to learn from engagement with various stakeholders in national, regional, and international constructive dialogues for the next transition in South Asia. SAPNA's approach to governance, participatory democracy, and development with equity is not one of marginal tinkering and ad hoc reforms with palliatives and rhetoric of a social charter. It is based on five interrelated fundamentals:

The long revolution and social transformation

The first premise that needs to be internalized is that social transformation and structural changes are required that go beyond simplistic growth, redistribution, and human face models. Structural change is more than mere financial and budgetary discipline and ad hoc redistributive justice. Such social transformation has to be conceived of as a long revolution implying a complex chain of long and short time frames – not a one shot 'big bang' revolution. Self-reliance is another fundamental transformative issue. South Asia has for too long depended on external inspiration and hegemonies. In retrospect, such structures have led to 'soft' societies where the majority of people, including the poor and the young, are alienated. The welfare societies that were to be created became unsustainable. Creativity, innovativeness and a problem-solving approach to life were ignored, although they have always been characteristics of South Asian societies. Therefore, de-alienation is an important dimension of the process of building self-reliance.

Perspective and values

The structural changes at the macro- and micro-levels outlined above have to start with a clear perspective and be value-led. This is fundamental for correct action. Before action is taken, the underlying values need to be made explicit. The perspective, from which to search for the underlying paradigm, is that participatory democracy and development are parts of the same holistic vision that has inspired human endeavour in different South Asian socio-cultural settings for more than 2000 years. Several fundamental values that existed in traditional South Asian societies must be identified and re-examined. Some critical values relate to looking at life in its totality and all its richness, people's participation in decisions that affect their lives, sharing and caring for the community, cooperative activities beyond individual self-interest, trust, innocence, simplicity, thrift, a work ethic with a fine-tuned balance between work and leisure, harmony with nature and a rational use of natural and financial resources, communal ownership of the commons, and complementarity between men and women as well as gender equity.

Countervailing power: a political approach to the transition

Another fundamental in rethinking past paradigms of development and democracy relates to the question of participatory democracy. In this regard, devolution of power and empowerment of poor and vulnerable groups, as opposed to representative democracy and highly centralized elite power, require clarification. Conventional thinking on both development and democracy was based on a harmony model. This needs to be demystified. The assumption of harmonious communities in a conflict-free social framework for change has no basis in reality, whether at local or national level in South Asia or at the global level. In South Asia deep-seated contradictions exist between groups with conflicts of interests, which have to be recognized, particularly in the transition from decolonization. Any meaningful approach to social change must be both political and transformative. It should not be a purely technocratic, fragmented or sectoral approach. The project approach with 'tool kits' is inadequate. A political process has to be initiated. The space for a political approach exists already in some countries, while in others it needs to be created. A great deal of social mobilization is required. This involves remoulding of elites as well as mobilizing and raising the consciousness of the poor and helping them to build their own organizations. Where formal power is in the hands of a few and power is not shared, but grossly misused, participation in the first instance results in building countervailing forms of power, leading ultimately to a healthier participatory democracy as opposed to representative democracy in the Westminster model. Countervailing power does not preclude new partnerships with sensitive institutions, either state institutions or others in the support system like government entities, banks, and donor NGOs. This kind of participatory democracy must have its counterpart in economic democracy.

Growth, human development, and equity: no trade-offs

As the multifaceted crisis in South Asia deepened, the accumulation process was set in motion, by means of private or state capital accumulation. This process was basic to the old concept of economic development and its reformist option, but as it turned out to be insufficient, the pressures mounted for an alternative accumulation process. It was not a matter of growth first and equity afterwards. Redistributive justice and 'trickle down' were simply not the issues. A fundamental difference between the new approach to poverty eradication and conventional approaches is that the poor are not considered as the problem, but as part of the solution, capable of generating savings and efficient investment. A second difference is that the new strategy for poverty eradication is based on a three-sector – public, private, and organizations of the poor – pro-poor growth strategy, and not on a redistributive strategy of welfare, safety nets, and charity, which at best can be residual. The pro-poor growth strategy is based on the observable evidence of the efficiency of the poor as subjects in the process. A sustainable development strategy needs to search for alternative driving forces for a self-sustaining accumulation process, requiring increased savings. The compulsion of seeking alternative driving forces for this kind of accumulation, even in this narrower conception, is therefore mounting. This is not a matter of giving credit to the poor. It is a matter of embarking on a new pattern of growth with the poor, where they save and invest. Growth, human development, and equity are in this pattern of development, not trade-offs, but part of the same complementary process. This pattern of growth provides the link between political and economic democracy through pro-poor growth, initially at the micro-level, complemented by a supportive macro-policy framework and a new financial architecture.

It also seems necessary for South Asian countries to adopt a more complex development strategy that combines development, growth, equity, and technological change with more creative use of local resources and knowledge. In such a strategy, people's creativity, locally available resources, local knowledge systems, and local savings become critical instruments. Imported capital and technology, the factors in short supply, can be supplementary. In this transition all countries will need to internally pursue a basically two-pronged strategy that will permit them to maintain the gains from past attempts at modernization and industrialization, to trade with appropriate damage limitation, and to make a direct attack on poverty in all its manifestations, with the poor as subjects rather than objects. Initially, two prongs of the strategy may have different time horizons and some contradictions, but over time they can be harmonized. Regional cooperation can reinforce national efforts with the building of global competitiveness, permitting

South Asian countries to adjust to the global system on more favourable terms.

Refocussing praxis and managing the knowledge system

Another fundamental that requires further elaboration is the methodology of praxis, and management of the knowledge system. Some systematic efforts are being made to break out of conventional social science methodologies into participatory action research by groups of South Asian scholars and activists working together. Social praxis, and participatory action research that goes with it, take off from the cultural and historical experiences of South Asia. It critiques a predetermined universalism and stresses pluralism, including geo-cultural specificity. Social sciences have evolved through the study of western societies, hypotheses and value judgements have emerged from that cultural world, and continue to influence a major part of the academic community, as well as educational, technical, and administrative systems.

These five interrelated fundamentals are critical to achieving social justice, greater self-reliance, and participation. In the new participatory democracy and accumulation, and growth process for development with equity, the knowledge system inherent in the culture must inform the whole process. The nature of knowledge, harder evidence collectively acquired, the method of the utilization of the wider stocks and flows of knowledge, and the choice of technology have to be probed further. This could help bridge the gap between real knowledge and wisdom, and catalyse the process of social change and development action in new terms, linking knowledge to power and action. Also, without vigorous and informed regional cooperation, no individual country could effectively manage the transition out of the contradictions and unmanageable polity to which it has descended.

A new social contract

Another critical element relates to the need for a new social contract between the state and the poor in South Asia. The failures of the past and the disarray in development thinking and action require a new major inspirational drive and dynamic, which can bring diverse social forces and communities into new partnerships. A social contract between South Asian states and the poor should provide inclusivity and pluralism in a universal sense in the ownership of the vision at the national as well as regional level. Such a contract is the only instrument which can help regenerate the trust which has been eroded. It goes beyond the old social contract between management and labour, the Keynesian consensus, which led to the welfare state. The design will be quite different from the proposal for a SAARC social charter. It should be carved in stone and have the moral and legal authority stemming from international law and a new global discussion on the link between development with equity, security, and human rights in a wider sense.

The Dhaka consensus on eradication of poverty by 2002, taken at the SAARC summit in 1993 and repeated at the SAARC summits of 1995 and 1997, was not an end in itself. It was the first step in the new social contract. It was envisaged that this contract should incorporate culturally relevant values such as 'sharing and caring' and also the right to food and the right to work. Such a contract would enable the states of South Asia to replace the welfare state concept with a more inspiring concept which could also help mitigate the violence and multifaceted crises in the region and within individual countries.

The knowledge-action-power nexus

To move in this transition from the dominant macro-framework of development and democracy towards the new school of thought, based on the interrelated fundamental premises and the micro-level development praxis, it is important to probe deeper and be unambiguous about the available knowledge system and its management. It must be clear what and whose knowledge is to be involved, and how culturally relevant knowledge is to be used in catalysing the transition to social transformation, sustainable development, and eradication of the worst forms of poverty, while also mediating the contradictions caused by globalization and the need to engage in global competitiveness.

This then becomes another element in the new school of thought. Without being 'simplistic', the concept of knowledge as an instrumentality in relation to power and development action would need to be analysed in-depth. In the South Asian cultural context this is not an easy task, due to the deep and complex metaphysical perennial philosophies, which provide the value framework, the integrity, and the intellectual underpinnings of the culture and knowledge system. There are no simplistic dogmas nor dialectics alone. It cannot be done in the Cartesian mould or based on values and visions from distant situations. The need for a relevant development with equity school of thought, rooted in the culture, compels an enunciation of several relationships, relating to knowledge, power, and action.

Three propositions are posed in the form of simple assertions:

1. The crisis of the modern knowledge system confirms the need for devising new methods of scientific inquiry for the next transition.
2. The availability of many stocks of knowledge in South Asia also means a greater choice of technology for sustainable development and poverty eradication.
3. The traditional knowledge system of the poor now assumes greater validity and relevance in relation to sustainable development with equity.

The modern knowledge system, incorporated into mainstream development thinking and action, was initially deeply wedded to economics and single discipline analysis, largely unrelated to wider to human needs. The concept and practice of modern economic development have now been questioned. Politically, they are inconsistent with the claims of equality and justice by disrupting local communities and polarizing society into those with access to resources and power, and those without. Knowledge and technology were critical elements in this process. Knowledge and choice of technology also become critical elements in reversing the process. Knowledge is power. The relationship between knowledge, the development action that flows from it, and power then become critical issues. The claim of modern knowledge was that the kind of development it generates can be extended to cover all situations and the entire globe. This has not happened.

The cultural dislocations that have taken place alongside economic development have confirmed that culture, knowledge, and development are intertwined. This was highlighted as early as in the 1950s, when the major 'economic development' intervention and the aid relationship were initiated.[5]

Further, the Cartesian knowledge system, being inherently fragmenting and having in-built obsolescence, creates an alienation of wisdom from technology and dispenses with the wisdom. In its preoccupation with quantitative analysis it further distorts reality and disregards aesthetic and human dimensions, experiential learning, and intuitive insights (Shiva 1989: 29).

A positivist orientation cannot provide cognitive validation (let alone connective or total validation) to all people in all situations. The scope of the problems in South Asia is too vast and complex. Furthermore, to disregard people's knowledge, derived from the aesthetic, experiential, and intuitive insights, is to disregard the essential links between knowledge, culture, and development. This linkage does not permit the intellectual processes to be divorced from values and will, under the guise of objectivity and only results in a narrow technocratic approach.

In South Asia social scientists of different disciplines are trying collectively to locate knowledge that is responsive to their socio-cultural realities. To move from the single discipline economic development model to a framework of participatory and sustainable development in holistic terms, it is not sufficient to merely critique the old model, and the knowledge system on which it was based, in general macro- or philosophical terms. There are some specific elements that need to be de mystified before homogenization can be replaced by pluralism, globalism by localism, economism by humanism, unlimited progress by notions of self-control, restraint, and simplicity. It has been assumed that the world has only a single stock of knowledge and technology. Post-Second World War technical assistance and the extension worker concept are both part of this old approach. The knowledge systems and technological choices available to South Asia and its people are, however, much wider.

Given the intrinsic interconnectedness of knowledge and power in every culture, it is necessary to examine the social basis of different knowledge systems. People in South Asia have a great deal of scientific knowledge which can be applied to their daily lives and problems. This knowledge has been acquired intuitively or by trial and error. It is not mere traditional romanticism or religious mysticism. Much of the available traditional knowledge and technology can be used as they are. Some traditional knowledge is half forgotten and needs to be revived. Such revival can only be undertaken through a participatory process within the culture. Some traditional technology needs to be upgraded in its own environment, and not in research institutes abroad, where the adaptation process itself is biased by different values. Furthermore, when repatriated, its use in the country of origin becomes very costly. Appropriate R & D systems, which do not exist or exist in a very fragile form, are also required for upgrading traditional knowledge and giving it further scientific validation. As this happens, the knowledge also has to be returned in the same cost-effective participatory process and in an idiom that people can understand.

A new process is emerging in the South Asian reality. As a result of a two-way interaction between committed South Asian 'experts' and people during participatory action research, a new technology is gradually being created in these countries, which does not exist in the categories referred to earlier, i.e. modern, intermediate, and traditional. The new technology results from another variant of the new and still fragile R & D system, gradually being built by committed experts and people in South Asia, living and working together to develop a more humane society, initially using locally available resources and knowledge. This process also reflects the interaction of different perceptions of life and knowledge between the two groups. It results from the committed expert or de-professionalized intellectuals, identifying with people and committing themselves to bringing sustainable development and social change (ibid.). These are the new kind of facilitators of people's praxis whose role will be analysed later, along with that of the animator.

Likewise, in industrial countries, as a result of alternative life style experiments, ecological movements, the energy crisis, ecological concerns, youth alienation, and search for human values, individuals and groups are experimenting with new technologies. These technologies are related to new values, and not to those which emanate from the market. In the process, people are creating a new knowledge base on renewable resources, food habits, and health. Sometimes, this represents reviving traditional knowledge, sometimes taking knowledge from South Asia (and other poor regions) and adapting it. This technology may in the long run be more relevant for development in South Asia, than unadapted transfers from the modern sector.

The fundamental argument here synoptically presented is that for sustainable development and poverty eradication, there is a plurality of 'stocks' of knowledge and a greater choice of technology than in the old framework of development. However, without a participatory process, this knowledge will not surface. As structural and value changes take place in industrial countries and a new international order emerges, a different and two-way knowledge transfer is possible between rich and poor countries.

Notes

1. Sapna means vision/perspective in several South Asian languages. The South Asian Perspectives Network Association (SAPNA) is an independent innovative action research, policy dialogue and capacity building catalytic network, composed of a critical mass of South Asians committed to renewing a vision after decolonization and to investigating South Asian governance and development problems from a South Asian perspective. SAPNA's actions are rooted in pluralistic South Asian values, culture, and the holistic civilizational rhythm, and are based on the micro-macro lessons from the ground.

Network members carry out their own programmes, based on similar fundamentals and values, thus contributing to an emerging South Asian school of
thought on governance and development. From its small beginnings in the
mid-1970s, SAPNA has expanded into a regional network of over 100 South
Asian individuals and institutions, with several thousand less visible participants. It is linked to several global development networks and international institutions.

2. The methodology of praxis and PAR should be distinguished from pseudo
methodologies in use like PRA, RRA, and logical framework analysis (LFA).
Praxis and PAR are located outside the dominant framework of positivist
knowledge and the fragmented Cartesian mould of knowledge management,
based on harder evidence, information and more scientific interdisciplinary
methods of enquiry (see Wignaraja 1991).

3. Particular attention can be drawn to two papers in Wignaraja and Hussain
1989. 'Ideology and the Status of Women in Hindu Society' by Gowrie
Ponniah, and 'Islam, Ethnicity and Leadership in Pakistan' by Akbar S.
Ahmed both emphasize cultural issues that have resurfaced in the current
discourse on development, security, and culture. Contradictions that could
have been resolved within a concept of 'unity in diversity', have instead been
sharpened.

4. This is what the 1948 UN Universal Declaration on Human Rights is about.
The underlying values for global governance were later supported by the
Covenants on Genocide (1948), the Covenant on Civil and Political Rights
(1966), the Convention on Elimination of all Forms of Discrimination based
on Religion or Belief (1981), the Declaration on Rights of Persons belonging
to National or Ethnic, Religious, and Linguistic Minorities (1992), and
others.

5. Wignaraja (1953) writes: 'While considerable thought has been expended in
recent years in attempting solutions to the numerous immediate problems
confronting developing countries, very little attention has been placed on
the reality that development takes places within an established cultural pattern. The process of culture change that is set in motion during economic
development tends for most part to be ignored. When it is recognized, it is
merely hoped that time will bring about the necessary adjustments.'

References

De Silva, G.V.S., Haque, W., Mehta, N., Rahman, A. and Wignaraja, P. (1988)
Towards a Theory of Rural Development, Lahore: Progressive Publishers.

The Expert Group on South Asian Financial and Payments Co-operation (1994)
Towards a Regional Monetary and Financial System in South Asia – Consensus
among the South Asian Expert Group, Report of the Expert Group Meeting on
South Asian Financial and Payments Co-operation, New Delhi, India, August
1994.

The German Foundation for International Development and the Federal
Ministry of Economic Cooperation and Development (1995) Poverty
Alleviation in South Asia. Report of the International Round Table, organized
by the German Foundation for International Development and Federal

Ministry of Economic Cooperation and Development, Konigswinter, March 1995.

SAARC (1992) *Meeting the Challenge*, Report of the Independent South Asian Commission on Poverty Alleviation, Kathmandu: SAARC, November 1992.

SAPNA Center (1991) SAARC: Moving Towards Core Areas of Co-operation, Report of the Independent Group on South Asian Co-operation, SAPNA Centre, September 1991.

Shiva, V. (1989) *Staying Alive: Women, Ecology, and Development*, New Delhi: Zed Books.

Wignaraja, P. (1953) 'The Conflict Between Economic Rationality and Cultural Values', *Civilizations* 3(1) (1953): 53.

Wignaraja, P. (1990) *Women, Poverty, and Resources*, New Delhi/Newbury Park/ London: Sage Publications.

Wignaraja, P. (1991) 'Reforcing Development Praxis in South Asia: Critical Instruments', in Wignaraja, P., Hussain, A., Sethi, H. and Wignaraja, G. (eds) (1991) *Participatory Development: Learning from South Asia*, Karachi/Oxford: Oxford University Press.

Wignaraja, P. (ed) (1993) *New Social Movements in the South: Empowering the People*, London: Zed Books; New Delhi: Sage Publications.

Wignaraja, P. and Hussain, A. (eds) (1989) *The Challenge in South Asia: Development, Democracy, and Regional Cooperation*, 1st edition: New Delhi/Newbury Park/ London: Sage Publications; 2nd edition: Karachi/Oxford: Oxford University Press.

Wignaraja, P., Hussain, A., Sethi, H. and Wignaraja, G. (eds) (1991) *Participatory Development: Learning from South Asia*, Karachi/Oxford: Oxford University Press.

Wignaraja, P. and Sirivardana, S. (eds) (1998) *Readings on Pro-Poor Planning through Social Mobilization in South Asia: The Strategic Option for Poverty Eradication*, New Delhi: Vikas Publications.

Wignaraja, P. and Sirivardana, S. (eds) (2004) *Pro-Poor Growth and Governance in South Asia: Decentralization and Participatory Development*, New Delhi: Sage Publications.

Wignaraja, Ponna and Sirivardana, Susil (eds) (forthcoming) *The Role of the Facilitator in Social Mobilization for Poverty Eradication*.

The World Bank and SAARC (1993) Poverty Reduction in South Asia. Report of workshop co-sponsored by the World Bank and SAARC, Annapolis, October 1993.

5
Environmental Load Displacement in World History

Alf Hornborg

It is frequently observed that globalization is not a new phenomenon in world history. Processes leading to greater societal connectedness over vast areas of the world can be traced centuries and even millennia back in time (Gills and Thompson 2006). A commonly neglected aspect of such processes is the inclination of more highly 'developed' regions – centres of 'civilization' – to establish asymmetric relations of exchange with their local or global hinterlands, leading to accumulation of resources in the centres and often to environmental deterioration in their peripheries. This chapter reviews some of the evidence for various kinds of such 'environmental load displacement' in different societies and cultures over the past few millennia. Rewriting global environmental history in these terms allows us to conceptualize contemporary concerns with 'sustainable development' and 'environmental security' in analytically more precise ways, integrating perspectives from social and natural science and illuminating continuities and discontinuities between successive cultural patterns of resource use and their accompanying cosmologies (cf. Hornborg et al. 2007).[1]

Theoretical background

Environmental historians have generally categorized their data in terms of a set of 'environmental problems' that have been generated by specific historical forms of human resource use, production, consumption, settlement patterns, and so on. Some have produced comprehensive and authoritative accounts of the history of *one* such problem, as in studies of the history of energy use (e.g. Debeir et al. 1991 [1986]), or in Williams' (2003) landmark volume on global deforestation. Others have tried to sketch world histories of a whole spectrum of environmental problems. Thus, in a wide-ranging and popular compilation, Ponting (1991) reviews vast quantities of data on the environmental impacts of agriculture, deforestation, hunting, fishing, urbanization, pollution, energy use, etc. in different historical periods from the Neolithic to the present.[2] Rarely, however, are environmental problems discussed specifically from the perspective of how they are *distributed* between different groups or sectors of society. Although such questions are often raised in modern discussions of 'political ecology' (Bryant and Bailey 1997; Martinez-Alier 2002) and 'environmental justice' (Harvey 1996), there has been little systematic treatment of the uneven social distribution of environmental burdens in world history (for exceptions, however, see Bunker 1985; Goldfrank et al. 1999). When geographical distances between points of consumption and environmental impacts are addressed in historical studies, it is generally merely to illustrate the widening spatial scale of environmental change, rather than to highlight issues of societal distribution. In this chapter, I will suggest an analytical framework for understanding the uneven distribution of environmental burdens as a social strategy that is integral to the political economy of world-systemic processes, rather than the incidental effect of certain patterns of production and consumption.

All biological processes have 'entropic costs' (cf. Clark 1997: 8–10) in the sense that they dissipate energy and materials. The earliest human societies did not differ much from our pre-hominid ancestors in terms of how these dissipative processes were organized. Local populations of hunter-gatherers derived their energy and material requirements from their immediate environment. Certainly there was inter-group competition over both resources and anthropogenic environmental impacts, but as long as neighbouring groups relied on the same kinds of resources, environmental degradation was no more of a *political* issue than among other species of mammals. The distribution of resources hinged on the ability of bands of foragers to gain and retain access to high-yielding territories, generally by defending their own presence in these areas. Social inequalities in resource distribution were primarily confined to local intra-group hierarchies based on age and gender. Technology was simple enough to rely almost exclusively on local resources and labour.

With cultural specialization geared to different ecological niches – such as coasts, floodplains, forests, and mountains – competition between human groups assumed new forms. Exchange of produce between different specialized zones introduced a new element in human-environmental relations: the possibility of systematically unequal transfers of resources *between* communities or regions (cf. Godelier 1969). For the sake of simplicity, 'unequal exchange' can be conceptualized in terms of asymmetric flows of embodied land (gauged, for instance, in hectare yields) and/or embodied labour (gauged in human labour time) that have been invested in the traded products. Communities or regions that are able to sustain a net import of embodied land and/or labour are potentially able to invest the 'surplus' in *capital*. Thus, capital *is* embodied land and labour. This relationship is well illustrated in Cronon's (1991) masterful study, although not phrased in these terms, of how the city of Chicago emerged from the accumulation of inexpensive land and labour assets that had been invested in grain, lumber, and meat from the American West.

To be precise, I use the concept of 'capital' to denote some kind of infrastructure for locally saving time and/or space by intensifying the productivity of labour and/or land. If such infrastructures are also recognized as *constituted* by embodied labour and land that have been appropriated through unequal exchange, we are able to postulate the following relation between the three 'factors of production': capital is a strategy for locally *saving* labour (time) and land (space) through the *appropriation* of embodied labour (time) and land (space) from elsewhere in the social system. This understanding of capital carries very different implications than the conventional economic doctrine that posits land, labour, and capital as substitutable. In material terms, the three factors of production are *not* mutually convertible into one another. Land can nourish labour, and land and labour can yield capital, but capital can create neither land nor labour.

Capital accumulation and environmental deterioration 4000 BC–AD 2000

Geographer Mats Widgren (2007) discusses the definition and global distribution of 'landesque' capital from several perspectives. Land improved for purposes of agricultural production is the main form of capital accumulation in pre-industrial societies on all continents, and simultaneously one of the most tangible ways in which humans for millennia have changed their natural environments. There are many varieties – e.g. irrigation or drainage canals, terraces, raised fields, forest clearance, stone clearance, soil improvement – but only one common incentive: to increase agricultural yield per unit of land. It is thus closely connected with sedentary settlement and often the object of violent competition or even military conquest. Although there are examples of landesque capital precipitating environmental degradation (e.g. salinization, or erosion following abandonment), Widgren points out that it has often permanently improved the conditions for sustainable land use. He also notes that the concept is in conflict with the notion of 'carrying capacity' as an immutable feature of a given environment. Although often attributed to central planning and hierarchical social organization, as in Wittfogel's classic discussion of 'Oriental despotism' and 'hydraulic' civilizations, Widgren observes that landesque capital can also be accumulated through the long-term labour investments of local communities, particularly under political, economic, and social conditions where investments in land are experienced as secure. The concept of landesque capital provides us with a foil against which to better understand what Amartya Sen has called 'laboresque' capital, i.e. machinery: while the latter saves labour, the former saves land. It also reminds us that land and labour are not as distinct factors of production as they are sometimes visualized, for landesque capital is so by virtue of representing embodied labour. The great variation in the quality and productivity of land presents a great challenge for modern methods of natural resource accounting based on units of land, e.g. that of ecological footprints.

The 'landesque' capital of early agricultural societies was generally accumulated by chiefs or monarchs through the appropriation of labour by means of slavery, *corvée*, kinship, or other obligations. Fertilizers were sometimes transported over considerable distances. Thus, the local intensification of agricultural production was generally made possible through the mobilization of human and natural resources from a much wider area. Local increases in productivity at times implied ecological and/or human impoverishment elsewhere. The advantages of agricultural intensification vis-à-vis foraging, however, were not so much a matter of saving time as of saving space. It made it possible to concentrate larger populations in restricted areas, a project that primarily served the interests of political–religious elites who sought control over ever larger workforces. For the majority of the population it implied more and harder work, less freedom, and poorer health (Hughes 2001: 25, 32). Although 'population growth' is often referred to as a driving force behind agricultural intensification (cf. Boserup 1988), it should be recognized that local demographic expansion need not primarily be a biological phenomenon, but can result from centripetal socio-political processes driven by elite strategies to accumulate rising numbers of servants, artisans, and soldiers.

If 'landesque' capital refers to various inalienable investments augmenting the productivity of land, we can also identify a specific kind of capital designed to assure the constitutional cooperativeness of labour. In order to be able to mobilize and control large populations, the rulers of early theocratic civilizations needed to invest in 'ideological' capital such as prestige goods, temples, palaces, and other public architecture. The production of such capital generally relied on resources far beyond the city limits. In the fourth millennium BC, for instance, the uplands to the north and east of Mesopotamia suffered from deforestation (and subsequent soil erosion) due to timber and charcoal extraction catering to the demands of lowland centres like Uruk (Redman 1999: 180–182; Hughes 2001: 36–37). Sumerian merchants also brought timber, ivory, and precious stones from as far as the Indus Valley, and copper from Cyprus. In the Indus Valley civilization (2300–1800 BC), mud bricks were dried in ovens that required great quantities of wood, and the resulting deforestation caused rapid soil erosion over a wide area. Early Indus Valley cities also imported cedar wood from the Himalayas, and both Sumer, Egypt, and Rome harvested cedars and other timber from Lebanon. Most of the Mediterranean area was deforested to provide grain, fuel, and construction materials for the urban centres of ancient Greece and Rome. Roman ships brought tin and other scarce resources from beyond the Straits of Gibraltar. Other, more local examples of deforestation and ecological deterioration largely due to the excessive construction of elite monuments include Easter Island and the classic Maya (Hughes 2001: 45–46). Such 'ideological' capital, the rationale of which is primarily symbolic, should be acknowledged not as superfluous luxuries but as an integral aspect of the 'technology' of early state power. No less than other forms of capital, also, it may generate tangible material repercussions, locally as well as throughout its hinterland.

Exports of foodstuffs and other perishable goods such as wool are difficult to trace archaeologically, but it is likely to have occurred in the Near East already around 7000 BC, in exchange for archaeologically documented imports such as obsidian, turquoise, and copper. The urban core area of lowland Mesopotamia in the fourth millennium BC increased its export production of grain, ceramics, and textiles in order to sustain imports of timber, minerals, and other resources not locally available (Redman 1999: 185–186). Agricultural intensification in the core area led to shortening of fallows, cultivation of marginal lands, and salinization. Meanwhile, the extraction of timber, stone, and metals in the peripheral uplands east of Mesopotamia also led to environmental degradation. Ancient Egypt exported grain, other foodstuffs, flax, and papyrus, and became the 'breadbasket' of the Roman Empire. Beginning in the third millennium BC, an increasing export production of olives and grapes around the Mediterranean reduced natural forest cover and transformed the landscape. In the Levant, these environmental impacts peaked during Roman colonial rule about two thousand years ago. Such environmental changes are reflected in the successive extinction of species such as elephants, rhinos, hippos, giraffes, and zebras in Egypt and North Africa, lions and leopards in Greece, and tigers in Mesopotamia (Ponting 1991: 161–162).

Deforestation in Europe reached a peak by 1300, although the bubonic plague was followed by two centuries of temporary regeneration (Hughes 2001: 86, 92). A few decades earlier, China experienced a similar episode of demographic collapse and temporary environmental recovery. At this time, Italian cities like Florence, Venice, and Genoa were drawing on resources from all over Europe and the Mediterranean basin, including wool from an increasingly deforested England (ibid.: 87–89). By the early fourteenth century, Florence had to rely on long-distance imports even of food, but these supplies were insecure and famine remained a real threat. The shortage of wood became increasingly severe in Europe as consumption increased in architecture, fortifications, heating, lighting, metallurgy, and the manufacture of glass, tile, bricks, pottery, carts, ships, weapons, musical instruments, dishes, shoes, barrels, and other products (ibid.: 90). The production of one ton of iron, for example, required the annual growth of 12 hectares of productive forest. Hansa ports such as Lübeck controlled a lucrative trade in timber and other forest products, such as furs, from around the Baltic. By the sixteenth century, almost all Portuguese ships were built in India or Brazil, while Spain imported timber from Poland in order to build the Armada, and England imported timber from Scandinavia and Russia (Ponting 1991: 278–279). Already by the late seventeenth century, British warships were being built in North America.

Agricultural intensification is customarily presented as a process of technological improvement designed to feed greater numbers of people, but as Ponting (1991: 108–109) reminds us, famine is generally not so much a matter of food shortage in absolute terms as of who is given *access* to food. In recent centuries, this has largely been a matter of who can afford to buy it. Intensification tends to be geared to export production, and food exports often continue from areas suffering from famine. This is particularly evident when agricultural intensification occurs in economically peripheral areas. Historical examples include fourteenth and fifteenth century France, nineteenth century Scotland and Ireland, India in 1876–1877, Russia in 1911–1912, Bengal in 1943, and more recent famines in Ethiopia and the Sahel. In all these cases, it is apt to speak of a displacement of environmental burdens from those regions where the exported food is consumed to the impoverished areas where it is produced. After about 1850, Europe had decisively shifted to such a displacement strategy through large-scale importation of food and fertilizers from its colonial periphery. Although this periphery – today known as the South – suffers recurrent famine and widespread malnutrition, it has long continued to export more food than it imports (ibid.: 214). The most recent surge of agricultural intensification – the so-called 'Green Revolution' in the economic periphery of the world-system – has been imbued with detrimental socio-political implications in terms of redistributing resources and environmental burdens at both the local and the global level (cf. Hughes 2001: 186–187).

The four centuries of European expansion between 1500 and 1900 have aptly been characterized as 'the rape of the world' (Ponting 1991: 161–193). Not only was this expansion – like those of previous civilizations – founded on slavery and other forms of forced labour, but the relentless pursuit of profitable resources from other continents wrought havoc on distant ecosystems and societies in order to satisfy European desires for, among other things, precious metals, ores, timber, plantation crops (e.g. sugar, tobacco, cotton, rice, tea, coffee, bananas, rubber, cocoa, palm oil), fertilizers, fish, whale oil, ivory, furs, and feathers (cf. Richards 2003). The most tangible environmental consequences of this global expansion of resource extraction include devastated mining landscapes, deforestation, soil exhaustion, collapsed fisheries, and a dramatic reduction in biodiversity. The specialized cultivation of cash crops for the international market not only exhausted the soil but also reduced local food security in countries such as Cuba, Fiji, Tahiti, Gambia, and the Philippines, increasing their reliance on food imports (Ponting 1991: 213). A very tangible example of how European accumulation brought impoverishment to its colonial periphery is the import of fertilisers such as guano from South America and phosphates from Nauru and other islands in the Pacific Ocean (ibid.: 218–221). Today, affluent countries are able to maintain fertile soils and productive forests by importing resources (e.g. oil, nitrogen, phosphorus) to alleviate pressure on the land, a 'development' strategy that can hardly be offered as an example for less affluent countries to follow.

The rise of European hegemony in the late eighteenth and the nineteenth centuries was founded on new possibilities of environmental load displacement provided by access to the New World and investments in industrial technology (Wilkinson 1973; Pomeranz 2000). 'Industrial' capital (i.e. machinery) can be distinguished from 'landesque' and purely 'ideological' capital in that it actually conducts work. Rather than merely improving the inherent productivity of land or cooperativeness of labour, industrial capital can *replace* labour in harvesting and refining the products of the land. In processing raw materials imported from elsewhere, moreover, it can locally also serve to replace land itself as a productive asset. To be sure, the three forms of capital are continuously interwoven with one another, but this analytical distinction remains valid. What is not generally recognized, however, is that the substitutability of industrial capital for labour and land is more apparent than real (Hornborg 2001). From a local perspective, for example, England in the nineteenth century, capital may seem to substitute for labour and land, but this illusion stems from an inability (or unwillingness) to grasp the logic of the entire global system from which this capital has been generated. The accumulation of capital in nineteenth century England represented vast quantities of embodied labour and land appropriated on other continents. For example, the exchange of £1,000 worth of cotton textiles for £1,000 worth of raw cotton on the world market in 1850 implied an exchange of 4,092 British hours of labour for 32,619 hours in the cotton plantations, and of the use of less than one hectare of British land for the use of 58.6 hectares abroad (Hornborg 2006). Moreover, in displacing fibre production for its textile industry from domestic sheep pastures to distant cotton plantations, England liberated large amounts of land and labour for other purposes. To import the raw cotton to generate £1,000 of income from textile production rather than relying on domestic wool, meant saving 20,091 British work-hours at the expense of 10,521 work-hours in America and saving 107.5 British hectares at the expense of 18.9 hectares in America.

The twentieth century brought new and even more dramatic technologies of environmental load displacement, through which 'developed' regions were able to shift much of the industrial degradation of soil, air, water, and vegetation to their 'developing' peripheries (cf. McNeill 2000). The most obvious innovation of the twentieth century was the massive increase in consumption of oil, which has generated environmental problems at every moment of processing from extraction and transport through consumption, garbage disposal, air pollution, and climate change. Whereas 'developed' regions such as North America, Europe, and Japan have the highest rates of per capita consumption of oil, it is the 'developing' regions that are hardest afflicted by the environmental consequences. Assuming that these consequences (e.g. floods, droughts, hurricanes) can be estimated in terms of economic 'externalities', Martinez-Alier (2002: 213–233) has calculated that the entire external debt of Latin America in 1999 (US$ 700 billion) would be cancelled by a mere twelve years of the United States' 'carbon debt' (US$ 60 billion per year). Taking this 'ecological debt' seriously would thus mean acknowledging that Latin America's foreign debt is a mystification of actual debtor-creditor relations.

Towards an analytical framework for understanding environmental injustice

This brief sketch of the history of environmental load displacement from ancient Mesopotamia to current concerns about global warming can provide us with the outline of an analytical framework for understanding the uneven distribution of environmental problems as a world-systemic process. Rather than lump all instances of environmental deterioration into a general category of ecological consequences of civilization (cf. Chew 2001; Diamond 2005), it is important to distinguish between the different structural conditions that in separate historical periods generate varieties of environmental change. Unfortunately, it is still possible to write respectable and best-selling volumes on the history of environmental problems without any reference to social science (Diamond 2005; cf. Hornborg 2005). From a social science perspective, however, it is crucial to specify the social units of analysis experiencing environmental deterioration and whether this deterioration is primarily the result of endogenous or exogenous factors.

What Clark (1997: 8–10) calls the 'entropic costs' of industrial metropoles should be clarified as comprising two dimensions: (1) the appropriation of 'negative entropy' (accessible, high-quality energy and materials) from elsewhere, and (2) the displacement of entropy (energetic and material disorder) to some unspecified hinterland. In the present world order, the first could be exemplified by the struggle of industrial powers to control vital sources of fossil fuels (Klare 2001), the second by controversies over various kinds of 'ecological distribution conflicts' (Martinez-Alier 2002: 258–260), recently best illustrated by the 'disproportionate' use of sinks for carbon dioxide, and the uneven share of the burden of its climatic consequences (ibid.: 213–233). One of the benefits of this analytical framework is that it would help us to distinguish between different kinds of environmental problems in world-system history. In view of the twin problems of importing available energy ('negative entropy') and exporting entropy, different historical and contemporary cases of environmental crisis require different analytical tools. There are cases, such as the Classic Maya or Easter Island, where ecological overshoot is not so much a consequence of long-distance resource extraction as of locally generated over-exploitation of resources. There are clearly also a great number of cases, such as the hinterlands of Sumer, Roman North Africa, thirteenth-century England, British North America, or twentieth century Sahel, where environmental degradation was the result of the systematic appropriation of local resources by distant centres. A third type of environmental problems would be represented by nineteenth century London or twentieth-century Moscow, where the accumulation of distantly derived resources was not sufficiently balanced by an export of the entropy (pollution, waste) generated in the process. Finally, the recent North-to-South export of the most polluting industries, as well as waste itself, suggests a fourth version of ecological crisis, where world-system peripheries are converted into dumping grounds for entropy generated by affluent core areas. This phenomenon, epitomized in 1991 by the so-called Lawrence Summers Memo, is particularly conspicuous around North–South boundaries such as the border between Mexico and the United States (cf. Heyman 2007). These different varieties of environmental degradation clearly illustrate that problems of 'environmental justice' and 'environmental load displacement' can have two distinct aspects, since peripheral areas can be exploited both as sources of 'negative entropy' and as sinks for entropy.

It seems that 'civilization' as we know it has generally been founded on processes of environmental load displacement and great disparities between affluent core areas and impoverished peripheries. The hinterlands of ancient Mesopotamia, the Indus Valley, Egypt, Greece, and Rome were all afflicted by deforestation, erosion, mining, and loss of biodiversity that ultimately contributed to the decline of the core areas. During recent centuries, emerging from the assets accumulated through European colonialism, the expansion of industrial capitalism has entailed more sophisticated and less obvious strategies of environmental load displacement, to the detriment of the global South. Current concerns with 'sustainable development' and 'environmental security' need to more explicitly address the political issues of how environmental problems are distributed in global society. To frame the discussion in terms of whether 'we' shall 'fail' or 'succeed' in achieving sustainability (Diamond 2005: 3) is to mystify the underlying political contradictions and represent environmental security as an uncontroversial managerial challenge for an unspecified social unit of analysis. When civilizations 'succeed' – which they all do for a time – they generally tend to do so precisely by exporting their environmental problems, and jeopardizing 'sustainability' elsewhere. When civilizations 'fail' – which they all ultimately do – core and periphery alike tend to suffer through the subsequent turmoil, but former peripheries are the more likely to emerge as future cores.

Environmental history as political ecology

We have seen that there are different ways of writing the history of environmental problems. The dominant mode has been to assume a common human history, a global 'we' experiencing the arrow of time through cumulative changes such as population growth, technological development, and new patterns of resource use. Ecological degradation, seen from this perspective, is the collective concern of a generalized humanity prompted to exploit new territories, harness new energy sources, and develop new transport technologies. Environmental problems, although alarming, are presented as the inevitable side-effects of 'our' global success story.

The purpose of this chapter is to explore another way of writing environmental history. Rather than focus on the abstract accretion of landscape changes or technological inventions as a collective human experience over time, it seeks to highlight how such changes are distributed in space. It acknowledges that humanity is not a single 'we' but deeply divided in terms of reaping the benefits versus carrying the burdens of development. This *distributed* aspect of environmental problems can be illuminated by approaching ecological changes from a world-system perspective, viewing the world as a social system much more inclusive than individual countries (Wallerstein 1974–1989). If the world-system for a long time has built on unequal power relations between rich 'core' areas and impoverished 'peripheries', this inequality can also be expected to show in how environmental burdens have been distributed.

Over the past few decades, the concept of 'political ecology' has become a useful shorthand for the growing recognition, in several disciplines, of the extent to which environmental changes and societal processes are intertwined. The many proponents of this approach, for instance in anthropology (Paulson and Gezon 2005), geography (Bryant and Bailey 1997), and the philosophy of environmental justice (Low and Gleeson 1998), focus on what Martinez-Alier (2002: 70) calls 'ecological distribution conflicts' in modern, often Third World settings. In integrating cultural, political, economic, and ecological perspectives on conflicts of interest between different social groups, political ecology requires trans-disciplinary analyses that are able to handle the great variety of factors that enter into any such socio-environmental conflict. Generally driven by an almost activist concern with the predicament of marginalized, local people in today's world, it has made great progress in understanding the political economy of contemporary environmental change. Although it is reasonable to assume that processes of environmental change were no less politicized in the past, studies of environmental history are much less frequently couched in such a political framework. The reasons for this are not hard to imagine. For one thing, environmental injustices seem less worthy of attention, and more difficult to document, when the victims are long gone. Nevertheless, there are many good reasons to apply the insights of political ecology to environmental history. Foremost, I would argue, is the importance of writing a politically valid environmental history of human civilizations, from the earliest agrarian empires to the present, industrial world order. The political ecology of human civilizations would no doubt present a completely different picture of 'our' global success story than mainstream historiography. In acknowledging the power inequalities and distribution conflicts framing the development of industrial civilization, it would ultimately provide a more realistic view of future prospects for 'sustainable' development at the global level.

It is important here to emphasize that what I am suggesting is not merely an environmental history that acknowledges ecological degradation as the flip side of economic progress. This would be very far from a new idea. Martinez-Alier (1987) has traced the modern history of 'ecological economics', emphasizing how human economies are ultimately constrained by ecological conditions, to the mid-nineteenth century, and some of its roots to the eighteenth-century Physiocrats. As Hughes (1994) has shown, such connections were obvious even in ancient Rome. Awareness of environmental limitations has no doubt always been part of human experience, whether hunter-gatherers' concern over game stocks or horticulturalists' concern over soil fertility. Much recent work in environmental history in fact remains analytically confined to such Malthusian worries about a fundamental contradiction between human society and the natural environment. Irrespective of their discipline of origin – e.g. whether geography, archaeology, or history – most authors of classical works on global environmental history, even when addressing European imperialism, thus tend to couch their concerns in the generalized 'we' mode mentioned above (e.g. Thomas 1956; Turner et al. 1990; Simmons 1993; Redman 1999; Diamond 2005). Rather than subject the internal structures of societal systems to critical scrutiny, such studies seem to assume a simple dualism of society versus nature and to account for environmental problems in terms of the inexorable progression of technology or demography.

Rarer are historical studies that explicitly investigate contradictions *within* global human society *over* the natural environment. These studies are generally concerned with European strategies of environmental load displacement during the sixteenth to nineteenth centuries and sometimes make explicit use of the world-system terminology (Wilkinson 1973; Wolf 1982; Mintz 1985; Worster 1988; Ponting 1991; Pomeranz 2000; Richards 2003). They demonstrate a more profound understanding of the societal dynamics responsible for unevenly distributed environmental degradation and often present direct continuities with studies of twentieth-century political ecology (cf. Bunker 1985; Goldfrank et al. 1999; Bunker and Ciccantell 2005). Yet, I am convinced that our understanding of how societal and ecological systems are intertwined can progress even further than this, not only by politicizing the environment, but also by ecologizing the world-system.

Unequal ecological exchange

A fundamental theoretical question, for any attempt to merge ecology and world-system analysis, is whether the global distribution of environmental deterioration is somehow structurally determined. If the answer is yes, does this structural determination hinge on the physical properties of the traded commodities? Are economic sectors specialized in the extraction of natural resources systematically disadvantaged – economically and/or ecologically – vis-à-vis sectors specialized in the production of industrial goods? Let us review some theoretical and methodological approaches to this issue. These contributions generally propose to deal only with 'modern' (capitalist) economic systems, but in the final section we shall consider the extent to which their analytical frameworks are applicable also to pre-modern societies.

Martinez-Alier (1987) traces the early dialogue between Marxism and natural sciences such as physics and agricultural chemistry on the material dimensions of economic productivity, illustrating the difficulties that continue to plague communication between the social and natural sciences on economic matters. Although Marx was keenly interested in the metabolic flows between urban and rural areas, he did not think of these flows as inherently exploitative or as a constraint on progress, as did Malthus, but was optimistic about new technological remedies such as chemical fertilizers. If Marx and Engels had paid more attention to Serhii Podolinsky's argument for an integration of thermodynamics and their notions of surplus exploitation, early Marxist theory might have incorporated the kind of socio-metabolic perspectives that today provide a foundation for discussions on unequal ecological exchange.

Bunker (1985) pioneered the integration of ecology and world-system analysis. He posited a structural asymmetry between extractive economies in the periphery and 'productive' economies in the core, which has been exacerbated with the increasing spatial separation of extraction and production. The structural polarizations of production versus extraction and of core versus periphery are in fact one and the same. One of his key points is that the dynamics of scale have inverse consequences for productive versus extractive sectors, yielding falling unit costs of production in the former but rising costs in the latter. Furthermore, as resources are depleted or technologies and market demand transformed, extractive economies are unable to sustain the continuous, cumulative development of labour and infrastructure that, by and large, have characterized productive core areas over the past two centuries. To account for such uneven development under capitalism, Bunker chooses to complement the Marxian labour theory of value with a notion of 'natural values', which, like labour, are systematically underpaid and realized by the industrial core areas to which they are transferred.

As mentioned above, I have elsewhere (Hornborg 2006) presented a similar understanding of the asymmetric relation between centres of industrial development and their extractive peripheries. The argument is based on previous theoretical work on the thermodynamic conditions of an industrial world order (Hornborg 2001), but focusses on the appropriation of land and labour 'embodied' in the raw materials imported to Britain in the mid-nineteenth century. Using historical statistics on the inputs of land and labour in cotton and wool production, I estimate the amount of British land and labour that were saved by displacing fibre production to North America. By comparing inputs of land and labour in the textile exports of England with those in some commodities imported from its periphery, and juxtaposing these data with exchange rates, I also estimate the unequal exchange of (natural) space and (human) time underlying the Industrial Revolution. Using such methods, it is possible to bring together the Marxist concern with unequal exchanges of labour time, on one hand, with the more recent concern with ecological footprints (i.e. the land requirements of a given level of resource consumption), on the other. Rather than using the contested notion of underpaid 'values', however, I am content to show that the earliest stages of industrial capitalism relied on an objectively measurable, unequal exchange of embodied land and labour. Another way of saying this is that technologies for locally saving time and space often tend to draw on investments of time and space (labour and land) in other parts of the world-system.

The economists Roldan Muradian and Stefan Giljum (2007) apply the concepts and methods of material flow analysis to investigate how environmental burdens are distributed between countries. Their first finding is that so-called 'polluting sectors' have generally increased their physical volume of export production in absolute terms over the past few decades, irrespective of world region. Second, they find that, in the period between 1978 and 1996, the proportion of total exports that derive from polluting sectors, measured in monetary value, has increased in South America and Africa while decreasing in Europe, the United States, and Japan. Third, they note that the European Union has remained a net-importer of products from polluting sectors during the whole period analysed.

These findings are highly relevant for assessing the economists' notion of 'dematerialization' – i.e. the proposition that economies will become less of a burden on the environment the more developed they are – and the sobering counter-proposition known as the 'pollution haven' hypothesis – i.e. that polluting industries tend to migrate toward poorer countries with weaker environmental standards. Much as the economist Lawrence Summers infamously suggested in 1991, there is an impeccable economic logic in advocating a migration of 'dirty' (i.e. polluting) industries to less developed countries. Although the appearance of a cleaner, seemingly dematerialized economy in affluent countries may suggest that economic growth is good for the environment, such a view may be the product of an illusion. An alternative interpretation is that economic growth makes it possible to shift a country's environmental burden to other, less affluent countries. Moreover, we have reasons to be sceptical of indices of sustainability that measure environmental burdens *relative to* GNP, suggesting that it does not matter if environmental loads increase in absolute terms, as long as GNP increases faster. The illusion of dematerialization thus simultaneously highlights the two main obstacles to understanding socio-environmental metabolism using the kinds of data conventionally available to economists: the fact that statistics on trade generally use the *state* as unit of analysis, and the fact that these statistics generally use *monetary value* as the only significant metric.

The significance of the nation-state in organizing socio-environmental metabolism is undisputable, but in different ways than economists and historians have generally recognized. In the age of globalization, it should no longer be possible to imagine that a country's geographical extent, its economic activities, and its environmental impacts coincide. Yet, to correlate national statistics on GNP and environmental quality in order to draw conclusions on the relation between economic growth and environmental performance is precisely to make such an unreasonable assumption. From a world-system perspective, on the contrary, it is only to be expected that one country's environmental problems may be the flip side of another country's affluence. Such connections are evident even where there are no indications of coercion or imperial ambitions. What, then, is the role of state boundaries in organizing the distribution of environmental resources and risks? They are obviously instruments of political agency, even when there are no attempts to expand them, simply by defining arenas within which power can be asserted in direct and uncontroversial ways. They may also define fields of responsibility and a minimum of social solidarity, prompting governments – to the extent that they are able and willing – to redistribute resources so as to cushion marginalized groups within their jurisdiction against the worst ravages of the polarizing tendencies of accumulative processes. Rural populations engaged in extractive activities within affluent countries can thus be financially subsidized by successful industrial sectors of the same countries, making it possible for them to enjoy high standards of living, healthy environments, and security, whereas their counterparts in poorer countries may be left virtually unprotected. The nation-state is thus the basic social unit capable of politically intervening in the socio-environmental, metabolic processes generated by the logic of capital accumulation. Not only can it decide to alleviate the impoverishment of its internal, national periphery; ever since the days of mercantilism, states have explicitly struggled to promote – as national interests – activities that serve to make their external positions within world-systems as advantageous as possible. For centuries, the more powerful nation-states have used trade policies backed up by military force to secure vital flows of resources from the outside. Not so long ago, in fact, nation-states regularly struggled to expand their boundaries to achieve such goals. As trade has replaced conquest and tribute, national boundaries have begun to appear more stable over time, but the use of military force to secure resource flows is far from obsolete. Increasingly, states have also made it a national interest to export environmental risks.

As anthropologist Joe Heyman (2007) shows, this gate-keeping function of nation-states, struggling to import resources and export risks, is most obvious on their borders. Focussing on the border between the United States and Mexico, he explores the many subtle ways in which this boundary zone serves to maintain the *difference* between citizens belonging to the two adjacent polities. This serves to remind us that the formation of nation-states involves a partly arbitrary construction of territorialized identity, but also that territorializations of socio-metabolic relationships have very tangible consequences for people who happen to be living on either side of the border. The polarizing structures of world-systemic processes of capital accumulation are not necessarily organized in spatial terms to begin with, but the medium of nation-states has historically projected such structures onto geographical territories. It remains to be seen how far the current surge of globalization can go in challenging our attachment to the nation-state as a source of identity and a category for understanding the structure of world society. Heyman's contribution illustrates the very real, material processes that continue to undergird the existence of nation-states precisely by asserting their boundaries. The environmental dimension of this particular boundary is epitomized by the *maquiladoras*, a highly polluting industry concentrated along the Mexican side of the border, where wages can be kept low and environmental considerations ignored, but the profits from which often wind up among owners and executives residing north of the border. It is difficult to think of a more straightforward verification of the 'pollution haven' hypothesis.

Anthropologist Bill Fisher (2007) takes us further south into modern Latin America, to the vast fields of soybeans industrially cultivated on the former savannas of Mato Grosso, Brazil. What locally is experienced as modernization and economic progress appears, in the light of social and environmental concerns as well as world-system analysis, as a highly dubious development. The transformation of the partly forested savanna landscape into treeless soybean monocultures has drastically reduced the unique biodiversity of the *cerrado* and turned impoverished and eroding soils into a medium for the conversion of imported fertilizers, pesticides, and other industrial inputs into exported crops. As much of the soybean exports are destined for livestock fodder in industrialized countries such as the Netherlands or Japan, these vast expanses of extractive surfaces clearly represent the ecological footprints – the displaced environmental loads – of distant and more affluent economies.

Even locally, soybean cultivation has increased economic inequalities. Great numbers of small farmers have been forced to give up their land, only a minority have found low-wage jobs on the soybean plantations, and decreasing food security has brought an increase in rural hunger.

Is the exploitation of the periphery a myth?

The metabolic rift between economic cores and their extractive peripheries can be identified from ancient Rome to nineteenth century England, and the tendency to displace environmental burdens ever further off from core areas is pervasive, irrespective of whether it implies extending or transgressing political boundaries. The ecological impacts of long-distance trade in the ancient world can be exemplified by the Roman appropriation of timber, grain, and metals from vast areas of Europe, Africa, and Asia. From the sixteenth century and on, such impacts are all the more obvious, e.g. in the extraction of timber and grain from eastern Europe, silver from the Andes, ivory from East Africa, and sugar from the Caribbean (see various case studies in Hornborg et al. 2007). The uncalculated, indirect environmental impacts (i.e. 'ecological rucksacks') of the extraction of e.g. silver, ivory, or sugar are important aspects of the 'ecological trade balances' of colonial Spain and Britain. The modern displacement of the most polluting industries from the European Union to Latin America thus has antecedents in sixteenth century silver mining. Loss of biodiversity in the periphery is a theme that can be traced from Roman North Africa to the savannas of modern Brazil (cf. Ponting 1991: 161–193; Richards 2003: 463–616). Another pivotal factor in human-environmental relations throughout the millennia is the accumulation, maintenance, and eventual abandonment of landesque capital, designed to produce e.g. grain, wine, olive oil, rice, silk, beef, sugar, cotton, or soybeans as commodities for impersonal, monetized markets. Equally ubiquitous is the lack of environmental foresight that characterizes most market-oriented extractive activities, whether conducted by Roman slaves or nineteenth century loggers.

It is obvious that many of the imports to core areas, from ancient Rome to nineteenth century Europe, were of negligible direct significance for the social metabolism of these areas. If we were to restrict our perspective to this observation, we might well agree with economic historian Paul Bairoch's (1993: 97) remarkable conclusion that 'the West did not need the Third World.' But in looking at early twentieth-century statistics to draw the conclusion that the dependence of the West on raw materials from the Third World prior to 1955 is a 'complete myth' (ibid.: 70),

Bairoch seriously distorts our view of the dynamics of economic development and industrialization. Let us look closer at Bairoch's position as a foil against which to consolidate the argument in this chapter.

First, as Bairoch (ibid.: 88–97) himself concedes, the consequences of incorporation as a world-system periphery can be destructive enough, even if the socio-metabolic significance of the exports for importing core countries seem insignificant. To use a modern expression, the 'ecological rucksacks' of such exports (e.g. spices, jewels, silver, gold, silk, ivory, feathers, sugar, tobacco, coffee, tea) were generally formidable, and this is but one of the ways in which the periphery was – and continues to be – forced to pay a high price for the economic development of the core.

Second, Bairoch's conclusion that the role of colonialism was unimportant in the birth of the British Industrial Revolution (ibid.: 80) underestimates the recursive relation between mercantile and financial profits, on one hand, and investments in mechanization, on the other (cf. Wolf 1982: 267–295.) His mechanistic, linear notion that 'during the eighteenth and nineteenth centuries colonization was primarily a result of industrial development and not vice versa' (Bairoch 1993: 82) fails to appreciate the complex ways in which these two phenomena were mutually reinforcing aspects of the same process.

Third, Bairoch's use of the category 'the West' as a static economic and/or political entity extending indefinitely backwards in time beyond 1955 is extremely misleading. Economic core-periphery relations are dynamic and multi-scaled and frequently shift over the course of history, not to mention the variously constructed political boundaries asserted by different governments so as to maximize advantages and minimize risks in particular historical contexts. The imperial projects of Rome, Spain, and Britain are obvious examples. A socio-metabolic perspective on the accumulation of industrial infrastructure must avoid being strait-jacketed into the fetishized nation-state categories that organize economic statistics. We do not need to go very far back in time to find large parts of Europe peripheral to the industrial and commercial developments in Britain and the Netherlands. Nor should we forget how recently North America was a source of cheap (largely slave) labour and land serving as a vast extractive zone particularly for Britain. If Bairoch (ibid.: 59–71) finds that, just prior to the First World War, the 'developed West' was basically self-sufficient in minerals and other raw materials, it certainly does not mean that the accumulation of industrial infrastructure within its present-day political boundaries has not historically been characterized by ecologically unequal relations of exchange between core regions and *what were then* their peripheries.

The fundamental structural relationship, if we are to understand the social metabolism underlying economic development, is the exchange between geographical spaces experiencing an accumulation of physical capital (cores), on one hand, and extractive areas suffering net exports of natural resources (peripheries), on the other. Political boundaries and national statistics frequently – if not systematically – distort and mystify this relationship. At certain times and places an industrial core region in a given country will find its domestic, national periphery more or less sufficient for its metabolic requirements, at other times not. Although national statistics would make them seem comparable entities, Canada and Singapore obviously have very different capacities in this respect. Although the basic structural imbalance, which Marx identified as the 'metabolic rift' between town and countryside, is as old and pervasive as urbanization itself (cf. McNeill 2000: 281–295), the past few centuries of globalization have seen an increasing ambition – and capacity – of nation-states to displace such imbalances beyond their own borders to the international arena.

Finally, our review of the historical evidence from the past two millennia clearly shows that developments in core areas, thus defined, have in fact systematically relied on imports of bulk commodities, the significance of which, although less voluminous per capita than today, was very far from negligible for their metabolism: foodstuffs, timber, metals, fuels, and fibres are only the most obvious examples. Even if the mid-twentieth century to Bairoch suggests a discontinuity in the sense that extraction of such resources for the 'developed West' (Europe and North America) was increasingly externalized beyond its modern political boundaries, there are clear historical continuities in the fundamental structures of unequal ecological exchange. Not only was the 'developed West' a rather recently constituted geographical and political category at that time, but, over the centuries, structures of unequal ecological exchange have frequently unfolded with little regard to political boundaries. As long as it is confined to statistics on the flows of exchange values crossing national borders, the discourse on development and underdevelopment will thus be severely constrained.

Notes

1. Much of the material in the following discussion derives from the work of contributors to two huge conference volumes currently in press, both deriving from the landmark Lund conference *World System History and Global Environmental Change*, largely funded by the Bank of Sweden Tercentenary Foundation through its task force on Culture, Security, and Sustainable

Development (Hornborg et al. 2007; Hornborg and Crumley 2006). Needless to say, I am very much indebted to the Tercentenary Foundation for this support.
2. Not all of these environmental changes can be unambiguously classified as 'problems' or 'degradation', however. For instance, deforestation has largely been a prerequisite for agriculture. I thank Mats Widgren for reminding me to point this out.

References

Bairoch, P. (1993) *Economics and World History: Myths and Paradoxes*, Chicago: The University of Chicago Press.

Boserup, E. (1988) 'Environment, Population, and Technology in Primitive Societies', in Worster, D. (ed) (1988) *The Ends of the Earth: Perspectives on Modern Environmental History*, Cambridge: Cambridge University Press: 23–38.

Bryant, R.L. and Bailey, S. (1997) *Third World Political Ecology*, London: Routledge.

Bunker, S.G. (1985) *Underdeveloping the Amazon: Extraction, Unequal Exchange, and the Failure of the Modern State*, Chicago: The University of Chicago Press.

Bunker, S.G. and Ciccantell, P.S. (2005) *Globalization and the Race for Resources*, Baltimore: The Johns Hopkins University Press.

Chew, S.C. (2001) *World Ecological Degradation: Accumulation, Urbanization, and Deforestation 3000 BC–AD 2000*, Lanham: AltaMira Press.

Clark, R.P. (1997) *The Global Imperative: An Interpretive History of the Spread of Humankind*, Oxford: Westview Press.

Cronon, W. (1991) *Nature's Metropolis: Chicago and the Great West*, New York: W.W. Norton & Co.

Debeir, J-C., Deléage, J.-P. and Hémery, D. (1991) [1986] *In the Servitude of Power: Energy and Civilization through the Ages*, London: Zed Books.

Diamond, J. (2005) *Collapse: How Societies Choose to Fail or Succeed*, New York: Viking.

Fisher, W.H. (2007) 'Surrogate Money, Technology, and the Expansion of Savanna Soybeans in Brazil', in Hornborg, A., McNeill, J. Martinez-Alier, J. (eds) (2007) *Rethinking Environmental History: World-System History and Global Environmental Change*, Lanham: AltaMira Press.

Gills, B.K. and Thompson, W.R. (eds) (2006) *Globalization and Global History*, London: Routledge.

Godelier, M. (1969) 'La monnaie de sel des Baruya de Nouvelle-Guinée', *L'Homme*, 9(2): 5–37.

Goldfrank, W.L., Goodman, D. and Szasz, A. (eds) (1999) *Ecology and the World-System*, Westport: Greenwood Press.

Harvey, D. (1996) *Justice, Nature, and the Geography of Difference*, Oxford: Blackwell.

Heyman, J. (2007) 'Environmental Issues at the US-Mexico Border and the Unequal Territorialization of Value', in Hornborg, A., McNeill, J. Martinez-Alier, J. (eds) (2007) *Rethinking Environmental History: World-System History and Global Environmental Change*, Lanham: AltaMira Press.

Hornborg, A. (2001) *The Power of the Machine: Global Inequalities of Economy, Technology, and Environment*, Lanham: AltaMira Press.

Hornborg, A. (2005) 'Review of Jared Diamond "Collapse: How Societies Choose to Fail or Succeed"', *Current Anthropology,* 46(S): 94–95.

Hornborg, A. (2006) 'Footprints in the Cotton Fields: The Industrial Revolution as Time-Space Appropriation and Environmental Load Displacement', *Ecological Economics,* 59(1): 74–81.

Hornborg, A. and Crumley, C. (eds) (2006) *The World System and the Earth System: Global Socio-Environmental Change and Sustainability Since the Neolithic,* Santa Barbara: Left Coast Press.

Hornborg, A., McNeill, J. and Martinez-Alier, J. (eds) (2007) *Rethinking Environmental History: World-System History and Global Environmental Change,* Lanham: AltaMira Press.

Hughes, J.D. (1994) *Pan's Travail: Environmental Problems of the Ancient Greeks and Romans,* Baltimore: The Johns Hopkins University Press.

Hughes, J.D. (2001) *An Environmental History of the World: Humankind's Changing Role in the Community of Life,* London: Routledge.

Klare, M.T. (2001) *Resource Wars: The New Landscape of Global Conflict,* New York: Owl Books.

Low, N. and Gleeson, B. (1998) *Justice, Society, and Nature: An Exploration of Political Ecology,* London: Routledge.

Martinez-Alier, J. (1987) *Ecological Economics: Energy, Environment, and Society,* Cambridge: Blackwell.

Martinez-Alier, J. (2002) *The Environmentalism of the Poor: A Study of Ecological Conflicts and Valuation,* Cheltenham: Edward Elgar.

McNeill, J.R. (2000) *Something New Under the Sun: An Environmental History of the Twentieth-Century World,* New York: W.W. Norton & Co.

Mintz, S. (1985) *Sweetness and Power: The Place of Sugar in Modern History,* New York: Penguin Books.

Muradian, R. and Giljum, S. (2007) 'Physical Trade Flows of Pollution-Intensive Products: Historical Trends in Europe and the World', in Hornborg, A., McNeill, J. and Martinez-Alier, J. (eds) (2007) *Rethinking Environmental History: World-System History and Global Environmental Change,* Lanham: AltaMira Press.

Paulson, S. and Gezon, L.L. (eds) (2005) *Political Ecology across Spaces, Scales, and Social Groups,* New Brunswick, New Jersey, and London: Rutgers University Press.

Pomeranz, K. (2000) *The Great Divergence: China, Europe, and the Making of the Modern World Economy,* Princeton: Princeton University Press.

Ponting, C. (1991) *A Green History of the World: The Environment and the Collapse of Great Civilizations,* London: Penguin Books.

Redman, C.L. (1999) *Human Impact on Ancient Environments,* Tucson: The University of Arizona Press.

Richards, J.F. (2003) *The Unending Frontier: An Environmental History of the Early Modern World,* Berkeley: University of California Press.

Simmons, I.G. (1993) *Environmental History: A Concise Introduction,* Oxford: Blackwell.

Thomas, W.L. Jr. (ed) (1956) *Man's Role in Changing the Face of the Earth,* Chicago: The University of Chicago Press.

Turner, B.L. II, Clark, W.C., Kates, R.W., Richards, J.F., Mathews, J.T. and Meyer, W.B. (eds) (1990) *The Earth as Transformed by Human Action: Global and Regional Changes in the Biosphere over the Past 300 Years,* Cambridge: Cambridge University Press.

Wallerstein, I. (1974–1989) *The Modern World-System I-III*, New York: Academic Press.

Widgren, M. (2007) 'Pre-Colonial Landesque Capital: A Global Perspective', in Hornborg, A., McNeill, J. and Martinez-Alier, J. (eds) (2007) *Rethinking Environmental History: World-System History and Global Environmental Change*, Lanham: AltaMira Press.

Wilkinson, R.G. (1973) *Poverty and Progress: An Ecological Model of Economic Development*, London: Methuen.

Williams, M. (2003) *Deforesting the Earth: From Prehistory to Global Crisis*, Chicago: The University of Chicago Press.

Wolf, E.R. (1982) *Europe and the People Without History*, Berkeley: University of California Press.

Worster, D. (ed) (1988) *The Ends of the Earth: Perspectives on Modern Environmental History*, Cambridge: Cambridge University Press.

6
Child Malnutrition. From the Global Protein Crisis to a Violation of Human Rights

Urban Jonsson

Introduction

During the last five decades, development theory has gradually changed from a pre-dominantly positivistic approach towards an increased acceptance of normative thinking. This has been the result of the increasing awareness and acceptance that in the construction of 'reality', not only scientific facts, but also values determine its meaning. Human decisions are results of both science and ethics.

The problem of young child malnutrition in developing countries provides an excellent example of how the changes in theory have resulted in dramatic changes in approaches to solve the problem. The problem has been redefined several times, with each new approach or paradigm reflecting broader and increasingly more normative content.

In this chapter different conceptualizations of the nutrition problem will be described and the changes will be related to changes in the relative influence of science and ethics, and in the relationship between theory and practice.

Since the end of the Cold War, and particularly after the launch of the United Nations Reform in 1997, the interest in human rights in general, and in the adoption of a 'human rights-based approach to development' in particular, has dramatically increased among scholars and activists from the areas of development and human rights.

It will be argued that a human rights-based approach to development will be the next step in the process of moving development theory and practice forward. Such an approach combines the need for achieving desirable development outcomes, e.g. the Millennium Development

Goals (MDGs), *and* the establishment of a normatively determined development process for this achievement.

The chapter will conclude by showing the advantages of adopting a human rights-based approach to the problem of malnutrition instead of the economic 'investment in nutrition' approach.

Protein-energy malnutrition

The analysis in this chapter will be limited to protein-energy malnutrition (PEM)[1] because it has the most severe short and long-term consequences, has proven to be very difficult to prevent and has been re-conceptualized several times during the last 50 years. It affects 15–30 per cent of young children in most developing countries, with dramatic short-term and long-term consequences, often irreversible.[2]

Protein-energy malnutrition manifests itself in compromised physical growth. For many years a debate took place among nutrition experts about whether all children would have the same physical growth pattern if they were kept healthy and well-nourished. The 'small-but-healthy' hypothesis was vigorously defended by some Asian experts, arguing that being small was not a problem, but an advantage in reducing the food needs of a country. Scientists, however, soon found that the real problem was not being small, but *becoming* small – the failure to grow as a child (Beaton 1989; 1990). After some work by scientists associated with the World Health Organization (WHO), the 'small-but-healthy' hypothesis was totally rejected (UN ACC/SCN 1989).

Protein-energy malnutrition has important short-term and long-term consequences. The synergistic relationship between infection and malnutrition had been known since the late 1960s (Scrimshaw et al. 1968). Malnutrition makes children more prone to infection, and infection, particularly diarrhoea, contributes to increased malnutrition. In a detailed analysis of all relevant nutrition surveys, Pelletier (1994) concludes that 25–50 per cent of child deaths are attributable to malnutrition.

Malnutrition at young age also has serious negative impact later in life. Children who are well-nourished have a better attendance rate in school (Scrimshaw and Gordon 1967; Alderman et al. 2001) a higher IQ (Grantham-McGregor et al. 1999; Pollitt et al. 1993) and when they grow up, they become adults with a higher productivity (Haddad and Bouis 1991). A unique longitudinal study on the linkages among early childhood nutrition, human capital formation, and economic output has been done in Guatemala between 1969 and 2004. This study shows that the child of below three years of age is irreversibly affected by malnutrition. Today, there is a general agreement that poor human development is both a consequence and a cause of poverty (World Bank 2000). These facts are the basis for claiming that 'poverty reduction begins with children' (UNICEF 2000; Feeny and Boyden 2003).

The problem of child malnutrition and its severe consequences have been known for a long time, although increasingly better understood as a result of scientific discovery. The perceived causes, however, have been debated intensively during the last 50 years. It is a fact that if there is no common understanding of the causes of a problem, there will most likely not be any consensus on how to solve the problem. Approaches to the 'nutrition problem' have changed several times in the last 50 years, reflecting well Hettne's idea of the parallel existence of a dominant 'mainstream approach' and a single or several 'counterpoint approaches' (volume 1). 'Mainstream approaches' have dominated specific periods since 1950, each of them being replaced by a 'counterpoint approach' that became the 'mainstream approach' in the next period. Results from scientific discovery, changing ethical and political positions explain to a large extent these changes. Before this is described and analysed, a brief discussion of the interaction between science and ethics, both in theory and practice, will be made.

Science and ethics – theory and practice[3]

Almost any issue, problem or phenomenon in society has both scientific and ethical aspects, and science as well as ethics is advanced through the interaction between theory and practice. Theory and practice are dialectically related, one lacking full meaning without the other. Unreflected practice is both dangerous and common, as pointed out by Hechter (1987: 2): 'Without explicit theories, there is no way to decide on the relative importance of facts.'

In science, theories explain causality, and consequences can often be predicted. Theories of ethics, in contrast, are normally derived from moral axioms that cannot be proven right or wrong. There are many competing ethical theories. Karl-Eric Knutsson (1997) repeatedly warned against any type of reductionism, emphasizing that the meaning of what we observe is influenced by both scientific facts and values (ethics) and that theory and practice must be understood together.

In efforts to capture the whole 'reality', problems in society have increasingly been described as multidisciplinary, interdisciplinary, holistic, and complex. Too often these concepts are used interchangeably, which leads to confusion.

Interdisciplinary research, or cooperation, emerged in the early 1970s (Törnebom 1974) and it was soon realized that it requires strong disciplinary research, but also an openness to incorporate ideas form other disciplines. The 'cross-fertilization' of theories contributed to many advantages, for example, in human ecology and in the study of hunger and malnutrition.

In many areas, for example child development, there has been a demand for *holistic* approaches ('the whole child'), implying that efforts are made to understand all important aspects of a societal problem in their totality. This is based on a recognition that the meaning of one aspect depends on the meaning of the others (Von Bertlanffy 1969) and that the meaning of each part depends on the 'whole'.

More recently, reference is made to *'complex'* problems, and complexity theory has become an established scientific discipline (Kauffmann 1993; Peak and Frame 1994; Prigogine and Stengers 1985; Luhmann 1995). One of the most important characteristics of 'complex' systems is that they are normally not 'complicated' (like a computer which is always totally predictable). 'Complex' systems, like the weather, are *in principle not predictable*, and most often non-linear and therefore very dynamic. Human communities and societies are 'open complex systems' (Jonsson 1997).

The gap between theory and practice manifests itself most dramatically in a gap between rhetoric and action. The process from theory to practice is driven or constrained by science and ethics, as understood by those who have the power to decide. It is often said that good plans (i.e. good theories) are not implemented because of 'lack of political will'. That is a very polite way of describing what amounts to 'wrong political choices'. The rhetoric/action gap exists because those who decide make a wrong decision, or no decision, because of their misunderstanding of science or their particular ethical positions. The fact that current economic globalization contributes to increasing inequalities is not because globalization is non-ethical; it is because globalization has been used and exploited for the wrong reasons; it is a result of the particular ethical base of the dominating free-market paradigm (Jonsson 2006).

Changing theory and practice of malnutrition prevention

The period before 1950

Famines have sometimes killed a substantial portion of populations, and more permanent – though less well known – hunger situations have sometimes affected whole populations. Studies reveal, for example, that the majority of the population in Medieval Europe was severely under-nourished for generations (Newman 1990).

In every culture, hunger has been described in novels, poems, and songs, and throughout history people have had ideas about why hunger exists. Most descriptions prior to the nineteenth century, however, reflected a deterministic and fatalistic perspective. Christianity pro-moted an ethical position that poor and hungry people were lucky, because they would be the first to enter Heaven, or as Thomas of Aquinas stated, 'Naked follow Naked Christ'. Centuries later Mahatma Gandhi promoted a similar position when he redefined the lowest caste in India as Harijan, 'Children of God'.

The development of science in the eighteenth and nineteenth centur-ies resulted in increased specialization. New discoveries in chemistry, biochemistry, and biology provided knowledge and the base for a new scientific discipline – *nutrition* (Lusk 1909).

The fact that certain foods have a remedying effect on disease had been known since ancient times. In 1922 Funk proposed that the lack of specific, not yet identified, factors was probably the cause of berib-eri, scurvy, pellagra, and maybe rickets – 'and we will call these factors *vitamins*' (Funk 1922). By 1915 several vitamins had been isolated and the first real 'paradigm' for nutrition created. *Malnutrition in society is caused by lack of certain vitamins in the diet.* This was a scientific fact, and the solution was straightforward – provide vitamins to people who are lacking them. This approach was the 'mainstream' for several decades.

A 'counterpoint' position was promoted by those who saw the import-ance of amino-acids (building blocks of proteins) in human metabol-ism. It had become known that certain amino-acids are essential because they cannot be synthesized by humans and must therefore be provided through the diet (Cathcart 1940). Soon new studies would change the picture towards this counterpoint position.

The era of protein deficiency (1950–1970)

Already in 1932, Cecily Williams had reported about a disease found in very young children in the Gold Coast (Williams 1935), and at about the same time Trowell (1941; 1950) reported similar cases from Uganda. In the late 1940s, scientists agreed that the two syndromes were the same, called it 'Kwashiorkor' (literally meaning 'the disease of the deposed baby when the next one is born') and found that skimmed milk could cure it.

The work on vitamins had convinced nutritionists that malnutrition was a result of something lacking in the diet, and research therefore focussed on what was missing in the food intake of children who developed Kwashiorkor.

During 1950, Brock from WHO and Autret from FAO (1952) made nutrition surveys in ten African countries, concluding

> Kwashiorkor presents a formidable problem, and it might be no exaggeration to say that in many parts of Central Africa the majority of children in the second and third year of life suffer from Kwashiorkor.

During the following period (1952–1955) an incredible amount of human nutrition research took place and results were published in the most prestigious scientific journals and presented at big conferences. It was agreed that Kwashiorkor was a result of protein deficiency at the cellular level, and in 1952 the Joint FAO/WHO Expert Committee on Nutrition decided to rename it 'protein malnutrition'. It was also concluded that protein malnutrition was a worldwide problem, which was totally against one of the leading nutrition experts, Dr Brock, who claimed that Kwashiorkor was an African or Bantu disease, that explained the backwardness of Black Africa; a wonderful example of how science may be distorted in order to validate a racist ideology.

By 1954 the protein deficiency paradigm had been well established and the period that followed (1955–1970) was characterized by 'puzzle-solving' as part of 'normal science', in which the protein deficiency paradigm was the totally dominating 'mainstream' approach.

A Protein Advisory Group (PAG) had been set up by the UN in 1955 to lead the 'war against the world protein crisis'. Unconventional sources of proteins were explored such as fish, soya, oilseeds, algae, leaves, and micro-organisms (FAO 1964a; Pirie 1969; Gray 1970; 1973). The excitement, or 'hysteria', culminated in 1967, when the United Nations issued the report 'International Action to Avert the Impending Protein Crisis' (ACAST 1968; see also FAO 1964b; 1970).

The dominance of the protein deficiency paradigm was almost total. Several scientists and practitioners who raised 'counterpoint' ideas were ruthlessly marginalized, by not being invited to important conferences, having their papers rejected by mainstream scientific journals or side-stepped in their expected research careers.

Since the early 1950s, however, a few scientists had criticized the protein deficiency paradigm of being too narrow and simple.[4] The criticism focussed on four issues. First, it was discovered that most diets in poor communities in developing countries were actually low in both protein and energy (calories), with the energy deficit being worse (Sukhatme 1970). At such low energy intakes, valuable proteins would be utilized as energy source, rather than as a source of essential amino-acids for protein synthesis (Miller and Payne 1961). Second, it is the 'protein quality' of the diet that counts, not that of individual food ingredients. If children have their energy needs met through their 'normal' diet, the protein content and the 'quality' were most often adequate to meet the protein needs (Platt et al. 1961). Third, an increasing number of scientists found that the estimates for daily protein requirements were far too high (Rivers et al. 1974; Beaton 1988). Fourth, nutrition scientists discovered that most malnourished children were also infected with diarrhoea and parasites, which significantly contributed to malnutrition.

In an article in *The Lancet* in June 1973, Harper, Payne, and Waterlow (1973) strongly criticized statements from within the protein deficiency paradigm:

> The most likely effect of such statements is simply to distract attention from the need for a broad-based attack on the social and economic deprivation of which ill-health and malnutrition are but symptoms.

In August 1974, McLaren (1974) initiated the 'final' debate with a letter to *The Lancet*, titled 'The Great Protein Fiasco'. Cecily Williams (1975), who had discovered Kwashiorkor 30 years earlier commented:

> I suggest it was not the clinicians with their modest observations and their non-existent research grants, but the scientists, who made the lamentable errors and wasted so much time, money, and personnel.

At the following year's World Food Conference there was not even one session on Kwashiorkor or the protein crisis, and in 1977 the Protein Advisory Group was abolished. Economic, social, and political causes of child malnutrition and world hunger were now emphasized.

In summary, scientific discoveries in human nutrition first created and then weakened the foundation of the protein deficiency paradigm. Practitioners and researchers in the social sciences criticized the protein deficiency paradigm for reducing child malnutrition from a social and political problem to a technical, particularly medical problem (Berg 1973).

It was increasingly argued that it is unethical to spend resources on producing protein-rich foods, when most malnourished children were denied their 'normal' diet as a result of poverty and exploitation.

Multisectoral nutrition planning and national nutrition policies (1973–1980)

As described earlier, long before the 'protein era' had collapsed, an increasing number of nutrition scholars, many with experience from developing countries, had realized that the problem of child malnutrition could not be solved by just providing proteins. Instead, a much broader approach was required, including social, economic, cultural, and political aspects (Berg et al. 1973). The science of nutrition was too narrow; a *Science of Nutrition Problems in Society* was required (Jonsson 1983). The new position formed the intellectual base for the explosive development and acceptance of 'multisectoral nutrition planning' (Joy and Payne 1975) as the new 'mainstream' approach. The theory was a very ambitious attempt to address the structural causes of malnutrition. As John Osgood Field (1987) summarized:

> The early proponents of multisectoral nutrition planning clearly defined protein-energy malnutrition as a structural problem embedded in poverty and underdevelopment: they recognized that multiple changes to socioeconomic conditions would be necessary to alleviate malnutrition [...] Multisectoral nutrition planning sought to go beyond technical fixes in favour of going to the heart of a country's development effort.

This paradigm shift coincided with, or was probably a result of, the change in development theory towards a stronger emphasis on political factors. Multisectoral nutrition planning also immediately adopted systems theory as the planning framework. The efforts to develop evidence-based multisectoral conceptual frameworks of causality resulted in unbelievably complicated maps of the nutrition problem (Pines and Anderson 1976; Cooke et al. 1973).

There were many who criticized the multisectoral nutrition planning paradigm (e.g. Field 1977) and its popularity fell dramatically before the end of the decade. No single clear 'counterpoint' emerged, however. The consensus was primarily on what was wrong with the approach. The major reasons for the failure to use it in practice were that (1) it required much more data than what any developing country could (or wanted) to provide, (2) the system analysis became far too complicated ('a holistic day dream') (McLaren 1978), and (3) the assumption that nutrition would become a political priority was false – most governments were not interested and the few that were, could not coordinate the different ministries. Many thought that the approach had become too technical, or as James Pines (1982) said, 'multisectoral nutrition planning, oversold and under-politicized from the start, stands discredited for failure to bring about nutrition improvement'.

At the end of the 1970s most nutrition scholars had left multisectoral nutrition planning, but there was no return to the 'old thinking'. The nutrition problem in developing countries continued to be seen as a 'problem in society', but now with a focus on national policies and monitoring.

Even if multisectoral nutrition planning had failed, some of its fundamental principles survived (Berg 1987). All agreed that child malnutrition was a result of social, economic, political, and cultural processes in society, and that efforts to solve the problem of malnutrition would have to address all levels of society, from national policy to the community and household levels. Even if multisectoral nutrition planning had failed to mobilize political leaders, the problem of malnutrition had been put on the political agenda.

From the mid-1970s to the mid-1990s many countries and agencies strongly promoted and supported the preparation on *national nutrition policies and strategies* (Hakim and Solimano 1976). The ideas, however, were again based on the false assumption that governments in developing countries would give priority attention to nutrition. Several governments prepared national nutrition policies and strategies in order to please donors and secure additional assistance.[5] Another weakness of most national nutrition policies was their strong food-bias, often referred to as 'food and nutrition policies'.

Experts from the era of multisectoral nutrition planning used systems theory to develop sophisticated data collection and monitoring systems of the nutrition situation; nutritional status and the key causes of malnutrition (Mason et al. 1984). Data from the surveillance system would be analysed and translated into information for national level decision-makers. Some of these systems worked well and continue to be useful in nutrition work (Pelletier and Shrimpton 1994). It is important to note, however, that an information system does not by itself improve nutrition; the information must be used for better decisions.

A strong 'counterpoint' position had existed since the downfall of the multisectoral nutrition planning era, claiming that emphasis should be given to *preventing* children from becoming malnourished, rather than rehabilitating already malnourished children. Also, preventive actions should be *community-based* since affected children all live in communities. Community-based nutrition programmes within a primary health care (PHC) approach took over the 'mainstream' position.

Primary health care and community-based nutrition (1974–1990)

After the World Food Conference in Rome 1974, the problem was no longer seen as a problem of protein but of food supply. FAO (1977) further showed that the problem was not total supply but unequal distribution, or lack of access to food by poor people. Poverty was singled out as the major cause of child malnutrition (Reutlinger and Selowsky 1976) and for some time the conclusion was that malnutrition is best prevented by reducing poverty. The 'counterpoint' position was based on new research showing that the link between poverty and *young* child malnutrition is not a simple cause-effect relationship (for a recent review, see Haddad et al. 2002). Therefore malnutrition should be addressed in all relevant sectoral policies and strategies, and interventions should be *coordinated* – though not integrated as during the time of multisectoral nutrition planning. This soon became the 'mainstream' at the macro-level (Berg and Austin 1984; Latham 1984).

In the late 1970s, the World Bank, UNICEF and many other development agencies adopted the new Basic Needs Approach. initially introduced by ILO. The need to be well-nourished was immediately recognized as a 'basic need', and a 'basic services concept' was proposed as the key nutrition strategy. The idea was to use a 'holistic' approach to promote and respond to *community* initiatives by providing training of community workers, appropriate technology, effective support and referral services.

The Primary Health Care (PHC) approach, launched in 1978, was based on similar ideas (WHO and UNICEF 1978).[6] It includes three major priorities, (1) it places health at the centre, and sees it as an outcome, of development, (2) it advocates low cost and practical knowledge, including the training of village health workers and low-cost services, and (3) it is based on community participation.

At an informal consultation in New York 1982 (UNICEF 1982), nutrition experts agreed that three major factors must be addressed, (1) proper infant and young child feeding, (2) control of major diseases, and (3) adequate access to food. Two strategies were suggested; primary health care and poverty reduction.

Unfortunately, however, instead of being holistic and participatory, as suggested by the PHC approach, most work in the area of health and nutrition became selective and 'top-down'. The best example of the adoption of selective PHC is the 'child survival and development revolution' campaign, launched by UNICEF in the early 1980s, focussing on four low-cost interventions: growth monitoring (G), oral re-hydration therapy (O), breastfeeding (B) and immunization (I) – GOBI.

The GOBI approach was criticized from outside and increasingly from inside UNICEF (Cash et al. 1987). During the 1980s nutrition experts and practitioners became increasingly aware of that unless people in communities are empowered to improve their own situation, the problem of malnutrition will not be solved in a sustained manner (Jennings et al. 1991).

Tanzania, along with Thailand, was among the first countries that in the 1980s developed and applied community-based nutrition intervention strategies with great success. Developed in Tanzania, the concept of community-based nutrition programmes (Yambi 1979; Maletnlema 1978; Jonsson 1980) was first used on a larger scale by WHO and UNICEF in the in Iringa region (1982–1988) (UN/ECOSOC 1982). It almost eliminated severe malnutrition and reduced moderate malnutrition by half in five years, and became a model in many African and Asian countries (Jonsson et al. 1993; Yambi and Mlolwa 1992; Pelletier 1991; The United Republic of Tanzania WHO and UNICEF 1988; Yambi et al. 1989; UNICEF 1993; UNICEF/ESARO 1986).

The two major innovations of the Iringa project were the further development and refinement of a *conceptual framework of causality* as a tool to understand 'what to do' in order to reduce the nutrition problem, and the *Triple A approach* for 'how to do it'.

As seen, most of the models of causality proposed during the period of multisectoral nutrition planning were far too complicated to be useful (Cooke et al. 1973; FAO 1974). The refined conceptual framework of causality, however, was adopted by UNICEF in 1990 (UNICEF 1990), and is now being used in various forms by most nutrition researchers, teachers and practitioners in the area of young child nutrition in developing countries.

'Triple A' is a mental construct of rational decision-making in society, seen as an iterative process of assessment of a problem; analysis of its causes; action to reduce or solve it; reassessment of the result of the action, reanalysis, new improved action, and so forth. At the heart is to strengthen the capacity of all players to engage in the process, and the approach implies a learning process, where the players' capability to cope is constantly improved. Information flows from assessment to analysis, action, and reanalysis (monitoring) fuel the process (Ljungqvist 1988; Jonsson et al. 1994; Jonsson 1985).

An emerging consensus (1990–1995)

1990 was an important year for the world's children. In September, the World Summit for Children (WSC), with 169 countries represented, agreed on a declaration including seven major goals and 20 supportive goals for women and children (United Nations 1990), eight of which aimed at reducing child malnutrition by the year 2000.[7] Also in September, the Convention on the Rights of the Child entered into force, codifying children's right to good nutrition. Both events explain the great interest in child nutrition during the following years.

Also in 1990, Dreze and Sen published their findings about hunger, arguing that hunger is most often not the result of inadequate aggregate food supply, but of a breakdown in people's entitlements, of people not having the resources to produce, barter or buy the food they require (Dreze and Sen 1990). There was an increasing consensus among many scholars and practitioners that hunger and malnutrition should be analysed and understood in the context of society (Latham et al. 1988).

At a milestone meeting in1990 (UN ACC/SCN 1991) guided by the UNICEF nutrition strategy, it was agreed that the nutritional status is determined by the level of household food security, infectious disease, and caring capacity. All three are necessary conditions for ensuring good nutrition, but neither is sufficient alone, and the degree to which they are not met determines the appropriate mix of interventions. This was fully endorsed at the International Conference on Nutrition (ICN) in 1992, as stated in the final report (FAO/WHO 1992):

> Although poverty is the root cause of malnutrition, nutritional status is affected by a wide range of factors which can be categorized into three main categories – food, health, and care.

This became the 'mainstream' approach during most of the 1990s and is still the dominant strategy for prevention of protein-energy malnutrition.

USAID had already in the early 1980s evaluated a number of community-based nutrition programmes, looking for 'success factors' (Drake et al. 1980). During the first half of the 1990s, the ACC/Sub-Committee on Nutrition achieved an unprecedented consensus on the causes of and strategies to prevent malnutrition. Further studies identified 'success factors' in nutrition policies, programmes, and projects (Jennings et al. 1991; Gillespie and Mason 1991; Gillespie et al. 1996; Jonsson 1995b) and a reasonable consensus was reached on 'lessons learnt' and 'best programming practices' (e.g. Mason, et al. 1995; Sanders 1999) – clearly reflected in and responded to by using a conceptual framework of causality and the triple A approach.

1. People should be recognized as key players in their own development, rather than passive beneficiaries of transfers of commodities and services.
2. Participation is crucial, as an end and a means. Rather than 'they' participating in 'our' programme or project, however, 'we' should behave so that 'we' are allowed and invited to participate in 'their' efforts.
3. 'Empowerment' is not a strategy in itself, but an important aspect, along with 'disempowerment', of any strategy, such as advocacy, capacity building or service-delivery.
4. Outcomes as well as the quality of the process behind them should be monitored, and the information used to improve decision-making and the design of the programme or project.
5. Stakeholder analysis can identify clear accountabilities, and is therefore very useful for social mobilization.
6. Programmes and projects should respond to basic needs, with a focus on vulnerable groups.
7. External development support should always build on and contribute to existing capacities. Local ownership of programmes and projects contributes to local funding and sustainability.
8. Poverty reduction should be the overarching goal in all development efforts, which often requires direct efforts to reduce existing disparities.
9. Pure top-down approaches deny the recognition of 'people as players', while pure bottom-up approaches are utopian. Therefore the synergism between the two should be promoted.
10. Repeated situation analyses should be made before and during implementation, as a local context and causes of malnutrition change. Priority problems thus identified, and their immediate, underlying, and basic causes, should be addressed, either simultaneously or in sequence.
11. Targets represent time-bound goals, and together with a valid baseline define the desirable trajectory, thus making monitoring and evaluation more possible and useful.

12. For nationwide results, 'pilot projects' must be scaled-up, which should be analysed, appraised, and decided upon *before* the start of the pilot.
13. Sustainability, including environmental sustainability, must be assessed *before* an intervention, since non-sustained/-sustainable nutrition programmes and projects are a waste of resources, apart from their possible short-term humanitarian impact.
14. Possible partnerships with strategic allies, including donors and NGOs/CBOs, should be explored, partly in order to attract additional resources through linkages to other development efforts.

A new focus on micronutrient malnutrition (1995–2005)

As seen, the key role of micronutrients (vitamins and minerals) was well known already 50–70 years ago. However, since the 'micronutrient strategy' was replaced as the 'mainstream' by the 'protein deficiency paradigm' in the early 1950s, it had played the role of a 'counterpoint'.

A conference in 1991, held to pursue the WSC-goals, was titled 'Ending Hidden Hunger' referring to the invisible frequent forms of mild and moderate micronutrient malnutrition. The conference managed to mobilize more resources from the international nutrition community to this rapidly growing field of nutrition, and by the mid-1990s, control of micronutrient malnutrition, particularly deficiencies in iodine, vitamin A, and iron, became the 'mainstream'.

Meanwhile, the interest in protein-energy malnutrition dramatically decreased and, apart from the new interest in micronutrients, the nutrition field in general got much less attention. When UNICEF in 1992 defined 'mid-decade goals' (Grant 1993; Shrimpton et al. 2002) reducing protein-energy malnutrition (PEM) was found to not qualify, which immediately resulted in reduced funding. Nutrition department or sections in agencies and developing country governments were also closed or merged with the health section; fewer and less competent staff was hired and scholarships for international nutrition training dried up.

In order to create an 'identity' for all those who worked in different sectors to improve nutrition, and to bring together the often uncoordinated policies, programmes, and projects, a small group of experts suggested to establish a new discipline. The first meeting on *Public Nutrition* (Mason et al. 1996) was held in 1997. From a public nutrition perspective, good nutrition is a 'public good', prevention of malnutrition is largely a state responsibility, solutions are normally very contextual, and local communities are key players. After a few years the discussion on 'public nutrition' died off, but by then it had contributed to preventing nutrition from being subsumed under 'health' and paved the way for an emerging 'counterpoint' strategy – *a human rights-based approach to nutrition* (see below).

Though it is difficult to understand the dramatic shift in focus from protein-energy to micronutrient malnutrition, several reasons can be identified. First, accumulated research results conclusively demonstrated the health impact of deficiencies in iodine, vitamin A, and iron (anaemia). Second, low cost technologies for providing these micronutrients on a large scale had been developed (e.g. salt iodization). Third, control of micronutrient malnutrition was estimated to be one of the most cost-effective interventions in the area of health and nutrition (Behrman et al. 2004). Fourth, the impact of many large-scale efforts to prevent protein-energy malnutrition had been far below expected (that the failures were results of *not* applying the 'lessons learnt' did not make any difference). The fifth, and perhaps most important, reason was that micronutrient control programmes can easily be implemented 'top-down', rarely requiring any change in social and political structures.

Control of micronutrient malnutrition is still the 'mainstream' strategy, while prevention of protein-energy malnutrition has become a rather silent 'counterpoint'. This situation, however, is likely to change.

Future scenarios in the field of nutrition

During the last couple of years there have been signs of a revived interest in nutrition, and of a new emphasis on prevention of protein-energy malnutrition. The economic rationale for 'investing in nutrition in developing countries' has been supported especially by the development banks (Behrman 1993; Hunt 2005; Mason et al. 1999). As part of the Millennium Project, a number of task forces have also been established, including a Task Force on Reducing Hunger and Malnutrition, whose final report strongly promotes 'investment in nutrition' (Millennium Project 2003). Based on that argument, the World Bank has launched a new 'Nutrition Initiative' (World Bank 2006) identifying three reasons for intervening to reduce malnutrition: (1) high economic returns and high impact on economic growth and poverty reduction, (2) the alarming shape and scale of malnutrition, and (3) markets failing to address the malnutrition problem in poor households. Three common myths are also criticized: (1) that malnutrition is primarily a matter of inadequate food supply, (2) that improved nutrition is a by-product of other measures of poverty reduction and economic advance, and (3) that, given the scarce resources, large-scale action on nutrition is hardly feasible, especially not in poor countries. The overall argument for preventing child malnutrition is that it is one of the best investments in human capital. The initiative was picked up by global mass media in February 2006, which is likely to result in renewed interest in nutrition.

In another World Bank report, it is argued that the key challenge in mobilizing strong and lasting investment in nutrition is the *lack of commitment* (Heaver 2005) and that there are three opportunities for strengthening such commitment: (1) by using the unprecedented interest in the MDGs, almost all of which are related to child nutrition, (2) by integrating nutrition-relevant interventions in poverty reduction strategy papers (PRSP) and using nutritional status as an overall outcome indicator, and (3) by building community capacity to choose cost-effective interventions. Again, ideas about nutrition, supported by the World Bank, are likely to become the 'mainstream' strategy.

The most recent initiative is 'Ending Child Hunger and Undernutrition' (ECHUI), originally conceived by the heads of WFP, UNICEF, and the World Bank, and then launched by WFP and UNICEF in 2006. The draft Plan of Action (WFP and UNICEF 2006) promotes an outdated strategy for the 'delivery of strategic packages of commodities and services' to communities and households most seriously affected. The approach, which is based on WFP's emergency work, does not include household food security and deliberately avoids any mentioning of human rights.

A 'counterpoint' to these initiatives was delineated already in the UNICEF Nutrition Strategy of 1990:

> Freedom from hunger and malnutrition was declared a basic human right in the 1948 Universal Declaration on Human Rights. [...] Human rights need not be defended from an economic perspective, although such an economic impact may be felt. Freedom from hunger and malnutrition is, therefore, a goal in nutrition strategies for countries that have ratified United Nations conventions.

The rest of this chapter will outline this 'counterpoint' strategy – a human rights-based approach to development and development programming (HRBAP).

Towards development ethics, values, and rights

While economics dominated development thinking in the 1960s, there was also growing criticism that even the best-intended policies and programmes could have a detrimental impact on poor people. A large number of philosophers, political scientists, and development economists gradually supported a call for 'development ethics': 'Development needs to be redefined, demystified, and thrust into the area of moral debate.' (Goulet 1971; Crooker 1991) The most influential promoter of development ethics, Amartya Sen, who also promoted a normative approach to development (Sen 1987; 1984) emphasized the need to develop 'cross-cultural moral minima' and to focus on building people's capacities.[8]

It has not been fully recognized, that James P. Grant, former Executive Director of UNICEF, was one of the greatest practitioners of development ethics, making a very clear distinction between science, which can tell us what is or what can be, and ethics, which tells us what *ought to be*. Without any reference to human rights, he criticized the world of being 'absurd' and 'obscene' when millions of young children die of easily preventable diseases. In trying to realize desirable, ethically defined goals, we can only proceed as fast as possible, and UNICEF should therefore select 'doable' interventions (Carter 2001).

In 1990, the Human Development Approach was convincingly launched in UNDP's first Human Development Report, and has since then dominated the work of most UN development agencies. The Human Development Report from 1997 also had a strong impact on development thinkers and practitioners, introducing the notion of 'Sustainable Human Development'. This notion emphasizes empowerment, cooperation, equity, sustainability, and security. More recently it has been extended to cover the sustainability of whole societies, and with the concept of 'sustainable social development' the discussion is broadened from ecology and humans to include social structure, political institutions, and culture (Hettne 2003). Culture, too, has increasingly been recognized as a key aspect of development (Hettne 1995).

The trend since the 1960s is clear. Development theories have increasingly become normative, reflecting the fact that human decisions are not based only on scientific facts about 'reality', but also on *values*, that are themselves part of 'reality'. One issue that currently divides development scholars, however, is whether there are, could be or should be *universal* values. Those who do not believe in universal values emphasize relativism and diversity, while those who do are further divided on whether such universal values are represented or not by human rights as codified in UN covenants and conventions.

Since the emergence of natural rights (Ishay 2004) human rights are based on the assumption that 'there are things that ought not to be done to *any* human being and other things that ought to be done for *every* human being' (Perry 1997). Although, in that sense, human rights are *universal*, it does not deny the full recognition of *pluralism*. There are many things that are good for some, but not for all. Thus – 'A conception of human good can be, and must be, universalistic as well as pluralist' (ibid.: 473).

A basic aspect of the human rights approach, that makes it different from other development approaches, is that a human right is not realized until there is a mechanism for the subject of the right to enforce and keep it realized. This is the fundamental difference between a right and a privilege.

A human rights-based approach to development

For a long time, there was only limited contact between human rights activists/scholars and (human) development activists/scholars. While the former group focused on civil and political rights, the latter was mainly interested in economic and social development – and rarely talked in terms of economic and social *rights*. The two groups had also developed very different languages, which made communication difficult.

By the early 1990s, however, the respective areas of interest of the two groups significantly broadened and started to overlap. Human rights scholars and practitioners were increasingly interested in economic, social, and cultural rights, and development people realized that the violation of civil and political rights often reduces economic and social development. Amnesty International, for example, expanded its mandate to include economic, social, and cultural rights, while UNICEF moved into protection of children's civil and political rights, focussing for example on child labour, child prostitution, street children etc. This resulted in strong efforts to conceptually and practically understand the relationships between human rights and (human) development, and how to work better together (Nelson and Dorsay 2003; Sano 2000).

The former Secretary-General repeatedly stated his position that human rights are the 'bedrock' of the United Nations, also underlined in the Millennium Declaration:

> We will spare no effort to promote democracy and strengthen the rule of law as well as respect for all internationally recognized human rights and fundamental freedoms, including the right to development.

The UN reform and in particular the former Secretary-General's enthusiasm to revive the UN Charter, started an unprecedented rush in most UN agencies to conceptualize a 'Human Rights-Based Approach to

Development', and within it to operationalize a Human Rights-Based Approach to Programming (HRBAP) (e.g. UNICEF 1998). In 2003 a Common Understanding of a Human Rights-Based Approach to Development was approved (UNDP 2003) providing the conceptual base for the work of all UN agencies, many bilateral agencies and international and national NGOs. It was summarized in three principles: (1) all programmes of development cooperation, policies, and technical assistance should further the realization of human rights, (2) human rights standards and human rights principles guide all development cooperation and programming in all sectors and all phases of the programming process, and (3) development cooperation contributes to the development of capacities of 'duty-bearers' to meet their obligations and/or of 'right-holders' to claim their rights.

The third principle is particularly important for the development and design of a Human Rights-Based Approach to Programming. A human right can be seen as a *relationship* between one individual (or a group of individuals) who has a valid claim and another individual (or group of individuals) who has correlative duties or obligations. The first individual enters into the role of a *claim-holder* and the second into the role of a *duty-bearer*. Since these are *roles*, into which individuals (or groups of individuals) may enter, an individual may be both a claim-holder and a duty-bearer.

Children have valid claims (rights) against their parents to be provided with adequate food, health, and care. The parents are therefore the first line duty-bearers. Often, however, the parents cannot meet these duties because they do not have access to cultivable land, salaries or other necessary resources. In other words, they cannot meet their duties to their children because some of their rights as claim-holders against the state are not realized. The state thus becomes the *ultimate or final duty-bearer*, which is important since it is the state that ratifies covenants and conventions and is legally bound to meet the obligations.

This shows that claim-duty relationships in society are linked and form a *pattern of human rights*. The identification and analysis of such patterns form the core of a Human Rights-Based Approach to Programming, in which the identification of duty-bearers and the determination of the extent of their accountability are crucial.

As touched upon, during the 1990s a dialogue was established, meetings were arranged, and a number of papers were published on the relationships between development and human rights (Sano 2000; Hamm 2000). Although there are different opinions about this relationship

(UNDP 2000: 19; Conant and Haugeland 2000) below follows an attempt to clarify it.

In whatever way 'development' is defined, it aims at *desirable outcomes*, and any outcome is the result of a *process*. It would therefore be a mistake to focus too much on either outcome or process. Rather, the aim should be to simultaneously and progressively achieve the desirable outcomes *and* establish a 'good' process.

This can be linked to human rights *standards* and human rights *principles*. Most scholars would agree that human rights standards usually refer to the minimum acceptable level of an outcome, while human rights principles specify conditions for an acceptable process. Typical human rights standards (outcomes) are adequate child nutritional status, universal basic education, access to water, and access to social justice. All MDGs are examples of outcomes and often referred to by donor agencies as 'results'. As for human rights principles, the following ones were agreed upon in the UN Common Understanding: (1) universality and inalienability, (2) indivisibility, (3) interdependence and interrelatedness, (4) equality and non-discrimination, (5) participation and inclusion, and (6) accountability and the rule of law.

More recently several NGOs have promoted a position that 'rights' should be defined and used outside the UN system of codification and ratification. What they call a 'Rights-Based Approach (RBA)' focusses more on the quality of the process than on the outcome. In such an approach, 'rights' become the overriding concern and it would make sense to talk about a 'human development approach to human rights' (Gready and J. Ensor 2005).

Nutrition as a human right

In Europe, the suffering of children during the First World War created a movement in favour of an international agreement to protect children. This resulted in the adoption of the *Declaration of the Right of the Child* by the League of Nations, specifying that a hungry child should be fed and a sick child should be cared for.

During the Second World War children as a group suffered even more. Increased awareness of the special needs of children also resulted in the adoption in 1959 by the United Nations of the *Declaration of the Right of the Child* introducing the principle of 'the best interest of the child'. The right to nutrition is explicitly mentioned in Principle 4 of the Declaration.

Though the 1959 Declaration contains the most important ideas, values, and principles regarding the rights of the child, it is only a moral and political declaration, and not legally binding in the framework of international human rights law. During the International Year of the Child (1979) Poland submitted a draft convention on the rights of the child, after ten years of debate it was adopted by the General Assembly, and less than a year later, in September 1990, the Convention on the Rights of the Child (CRC) came into force. By 2000 all countries except Somalia and the US had ratified it. No other convention has been ratified by so many states and in such a short period of time.

Since 'malnutrition' is basically seen by some as hunger or lack of food, 'nutrition' is not explicitly mentioned in many of the earlier human rights instruments. In the International Covenant on Economic, Social and Cultural Rights (ICESCR) from 1966, for example, the parties recognize 'the right of everyone to an adequate standard of living for himself and his family, including *adequate food* ...' (article 11.1) and 'the fundamental right of everyone to be *free from hunger* ...' (article 11.2) (author's emphasis).

In the CRC, despite its great importance for children's survival and development, nutrition is mentioned only twice, in article 24.2 (c) and (d), the first time reflecting the idea that malnutrition is mainly a result of lack of 'nutritious foods'. If, however, 'food', 'health', and 'care' are seen as necessary, and together sufficient, conditions for good child nutrition, there are many articles in the CRC that recognize the right to nutrition (Jonsson 1996).

The single most important shift in the conceptualization of the nutrition problem when moving from a basic needs to a human rights approach, is that from a human rights perspective, children are no longer seen as passive beneficiaries of transfers of commodities and services, but recognized as *subjects of rights, with valid claims on others, who have duties* to ensure that the rights are realized.

The WSC Declaration was a *promise* by the world's leaders to its children to improve their lives by achieving a set of agreed development goals by the year 2000. Ten years later it was clear that they had not kept their promise, and nobody could do anything about it. The countries that had ratified the CRC, however, had gone beyond 'promises', and accepted legally binding *obligations* to ensure that all children's rights enshrined in the CRC are realized.

A human rights-based approach to programming applied to child malnutrition[9]

As discussed, the third principle in the UN Common Understanding from 2003 gives a clear direction for the design of a Human Rights-Based

Approach to *programming*, further elaboration:

> In a Human Rights-Based Approach human rights determine the relationship between individuals and groups with valid claims (right-holders) and State and non-state players with correlative obligations (duty-bearers). It identifies *right-holders* (and their entitlements) and corresponding *duty-bearers* (and their obligations) and works towards strengthening the capacities of right-holders to make their claims, and of duty-bearers to meet their obligations.

During the development of HRBAP (in both theory and practice) it became increasingly clear that the 'good programming practices' from years of learning are no longer optional.[10] The application of 'good programming practices', however, does not by itself constitute a HRBAP. They are necessary, but not sufficient conditions.

Based on the UN common understanding, a method has been developed of applying a HRBAP. It was first applied in UNICEF supported programmes and projects in East and Southern Africa in the late 1980s, and has since been adopted and used to different degrees in several UN and bilateral agencies and NGOs. The HRBAP methodology consists of five consecutive steps.

Step 1: Causality analysis

Once consensus has been reached that a particular problem exists and needs to be addressed, a causality analysis should be undertaken by those who are likely to enter into roles of claim-holding and duty-bearing in the required improvement process. In the analysis, the causes will be identified of the non-realization of children's right to good nutrition in a specific context, together with a list of candidate claim-holders and duty-bearers.

Step 2: Pattern analysis

The next step is to, in the particular context, identify the most important relationships between the likely claim-holders and duty-bearers identified in the causality analysis in the particular community or society that has been chosen. As discussed, the same individuals or groups may enter into both roles. The pattern analysis should be undertaken by representatives of the key claim-holders and duty-bearers, and each claim-duty relationship must be recognized as a human right in a covenant or convention, ratified by the state.

Step 3: Capacity gap analysis

The next step is to analyse why a specific right is not realized. This is called capacity gap analysis, since a basic assumption is that the reason is that claim-holders lack the capacity to claim the right and/or duty-bearers lack the capacity to meet their duties.[11] Situations where duty-bearers do not meet their duties due to deliberate action, or where there is no obvious duty-bearer (e.g. failed states), cannot be dealt with by this method.

Capacity is defined in a broad sense, including: (1) responsibility/motivation/commitment/leadership, referring to the acknowledgement by an individual that she/he should do something about a specific problem, i.e. acceptance and internalization of a duty, (2) authority, referring to the legitimacy of an action, i.e. that an individual or group knows that it is permissible for her/him/it to take action, (3) access and control of resources – human, economic, and organizational – referring to capacity to act, (4) capability of rational decision-making and learning, requiring evidence-based assessment and logical analysis of the causes of a problem – leading to action, reassessment, improved analysis, better action..., i.e. a triple A approach (see above), and (5) communication capability which, along with access to information and communication systems, is crucial for individuals and groups in their efforts to claim their rights or meet their duties.

Step 4: Identification of candidate actions

Then actions should be identified that are likely to reduce or close the capacity gaps of claim-holders and duty-bearers. Such capacity actions should aim at increasing the players' responsibility, authority, resources, and decision-making and communication capabilities.

Step 5: Programme design

Priority actions should be clustered into projects, and projects should be clustered into programmes, both with clear objectives.

Though this is the reverse of most current programming practices – where programmes are disaggregated into projects, and projects into activities – the final programme may not be very different from 'traditional' development programmes. The process by which the programme has been developed is, however, totally different from 'traditional' ones. Since players in their claim-holding and duty-bearing roles have participated in the analyses and in the identification of actions, they are fully aware of all aspects of a problem and of who is accountable for what.

Conclusions

During the last 50 years different approaches to understanding and preventing malnutrition have replaced each other as the 'mainstream'.
Normally, this has happened as new scientific knowledge has turned a
former 'counterpoint' approach into the 'mainstream'. Proponents of
the 'mainstream' have always tried to stop such change, through scientific counter arguments as well as political pressure and lobbying.
Meanwhile, ethics, often translated into ideological and political arguments, have also been used to accelerate the change (Grant 1992;
Schuftan 1982).

Most 'paradigm shifts' have been caused by failures to make a theory
work in practice. Theories have normally been based on scientific discoveries made in research institutions, and when their applications
have failed, the demand for a shift has usually increased.

Moreover, changes in the approach to malnutrition have reflected
changes in general development theories. The trend towards increasing
normality, for example, has influenced malnutrition approaches, and
'Sustainable Human Development' incorporates good child nutrition as
a necessary component.

When the Convention on the Rights of the Child (1989) was rapidly
and almost universally ratified, some scholars had already promoted
'food as a human right' for a long time (Eide et al. 1984; Alston and
Tomasevski 1984). Now, from the mid-1990s and within the context of
renewed interest in human rights, a 'human rights-based approach to
nutrition' emerged (e.g. Linusson et al. 1994; Eide 2001) and has since
then become an increasingly strong 'counterpoint' to the 'mainstream'
approach of 'investment in nutrition'. It is argued in this chapter that
such an approach is superior to current development approaches and
ought to take the 'mainstream' position.

Most analysts today agree that a human rights-based approach
departs from some current strategies and reinforces others. One of
the more important improvements is that a human rights-based
approach to development and development programming, as
described above, makes 'good programming practices' obligatory.
Other advantages to, for example, a sustainable human development
approach are:

First, in a human rights-based approach, the individual is the *subject
of a right* with valid claims on others, who are the objects of the right
with duties or obligations. This is very different from 'entitlements'
that entail no specific duty-bearers. While a pattern analysis recognizes

duties, a stakeholder analysis recognizes 'interests'. Children are thus subjects of rights to adequate nutrition, rather than 'beneficiaries' or 'targets' of interventions, and preventing young child malnutrition is an obligation rather than a voluntary act of charity. With a human rights-based approach to nutrition there is no acceptable level of malnutrition.

Second, and as a corollary to the first, as duty-bearers are identified, so are *accountabilities*. The degree to which somebody can be held accountable, however, depends on what capacity she/he has to meet the duty in question. Ratification of a UN human rights covenant or convention is dramatically different to the numerous government commitments to nutrition goals and targets at various conferences over the last decades. While the latter imply absolutely no accountability or penalty for non-performers by the former, states are legally bound to act.

Third, a human rights-based approach to development pays equal attention to 'outcome' and 'process'. The outcome must represent a standard of a recognized human right and the process must adhere to human rights principles. The achievement of a human rights standard (desirable outcome, e.g. the MDGs) does not necessarily constitute the realization of the right. Rather, a mechanism must be established by which the right-holder can enforce the right. Without such a mechanism, the achievement of the outcome may represent only a privilege.

Fourth, a human rights-based approach aims at empowering claim-holders to claim their rights. Justice is seen as a *social* process, not merely a legal one, obtained through formal as well as informal mechanisms. In many cases, poor claim-holders have valid claims on less poor and much more powerful duty-bearers. A human rights-based approach therefore offers protection from abuse of power, and can be used to challenge power, reject impunity, expose corruption, and ensure access to justice much more effectively than other development approaches.

Notes

1. Protein-energy malnutrition (PEM), iodine deficiency disorders (IDD), vitamin A deficiency (VAD) and iron deficiency anemia (IDA) are the four most widespread and important types of malnutrition in developing countries. In a recent report on the nutrition situation about 660 million people, of which 160 million children, are underweight, i.e. affected by protein-energy malnutrition, almost 2 billion people are iodine deficient, half a billion

under-fives are vitamin A deficient, and about a billion, mostly women, are suffering from IDA (UNSCN 2004).

2. Child malnutrition is however difficult to see. Only one to two per cent of the world's children exhibit signs of malnutrition.

3. From Jonsson 1995a.

4. A good summary of the criticism can be found in Waterlow and Payne (1975). See also Latham (1969).

5. The World Bank, for example, often demanded a new or updated National Nutrition Strategy before any loan to nutrition was approved. See also Pinstrup-Andersen (1993).

6. PHC is defined in the Declaration as follows: 'Primary Health Care is essential health care made universally accessible to individuals and families in the community by means acceptable to them, through their full participation and at a cost that the community and country can afford. It forms an integral part of both the country's health system of which it is the nucleus and of the overall social and economic development of the community.'

7. These are: reducing severe and moderate malnutrition by half; reducing low birth weight to less than ten per cent; reducing iron deficiency anaemia in women to one third; virtual elimination of iodine deficiency disorders; virtual elimination of vitamin A deficiency; empowerment of all women to breastfeed exclusively 4–6 months; growth promotion institutionalized; dissemination of knowledge on household food security.

8. For a detailed review of Sen's contributions to human rights, see Vizard (2006).

9. For a detailed description of the HRBAP methodology, see Jonsson (1996: 79–108).

10. For the list of 'good programming practices', see Jonsson (1996).

11. Capacity is increasingly recognized as an important aspect of development also in non-human rights approaches. See Heaver (2002).

References

ACAST (1968) International Action to Avert the Impending Protein Crisis.

Alderman, H., Behrman, J., Lavy, V. and Menon, R. (2001) 'Child Health and School Enrolment: A Longitudinal Analysis', *Journal of Human Resources*, 36(1): 185–205.

Alston, P. and Tomasevski, K. (eds) (1984) *The right to Food*, Martinus Nijhoff.

Beaton, G. H. (1988) 'Nutrient requirements and population data', *Proc. Nutrition Society*, 47: 63–78.

Beaton, G. (1989) 'Small but Healthy? Are We Asking the Right Question?', *Human Organization*, 48(1): 30–39.

Beaton, G. (1995) 'Which age groups should be targeted for supplementary feeding?', in *UN ACC/SCN Nutrition Issues in Food Aid*. Symposium Report no. 12: 37–54.

Behrman, J. B. (1993) 'The Economic Rationale for Investing in Nutrition in Developing Countries', *World Development*, 21(11): 1749–1771.

Behrman, J., Alderman, H. and Hoddinott, J. (2004) 'Nutrition and Hunger', in Lomberg, B. (ed) (2004) *Global Crises, Global Solutions*, Cambridge: Cambridge University Press.

Berg, A. (1973) *The Nutrition Factor*, Washington: The Brookings Institution.

Berg, A. (1987) 'Rejoinder: Nutrition Planning is alive and well, thank you', *Food Policy*, November 1987: 365–375.

Berg, A. and Austin, J. (1984) 'Nutrition policies and programmes. A decade of redirection', *Food Policy*, November 1994, 304–312.

Berg, A., Scrimshaw, N. S. and Call, D. (1973) *Nutrition, National Development, and Planning*, Cambridge, MA: MIT Press.

Brock, J. F. and Autret, M. (1952) *Kwashiorkor in Africa*, WHO Monograph Series no. 8, Geneva.

Brock, J. F. (ed) (1961) *Nutrition*, London: Churchill.

Carter, J. (2001) *Jim Grant – UNICEF Visionary*, Florence: UNICEF Innocenti Research Centre.

Cash, R, Keusch, G. T. and Lamstein, J. (1987) *Child Health and Survival. The GOBI-FFF Programme*, London: Croom Helm.

Cathcart, E. P. (1940) 'The Mystery of Alimentation', *The Lancet*, 27 March 1940: 531–537.

Conant, J. and Haugeland, J. (2000) *The Road since Structure*, Chicago: University of Chicago Press.

Cooke, T. et al. (1973) *Planning National Nutrition Programmes: a Suggested Approach*, Washington: USAID, Office of Nutrition.

Crooker, D. A. (1991) 'Towards Development Ethics', *World Development*, 19: 457–483.

Drake, W. D., Miller, R. and Grant, M. H. (1980) volume 1. Final Report: Analysis of Community-Level Nutrition Programmes, Journal of Nutrition Planning, document no. 1426.

Dreze, J. and Sen, A. (1990) Hunger and Public Action, Oxford: Clarendon Press.

Eide, A., Eide, W. B., Goonatilake, S., Gussow, J. and Omawale (1984) *Food as a Human Right*, Tokyo: UNU.

Eide, W. B. (2001) 'Breaking Conceptual and Methodological Ground: Promoting the Human Right to Adequate Food and Nutrition', *Ecology of Food and Nutrition*, 40(6): 571–595.

FAO (1964) Report of the FAO/UNICEF Meeting with the Food Industries on Protein Rich Foods for Developing Countries, Rome: FAO.

FAO (1964b) *Protein – At the heart of the World Food Problem*.

FAO (1970) *Lives in Peril*.

FAO (1974), *Food and Nutrition Strategies in National Development*, Ninth Report of the Joint FAO/WHO Expert Committee on Nutrition, Rome, 11–12 December 1974.

FAO (1977) *Fourth World Food Survey*, Rome: FAO.

FAO/WHO (1992) *International Conference on Nutrition. Final report of the Conference*, December 1992.

Feeny, T. and Boyden, J. (2003) Children and Poverty. A Review of Contemporary Literature and Thought on Children and Poverty, Christian Children's Fund , Children and Poverty Series.

Field, J. O. (1977) 'The soft underbelly of applied knowledge. Conceptual and operational problems in nutrition planning', *Food Policy*, August 1977: 228–239.

Field, J. O. (1987) 'Multisectoral nutrition planning: a post-mortem', *Food Policy*, February 1987: 15–28.

144 *Sustainable Development in a Globalized World*

Funk, C. (1922) *The Vitamins*, Baltimore: Williams & Williams Company.

Gillespie, S. and Mason, J. (1991) *Nutrition-Relevant Actions*, ACC/SCN Nutrition Policy Discussion Paper no. 10, September 2001.

Gillespie, S. Mason, J. and Martorell, R. (1996) *How Nutrition Improves*, Geneva: ACC/SCN.

Goulet, D. (1971) *The Cruel Choice: A New Concept in the Theory of Development*, New York: Athenaeum.

Gray, W. D (1970 and 1973) *The Use of Fungi as Food and in Food Processing* (parts I and II), Cleveland: Cranwood Parkway.

Grant, J. P. (1992) *Nutritional Security: An Ethical Imperative of the 1990s*, address at the International conference on Nutrition, Rome, December 1992.

Grant, J. P. (1993) *Accelerating the Child Survival and Development Revolution*, News on Health Care in Developing Countries 4/93(7): 4–8.

Grantham-McGregor, S., Fernald, L. and Sethuraman, K. (1999) 'Effects of Health and Nutrition on Cognitive and Behavioural Development in Children in the First Three Years of Life. Part 2. Infections and Micronutrient Deficiencies: Iodine, Iron and Zinc', *Food and Nutrition Bulletin*, 20(1): 76–99.

Gready, P. and Ensor, J. (eds) (2005) *Reinventing Development? Translating Rights-Based Approaches from Theory into Practice*, London and New York: Zed Books.

Haddad, L., Alderman, H., Appleton, S., Song, L. and Yohannes, Y. (2002) *Reducing Child Malnutrition: How Far Does Income Growth Take Us?* International Food Policy Research Institute.

Haddad, L. and Bouis, H. (1991) 'The impact of nutritional status on agricultural productivity: Wage evidence from the Philippines', *Oxford Bulletin of Economics and Statistics* , 53(1): 45–68.

Hakim, P. and Solimano, G. (1976) 'Nutrition and national development. Establishing the connection', *Food Policy*, May 1976: 249–259.

Hamm, B. I. (2000) 'A Human Rights Approach to Development', *Human Rights Quarterly*, 23: 1005–1031.

Harper, A. E., Payne, P. and Waterlow, J. (1973) 'Human Protein Needs', *The Lancet*, June 1973.

Heaver, R. (2002) *Improving Nutrition. Issues in management and Capacity Development*, Washington: The World Bank.

Heaver, R. (2005) *Strengthening Country Commitment to Human Development: Lessons from Nutrition*, Washington: The World Bank, Directions in Development.

Hechter, M. (1987) *Principles of Group Solidarity*, Berkeley: University of California Press.

Hettne, B. (1995) *Development Theory and the Three Worlds*, London: Longman.

Hettne, B. (2003) *Culture, Security and Sustainable Social development*, Sector Committee for Research on Culture, Security, and Sustainable Development, Stockholm: The Bank of Sweden Tercentenary Foundation, Gidlunds.

Hunt, J. M. (2005) 'The potential Impact of Reducing Global Malnutrition on poverty reduction and Economic development', *Asia Pac Clinical Nutrition*, 14(S): 10–38.

Ishay, M. R. (2004) *The history of human rights: From Ancient Times to the Globalization Era*, Berkeley: University of California Press.

Jennings, J., Gillespie, S., Mason, J., Lofti, M. and Scialfa, T. (1991) *Managing Successful Nutrition* Programmes, ACC/SCN Nutrition Policy and Discussion Paper no. 8 Geneva: ACC/SCN.

Jonsson, U. (1980) 'Toward a Food and Nutrition Policy in Tanzania', *Food Policy*, May 1980: 143–147.

Jonsson, U. (1983) 'A Conceptual Approach to the Understanding and Explanation of Hunger and Malnutrition in Society', chapter 2, in *Hunger and Society*, Cornell International Nutrition Monograph Series, no. 17.

Jonsson, U. (1985) 'Towards an Improved State of Nutrition Surveillance', *Food and Nutrition Bulletin*, 16(2). 2 June 1985.

Jonsson, U. (1995a) 'Ethics and Child Nutrition', *Food and Nutrition Bulletin*, 16(4), December 1995: 293–298.

Jonsson, U. (1995b) *Success Factors in Community-based Nutrition-oriented Programmes and Projects*, Kathmandu: UNICEF.

Jonsson, U. (1996) 'Nutrition and the Convention on the Rights of the Child', *Food Policy* 21(1),1996: 41–55.

Jonsson, U. (1997) 'Nutrition, Complexity Theory and Society Evolution', Paper presented at the Public Nutrition Meeting, Montreal, 24–26 July 1997.

Jonsson, U. (2006) 'MDGs and Other Good Intentions. How to translate rhetoric into action', in Pinstrup-Andersen, P (ed) (2006) *Ethics, Globalization and Hunger: In Search of Appropriate Policies*, New York: Springer Publishing Company.

Jonsson, U., Ljungqvist, B. and Yambi, O. (1993) 'Mobilization for Nutrition in Tanzania', in Rohde, J., Chatterjee, M. and Morley, D. (eds) (1993) *Reaching Health for All*, Oxford: Oxford University Press.

Jonsson, U., Pelletier, D. and Shrimpton, R. (1994) *A UNICEF Nutrition Information Strategy. Improving Decision-Making at Household, Community and National Levels*, UNICEF Staff Working Papers, Program Division, New York: UNICEF.

Joy, L. and Payne, P. (1975) *Food and Nutrition Planning*, Rome: FAO.

Kauffmann, S. A. (1993) *The Origins of Order: Self-organization and Selection in Evolution*, Oxford: Oxford University Press.

Knutsson, K. E. (1971) 'Malnutrition and the Community', in Vahlquist, B. (ed) (1971) *Nutrition. A Priority in African Development*, Uppsala: The Dag Hammarskjöld Foundation.

Knutsson, K. E. (1997) *Children: Noble Causes or Worthy Citizens?*, UNICEF, International Child Development Centre, Florence, Italy; 96–101.

Latham, M. C. (1969) 'Starvation of Politics, or Politics of Starvation?' *The Lancet*, 8 November 1969: 999–1000.

Latham, M. C. (1984) 'Strategies for Control of Malnutrition and the Influence of the Nutritional Sciences', *Food and Nutrition Bulletin* 10(1): 5–31.

Latham, M. C., Bondestam, L. and Jonsson, U. (1988) *Hunger and Society, vols. 1–3*, Cornell International Nutrition Monograph Series nos. 17–19, New York: Ithaca.

Linusson, E., Beaudry, M. and Latham, M. (1994) *The Right to Food and Good Nutrition*, Cornell International Nutrition Monograph Series no. 26.

Ljungqvist, B. (1988) *The Making of a Nutrition Programme*, in Latham, M. C., Bondestam, L. and Jonsson, U. (1988) *Hunger and Society, vols. 1–3*, Cornell International Nutrition Monograph Series nos. 17–19, New York: Ithaca.

Lomberg, B. (ed) (2004) *Global Crises, Global Solutions*, Cambridge: Cambridge University Press.

Luhmann, N. (1995) *Social Systems*, Stanford: Stanford University Press.

Lusk, G. (1909) *The Elements of the Science of Nutrition*, Philadelphia and London: W.B. Saunders Company.

Maletnlema, T. N. (1978) *General Considerations Relating to a National Food and Nutrition Policy*, TFNC Report no. 293.

Mason, J., Habich, J-P., Tabatabai, H. and Valverde, V. (1984) *Nutritional Surveillance*, Geneva: WHO.

Mason, J., Habich, J-P., Greaves, P., Jonsson, U., Kevany, J., Martorell, R. and Rogers, B. (1996) 'Public nutrition', *American Journal on Clinical Nutrition*, 63: 300–400.

Mason, J., Hunt, J., Parker, D. and Jonsson U. (1999) 'Investing in Child Nutrition in Asia', *Asian Development Review* vol. 17, nos. 1, 2, Asian Development Bank.

Mason, J., Jonsson, U. and Csete, J. (1995) *Is Malnutrition Overcome?* Hunger Report, 1995, World hunger programme, Brown University.

McLaren, D. S. (1974) 'The great protein fiasco', *The Lancet*, 13 July 1974: 93–96.

McLaren, D. S. (1978) 'Nutrition planning daydreams at the United Nations', *American Journal of Clinical nutrition*, August 1978: 1295–1299.

Millennium Project (2003) *Halving Hunger by 2015: A Framework for Action*, Interim Report, New York: The Hunger Task Force.

Miller, D. S. and Payne, P. (1961) 'Problems in the Prediction of Protein Values of Diets: Caloric Restriction', *Journal of Nutrition*, 75: 225–230.

Nelson, P. and Dorsay, E. (2003) 'At the Nexus of Human Rights and Development: New Methods and Strategies of Global NGOs', *World Development*, 31, 2003: , 2013–2026.

Newman, L. F. (1990) *Hunger in History*, Cambridge, USA: Basil Blackwell.

Peak, D. and Frame, M. (1994) *Chaos Under Control*, New York: W. H. Freeman and Company.

Pelletier, D. (1991) *The Uses and Limitations of Information in the Iringa Nutrition Program, Tanzania*, Cornell Food and Nutrition Policy programme Working Paper no. 5, February 1991.

Pelletier, D. (1994) 'The Relationship Between Child Anthropometry and Mortality in Developing Countries: Implications for Policy, Programmes and Future Research', *The Journal of Nutrition*, 124(10S).

Pelletier, D. and Shrimpton, R. (1994) 'The role of information in the planning, management and evaluation of community nutrition programmes', *Health Policy and Planning*, 9(2): 171–184.

Perry, M. J. (1997) 'Are Human Rights Universal? The Relativist Challenge and Related Matters', *Human Rights Quarterly*, 19: 461–509.

Pines, J. M. (1982) 'National nutrition planning. Lessons of experience', *Food Policy*, November 1982: 275–301.

Pines, J. and Anderson, M-A. (1976) *Nutrition Planning in the Developing World*, New York: CARE.

Pinstrup-Andersen, P. (ed) (1993) *The Political Economy of Food and Nutrition Policies*, Baltimore and London: The Johns Hopkins University Press.

Pinstrup-Andersen, P. (ed) (2006) *Ethics, Globalization, and Hunger: In Search of Appropriate Policies*, New York: Springer Publishing Company.

Pirie, N.W. (1969) 'Complementary ways of meeting the world's protein need', *Proc. Nutrition Society*,28: 255–263.

Platt, B. S., Miller, D. S. and Payne, P. (1961) 'Protein values of human food', in Brock, J. F. (ed) (1961) *Nutrition*, London: Churchill.

Pollitt, E., Gorman, K. S., Engle, P.L., Martorell, R. and Rivers, J. (1993), *Early Supplementary Feeding and Cognition,* Monograph of the Society for Research in

Child Development, 58/7, Serial no 235, Chicago: The University of Chicago Press.

Prigogine, I. and Stengers, I. (1985) *Order out of Chaos: Man's New Dialogue With Nature*, London: Fontana.

Reutlinger, S. and Selowsky M. (1976) *Malnutrition and Poverty. Magnitude and Policy Options*, World Bank.

Rivers, J., Seaman, J. and Holt, J. (1974) 'Protein requirement', *The Lancet*, October 1974: 947–949.

Sanders, D. (1999) 'Success Factors in Community-based Nutrition programmes', *Food and Nutrition Bulletin*, 20(3): 307–314.

Sano, H. O. (2000) 'Development and Human Rights: The Necessary, but Partial Integration of Human Rights and Human Development', *Human Rights Quarterly*, 22: 734–752.

Schuftan, C. (1982) 'Ethics, ideology and nutrition', *Food Policy*, May 1982: 159–164.

Scrimshaw, N. W., Taylor, C. E. and Gordon, J. E. (1968) *Interaction of Nutrition and Infection*, WHO Monograph Series, no. 57, Geneva.

Scrimshaw, N. S. and Gordon, J. E. (eds) (1967) *Malnutrition, Learning, and Behaviour*, Proc. Int. Conf. Cambridge, Mass. US.

Sen, A. K. (1984) *Resources, Values and Development*, Blackwell, MA: Harvard University Press.

Sen, A. K. (1987) *On Ethics and Economics*, Oxford: Basil Blackwell.

Shrimpton, R., Macleod-Omawale, J., Metz, P. and Belbase, K. (2002) *UNICEF Nutrition Portfolio Review (1980–1999)*, New York: UNICEF.

Sukhatme, P. V. (1970) 'Size and Nature of the Protein Gap', *Nutrition Reviews*, 28(9): 223–226.

Törnebom, H. (1974) *An Essay on Knowledge Formation*, Report from the Department of Theory of Science, University of Gothenburg.

Trowell, H. C. (1941) 'Infantile pellagra', *Trans. Royal Tropical Medicine and Hygiene*, 1941, 33: 389–404.

Trowell, H. C. (1950) 'Problems raised by Kwashiorkor', *Nutrition Reviews*, 8(6): 161–163.

UN ACC/SCN (1989) 'The Significance of Small Body Size in Populations', in Report on the 15th Session of the SCN and the AGN, New York: United Nations.

UN ACC/SCN (1991) *Some Options for Improving Nutrition in the 1990s*, Supplement to SCN News no. 7 (Mid-1991)

UN ACC/SCN (2004) *5th Report on the World Nutrition Situation*, Geneva.

UNDP (2000) *Human Development Report 2000*.

UNDP (2003) *Report from the Second Inter-Agency Workshop on Implementing Human Rights-Based Approach in the Context of UN Reform*, Stamford, USA, 5–7 May 2003.

UN/ECOSOC (1982) Joint WHO/UNICEF Support to the Improvement of Nutrition. Proposed Five-Year Programme of Work, 1982–1986.

UNICEF (1982) *Current Views on Nutrition Strategies*, Report from an Informal Consultation in UNICEF Headquarters, New York, 25–26 September.

UNICEF (1990) *Strategy for Improved Nutrition of Children and Women in Developing Countries*, A UNICEF Policy Review, 1990–1991, New York: UNICEF.

UNICEF (1993) *'We will Never Go Back'. Social Mobilization in the Child Survival and Development Programme in the Republic of Tanzania*, New York: UNICEF.

UNICEF (1998), *Guidelines for Human Rights-Based Programming Approach*, Executive Directive CF/EXD/1998–04, 21 April 1998.

UNICEF (2000) *Poverty Reduction Begins with Children*, New York: UNICEF.

UNICEF/ESARO (1986) *UNICEF Programme Audit Evaluation of WHO/UNICEF JNSP Support to the Iringa Nutrition Programme*, Nairobi.

United Nations (1990) World declaration and plan of action. World Summit for Children, New York: United Nations.

The United Republic of Tanzania WHO and UNICEF (1988) *The Joint WHO/ UNICEF* Nutrition *Support Programme in Iringa, Tanzania, 1983–88. Evaluation Report*, Dar es Salaam: Government of Tanzania, WHO, and UNICEF.

Vahlquist, B. (ed) (1971) *Nutrition. A Priority in African Development*, Uppsala: The Dag Hammarskjöld Foundation.

Vizard, P. (2006) *Poverty and Human Rights: Sen's 'Capability Perspective' Explored*, Oxford: Oxford University Press.

Von Bertlanffy, L. (1969) *General Systems Theory: Essays on Its Foundation and Development*, New York: Braziller.

Waterlow, J. C. and Payne, P.R. (1975) 'The Protein Gap', *Nature*, 258, November 1975: 113–117.

WFP and UNICEF (2006) *Ending Child Hunger and Undernutrition. Global Plan of Action*, Draft for Review.

WHO and UNICEF (1978) *Primary Health Care*, Geneva: WHO.

Williams, C. D. (1935) 'Kwashiorkor: a nutritional disease of children associated with a maize diet', *The Lancet*, 1935, ii: 1151–1152.

Williams, C. (1975) 'On that fiasco', *The Lancet*, 5 April 1975: 793–794.

World Bank (2000) *Entering the 21st Century*, World Development Report 1999– 2000, New York: Oxford University Press.

World Bank (2006) *Repositioning Nutrition as Central to Development. A Strategy for Large-Scale Action. Overview*, Washington: The World Bank Directions in Development.

Yambi, O. (1979) *Nutritional Problems in Tanzania: Potentials of a Food and Nutrition Policy in Their Eventual Solution*, MA Thesis Paper, Cornell University, May 1979.

Yambi, O., Jonsson, U. and Ljungqvist, B. (1989) *The Role of Government in Promoting Community-Based programmes: Experiences from Tanzania and lessons learnt for Africa*, PEW/Cornell Lecture series on Food and nutrition policy, 24 October 1989.

Yambi, O. and Mlolwa, R. (1992) *Improving Nutrition in Tanzania in the 1990s: The Iringa Experience*, UNICEF Innocenti Occasional Papers no. 25, March 1992.

7
Culture and Human Rights*

Thoraya Obaid

Introduction

The subject of this essay raises many questions based on assumptions that might not be clearly studied. It also provokes reactions as people interpret a discussion of culture within the context of human rights as an attempt to be relativist, in other words justifying whatever cultural values and practices exist, resulting in depriving individuals of their human rights. I fully understand this fear of relativism because it could negate the essence of what has come to be accepted as the 'universal' character of human rights.

However, this article is not about the supremacy of culture but about how we can promote human rights by understanding the context in which they are to be promoted by the people who are to believe in these rights and benefit from their application. It is about how we unpack *collective rights* that exist in communities and countries in order to identify *individual rights* that can be exercised by people. It is about how we deal with diversity and identity at the same time, with an attempt to see both as positive elements of healthy mental, physical, and behavioural processes of individuals as well as of communities and nations. It is about how we address our own desires to benefit from globalization that has changed the world and made it a village, and yet retain something that is still very much ours, a private thing called identity, but an identity that is open and strong and not vulnerable and fearful.

What drove me to start raising these difficult issues is the continuous debate and until-daybreak negotiations in international fora on sensitive

* Based on the lecture delivered at the Traverse of the Swiss Development Cooperation on Culture Matters to Development: 'It Is the "How" and Not the "Why" and "What"', in Bern, 13 December 2005.

social issues such as empowerment of women and gender equality, sexual and reproductive health and reproductive rights, violence against women, and young people and their rights to sexual and reproductive health information and services. The debate is rarely about technical issues, but mostly about the cultural implications of the universal rights that have been adopted globally, beginning with the Declaration of Human Rights in 1948.

Using reproductive health as an example, Abdullahi Ahmed An-Naim, Professor of Human Rights and Religion at Emory University in the United States, rightly points out, in his Facilitator's Report to UNFPA (An-Naim 2004) that

> the most fundamental principle that dignity and well-being of every single human being, man, woman or child, is the only end and everything else is a means to that end. That means that religion, culture, human rights, other social institutions, and legal and political processes, are means to that end, and must be conceived in ways that are consistent with the dignity and well-being of every human being. It would therefore follow that the people and communities UNFPA staff works with are entitled, as a matter of principle and not only expediency, to define and practice reproductive health and rights for themselves. But this entitlement must also be limited by the rights of other persons, and that of the community limited by the rights of its members. (An-Naim 2004: 2)

Taking this principle of individual rights versus collective rights within a particular context and trying to demonstrate what I mean, I would like to refer to two examples. The first deals with how societies relate to the word 'rights'. The term 'rights' may not exist in many cultures, but different words are used to connote it. For example, the rich cultures of Asia and Africa express matters of human dignity in terms other than 'rights'. These cultures 'value a sense of community and stress duties to family and community more than they emphasize individualism and rights' (Leary 1990: 16). And this is a recurring theme – collective responsibility seemingly in conflict with the rights of individuals.

Another example is an article in *The New York Times* of 30 December 2005, entitled 'Women's Rights Laws and African Custom Clash' by Sharon La Franiere. It is about the South African Zulu tradition of controlling young women's virginity in a public ceremony. While laws have been put in place to stop such practice, the practice has not ceased. The article goes on to say that similar practices exist in other countries on other issues such as female genital cutting/mutilation. However, 'measured by laws and political status, women are making solid, even extraordinary, gains toward equality' (La Franiere 2005). Yet, the article also says that in Africa, where half of the women are illiterates, and courts and legal aid is often away from communities, 'it is often tribal leaders, not members of Parliament, who decide what is law. Almost invariably men, tribal leaders are rural Africa's cultural arbiters' and often their interpretations overrule civil and criminal statutes (ibid.).

This example is about power relations, social status, and probably about the income of the women who undertake the inspection, if they are paid. But it is also about what appears as a contradiction between contemporary systems and concepts of human rights and traditional values, systems, and practices, as well as collective rights that are supposed to protect the dignity of individuals and thus the community. It is also about identity and the fear of getting lost in a changing environment that is perceived as the 'unknown'.

This example demonstrates the dilemma one faces – do we just ignore or dismiss cultural practices and insist on the recognition only of the modern legal system, which does not have an immediate impact? Or do we work with both traditional and modern systems to ensure new positive interpretations of cultural values, leading to more positive practices that reinforce respect for laws and ensure their implementation and a movement towards the contemporary human rights standards?

The traditional versus modern tension can be positive as well, rather than negative as in the example above. When Bolivia elected the first indigenous president in the Latin America region, Evo Morales, his inauguration was celebrated in two ways. He first participated in a traditional ceremony of his indigenous group, and then the following day he was formally sworn in as a president in a modern ceremony. Thus he recognized both traditions as they exist side by side and made the best of both, by making the indigenous population feel included, their traditions respected and their identity protected as citizens, as well as bringing all people together as one nation.

I have personally witnessed the same positive example in New Zealand, where I was welcomed to the Ministry of Development Cooperation by a traditional ceremony, including song and prayer, by the staff who are of indigenous and European origin. This symbolized a unified nation that respects its entire population and recognizes the different identities, yet acts as a unified body.

In the last two examples (Bolivia's president and New Zealand's welcome to guests) the *We* and the *Other* are meshed positively, while in the first example (the South African tradition) the emphasis is on the *We* and the fear of the external *Other*. It is a negative reaction to new ways of doing things and new systems that are taking over. It is the self-protective collective identity of *We, the community.*

To bring the issue into more focus, we need to recall the controversy in Denmark about the drawings of the Prophet Muhammad (Peace be Upon Him). While Muslim communities objected not only vigorously but in some instances violently, saying that the drawings were offensive, the Danish government claimed it was an issue of freedom of speech. This story demonstrates how issues of belief, identity and diversity impact on social cohesion and social peace and how the *We* and the *Other* can be confrontational and destructive, if the relationship between them is not managed well and with great wisdom.

The issue of diversity and identity has become more pronounced with the increasing process of globalization and its impact. Today's world is characterized by the forces of globalization, ever-faster communication across space and time, the fragile process of 'democratization' underway in many countries, the economic interdependence that binds our world together, rising levels of migration and urbanization, and changes in the size, form and function of families. Globalization, as an economic phenomenon, is spreading over many parts of the world, but what is it activating in people and communities? I keep asking myself: what is *the* critical ingredient for the success of this kind of globalization? The repeated response is cultural globalization. Is this what is making people in developing countries respond violently to the rapid movements of change and to economic and cultural hegemony?

Then I see a mental image of a young girl and boy, seeing a world of opportunities on the television screen, while no such opportunities exist for either one of them. Despite advances on many fronts, widespread poverty, disease, gender discrimination, and conflict continue to take a titanic toll on them. There remains an untenable gulf between the powerful and the powerless, the rich and the poor. And the poor are abstracted into concepts and their reality is submerged into strategies, plans, policies, systems, conventions, statements, speeches, and the like. Progressively, they become more and more invisible for immediate action. Governments, donors and multilateral organizations seem more and more remote from the realities of people as they focus on national policy dialogue in order to ensure healthy macro-level action, and could lose contact with the communities, who are the *real change agents* through their institutions, which are the vessels for sustainable change. Eventually, one has to find a balance between these two types of intervention. And those of us who work in the development field must ensure that our policies make the poor visible as the true agents for change and that we act as we should – not as agents for change, but as *facilitators and supporters of change*. This is what empowerment and ownership is about. We can thus link the local with the national and eventually with the global.

Human versus economic, social and cultural rights

The contemporary debate on human rights is not new, but goes back to 1948 with the formulation and adoption of the Declaration of Human Rights. The history of this important document is interesting to summarize here, since it provides the backdrop of the conflict that we are facing between human rights standards and their adoption and application in developing countries.

There are many writers who have written on the history of this Declaration, as being universal and representing a global consensus, and thus being applicable to all nations and individuals. A smaller number of writers have taken another angle, trying to see the link between human rights and identity, diversity and the cultural context. Virginia A. Leary in her chapter on 'The Effect of Western Perspectives on International Human Rights' gives a good perspective on this history (Leary 1990: 15–30).

Leary points out that the Declaration of Human Rights was developed mostly by representatives of western countries and a few developing countries, while many other countries were still under colonial rule or just emerging from it. Only four African and less than eight Asian states were members of the United Nations in 1945. Western countries, many of whom were colonial powers, dominated the formulation of the early international standards of human rights and thus the 'undeniable effect of western perspectives' on the formulation of the human rights standards. This has 'cast doubt on the universality of those norms and their suitability for application in non-western cultures' (ibid.: 15).

Human rights were introduced in the legal systems of non-western cultures through colonialism and through the influence of the West by the modernization process. This introduction has not always been easy. To many in the developing countries, human rights have remained alien and a symbol of cultural imperialism as well as a pretext for continued intervention by the former colonial powers. The example given above of the adoption of laws, and their ineffectiveness due to customary law, is one demonstration of how the modern legal system is sidelined in traditional settings, and seen as alien and ineffective. In fact, the President of the Congress of Traditional Leaders in South Africa, in the example above, said to *The New York Times* reporter, Sharon La Franiere, that 'we will uphold our traditions and customs. There are laws that passed that do not necessarily have any impact on the lives of people' (La Franiere 2005).

Actually, Amartya Sen confirms this tension between developed and developing countries. He asserts that

> the notion of human rights builds on the idea of a shared humanity. These rights are [...] taken as entitlements of every human being. The concept of universal human rights is, in this sense, a uniting idea. Yet the subject of human rights has ended up being a veritable battleground of political debates and ethical disputes, particularly in their application to non-western societies. (Sen 1998: 41)

To respond to the 'western-loaded' Declaration of Human Rights, the developing countries actively promoted self-determination and rights from their own vision and context in two main important documents: *The International Covenant on Economic, Social, and Cultural Rights* and *The International Covenant on Civil and Political Rights,* which were both adopted and opened for signature, ratification, and accession by the General Assembly resolution 2200A (XXI) of 16 December 1966. This was met with resistance from western countries in the negotiations in the United Nations' General Assembly, because they saw these concepts as diluting the principles of individuality, which is the basis of human rights and/or because they saw them as disguises for justifying abuses.

However, progressively and through many years of discussions and negotiations, this process was not one-way, and 'despite the conceptualization of human dignity in terms of human rights (originally a western concept), the present concept of international human rights has become a universal one that is not inimical to non-western cultures', concludes Leary (1990: 17). To be more accurate, I would say that the principles of human rights are becoming more acceptable in non-western countries in both policy and practice, although there are contentions with regard to some of the rights that link directly to issues that are culturally taboos, theologically unacceptable, or economically biased against them.

One would ask what is at the heart of this difference. It is in the definition of the concept of rights itself. According to traditional western views, social, economic, and cultural rights are entitlements to be provided by the state, while rights in non-western areas are regarded as demands or claims that need to be protected.

> It is contended that there is an intrinsic difference between the two sets of rights, particularly in the means of implementing them. Economic and social rights, it is claimed, require positive state action and are not justifiable. Civil and political rights, however, require only the state to refrain from action, are negative and can be enforced more easily, and do not depend on the economic development of a nation. (ibid.: 26)

With specific monitoring and reporting mechanisms being put in place for civil and political rights, it was deemed that economic, social, and cultural rights were relegated to a lower position.

The world community has come a long way since 1948. The processes of modernization and globalization with the movement of ideas, technology, knowledge, and people have led to a 'rights discourse' being adopted widely throughout the world. However, since the present debate on rights links it with human rights practices and the implementation of justice and achievement of peace, it is necessary now more than ever to widen the debate and make it more interdisciplinary.

> This is important because local concerns continue to shape how universal categories of rights are implemented, resisted, and transformed. [...] However, despite the global spread of rights-based political values, the specificities of any particular struggle cannot be grasped empirically through a methodological focus on local community alone. For in the process of seeking access to social goods (ranging from land, work, and education to freedom of belief and recognition of distinctive group identity) through a language of rights, claimants are increasingly becoming involved in legal and political processes that transcend nation-state boundaries. (Cowan et al. 2001: 1)

Debate is still ongoing on the opposition of culture and rights, focussing on four streams of thinking. The first one is about *rights versus culture,* which basically says that recognizing rights entails denying, rejecting or overriding culture. This also means that recognizing culture prohibits the pursuit of universal individual rights. The tension here is between the universality of rights and the recognition of cultural differences, with no possibility of finding common ground on which to base the rights. This tension can be summarized as a choice between universalism of rights and relativism of cultural values.

The second stream of thinking deals with *rights to culture*, which focusses on the legal and political status which 'a culture' has or should have. It is a debate that often takes place in national and international institutions rather than in academia.

The third stream focuses on *rights as a culture*, which is an anthropological perspective used to the study of rights and legal processes generally, to delineate their structuring qualities and their connection to other aspects of social life. It is a perspective that can illuminate many aspects of rights processes.

I would like to join other writers who are preoccupied with this subject to introduce a fourth approach, of *culture as*

> *a heuristic analytical abstraction through which to think about rights.* [...] culture, rather than being solely an object of analysis, can be employed as a means of analysing and better understanding the particular ways that rights processes operate as situated in social action. (ibid.: 4)

This fourth attempt basically means that it is more illuminating to think of culture, not as static, but as 'a field of creative interchange and contestation, often around certain shared symbols, propositions or practices, and continuous transformation' (ibid.: 5). An-Naim points out that 'instead of insisting on a sharp dichotomy between universality and relativity, it is better to perceive issues in terms of a constant mediation between the two poles' (An-Naim 2001: 95).

The tension mentioned above is a result of having general principles and applying them in specific contexts. Therefore, one does not need to imprison one's mind on choosing between universalism and cultural relativism as the only alternatives. Rather, one should see the tension

> as part of the continuous process of negotiating ever-changing interrelated global and local norms. It is inescapable as long as flux and change exist in the world. The tension is inevitably magnified in our era where there is a drive to set and to implement global standards for humanity. (Cowan et al. 2001: 6)

Abdulahi An-Naim and Frances M. Deng tell us that there are researchers who believe that it is not possible to use the contextual cultural approach to promote universal recognition of human rights. They think that it actually 'retards the evolution of international standards'. They argue that the cultural approach fosters a relativism that is opposed to universalism, whether it is because of a sincere commitment to local cultures or a purposeful manipulative effort to justify violation of human rights at the local and national level. Whatever the case, it is nearly always the elite, or I might add the 'power structures or the gatekeepers in communities' that interpret the culture and use it for their own ends. Those who fall victims to such abuse can hardly be expected to reject international human rights standards by invoking local cultures (An-Naim and Deng 1990: 1).

Actually, Leary explains that often the objection is not so much to universalism as to the western character of the international standards, which has led some people to question the 'universality of those norms and their suitability for application in non-Western cultures' (Leary 1990: 16).

Culture in human rights promotion

I know that this theme is of increasing concern to all of us working in development. The Nobel Prize-winning economist, Amartya Sen, who, defined development as freedom, said in an essay:

> The issue is not whether culture matters [...] That it must be, given the pervasive influence of culture on human life. The real issue, rather, is how – not whether – culture matters. What are the different ways in which culture may influence development? How can the influences be better understood, and how might they modify or alter the development policies that seem appropriate? The interest lies in the nature and forms of the connections and in their implications for action and policy, not merely in the general – and hardly deniable – belief that culture does matter. (Sen 1999a)

Amartya Sen rightly points out the need to better understand the connections between culture and development. He goes on to say that 'cross-cultural communication and appreciation need not necessarily be matters of shame and disgrace' (ibid.: 242). They are about individuals and communities are empowered to bring about change.

The World Commission on Culture and Development, established by the United Nations, confirmed the same position. In its report, 'Our Creative Diversity' (UNESCO 1995), the Commission stated that the relationship between culture and development should be clarified and deepened in practical and constructive ways.

In this chapter, I would like to explore that relationship as well as the added value of cultural sensitivity in promoting human rights. I will explore how culture matters to the United Nations Population Fund (UNFPA) and explain the dynamics of and steps to institutionalize a culturally sensitive approach to promoting human rights.

The second part will discuss how culture matters to the implementation of the agreements that guide our work – the Programme of Action of the 1994 International Conference on Population and Development – with its focus on gender equality and the right to sexual and reproductive health, and also the outcome document of the recent World Summit and the Millennium Development Goals (MDGs). I will conclude by discussing how culture matters in our collective efforts to improve aid effectiveness, as articulated in March 2005 by developed and developing nations in the Paris Declaration on Aid Effectiveness (2005).

Culture and religion in development cooperation

The following quotations may provide some insight into the United Nations' environment with regard to culture and religion.

Speaking in 1998 at the Tanenbaum Centre for Interreligious Understanding, UN Secretary-General Kofi Annan said: 'You may be wondering what a Secretary-General of the United Nations is doing in a synagogue, speaking about religion'. In answering his question, he went on to say: 'The United Nations is a tapestry, not only of suits and saris, but of clerics' collars, nuns' habits and lamas' robes – of mitres, skull-caps and yarmulkes'. Then he cited Pope John Paul II's speech at the fifty-ninth anniversary of the United Nations saying, 'The politics of nations [...] can never ignore the transcendent, spiritual dimension of the human experience'.[1]

Another quote from the Park Ridge Centre study on 'Religion and Public Opinion at the UN' provides a thread in the tapestry that I am weaving:

> No one coming to the UN is neutral. Every one comes here with moral values, ideas they believe in. The lesbians and the communists come with moral values, as do those organizations that come with a belief in the [traditional] family. Every one has a right to be here. That was the principle founding of the United Nations in the first place.

That is a quote from a leader of a conservative 'family values' NGO (Park Ridge Centre for Health, Faith, and Ethics 2002).

In the 1990s global conferences on the environment, population and development, women, human rights and social development, and religion moved to the forefront of United Nations advocacy. Public awareness of religion at the United Nations also increased dramatically as a result of media coverage surrounding the 1994 International Conference on Population and Development (ICPD) in Cairo and subsequent United Nations global conferences. The charged religious atmosphere that emerged gave many observers pause to think about the role of religion in international dialogue.

A study by Paul D. Namrich undertaken for The Park Ridge Centre for the Study of Health, Faith, and Ethics described what happened at the ICPD:

> People of [religious] conviction shocked each other and a watching world as they clashed over some of the most volatile topics of the day: family planning and the nature of the family, the rights of women, gender and sexuality, and abortion and birth control. (Park Ridge Centre for Health, Faith, and Ethics 2001)

In response, 'Religion Counts' was established by the Park Ridge Centre as an international representation of scholars, experts, and leaders. They participated in and monitored religious activities at the United Nations, especially the five-year reviews of ICPD+5 and Beijing+5. In its report, the group concluded that religion was indeed present at the United Nations; that its role at the United Nations was unclear to many people; and that religious individuals and groups at the United Nations did not have a unified perspective on either the issues before the United Nations or the appropriate role of religion in the United Nations (Park Ridge Centre for Health, Faith, and Ethics 2002).

The same report points out that the problems of development persist and that

> religion should neither be ignored nor seen as an obstacle in these debates. The wisdom, compassion, and experience of people of faith can be a powerful source of tradition – or of change – when it comes to these pressing human issues. (ibid.)

The objective of the Religion Counts project is to propose ways in which religious voices can be heard effectively in debates over population, development, and other crucial issues.

In the pre-appointment interview in October 2000, the Secretary-General asked me what I would bring to UNFPA as the Executive Director. I told him that I would not bring a new agenda because the ICPD Programme of Action is a holistic agenda, focussed on the interactions among people, development, human rights, and gender. My duty is to ensure quality implementation. However, I told him, I would bring a new way of dealing with controversial issues, namely through culturally sensitive approaches to human rights. I explained that the international debate on reproductive health and rights and gender equality is rarely technical, it is about values and beliefs. Therefore, we must understand both culture and religion as they affect human experiences and lives, and work from within to bring about positive change.

I hold the position that all 'isms' are value-laden, that democracy is about the interaction of such 'isms', and that the product is either conflict or consensus, reached through contestation, mediation, and negotiation, as practiced in every society. The Cairo agreement itself was a product of consensus-building that emerged from the world's diversity of values, cultures, and religions. It was the natural product of the tensions between human rights principles and cultural values and religious beliefs. I believe that the implementation of the Programme of Action could be further facilitated by negotiation and mediation, by being attuned to religious and cultural dynamics, including power dynamics, and by working with local power structures and local allies to foster understanding and, thus, respect for human rights.

Our thinking about the role of culture in development has undergone a remarkable change in the last four decades. In spite of occasional declarations to the contrary, early thinkers regarded traditional cultural attitudes and practices as obstacles to development. The implication was that, unless people in developing countries adopt the norms and standards, and thus the behaviours, of the developed countries (all western in culture), there is no hope of improvement in the quality of their lives.

The pendulum has since swung in the opposite direction, sometimes to extreme forms of self-assertion. The move from condemning to celebrating cultural diversity, both among and within cultures, has been an illuminating change. It reminds us that development can take many forms and that there are different approaches to it. We are just beginning to realize that we are not all destined to be consumers of Starbucks coffees or McDonalds food as life necessities, or to find joy only in MTV music and images, even though a good part of the youth culture in developing countries conveys that message. We recognize that cultural globalization is not necessarily a win-win contribution to sustainable development and that cultural diversity and identity are critical contributions to development.

James Wolfensohn said in an address at a conference on 'Culture and Sustainable Development: Investing in the Promise of Societies' in Washington, DC, in September 1998:

> The issue of culture and development is not one that we regard as controversial. We start from the proposition that you cannot have development without recognition of culture and history. In a world that is becoming increasingly globalized, in a world where there are pressures for cultural homogeneity across all countries, what is abundantly clear is that it is essential for us to nurture, to prize, to revere, and to support the culture and the history of the countries in which we operate. Very simply, we do not believe that you can move forward unless you recognize the base and the past from which we have come. [...] This is not some wild, exotic idea. This is not a view of an elitist. This is a view that you find in villages and in slums and in part of countries where people, however bereft of physical resources, are turning back to their culture and their history. (Wolfensohn 2005: 174)

Having asserted the right of people to an identity, and to enjoy their identity and culture, I have to make it clear that there are cultural practices that are harmful to women and young people and that deny their human rights. Therefore, it is important to distinguish between value judgements about cultures, and judgements about harmful practices. It is also true that culture and the differences between and within groups can be hijacked for political gain and manipulation.

There is a growing consensus that cultural diversity must be accompanied by equal opportunity, equitable treatment, and respect for all, with full adherence to the rule of law, not only among individuals and communities, but also among and within nations. In the Universal Declaration of Cultural Diversity, adopted by UNESCO in 2001, cultural diversity is for the first time recognized as a 'common heritage of humanity' and its protection considered an ethical imperative, inseparable from respect for human dignity. The Declaration states that no one may invoke cultural diversity to infringe upon human rights guaranteed by international law or to limit their scope.

In 2004, the Human Development Report was devoted to the importance of culture in human development (UNDP 2004). It concluded that poverty, a central economic idea, cannot be understood, or combated, without addressing cultural considerations. There is growing awareness that social and cultural analysis – which has often been ignored by development policy – must be on the same footing as political and economic analysis. The report is right, for we have seen the failures when solutions are imposed from outside without listening to voices from within.

On 18 May 2002, the World Bank held a conference on culture and public action, in which participants pointed out the need to always use poor people's realities, including cultural ones, as the starting point for policy formulation. Whether policies are about trade, decentralization, education or health, they need to be based on the realities that people face.[2]

The World Bank publication 'Voices of the Poor' (Narayan and Petesch 2004) states that across all cultures, poor people feel that they are 'invisible' – excluded from institutions, assets, decision-making, and opportunities to improve their lives. Making the invisible visible and fostering participation and inclusion are key to development. I would add that the approaches to bringing about such much-needed visibility – the 'how' – must be culturally sensitive, and promoting human rights.

Overall, it has become clear that culture is not a sort of 'primordial constraint' from the past that hinders economic and social progress. Culture is constantly being changed by the people who construct it in the first place.

The only way for the human rights content to be universalized is to allow it to be articulated by people themselves, through their own context, suffering, and understanding. Only when people take action to respond to their immediate needs, or to a violation of some aspects of their lives, can they move to a higher level of conceptualizing the principles of human rights. For example, the right to have a health clinic becomes a concrete realization of the right to health of all women, and thus of every single woman, and, eventually, it is linked to human rights in general. Ownership of the right to health allows its internalization into the experiences of the communities and moves them into deeper understanding of the universality of human rights, from the collective right of the community to a better life, to the individual's right within that community to a better life.

This is where communities can universalize human rights. Diversity means that there is not one culture in the world, but a scope of values within small groups. Human rights are about fitting the smaller scale into the larger – what changes is the level where human rights are applied.

This discussion aims to pinpoint the implication of 'universality of human rights'. In his article on 'Democracy as a Universal value', Amartya Sen says that we must deal with the question of what universal values mean:

> For a value to be considered universal, must it have the consent of everyone? If that were indeed necessary, then the category of universal values might well be empty. I know of no value – not even motherhood [....] – to which no one has ever objected. I would argue that universal consent is not required for something to be a universal value. Rather, the claim of a universal value is that people anywhere may have reason to see it as valuable. (Sen 1999b: 12)

Abdullahi Ahmed An-Naim also states that there is a continuous tension between human rights and cultural values and religious beliefs. Therefore

> every culture is characterized by **diversity, contestability, contingency, and negotiation.** Since cultures and religions do not hold uniform and monolithic views on social and moral issues, it is possible to challenge dominant views or practices regarding any issue from within the same frame of reference.[3]

This is where people can become active agents of change from within their communities. It is where organizations, such as UNFPA, can become active facilitators of dialogue for change and mediators of consensus-building within communities. It is through this role that we can support communities as they create 'safe spaces' for mediation, dialogue, negotiation, and consensus-building at the local and national levels, to achieve the human rights of communities and individuals.

Culture in UNFPA

To all governments, multilateral organizations, and civil society institutions, the Millennium Development Goals, known as MDGs, constitute a minimum framework for development action. Many of these goals are reflected in the Programme of Action from the 1994 International Conference on Population and Development (ICPD), which provided an important international forum for dialogue among civilizations to create the necessary consensus on highly controversial issues. UNFPA has, since it became operational almost 40 years ago, had to navigate its way through culturally difficult issues – including sexual and reproductive health and reproductive rights, family planning, female genital mutilation/cutting, women's empowerment, and gender equality, issues within the private spheres of individuals and families, that have been brought under scrutiny in the public arena at national, regional and global levels.

Rebecca Cook, Bernard J. Dickens, and Mahmoud F. Fathalla assert that

> the field of reproductive health is different from other fields of health care. The inputs from society at large, and the consequences for that society, vary markedly from other areas of medicine and health, not least because human reproduction is the means by which each society perpetuates itself and its traditions. No society, no religion, no culture, and no system of national law has been neutral about issues of human reproduction. Advancing reproductive health, much more than other fields of health, requires inputs from health care providers, health policymakers, legislators, lawyers, human rights activists, women groups, and the society at large. (Cook et al. 2003: 3)

The authors explain that the motivating factor in writing the book is their recognition that 'reproductive and sexual ill-health does not occur in a vacuum, but is conditioned by cultures, laws, and values' (ibid.: 4). They add that the reproductive health of women is often compromised 'not because of lack of medical knowledge, but because of infringements of women's human rights. Powerlessness of women is a serious health hazard' (ibid.: 11). Their statement that 'inequity in reproductive health is [... another] compelling reason for international concern about social injustice. There is no area of health in which inequity is as striking as in reproductive health' (ibid.: 13). This is one of the main reasons why I believe that culture matters.

Over the years, UNFPA has made progress, through patient advocacy, mediation, and negotiations, as well as through engagement with national governments and local communities, to promote the ICPD Programme of Action, and the human rights and gender principles upon which it is grounded. We recognize the need to work through positive values that exist in all countries and in all cultures to realize further progress. We know that UNFPA needs to identify, engage, and cooperate with local power structures and religious institutions to strengthen alliances and partnerships.

We have learned through country experiences that culture matters in order to promote a human rights-based approach. Therefore, we are committed to *deliberately, systematically, and strategically* institutionalizing a culturally sensitive approach to development, based on human rights. UNFPA's work on culture is based on eight assumptions:

1. Cultures are the realities within the contexts in which development takes place.
2. Individuals are not only the products, but also the creators of their cultures. As such, they are not simply passive receivers but also active agents who can reshape cultural values, norms, and expressions.
3. Cultures are neither static nor monolithic. Every culture is characterized by diversity, contestability, and private and public space for mediation and negotiation.
4. Cultures have a strong impact on social sectors and relations, and especially on gender power relations.
5. It is from within societies/communities that cultural norms, traditions, and expressions are challenged and thus changed.
6. Cultural independence and cultural diversity must be respected, with the acknowledgement that change can be mediated in favour of human rights and gender equality.
7. Cultures and religions share common denominators with universal standards, such as human equality, compassion, and tolerance.
8. Human rights can be recognized and internalized through a culturally sensitive approach that gives social basis and support to the legal approach.

The last point is spelled out in a policy note issued by me as the Executive Director, circulated to UNFPA staff in January 2004:

> We must distinguish between theoretical references to human rights in policy development and concrete applications at the programming level. As part of the process [...] we need to review reservations to treaties, and share comparative jurisprudence in customary and religious traditions, law reform, and research within communities, in order to understand the evolving, changing nature of cultural norms and religious interpretations. Such effort would allow us to dialogue with the communities, express respect and win their confidence. In turn, it would allow them to feel their ownership of the change process itself because it is built on greater understanding of the complexities of the necessary interaction that would bring about change. (UNFPA 2004a)

Success, we have learned, requires patience, a willingness to listen carefully, and respect for cultural diversity. Changing attitudes, behaviours and laws – especially those dealing with gender relations and reproductive health – has proven to be a long-term and complex task. The point is that we cannot achieve human rights for people, *achieving human rights is the responsibility of people themselves*, but we can support their efforts in the process. The question is how to identify the appropriate entry points for bringing about change through a human rights based approach. For example, there is a fundamental operational problem with exercising human rights protection. The mechanisms for addressing human rights violations are at the national level. However, most often, violations occur at the micro-level, within the family and the community. We know the *'why'* and the *'what'* for an appropriate intervention, but for the *'how'* we need to know the context.

Therefore, human rights-based programming must be culturally sensitive in all its aspects and levels of action for the promotion and sustainability of human rights. It is about transforming values and practices from within, rather than displacing or discarding them. I would argue, though, that sometimes through this *process of contestation, mediation, and negotiation*, people themselves decide to let go of practices that do not serve them any more and to transform values to meet their new context.

Developing the culture initiative 2002–2006 was a new theme in UNFPA, and thus required discussions, debates, and patience.

The project has three phases. In phase one, we conducted field-based research of UNFPA programmes in nine countries in different parts of the world, aiming to provide hard evidence for how culture matters (UNFPA 2004b; c).[4]

Based on the case studies, we documented many interesting lessons. In Yemen, for instance, UNFPA has helped produce a guide for imams and other religious leaders that relates family planning and reproductive health to the Quran and stresses the teachings of the Prophet (Peace Be Upon Him) on the equality of women and men. In Cambodia, we documented how UNFPA is exploring partnerships with Buddhist monks and nuns to address the emerging threat of the HIV/AIDS epidemic and the vulnerability of young people. Two case studies from Uganda show how UNFPA won the support of traditional custodians of culture, the Sabiny elders, to promote healthier behaviours and eliminate harmful traditional practices, such as female genital mutilation/cutting. They also present the work done to support the Muslim community to ensure that reproductive health services improve the quality of women's lives.

In the second phase, UNFPA applied the knowledge and wisdom that we had gained to develop learning, training, and capacity-building for a culturally sensitive approach to programming for UNFPA staff, and hopefully for development practitioners.

Another important component of this phase was an in-depth analysis of the cultural dimension of the global survey, that was undertaken for the ICPD+10 review to measure progress and determine challenges (UNFPA 2005b). The survey showed diversity of regional responses. It shows that culture and religion are seen as powerful forces, with both positive and negative impacts on programming. Sex and sexuality are widely regarded as taboo, especially adolescent sexual and reproductive health. A number of harmful practices related to marriage were identified: child marriage, polygamy, widow inheritance, sex selection as related to son preference, and many others.

The third phase is ongoing and includes building the capacity on this approach of staff at the country level as well as at the headquarters. It includes training of trainers and expanding their constituency to national and regional partners, depending on the regional. UNFPA is also finalizing another set of case studies on gender-based violence from a cultural perspective, with the specific goal of understanding the underlying causes, and thus supporting stakeholders as they formulate appropriate action to stop such violence.

In our continuous effort to promote this approach, UNFPA continues to have rich discussions on religion and the role of religious institutions. I believe that there are many reasons for working with religious and faith-based organizations: they are present in the communities and have access to people, they have legitimacy and credibility among those who seek their advice and counsel, strong structures and outreach programmes, as well as institutional, human, and financial resources. They also deal with the well-being of local communities, just as we do – this objective should bring us closer to one another.

Culturally sensitive approaches to the promotion of human rights is about opening spaces for the vulnerable to express themselves in their own ways and through their own institutions, including religious ones. At its heart, it is a political process and a true struggle for participation and representation, a struggle for democracy.

I am confident that this approach is not only an effective strategy, but also a prerequisite for the achievement of the ICPD and Millennium Development Goals and increasing aid effectiveness.

Culture in improving aid effectiveness

The 'Paris Declaration on Aid Effectiveness: Harmonization, Alignment, Results', endorsed in 2005 by developed and developing countries, represents the latest consensus on what is needed to achieve greater effectiveness in development cooperation. It focusses on five key principles: national ownership, alignment, harmonization, managing for results, and mutual accountability. There is an emphasis on a multi-stakeholder approach, which involves civil society. It introduces a new environment for development assistance and for how it is to be channelled to developing countries.

This new framework for aid effectiveness challenges all of us who work in development and humanitarian assistance to change the way we do things. I believe that increased social and cultural intelligence is critical to this new endeavour.

Greater flexibility and innovation, multiple lines of accountability and the development of skills for relationship-building, such as language and cultural understanding are required more than ever. Internally, new organizational norms, based on learning, growth, and mutual respect, are needed to encourage teamwork and innovation, and to support the development of country programmes that empower communities and ensure ownership.

Playing the role of the honest broker – through promoting safe space for contestation and negotiation – is central to breaking down power imbalances, opening up communication channels, and developing trust. These elements are fundamental to developing an international aid system that recognizes complexity, and accordingly evolves into a system that will be more effective in reducing poverty. For some, this means that development assistance should focus on supporting the freedom and capacity for action of local players – and what emerges, in terms of development action, will be suitable to the context in which it is being developed. At the same time, issues of power appear at every level, from apparently taking for granted cultural practices, to global economic and political structures, to unequal relationships among and within countries. Local players who understand a particular situation are well-placed to bring an informed knowledge of local conditions to their own development. However, this kind of interaction is also necessary at the national and international levels.

The United Nations as a whole has a critical role to play in fostering dialogue and building consensus. Beyond designing new assistance architecture to finance development, and building a real partnership for development, the success of our development-oriented actions will partly depend on how we promote the creation of space for interaction and cultural diversity; how we work at the macro-level and how we ensure empowerment and ownership at the micro-level.

Clearly, building partnerships and alliances is about finding common space and objectives to work together to serve the vulnerable and excluded. Therefore, alliances are not about 'us', the international organizations and development practitioners, but about 'them', the individuals and communities who will bring change from within. It is about finding the best kind of support. It is not about our own conceptual powers, intellectual muscles or organizational positions, but about our moral obligation to make vulnerable people visible. So, it is their own agenda that matters. We have to ensure that we do not usurp their right to decide, by deciding for them and imposing our agenda.

This said, I would conclude with the words of the great Nigerian writer and Nobel Laureate, Wole Soyinka (1999), asserting that

> Culture is a matrix of infinite possibilities and choices. From within the same cultural matrix we can extract arguments and strategies for the degradation and ennoblement of our species, for its enslavement or liberation, for the suppression of its productive potential or its enhancement.

All development workers who promote human rights, must believe that *it is all possible*, for without this belief, none of us would uphold the courage and the patience to be active supporters of human rights and respectful of both diversity and identity. So, we have to always remind ourselves that it is truly possible, even though it might take longer than we wish.

Notes

1. Secretary-General Kofi Annan at the event Challenge of Diversity, convened by the Tanenbaum Centre for Interreligious Understanding, 27 April 1998.
2. Vijahendra Rao, Senior Economist for Development Research Group and Michael Walton, Regional Adviser for Poverty Reduction and Human Development for the Latin America region, delivered a lecture on culture and public action, basing their arguments on the special attention given to culture in development by The World Bank President, James Wolfensohn.
3. Abdullahi Ahmed An-Naim at a UNFPA retreat for the Arab States region: 'Promoting Human Rights: culturally sensitive approaches', Retreat, Sharm El-Sheikh, Egypt, 16–18 September 2004.

4. Based on the case studies, 24 tips were formulated (UNFPA 2005a) intended to help development practitioners understand and apply culturally sensitive approaches to their community mobilization work. The tips include: invest time in knowing the culture, listen to the community, demonstrate respect, show patience, gain the support of local power structures, be inclusive, work through local allies, find common ground, accentuate the positive, celebrate achievements, and do not expect to accomplish everything at once.

References

An-Naim, A. A. (2001) 'Human Rights', in Blau, J. R. (2001) (ed) *The Blackwell Companion to Sociology*, Oxford: Blackwell Publishers.

An-Naim, A. A. (2004) *Facilitator's Report: Africa Regional Retreat on Promoting Reproductive Rights, Gender, and Human Rights through a Culturally Sensitive Approach*, convened by UNFPA, Accra, Ghana, 8–10 April 2004.

An-Naim, A. A. and Deng, F. M. (eds) (1990) *Human Rights in Africa: Cross-Cultural Perspectives*, Washington, DC: The Brookings Institution.

Cook, R., Dickens, B. J. and Fathalla, M. F. (2003) *Reproductive Health and Human Rights: Integrating Medicine, Ethics and Law*, New York: Oxford University Press.

Cowan, J., Dembour, M-B. and Wilson, R. A. (2001) *Culture and Rights: Anthropological Perspectives*, Cambridge: Cambridge University Press.

Leary, V. A. (1990) 'The Effect of Western Perspectives on International Human Rights', in An-Naim, A. A. and Deng, F. M. (eds) (1990) *Human Rights in Africa: Cross- Cultural Perspectives*, Washington, DC: The Brookings Institution.

Narayan, D. and Petesch, P. (eds) (2002) *Voices of the Poor. From Many Lands*, Washington, DC: The World Bank, New York, NY: Published for the World Bank, Oxford University Press.

Paris Declaration on Aid Effectiveness (2005) High Level Forum on Joint Progress Toward Enhanced Aid Effectiveness, Paris, 28 February – 2 March 2005.

Park Ridge Centre for Health, Faith and Ethics (2001) 'United Religions at the United Nations: Why should anyone expect that?', *Second Opinion*, number 8, Chicago.

Park Ridge Centre for Health, Faith and Ethics (2002) *Religion and Public Opinion at the UN: A Religious Counts Report*, Chicago, April 2002.

Sen, A. (1998) 'Universal Truths: Human Rights and the Westernizing Illusion', *Harvard International Review*, 20(3).

Sen, A. (1999a) *Development as Freedom*, New York: Random House, Inc.

Sen, A. (1999b) 'Democracy as a Universal Value', *Journal of Democracy*, 10(3).

Soyinka, W. (1999) Keynote address on Culture, Democracy and Renewal, given at the annual meetings of Boards of Governors of the World Bank Group and the International Monetary Fund, 27 September 1999.

UNDP (2004) *Cultural Liberty in Today's Diverse World. Human Development Report, 2004*, New York: UNDP.

UNESCO (1995) Our Creative Diversity: the Report of the World Commission on Culture and Development, Paris: UNESCO.

UNFPA (2004a) Circulars nos: UNFPA/CM/04/7; UNFPA/REP/04/8; UNFPA/ RR/04/8, 22 January 2004.

UNFPA (2004b) *Culture Matters: Working with Communities and Faith-based Organizations. Case Studies from Country Programmes*, New York: UNFPA.

UNFPA (2004c) *Working from within: Culturally-Senstive Approaches in UNFPA Programming*, New York: UNFPA.

UNFPA (2005a) *Guide to Working from Within: 24 Tips for Culturally Sensitive Programming*.

UNFPA (2005b) *Culture in the Context of UNFPA Programming: ICPD + 10 Survey Results on Culture and Religion*, New York, UNFPA.

Wolfensohn, J. D. (2005) *Voice for the World's Poor: Selected Speeches and Writings of the World Bank President, James D. Wolfensohn, 1995–2005*, Washington, DC: The World Bank.

8
Words as Moral Badges. A Flow of Buzzwords in Development Aid

Gudrun Dahl

—

International aid organizations, voluntary associations, social science and neo-liberal reform programmes have in the last decade turned out to use more or less the same vocabulary. Buzzwords such as 'empowerment', 'participation', 'mobilization', 'civil society', 'capacity building', 'local knowledge', 'community-based', 'ownership' etc. convey in different ways emancipatory ambitions to involve citizens or beneficiaries of aid to more actively take part in decisions and policymaking, and to share power and responsibility. In this chapter I will discuss some of these words in their use as organizational cultural capital and moral emblems.[1]

The chapter is organized into three parts. It starts with a general discussion of the moralization of development discourse and of the ambiguous nature of policy language. This is followed by a presentation of some concepts pertaining to the overarching relations between developers and their assumed beneficiaries. Finally, I will discuss concepts denoting the hopefully emancipating nature of the involvement of beneficiaries in development activities.

The terminology and linguistic forms of international development is increasingly homogenous, but the uses and readings of certain terms always articulate with national cultures, often in revealing ways. Therefore, reference will mainly be made to the Swedish aid discourse, though recognizing that it is heavily influenced by an international language of development. An attempt will be made to trace the ambiguities of meaning of some terms that allow seemingly political opponents to share the same discursive tools, and to identify how the terms reflect basic underlying notions of differences in the distribution of knowledge, agency, and moral worth.

Here, the definition of morality used should not be taken as normative in itself. The chapter attempts to make morality an object of a distancing 'epoché'(cf. Husserl 1913/1949: 63). I will take as my point of departure the idea that what is moral is what is socially constructed as moral. This is nothing unexpected in anthropology, but still needs to be said as most of what is written on the topic of morality is written from a moralist standpoint.

I will also leave aside the issue of how efficient the motivational force of moral language is, i.e. whether moral terms or judgments themselves have a force to motivate the believers also to act on them. I am not so much concerned here with whether contemporary developmentalists are being moved to 'act good' by certain precepts, nor with how they situationally use moral exhortations to address particular others, or make moral judgements about the latters' behaviour. Instead, I am interested in the capacity of language to convey a favourable impression about the speakers' own moral identity, and mainly concerned with collective, organizational speakers. Morally loaded terms are mobilized to give accounts for action, to claim positions, and present identities. Such claims demand an audience. Hence the notion of intersubjectivity enters, a necessary and defining element of culture. Claims are meaningless if they do not resonate with the precepts of the audience. In traditional 'moral science', the social processes forming moral positioning are relatively under elaborated. Morality is seen as based on either universal, natural rules of morality or on the rational deliberations of an autonomous individual over what is right or wrong in a particular situation. However, at least for analytical purposes, morality can also be regarded as socially constructed and historically and culturally contingent. Morality is both expressed in, and reproduced by, language use.

Moralism and development

Notions of morality are central to activities of international development. Anthropologists have long analysed the role of the Christian mission in preparing ground for colonialism. Reforms of personal morality, body discipline, and time handling were part of western expansionism. Similar aspects are presumably relevant to current interaction between donors and receivers of international aid, but have largely disappeared from official organizational discourse, which has become increasingly sensitive to accusations of desultory 'othering'. Moralism has taken on a new clothing, expressed in calls for the development of 'social capital', 'responsibility', 'trust', and 'agency', even if the moralizing dimension of such talk is easily concealed by the fact that bureaucratic culture defines itself as value-neutral. There are both similarities and differences between missionary discourse on e.g. Africa, and modern, secular development discourse. As Karp (2002) notes, the differences mainly relate to how explicit the moral colouration is. For example, 'discipline' in colonial rhetoric has its correspondence in the idea of 'social training' and the 'development of social capital', e.g. to create trust, trustworthiness, social commitment, and similar values as necessary parts of development work. Much development work is in itself still focussed on transforming the individual, not only in terms of knowledge and skills but also morally, as a way of transforming society. With the breakthrough of the 'good governance' discourse and the increased importance of NGOs in international aid, the scope is widened for explicitly normative frameworks of interaction. The distinction between missionary/religious activities and 'secular aid' is not all that clear, particularly when, as in Sweden, mission organizations channel substantial parts of the bilateral help.

In Karp's analysis, development discourse ties up with orientalist and colonialist thinking by the way it defines the 'other' in terms of agency, morality, and personhood. Yet, he argues, it has a particular twist by doing so by implications and assumptions rather than by outspoken stereotyping. Modern development discourse works not by simply exoticizing the 'others' but by defining them as exceptions to the universal rules that govern human history.

> Development discourse [...] can not explicitly exclude or marginalize the very agents whom it addresses and strives to transform. Instead it defines the subjects of development as exceptions whose very exceptional nature is the problem that development theory seeks to understand and development practices seek to transform. (Karp 2002)

The truth of this solidifies with the increased awareness of the moral hazards of discourse itself, leading to a decreased use of terms which are explicitly denigratory. However, images of differences in moral quality are important explanatory assumptions in the interpretations that various ideologies offer of patterns of history – 'blaming the victim' is a widespread temptation. It is a realistic worry that older master narratives of development discourse, as well as more popular versions of an orientalizing cultural heritage, may remain a silent potential backdrop to modern talk of international cooperation.

The social field of development work actualizes moral issues at a number of levels. Staff who in their daily work embody the interface between international bureaucracy and local norms are classic carriers of moral dilemmas. Moralized interpersonal conflicts evolve over trivialities in everyday encounters with representatives of unfamiliar social settings, and in the structurally unequal situation of expatriate 'helpers' with local counterparts of various positions, around the nature of the exchange and of the involved roles. Is the aid worker a loyal friend, a protective patron or a bureaucrat with disinterested integrity? Are people givers and receivers or equal partners (cf. Eriksson Baaz 2005)? Does the client or partner claim human rights or the status of a deserving case for alms? Perceived failures to change may be explained by donors or receivers by lack of morality in the counterpart. To qualify as good receivers, recipients may have to adapt to moralized schemes involving demonstrations of e.g. self-restraint, humble behaviour, time consciousness, develop-mindedness, eco-awareness or freedom from sexism. People involved in such encounters relate to each other as individuals, but also as representatives of macro-level categories.

The other obvious level where moral discourse in development work is actualized is the one of organizational debate and text production. Development organizations are prone to mobilize moral language. They are public organizations, supported by taxes rather than direct payments from consumers. Their benefit to the taxpayers is formulated largely in moral rather than material terms (Hannigan and Kueneman 1977), even if Swedish legitimating rhetoric increasingly emphasizes 'enlightened self-interest' as a supplementing reason for Sweden to engage in programmes for global development. This can for example be seen in 'Partnership for Africa' (1997) and 'For a Just World without Poverty' (2002), two major policy-elaborating parliamentary commission reports.

Contested buzzwords and the rhetoric of development

'Development discourse' as a general category comprises many different kinds of utterances, ranging from individual statements on an ad hoc basis during the work in the organization, to carefully authored texts outlining a policy or presenting the organization to various audiences. At the interpersonal level, speech is generated as we talk along. One can analyse the functions of such spontaneous improvisations along different dimensions. Speech both pushes various instrumental goals, describes the world, and states something about the speaker. These aspects do not exclude each other but exist simultaneously. The degree of conscious and reflexive deliberation over the language choices involved in interpersonal talk is somewhat problematic, even if the speaker at some level is always adapting to the audience.

A reflected use of words is a more unquestionable characteristic in policy text production and organizational self-presentations. The authorship for a policy document is not always easy to pinpoint, since in many cases the document is created by a long series of consultations and negotiations. Similarities in the vocabularies and basic arguments with what is found in other documents, in similar organizations within the same field, or with the public debates of the surrounding society, arise out of conscious organizational strategizing in relation to what are the hot issues of today. They may also arise from individual strategies by the participants in the authoring process to perform as timely, informed, and moral persons to beneficiaries, clients, partners, and tax-payers. The report as a final product both reflects some of the discursive fads of its time, and functions as a kind of normative model, to which subservient organizational levels and also individuals may adjust their vocabularies.

In these performances, 'buzzwords', 'keywords' or 'fad-words' appear to play a particular role. Many external observers as well as staff members have noted the predilection found in Sida, the Swedish government authority dealing with international aid, for catchwords which follow each other in a steady stream, always promising a radical break with whatever is seen as a problem of former policies. (In fact, this seems to be an established part of the organization's self-image.) The slogans tend to change over time with political exigencies. As with all political rhetoric, they are abstract in the sense that they allow for extended interpretation and multi-layered references, based on the need for enrolling large support by linking specific issues to encompassing programmes. Arguments about their vagueness or difficulties of definition are common. They are words such as 'participation', 'empowerment', 'partnership', 'sustainable development', and 'integrated rural development'. Some emanate from the idiom of public and media discourse, others from the international development lingo, yet others from the applied sub-branches of varying disciplines. Social science is by no means immune to the temptation to adjust to fashionable public debate, in order both to get financed and to appear socially and morally relevant. Surprisingly enough, what is not always evident to those who take an interest in development discourse is the close parallels between the terms applied in international aid and those used in social work.

Some of them abound in social science and in radical politics of recognition and identity. Although their prominent place in development discourse is undeniable, the assumption that such words flourish more in the international aid business than in other contexts perhaps needs to be investigated. One could nevertheless argue that international organizational conversation, even more than national debates, tends to promote de-politicized key symbols that can work as bridges between different contexts. Alternatively, it is only essentially neutral or ambiguous value terms that survive processes of common policy formulation. In these processes, each phrase or sentence is adjusted and polished to suit everybody's political agenda in the home base. The ambiguities of such words underline the old truth that words do not have fixed meanings, but must be understood in their particular contexts. However part of my argument is that the very span of possible semantic interpretations is part of the magic of such buzzwords.

Among those who have worried about the ambiguities of words, is the political scientist W. B. Gallie (1956), the originator of the term 'essentially contested concepts'. His argument was that certain political terms – that is words, rather than cognitive concepts – cannot be narrowly defined for the purpose of analysis and/or correct usage, as they are basically open to normative contestation. They are terms which, as terms, all political players appear to agree on, but which each side tries to hijack for their own purposes, operationalizing them in very different ways. Gallie held that the meaning of such words is by necessity informed by the political ideology of those who use them. They can thus not be narrowly defined, and only by considering how they are mobilized by politically and existentially differently positioned players, can one improve their usefulness as analytical terms. Political science texts, where the concept of 'essential contestedness' is used, tend to see the problem of the interaction between normative and analytical terms as a methodological problem rather than a social fact that needs to be analysed. Our approach is to look at how such terms work, at the role of words as social phenomena in themselves. At the core then is not just to take notice of their vagueness, but to problematize how new terms enter dominant public debates and what makes certain terms more prone to be used.

Looking closely at any of the terms I have mentioned, dispute is likely to be discerned. There is in 'empowerment' the tension between being given tools to legally and politically combat oppressive structures, and being given strength by self-confidence gained from autonomous action and from rejection of subjugating discourse. There is in 'participation' (and in 'democracy'!) the tension between definitions which emphasize the technical process and those which give weight to substantial issues of influential involvement. There are those who see 'participation', and the more recently popular term 'civil society', as the bases on which good states can be built, and those who see them as a civil counterbalance to a necessarily oppressive state. There are those who see the 'partnership' discourse as the final chance for the representatives of the South to get listened to, and there are those who see it as a way to put strength behind the demands from the West on recalcitrant Third World states.

In the contestation over buzzwords, competition takes place over their meaning – launching perhaps, under the same form, different political, philosophical or cognitive concepts. However, struggles also take place over the claim to be associated with a value-loaded word as an identity label. Why do people want to hijack these words and why do contradictory political interests rally around such words in apparent agreement? Why not just use a new word if the connotational content of an old one does not fit? In the first instance, it is certainly the ambiguity that creates their potential appeal – these are words which seemingly offer 'the lowest communication factor' to be used in organizing 'the experiences of the listeners so that they see their interests as reflected in the words of the speaker' (Parkin 1984: 353; Paine 1981; also cf. Callon 1986). As it seems, for the word to become really popular, it has to be incontestable in form but contestable in terms of content and ownership. It must resonate well with trends in the surrounding cultures. Explanations of the appeal of a particular symbol, from an anthropological point of view, often relate to side connotations. In this case they do not relate to the precise definitions that are subject to contestation, but to complex semantic fields, cross-cutting societal spheres and often loaded with identity politics. An anthropological issue of interest in this context is the way, for example, political oratory or public rituals are part of the charging process.

Basically, however, a monolithic power perspective cannot be used in order to explain why a certain verbal key symbol becomes pervasive. Its form is cemented by the fact that different groups fight over the interpretation of meaning. Concepts survive through the very practice in which different interest groups use them and give them a value – a process which does not necessarily reflect hegemony but rather perhaps a contest over power. Counter-discourses are essentially formed by the discourses that they oppose, and therefore continuously refer to and confirm the symbol. That may also be the process that makes a buzzword preserve its ambiguity and retain its efficiency as capable of broad mobilization. If some party was able to monopolize the term, it would in the long run be compromised. Goal concepts that are on the surface apolitical lend themselves particularly easy to become 'essentially contested concepts' tied to opposite strategies and interests of action. The use of new terms is, furthermore, marked by fashion trends, where a new term can be used to mark an exclusivity and identity whose capacity declines over time. This stimulates the continuous flow of new buzzwords. There are however also processes which lead to inertia in the system, or if you like, to the cementation of a temporally fashionable catchword in organizations and texts which inter alia their sheer materiality are less prone to change.

Value terms with a definite form can thus be related to different normative contents, if we with norm mean a preferred way of looking at the desirable value. In fact, there are many situations when such keywords function to gloss over paradigmatic conflicts by reference to higher values. The argument here lies close to Parkin's views on the relation between symbolic form and meaning in situations of rapid change. Parkin draws our attention to the possibility for the connotations of a symbol to change under persistence of form and vice versa. His concern is with how formalized political language, based inter alia on the repetition of key verbal concepts, can gloss over cultural change and its inherent tensions. In the phrasing of Parkin, quoted by Stade (1999), retaining an unchanging form, they can smuggle new meanings into the cultural context of which they are a part. That is, the keywords of cultural debates go through semantic changes, some of which may be apparent and contested, but some of which may occur at the level of what seems self-evident and therefore pass unnoticed.

Far from just expressing neutral, instrumental values, as popular stereotypes of bureaucratic rationality would have it, bureaucratic language mobilizes virtues and values. It does so with temporally contingent terms, which offer an idiom in which both timeliness and moral value can be claimed. The balance between technicality and moral value has, however, to be carefully guarded. In development discourse, important concepts often have a double reference, where a purely technical definition coexists with a much more obviously morally loaded meaning. 'Commitment' has double references to a technical financial promise and to an intense involvement. 'Ownership' has a sense of legal responsibility and another one referring to an emotional undertaking. 'Partnership' has senses of contractuality and of companionship. The meaning of 'participation' ranges from being given the chance to take part in the increasingly formalized and standardized routines of Participatory Rural Appraisals (PRA) to having a sense of social sharing. The moral charge of the mentioned terms is obvious, particularly when they refer to the relations between development activities and the presumed beneficiaries. Other words that in academic writing can be relatively neutral and descriptive, such as 'identity' and 'community', are in development rhetoric almost always positively loaded. 'Local knowledge', for example, can be used as an easy and neutral way of saying 'cognitions situated in or pertaining to a particular spatial location', but its elements, both 'local' and 'knowledge', have strong overtones of value. These overtones sometimes resound also in academic anthropology, but do so in a more obvious way in development discourse. Although vocabularies of academic writing and development policy texts often overlap, the value load of a term appears to be stronger in policy texts.

Language and moral cleansing

A significant trend in public discourse in the 1990s and early 2000s has been the emphasis on discursive morals, revealing structures of ideological subjugation and leading to a search for policies of recognition.[2] In Swedish development aid, the concern with how to achieve a socially and morally appropriate language in talking about social issues was not new, but it gained momentum when insights from the social sciences, where discursive and constructivist trends had made headway already in the 1980s, filtered into policy formulation and organizational self-presentation. Sida has a long record of attempts to establish a less condescending way of talking about the 'other' and to achieve more egalitarian relations with the recipients of international aid. There is thus a kind of moralizing self-reflection over the language used, adding to the evident need for organizational self-presentation and public relations concerns.

The awareness about linguistic strategies of power has been raised not only among social scientists, but also among the subjects and superordinates involved in such games. Moral sentiments around linguistic practice are often part of the culture of both professional and recreational groups in modern society: the choice of wording is an important part of group identity practices. The substitution of innocent or more morally acceptable expressions for words that are tainted by past praxis is most common. As we shall see further on, we find in the development context a gradual change from talking about 'aid' to talking about 'partnership' (Dahl 2001) as if this would imply a radical social reconstruction of the basically unequal relation between rich donors and poor recipients. The words that most clearly stimulate reflection over the 'othering' force of language and the morality of language itself appear to be words that categorize other people. This is where I suggest that Karp's observation was right: official development discourse has become more circumscribed than before. It is based more on universalist categories that on the surface treat all human beings as subjects to the same evaluative criteria. There are no more 'natives', only 'citizens', no 'tribes', only 'ethnic groups'.

My aim is not to enter into the moral debate about which linguistic forms may be more or less correct, but rather to treat this phenomenon as an ethnographic fact. However, I would like to draw attention to the difficulties that the analyst has by necessity in writing about contemporary discourse in her own society. As one has to distance oneself from common words to be able to look at them, one cannot use the very same words as analytical tools. How can one write about the effect that certain labels have on our perceptions of certain phenomena, without using the very same labels to denote them? In writing this, I am myself at loss of how to label the activities addressed by the Swedish government, through Sida and voluntary organizations towards resource-poor countries and their inhabitants. Although I do as a private person have my own preferences, I would not like to reproduce the connotations of the discourses at hand in my analysis, appearing to take a stand. Nor do I wish to trap myself into incomprehensible neologisms. How shall I name the partakers in these activities without myself implicating the different levels of activity or passivity, hierarchy, moral virtue, and accountability that I claim that the terms refer to? The problem is not limited to the moralized context of international assistance, but holds valid whenever we try to analyse linguistic forms that come close to the forms that we need to use for our analysis. Furthermore, whatever is peculiar to our time is often so self-evident ('doxic' in Bourdieu's terminology (1977)) that it appears trivial. In due time, our own modes of expression as well as the discourse we look at will appear outdated, and their temporal contingency becomes transparent. The reader will have to bear with this present triviality and take it as an attempt to put current usage into perspective.

Something also needs to be said about the difficulties of translation at a more simple level. Words do not always have one-to-one translations, and some offer stronger resistance to translation than others, illustrated for example by 'partnership' and 'empowerment'. 'Partnership' is difficult because 'partner' was until recently a more emotionally cold and businesslike word in Swedish than in English. Words that share form over languages may not share the same connotations. 'Empowerment' creates even greater problems since the word 'power' has two different translations in Swedish, as in German, – suggesting 'influence over' (*'makt'*) and 'energy' (*'kraft'*). Furthermore, 'empowerment' has the additional sense of a legal transference of rights to do something, which in Swedish is translated by *'befullmäktiga'*, containing the root *'makt'* only in a rather intransparent way. Because of the unwieldiness of any translation, the word is therefore imported in its English form.

For the purpose of legibility, I have in this chapter limited the use of Swedish word forms to cases where there exists a particular Swedish connotation.

How to frame Swedish aid

The social field in which Swedish development discourse is elaborated consists mainly of the political system and the governmental bodies concerned, i.e. pre-eminently the Ministry of Foreign Affairs and Sida. However, it also includes a number of consultancy firms and the national organizations representing prominent NGOs and voluntary organizations. Between Sida and the Ministry of Foreign Affairs, a considerable degree of staff circulation has taken place over time, and the structure of project financing tends to turn not only consultants but also NGOs into clients of Sida. The total value of aid conveyed by Swedish NGOs and voluntary associations was 1.1 milliards in 2004 (Sida 2006) In 1979, Sida introduced a rule whereby they would add four times the sum that a voluntary organization offers for international projects, after a further adjustment referred to as the 10/90 rule. About a tenth of the Sida funds is spent in this way. Consultancy work is widely drawn on for information gathering and auditing, but also for implementation. A lot of 'outsourcing' is thus going on especially at project level, intensifying the circulation of buzzwords.

It has also been claimed that the very future-orientation of the development concept means that it constantly projects the evaluation of actual results of development-labelled activities into the future. However, it is evident that the basic catchwords of such activities are often changed. This goes not only for those very general and overarching terms which define the field of activity and with which I am concerned in this chapter, but also more specific terms indicating methods and sub-goals. 'Development' is a near-synonym of 'modernity'. Apart from more technically social scientific uses, 'modernity' as a folk-concept refers to a time-oriented value that emulates what is supposed to lie nearest in the future on a linear stream of progress. Modernity in this sense is certainly not dead in Sweden, and in itself creates a demand for new and inspiring buzzwords. The meaning of an idealizing buzzword absorbs over time some of the connotations of the shortcomings that always pertain to practice. By changing the buzzwords, a sense of achievement is reached. Narratives of improvement of organizational virtue are also created by devaluing former policies.

In order to address the direction of change, one must first identify some factors that have historically constrained the Swedish developmental practice and discourse. These are the central position of popular movements (*'folkrörelser'*) in the creation myth of the Swedish welfare society, the social engineering tradition of social democratic Sweden, and the heritage from various mission organizations and their particular links to developing countries (Rosander 1992; Tokura 1994). More recently, there is the influence of emotional charges of environmentalist and gender-equality discourses, which form strong elements of the Swedish self-image. Such constraining frames, however, have not made impossible the use of international keywords like the abovementioned 'empowerment' and 'partnership'. Rather, the Swedish context allows alternative understandings and uses of international words, which are reinterpreted as Swedish in ways which, in turn, often conceal the transnational origin and diffusion of key concepts, and the modes of their circulation. Of particular interest are the terms that are used to denote the international aid activity as a whole, the basic categorization of the relations and statuses involved.

The term most commonly heard in Sweden for international assistance is presumably *'bistånd'* (assistance). The literal, etymologically based translation of this term would be 'by-standing', somehow suggesting support given from somebody standing at the same level. When it was introduced in the 1970s, the purpose was to substitute it for *'u-hjälp'*, a term which is however also still widely in circulation. While *'hjälp'* is 'help', the *'u-'* ambiguously and conveniently stands for the two words *'utveckling'* (development) and *'underutveckling'* (underdevelopment, in its two semantic meanings 'de-development by exploitation' and 'deficient in progress'). When the concept *'u-hjälp'* was criticized, it was because of the potential paternalistic tune of 'help', as well as the suggested derogatory notion of being underdeveloped. 'Assistance' (*'bistånd'*) was initially conceived of as more neutral and egalitarian, but is now regarded as sharing the humiliating connotations of passive recipiency, and in fact treated as more or less synonymous with both *'u-hjälp'* and the negatively loaded term *'välgörenhet'* ('charity'). In the 1990s, the expression 'development cooperation' gained a place. Because of its relative unwieldiness and because it is often considered, rightly or wrongly, to be too complicated for the average layman to handle, this expression has not been able to oust the terms *'u-hjälp'* and *'bistånd'* from the discourse, despite the fact that it is frequently repeated by Sida that the previous terms are outdated. According to the official Sida homepage (2004), the concept 'development cooperation' stands for

> a process that takes a more holistic approach, is more far-sighted and marked by a different level of insights about mutual usefulness than what was comprised by earlier *'u-hjälp'* and *'bistånd'*. (My translation from Swedish)

Correspondingly, the preferred expression for the other party to the relation was changed from 'recipient country' to 'country of cooperation'. The Sida homepage emphasizes that these words express *'"jämbördighet"* (equal social rank) and also a far-sightedness far from the *"u-hjälp"* of old times', adding that 'in the increasingly global society we expand the concept and talk about a Policy for Global Development (PGU)'.

Judging from its self-presentations, Sida takes a considerable pride in its change of labelling practices. Describing this discursive history, the Sida homepage optimistically claims that never before have the conditions been so favourable for improvement as now: there is

> a global consensus that we are all interdependent. The Swedish involvement in international issues and assistance has contributed. The work that was started by Christian missionaries in the nineteenth century was developed to expert help, further to *'u-hjälp'*, *'bistånd'* and development cooperation up to the present-day Policy for Global Development. (My translation from Swedish)[3]

The last concept refers to a recent commission report, 'Towards a More Equitable World Free from Poverty' (En rättvisare värld utan fattigdom, SOU 2001: 96), referred to as the 'Globkom Report', outlining the basis for a Swedish 'Policy for Global Development'. This report states that all policy fields, not only that of international aid, should be streamlined in their implications for international development.[4] The Globkom Report requested inter alia that more of Sweden's efforts of international cooperation should go into multilateral work for the protection and improvement of 'global public goods' (see the chapter by Gun-Britt Andersson in the second volume of this book).

In an article on the Swedish policy on the country's relation to Africa, launched in 1997, I have discussed the concept of 'partnership' (Dahl 2001). *'Partnerskap'*, obviously imported from international development language, was launched as something that would radically change Swedish policy: the notion that it was supposed to change was that of charity (*'välgörenhet'*), which has rarely acted as a mobilizing buzzword in Swedish aid. In the materials preparing for and promoting the policy proposal, little mention was made of solidarity (*'solidaritet'*). This term has, in contrast, historically had a strong motivating resonance in Sweden, a country that in the twentieth century was ruled for 40 years consecutively by the Social Democratic Party. The word has been prominent in the context of international aid, particularly in the voluntary organizations that talk about international aid as 'solidarity work'. Together with *'jämlikhet'* (equality, equitability, see Rabo 1997) and *'trygghet'* (security), 'solidarity' was for many years a key political slogan, yet became used gradually less frequently throughout the 1970s and 1980s (Boreus 1994). When the commission report 'Partnership for Africa' in 1997 referred to 'charity', rather than 'solidarity', as the value that lamentably had characterized earlier international assistance, it could be seen as a rewriting of the past in a derogatory way, in order to strengthen a story of moral improvement. I will return to the negative value of charity below.

In fact, the values that new terms such as 'development cooperation' and 'partnership' are supposed to convey, figured prominently already in earlier versions of Swedish development discourse. This can be illustrated for example by the slogan 'assistance at the conditions of the recipient', launched in the 1970s (Wohlgemuth 1976). Contemporary official Sida discourse puts strong emphasis on the value change implied by a shift to 'cooperation' and 'partnership', tuning down the fact that a concern for the recipients' own wishes has been part of Sida self-presentations for decades.

Another positively charged word is 'dialogue', which is supposed to mean a discussion, leading to a synthesis rather than one party imposing its will on the other (see Edgren 2003a). The terms 'partnership' and 'dialogue' can be used to emphasize demands and views on both sides. While they are often used in the marketing of development assistance to the Swedish public to put a stress on the care for the counterpart's wishes, they are also often used internally to actually criticize Sida for having a too laid-back attitude: of being too passive in enforcing Swedish wishes.

> Making good use of the policy dialogue entails walking a tightrope between passivity and intervention, and in order to ensure national ownership Sida may have been erring on the passive side. A clear policy directive that explains the roles and legitimate concerns of the partners may be required. (Farrington et al. 2002)

Thus counter-narratives to what the change of terms implies also occur. One of the staff at the Swedish embassy in Hanoi argued that development based on 'partnership' is an improvement from 'assistance on the conditions of the recipient', because it allows the Swedish partners to make more explicit demands. The vagueness of the concept of partnership certainly allows for such an interpretation, which resonates with the international emphasis on aid conditionality that was contemporary to the launching of this term as a buzzword. However, popular presentations of Sida work, addressing the Swedish public rather tell the story of a new concern for listening to the objects/beneficiaries/partners, a growing moral insight put to practice. My point here is that sometimes little is new, if a reading is made in terms of the value that a discarded concept had when it was minted. While underlying values may remain the same, the linguistic vessels supposed to convey them become tainted by time: ideals can always rest in the future, but history is evaluated by what was actually achieved. A demand is created for untainted substitutes whose realization still lies in the future.

Sida and its clients

Sida's client organizations in their self-presentations often echo the concerns of the former body for linguistic straightening-up. Each of them have their own twist depending e.g. on whether it is an organization for the functionally impaired, a Christian charity etc. So for example, the National Sports Association (*Riksidrottsförbundet*) writes on its homepage about talking about 'international cooperation' instead of 'assistance activities' in order to emphasize egalitarianism, cooperation, and two-sided engagement.

The Swedish Mission Council (Svenska missionsrådet, SMR) in its handbook for development assistance elaborates on how to engage in development cooperation 'based on honest dialogue and partnership rather than notions of passive recipients (Svenska missionsrådet 2003; my translation).

A homepage text (*Hela världen ska leva. En rapport om utvecklingssamar-bete*) presented by the Centre Party University Organization (2004) illustrates this close relation between the Sida discourse and the discourse of client organizations, but also the limited effect that an express wish to change the terms of discourse may have on actual phrasing. The text heralds the change of terms:

> Assistance is help that is not necessarily mediated between two equal partners, while development cooperation builds exactly on the thought of cooperation and partnership. The Centre Party University Organization considers the development from 'help' to 'assistance' to 'cooperation' to be correct. The primary purpose, disregarding the choice of words, has been the same all the time: that is, to help people who have worse conditions than we have. (My translation from Swedish; Centerpartiets högskoleförbund 2004)

As the last sentence indicates, the explicitly made choice of a particular preferred policy term does not change the way people spontaneously express themselves even in the immediate context of the proposed change. Neither have any attempts succeeded in changing the terms 'donors' and 'recipients', although 'donorship' (in English) has recently been launched as yet another term with derogatory implications (Edgren 2003b).

In a report from a course in communicating about issues of international assistance (Gunnarsson et al. 1999), the authors similarly note that many organizations claim that they do not want to use the word 'assistance', but still do so in their information materials. Some of the NGO communicators interviewed argue that the same applies to Sida, rejecting the word 'assistance' but encouraging NGOs to apply for support to 'assistance projects'. Words connoting help, aid, and giving are difficult to dispose of. What is actually said in different situations is obviously constrained by the opportunities that everyday language offers for simple and precise communication.

Communion and exchange

The different words that are summoned in the self-presentation of Sida can be elucidated by relating them to the two basic forms of interpreting human cooperation that are well-known in anthropology.

One is transactional and based on reciprocity and exchange between two autonomous and distinct units or carriers of agency, be they individuals or social groups. The other form of cooperation is based on mutual sharing between people defined as belonging together on the basis of some form of spiritual or material con-essentiality. This basic form ranges from the relationship between a mother and her children, at the most concrete level, to ideological claims for universal human solidarity, at the most abstract level.

Simmel who uses the term 'organic solidarity' for the latter type of con-essentiality juxtaposes such organic solidarity – which he claims to give more secure rights to the poor – to help that is given with 'suitability' or an instrumental purpose in mind, even if the instrumental purpose is to achieve an abstract religious value (Simmel 1971: 153, see Johansson 1992: 185 for a discussion). Divine blessing enters a force outside the particular link between the giver and the recipient, and the relation has nothing to do with human reciprocity. Help which is motivated by external rewards or suitability should thus make up a third category of cooperation, what moral philosophers define as 'enlightened self-interest', a term which we shall return to below. There is of course a fourth possible frame of interpretation – that of exploitation. For obvious reasons, this is not part of the vocabularies of self-presentation by the players in development aid/assistance/cooperation, and will therefore not be considered here.

The principles of rightful sharing versus exchange versus 'enlightened self-interest' are important points of departure when considering the changing moral overtones of international assistance or social work within modern society. In the present context, they should not be seen as exclusive and absolute categories of cooperation, but rather as paradigms of interpretation, between which the various ideological readings of assistance may be swerving, offering alternative arguments to the involved partners. Their limits are not clear-cut and the situational use of one term does not necessarily compromise the use of another term in another context for exactly the same transaction. In particular, the distinction between con-essential sharing and reciprocity is additionally blurred by the fact that the acceptance of a gift in itself involves inferiority and loss of agency and power (Mauss 1990: 74, Blau 1964: 28). Read with inverse signs, this is transfer of hierarchical status, gratitude, and prestige which may be seen as reciprocal compensation.

An example of how these understandings are expressed in the context of international aid is provided by the handbook of the Swedish Mission Council:

The concept reciprocal is used to describe a relation between different parties. [...] A sound and genuine reciprocity demands clarity and an expressed own identity. Reciprocity does not depend on having no opinion or on subordination, but on partners being distinct. (My translation from Swedish, Svenska missionsrådet 2003)

The same source however also defines solidarity with a definition that it literally shares with other organizations such as the network of voluntary organizations Forum Syd or 'The Africa Groups', the leading Swedish solidarity association that used to deal with South African issues in apartheid times:

> Solidarity stands for a shared responsibility and for deeply defending other people's rights. Solidarity means to be able to identify with exposed people and let their situation influence one's own action. [...] Humanity is one, and it is all about a rightful management and sharing of the resources of the earth. Many problems are global and threaten us all, therefore we need to find common, reciprocal solutions based on a rights perspective. (My translation from Swedish, Svenska missionsrådet 2003)

The debate on whether we are talking about 'aid' or 'assistance' or 'solidarity work' reflects the possible ambiguities of interpreting international development activities. Partnership may in this context be seen as a new rhetoric alternative to 'solidarity'. It has ideological connotations of equality but no element of suggested identity or shared membership in any larger collectivity. Instead, it suggests a contractual relation based on reciprocal exchange, and limited to the time that such conditions are met. 'Solidarity' too is supposed to suggest equality, but in the form of egalitarian sharing within a larger con-essentiality. Which unit is implied, is not always spelt out, but at the general level, where Swedish aid organizations offer self-presentations, the explicit reference is often to humanity as such, as in the above quotation.[5] In a report on development cooperation, published by the Centre Party University Organization, the author quotes a poem by Saadi (1215–1292).

> All humans are members of the same family sharing origin in Creation if one limb is aching the others are caught by worry. If you are not hurt by other people's suffering you do not deserve the name of human

'Collectivism' is sometimes juxtaposed with 'individualism' as its conceptual opposite. Swedish culture, although often claimed to be 'collectivistic' by external observers, is not particularly collectivistic at the level of everyday interaction: on the contrary, it can be claimed to have an extreme emphasis on the autonomy of the individual, for which collectivism at the state level is a precondition. Sweden has a tradition of giving political influence to strong membership organizations within the labour movement, the teetotallers movement and the 'free churches'. Many of these organizations however, currently struggle with problems of new membership, of recruitment of new generations, and of engaging the members in their activities, reflecting that personal collective commitment beyond the nuclear family is becoming weak. On the level of official development discourse, globalism or humanism are often used as rhetorical resources. Overt nationalism has become more widespread and accepted in Sweden than since before the Second World War, but the rejection of nationalism as harmful and anachronistic is also widespread. Official Swedish self-presentation reflects the paradox that even internationalism can be launched as a symbol of national pride.

Utopias of involvement

So far I have mainly discussed concepts that relate to the frame of interpretation, intended by governmental bodies to be used for the relationship between Sweden and the counterparts in its international cooperation with poor countries. There are however another set of interesting concepts that relate not to the relationship as such, but to the expected quality of recipient involvement in particular aid activities. Of these terms, I will take a closer look at the three terms participation, ownership, and empowerment.

Participation

'People's participation' figured prominently in Swedish development discourse of the 1980s, linked with social democratic ideas that, in line with a century-old tradition, cherished political influence through popular associations, yet certainly did not rule out the idea of the good state. Rosander (1992) has described the difficulties that policymakers in Sida had in conveying to field staff that the expression was not used as simple rhetoric, but had a relevance to how work was to be carried out. Nevertheless, at the level of rhetoric, the concept was an important part of Sida ideology throughout the 1980s. Within Sida, many officers interpreted the term mainly in the 'instrumental means' mode, but its central position in official ideology and self-presentation is more likely to have its roots in the 'ends-in-itself' dimension, legitimizing develop-ment practice to notions central to Swedish values of equality and democracy. When the World Bank took the concept to its heart in around 1990, this was heralded in Sweden as a breakthrough of Swedish influence. However, it appears more realistic to place the international flourishing of the concept in the context of neo-liberal international streams of thought, linked to views of state influence as primarily ham-pering individual initiative, and of 'civil society' as the proper location of participation, mutual support and influence. Though such cultural differences in the model of the good state may appear evident once they are explicitly formulated, for most people partaking in development debates, they are presumably confined to the silent and taken for granted. Today, participation, like democracy, is emphasized by Sida to be both an end in itself and a means to achieve more efficient aid.

Participation, like other fad-words, is notoriously vague in its refer-ence, to begin with because it wavers between being seen as a goal in itself, a tool of achieving higher efficiency, and a tool of mobilizing the support of ('co-opting') a population by making people identify with a project and feel accountable for it. At the most general social level, the concept becomes synonymous with that of social inclusion. Henkel and Stirrat (2001: 172) write about the term:

> On the one hand it refers simply to people taking part in decision-making [...] On the other hand, however, 'participation' has much more far-reaching connotations involving a specific vision of society as 'communitas' and, at times, of evangelical promises of salvation.

Already in the 1970s and 1980s, researchers remarked that it is often unspecified to what part of a process of planned improvement the term participation refers – data supplying, problem formulation, decision-making, practical implementation, cost splitting, and so on (Paul 1987; Cohen and Uphoff 1977).

The use of the term has also inspired several development researchers to reflect upon the discrepancy between the assumed ideological con-tent of the term and its different de facto functions in various local contexts, for example, as an instrument of recruiting cheap labour for infrastructural projects (Chambers 1995: 37; Peters 1996). An early cri-tique came from Cardoso (1982, cited in Wolfe 1983) who warned that participatory efforts usually were too confined to solving problems at a narrow local scale, distracting from the concern with popular influence at a more significant national level. Participation has furthermore been seen as a general instrument to circumvent the issues of how to create a functioning formal political democracy. The relation between 'participation' and the concept 'democracy' is arguably unsettled (Abrahamsen 2000). The two concepts often seem to belong to separate discursive spheres. Participation, it is said by its critics, is considered to be something that takes place in the de-politicized sphere of local development projects, run either by official international development agencies or increasingly by NGOs, while official aid withdraws from local engagement and concentrates on macro issues. Participation in such contexts is not conceptualized in terms of democracy, perhaps because development agencies and NGOs do not usually self-identify as part of power structures. Rather than strengthening democracy within the framework of the state, the discourse of participation is thus part of what Fergusson has termed 'the anti-politics machine' (1990). Among the silent issues of participation, rarely raised in the present international ideological regime, is that of workers', customers', neighbours', and suppliers' participation in production decisions within enterprises, or beneficiary participation in the internal decision-making of NGOs beyond particular project concerns. The notion of popular participation implies ideas about the 'people', a category normally separated from the speaker, often conceived of as a particular category of mainly rural-based persons for whom exclusion from planning issues is a major problem – mainly categorical exclusions from influence on planners and planning. The agenda usually remains silent on issues of decision that refer to economic control and differentiated access to land and other bases of production, which are protected by the notion of unalienable property rights as central human rights enjoyed by the formal owners. In the neo-liberal model, the participating people are further not conceptualized as citizens that form part of a state, but in opposition to the state (cf. Trägårdh 1999). Exclusion can in this way almost be seen as part of the definition of the 'people', turning the idea of 'people's participation' into a moving target, one of these utopian values which can never be an end state. Such excluded 'people' are seen as people who have knowledge and a potential, yet unrealized capacity for action. That is, they are not seen as people who now have real agency, but as people whose agency must be liberated. This limited recognition of agency reserves a role for the external intervener, that of a catalyst creating new spaces for community discussion and encouragement. Development aid at the project level has increasingly become a matter for NGOs. Their solution has often not been to strengthen the 'people's' participation as citizens of a state, but rather to solve local problems bypassing state structures, or at best enabling the 'people' to negotiate with the state and with each other.

The emphasis on local participation has, somewhat paradoxically, been matched by a decrease of international interest in local projects, at least by governmental aid organizations. This is in fact what has left a scope for NGOs to step in. Another dimension which is not spelt out in the concept itself (but always assumed) is that participation takes place in a local context.

Ownership

A concept related to 'participation' that also became common internationally and in internal Sida talk in the 1990s is 'ownership'. The term is normally given in English rather than in Swedish (*'ägarskap'*). It is formally translated as 'the exercise of control and command over development activities' (Edgren 2003b; Weeks et al. 2002). Nonetheless, it is often used in the sense of a sincere emotional commitment to a project from the stakeholders concerned, a desirable stance taken rather than the exercise of formal rights. Such a commitment is expected to involve a sense of responsibility for the project, even when it has been conceived elsewhere, and it can thus be seen as an intensified level of desired participation. 'Ownership' discourse links up with some traditions of 'participation' which can be traced back to school of psychologically oriented industrial managerialism founded by Kurt Lewin in the 1940s, stressing that people are more ready to change if they have themselves taken part in identifying problems and deciding on solutions. 'Ownership' should thus not be taken in the sense of proper proprietary rights. One can however reflect that its lavish use as a metaphor contributes to reinforce ideas of property and sense of responsibility as inalienably related (e.g. Hardin's classic article on the 'tragedy of the commons' 1968).

Empowerment

Empowerment started to appear in international development discourse around 1990, and soon spread also to Swedish texts on development. In the mid-1980s, new policies for social welfare were launched in several western countries by political leaders of the New Right, such as Thatcher and Reagan, drawing their inspiration from economists like Hayek and Friedman. A number of studies (e.g. Stewart and Taylor 1995; Hyatt 1997) by critical sociologists and anthropologists particularly in Britain mention the 'empowerment' idiom as part of the ideological draping of urban renewal programmes in Britain in the late 1980s and early 1990s.

Neo-liberal reform programmes of the belt-tightening mode were sold by a rhetorical emphasis on client choice, responsibility, partnership, and empowerment, while frequently a reality of responsibility, workload and the carrying of costs was pushed over to hesitant, economically and educationally disadvantaged clients.

The state that empowerment is expected to redress can be read in contrasting ways. The English language here appears to gloss over distinctions that Scandinavian language would make between lack of power, powerlessness, and effeteness. In Swedish, the concept *'maktlöshet'* (powerlessness) suggests a conscious player with a defined, already explicit preference that cannot be fulfilled, indicating a subjective experience of being victimized. Lack of power need not be the same as powerlessness, nor lack of energy. However, these states are conflated in relation to 'empowerment'. The concept thus has reference to two types of 'power' – power seen as resting in the nature of a relationship between different players or a player and his/her environment, and power seen as energy, a force inherent in the individual player. This basic ambiguity makes it possible to talk about empowerment both when the agent structurally lacks a range of action due to external constraints, and when the lack of agency and influence relates to personal weakness. While the first version may call for tools such as legal rights, knowledge, and skills, the second version sees self-confidence and positive thinking as central goods to deliver – nothing bad in themselves, as long as they do not distract from structural considerations. However, as with the ambiguities implied in the 'partnership' notion, the empowerment idiom is entangled in a neo-liberal overvaluation of individual choice and agency which opens for 'blaming the victim' by implication.

Conclusion

Swedish discourse on development work puts a strong emphasis on siding with the underprivileged. In the Globkom Report this is expressed as 'taking the southern perspective' and presented as a radical rethinking, although from the point of rhetoric, it is nothing new. However, having become a member of the European Union, Sweden is no longer autonomous from the perspective of foreign relations policy. When in around 1990, the term 'popular participation' was taken up as a major developmental buzzword by the World Bank, Swedish development thinkers took it to be a success for Swedish thinking, based on the particular national myth that Swedish democracy was built on the close link between government and popular movements. Buzzwords circulating in the international arena can still be picked up and read as if they stood for autonomous national values. 'Partnership' was in this way launched as a term with a particular Swedish meaning of egalitarianism (Dahl 2001). That the adoption of international terms is seen as an expression of national traditions also occurs in the context of 'civil society' and 'NGO' discourses, where references of civic engagement resonate with the image of Swedish associational life as it figures in the national myth rather than in contemporary reality. In an international perspective, many terms used in the neo-liberal discourse on development coincide with words, which also have a basic appeal to social movements and voluntary organizations engaged in emancipatory work, and which (for different purposes) also have a basic anti-statist attitude. The financial dependence of Swedish voluntary organizations on official support, and the dependence of Sida on NGOs to implement much of its international engagement, contribute to blur the boundaries between discursive fields. The general ambiguity of buzzwords contributes to making such syncretism unproblematic.

The moralization of language in development work takes different forms. It is expressed in subtle ways by the selective and preferential use of certain words, which point at moral values with which the speaker wants to be associated. Such less explicit moral aspects of language serve the purpose of individual or organizational moral impression management, but do not necessarily involve any conscious reflection over the vocabulary as having moral dimensions. Yet, the normative aspects of buzzwords are continuously endorsed by their frequent repetition. At a more conscious level, verbalized arguments about the morality of language use have become more common, and led to a continuous turnover of vocabulary as practice fails to meet the ideals, and as the idea of an ongoing improvement or imminent change for the better must be maintained.

The terms that regulate the contemporary morality of recognition (Honneth 1995) carry inherent and apparently insolvable paradoxes. For example, the emphasis on recognizing agency also contributes to reinforcing the notion that degrees of activity can be used as moral rods of measurement for the evaluation of subordinated and underprivileged groups. 'Empowerment' is thought of as something that is given to you and defines a place for external agents to act as catalysts. Projects of emancipation cannot escape the inequality inherent in notions of assistance, making the project of linguistic cleaning hopeless. Chambers, the international prophet of the participatory movement, presents these methods primarily as reversals of the direction of dominance in planning and research, but also as techniques that 'enable local people to share, enhance, and analyse their knowledge of life and conditions, to plan and to act' (1995: 45). This quote provides an example of the difficulties of discursive emancipation. It can be read as yet another example of denigrating othering, a statement that 'local people', before access to the technique, lacked the capacity to share and analyse their knowledge.

The ideological strands that activists and establishment developmentalists represent do not make up independent and coherent units, but have fuzzy edges. In this field of blurred boundaries and diffuse and moralized terms, the discourse of power more and more comes to use terms which look like those of the supposedly intellectually critical discourse of social science or political language of activism. Power uses signal terms that convey the same commitments as critical discourse does – commitment to the morals of recognition, fair distribution, non-interference, and freedom. Language then becomes less and less transparent semantically. At the same time, the implications and consequences of political language can never be evaluated only from a semantic analysis, but only post-hoc and seen in its practical context.

Notes

1. This text emanates from a research project funded by Sida, concerned with the social biography of words in development discourse, undertaken together with Ronald Stade.
2. Parallel to this new emphasis on discursive morals, a corresponding public silencing arose on issues of distributive justice. This was linked to the fall of eastern European regimes, whose ideological draping, if not governmental practice, was ultimately based on distributive morality.
3. Curiously, the presentation leaves aside the important role of the popular movements.
4. In 2006, one can conclude that this streamlining has not yet been accomplished, as Swedish restrictions on foreign imports are still at odds with the purposes of international poverty reduction.
5. More narrow con-essentializations are of course also done by some organizations, perhaps on the definitions made by the struggle for a common goal, which motivates the helper's presence and structures how she/he defines and labels the recipients. Given that the original mobilization in NGO activities is often based on some kind of moral cause, the recipient is often expected to stand for the values which ideologically motivate the assistance. Perhaps it should also be mentioned that among young Swedes, there is an increasing recognition of a unit larger than humanity as animal rights pro-activism and veganism are strong. This has not had any discernible impact on Swedish development discourse so far.

References

Abrahamsen, R. (2000) *Disciplining Democracy: Development Discourse and Good Governance in Africa*, London: Zed Books.

Amnå, E. (ed) (1999) Civilsamhället. Demokratiutredningens forskarvolym, SOU 1999: 84.

Blau, P. (1964) *Exchange and Power in Social Life*, New York: John Wiley and Sons.

Boreus, K. (1994) Högervåg. Nyliberalism och kampen om språket i svensk offentlig debatt 1969–1989, Stockholm: Tidens förlag.

Bourdieu, P. (1977) *Outline of a Theory of Practice*, Cambridge: Cambridge University Press.

Callon, M. (1986) 'Some elements of a sociology of translation: Domestication of the scallops and the fishermen of St Brieuc Bay', pp. 196–233 in Law, J. (ed) (1986) *Power, Action and Belief: A New Sociology of Knowledge*, London: Routledge and Kegan Paul.

Cardoso, F. H. (1982) 'Las politicas sociales en la decada del 80: neuvas opciones' (E/CEPAL/IPES/ SEM 1/R.r, 12 April 1982) cited in Wolfe, M. (ed) (1983) Participation: The View from Above, Geneva: UNRISD.

Centerpartiets högskoleförbund (2004) Hela världen ska leva. En rapport om utvecklingssamarbete http://fc.centerpartiet.se/chf /Let the whole world live/

Chambers, R. (1995) 'Paradigm Shifts and the Practice of Participatory Research and Development', in Nelson, N. and Wright, S. (eds) (1995) *Power and Participatory Development: Theory and Practice*, London: Intermediate Technology Publications.

Cohen, J. N. and Uphoff, N. (1977) *Rural Development Participation: Concepts and Measures for Project Design, Implementation and Evaluation*, Ithaca: Cornell University Press.

Cook, B. and Kothari, U. (eds) (2001) *Participation. The New Tyranny*, London and New York: Zed Books.

Dahl, G. (2001) Responsibility and Partnership in Swedish Aid Discourse, Nordic Africa Institute, Discussion paper 9 ISBN 91-7106-473-7.

Dahl, G. and Rabo, A. (eds) (1992) Kam-Ap or Take-Off: Local Notions of Development, Stockholm Studies in *Social Anthropology*, 29.

Edgren, G. (2003a) 'The Unequal Dialogue', in Olsson, J. and Wohlgemuth, L. (eds) (2003) *Dialogue in Pursuit of Development*, Stockholm: Almqvist & Wiksell.

Edgren, G. (2003b; draft) Donorship, Ownership and Partnership. Issues Arising from Four Sida Studies of Donor-Recipient Relations.

SOU 2001: 96, En rättvisare värld utan fattigdom, Stockholm: Fritzes.

Erikson Baaz, M. (2005) *The Paternalism of Partnership: A Postcolonial Reading of Identity in Development Aid*, London: Zed Books.

Farrington, J., Blench, R., Christoplos, I., Ralsgård, K. and Rudqvist, A. (2002) *Evaluation of Sustainable Poverty Reduction through Area Development Projects*, Stockholm: Sida Studies in Evaluation.

Fergusson, J. (1990) *The Anti-Politics Machine. 'Development', Depoliticization and Bureaucratic Power in Lesotho*, Cambridge: Cambridge University Press.

Gallie, W.B. (1956) 'Essentially Contested Concepts', Proceedings of the Aristotelian *Society*, 56: 167–198.

Gunnarsson, S., Hatt, K. och Åberg, E. (1999) GI/IHRs och Biståndsinfoakademins kommunikationsutbildning. 'Starka och Handlingskraftiga Människor?!' En studie om den u-landsbild några organisationer i biståndssektorn förmedlar. Forum Syd, Sweden.

Hannigan, J A. and Kueneman, R. M. (1977) 'Legitimacy and public organizations: a case study', *Canadian Journal of Sociology*, 2: 125–136.

Hardin, G. (1968) 'The Tragedy of the Commons', *Science*, 162: 1243–1248.

Henkel, H. and Stirrat, R. (2001) 'Participation as Spiritual Duty: Empowerment as Secular Objection', in Cook, B. and Kothari, U. (eds) (2001) *Participation. The New Tyranny*, London and New York: Zed Books.

Honneth, A. (1995) *The Struggle for Recognition. The Moral Grammar of Social Conflicts*, Cambridge: Polity Press.

Husserl, E. (1913/1949) Husserliana: Edmund Husserl, Gesammelte Werke bd 3, Haag: Springer.

Hyatt, S. B. (1997) 'Poverty in a "post-welfare" landscape. Tenant management policies, self-governance and the democratization of knowledge in Great Britain', in Shore, C. and Wright, S. (eds) (1997) *Anthropology of Policy: Critical Perspectives on Governance and Power*, London and New York: Routledge.

Johansson, G. (1992) *More Blessed To Give: A Pentecoastal Mission to Bolivia in Anthropological Perspective*, Stockholm Studies in Social Anthropology.

Karp, I. (2002) 'Development and personhood: tracing the contours of a moral discourse', pp. 82–104 in Knauft, B. M. (ed) (2002) *Critically Modern: Alternatives, Alterities, Anthropologies*, Bloomington: Indiana University Press.

Knauft, B. M. (ed) (2002) Critically Modern: Alternatives, Alterities, Anthropologies, Bloomington: Indiana University Press.

Law, J. (ed) (1986) *Power, Action and Belief: A New Sociology of Knowledge*, London: Routledge and Kegan Paul.

Lewin, K. (1948) *Resolving Social Conflicts. Selected Papers on Group Dynamics*, New York: Harper & Row.

Mauss, M. (1990) *The Gift: The Form and Reason for Exchange in Archaic Societies*. Foreword by Mary Douglas, London: Routledge.

Nelson, N. and Wright, S. (eds) (1995) *Power and Participatory Development: Theory and Practice*, London: Intermediate Technology Publications.

Olsson, J. and Wohlgemuth, L. (eds) (2003) Dialogue in Pursuit of Development, Stockholm: Almqvist & Wiksell.

Paine, R. (1981) Politically Speaking: Cross-Cultural Studies of Rhetoric, Philadelphia: Institute for the Study of Human Issues.

Parkin, D. (1984) 'Political Language', Annual Review in *Anthropology*, 13: 345–365.

Paul. S (1987) Community participation in Development Projects, World Bank Discussion Paper 6, Washington DC.

Peters, P. (1996) 'Who's Local Here? The Politics of Participation in Development', *Cultural Survival Quarterly*, 20: 3.

Rabo, A. (1997) 'Free to make the right choice? Gender equality policy in post-welfare Sweden', pp. 107–131 in Shore, C. and Wright, S. (eds) (1997) *Anthropology of Policy*, London and New York: Routledge.

Rosander, E. E. (1992) 'People's Participation as Rhetoric in Swedish Development Aid', in Dahl, G. and Rabo, A. (eds) (1992) *Kam-Ap or Take-Off: Local Notions of Development*, Stockholm Studies in Social Anthropology, 29.

Shore, C. and Wright, S. (eds) (1997) *Anthropology of Policy: Critical Perspectives on Governance and Power,* London and New York: Routledge.

Sida (2006a) http://www.sida.se/Sida/articles/500-599/506/uhjalp.html, 'Från uhjälp till utvecklingssamarbete'.

Sida (2006b) http://www.sida.se/sida/jsp/sida.

Simmel, G. (1971) *George Simmel on Individuality and Social Forms,* Chicago: University of Chicago Press.

Stade, R. (1999) 'Cosmopolitical Studies: The Refiguration of Cultural Thought', paper presented at the Swedish Collegium for Advanced Study in the Social Sciences, Uppsala, Sweden, 14 October 1999, and at the Department of Social Anthropology, Stockholm University, Sweden, 8 November 1999.

Stewart, M. and Taylor, M. (1995) *Empowerment and Estate Regeneration: A Critical Review:* Bristol: Policy Press

Svenska missionsrådet (2003) Utvecklingssamarbete Syd – SMRs handbook – / Development Cooperation South, Handbook of the Swedish Missionary Council,/ updated 28 January 2003.

Tokura, C. (1994) Swedish Discourse on NGOs in Development Aid, Stockholm International Studies, 94: 2.

Trägårdh, L. (1999) 'Det civila samhället som analytiskt begrepp och politisk slogan', pp. 13–59, in Amnå, E. (ed) (1999) Civilsamhället. Demokratiutredningens forskarvolym, SOU 1999: 84.

Weeks, J. et al. (2002) Supporting Ownership: Swedish Development Cooperation with Kenya, Tanzania, and Uganda, volume I, Synthesis Report, Sida Evaluations 02/33, Stockholm: Swedish International Development Cooperation Agency.

Wohlgemuth, L. (ed) (1976) Bistånd på mottagarens villkor, Stockholm: Sida.

Wolfe, M. (ed) (1983) *Participation: The View from Above, Geneva:* UNRISD.

9
Civil Society, Faith-Based Organizations and Development in the Arab World

Saad Eddin Ibrahim

Introduction

The last three decades have witnessed growing recognition that if development is to be sustainable, more is required than following state-led prescriptions for economic growth. The latter is now understood as one dimension of development which can neither take root nor progress apace while cultural, social, and political development remain stagnant. Theoretical work on the subject of civil society has been essential to understanding the role played by cultural norms and social capital in both economic and democratic development (Putnam 1993; Fukuyama 2002). Indeed, freedom and thus democratic governance have become synonymous with development (Sen 1999). Notions of participation and empowerment have rendered civil society a third essential agent of development in theory and practice, though in no way a substitute for the state (public sector) or the private sector.

Civil society demonstrated its capacity to oust military dictatorships in Latin America and help end communist rule in eastern Europe. Throughout the 'third wave' of democratization, the people, organized in freely associative entities, have been indispensable in extracting greater political, social, and economic freedoms from the state, fostering good governance, alleviating poverty, and empowering the marginalized.

Why, however, has this wave of democratization so meekly broken on the shores of the Arab world? Impatient observers in the global community, and in Arab countries alike, desire an explanation for the lack of freedom and economic advancement in this part of the world. Some analysts have maintained that despotism is a culturally ingrained reality of the Arab or Muslim psyche, rendering them content with the status quo and incapable of achieving the freedom associated with western civilization. In this case, one might assume that civil society, the realm in which social capital is built and resides, and which is now considered requisite for development and democratization, has either never developed due to Islam or remains stunted to such a degree as to preclude further progress.

Little credence should be lent to theories that the citizens of the Arab world are any less willing or able than those of other cultures to pursue the freedom and dignity afforded to them as part of humanity. It should be noted, with emphasis, that the same was posited of German and Japanese societies until the Second World War. With respect to civil society, there is a tradition in the Arab world which predates contact with the West and the formation of the modern state. Civil society in this region has undergone ebbs and flows, and has been stunted only to the extent that authoritarian regimes have sought to stamp out its role in the public space. The resurgence of civil society since the 1970s, its burgeoning capacity in recent years, and more vocal calls for political reform are cause for optimism.

This chapter will examine the composition of civil society in the Arab world, with special attention to recent events in Egypt, the region's most populous state and the widely accepted cultural leader. An assessment of civil society's potential as a vehicle for development and democratization will be offered with emphasis on the increasingly important role played by faith-based organizations (FBOs), most notably the Muslim Brotherhood.

Conceptual framework

Development

Development is a multifaceted cluster concept which is no longer limited to material well-being. It is not within the scope of this work to critique the prescriptions of international financial institutions. Suffice it to say that most remain necessary for advancement in the globalized market economy, and require that the state, as well as the political and economic elite, retain their function in carrying out economic policy. Our goal here is to examine the socio-cultural factors which have until recently been underestimated, and are most appropriately encompassed by the United Nations in the term 'human development'. The latter includes 'human goals and aspirations: freedom, justice, and dignity' (Arab Human Development Report 2004). Economic growth, though a crucial element, is only part of this more inclusive definition of development.

Liberalization, democratization, and democracy

Political liberalization is taken here to imply political change which is initiated and managed by elites. It may leave the fundamental character of an authoritarian regime intact. Liberalization manifests itself in a greater openness to political freedoms, rights, and civil liberties such as a wider margin for free speech, a less censored press, and less stringent control over formation and free activity of voluntary organizations and political parties. Certain autocrats in the Arab world have learned to 'temper authoritarianism with pluralism' in a way that allows opposition groups and civil society to 'blow off steam' (Brumberg 2005). Thus, regimes in Morocco, Egypt, and Jordan exhibit greater pluralism than Tunisia, Libya, Saudi Arabia, and Syria where very little is tolerated. The defining characteristic of political liberalization is that it intentionally stops short of the fundamentals of democratization.

Democratization is a process which is characterized by the extension and institutionalization of individual and collective rights well beyond that of liberalization. Democratization would entail authentic political reform that holds elites accountable, institutionalizes democratic decision-making mechanisms, and redistributes power such that the share held by civil society is enhanced, the arbitrary use of power by the state is reduced, and the power of popular forces increased to a stable equilibrium. As democratization progresses, governance is increasingly undertaken by bargaining and compromise with a vibrant civil society. The end goal of democratization is, of course, a genuine democracy as largely practiced in the West.

Democracy can be defined as the set of rules and institutions – namely the rule of law, free and fair elections, and rotation of power – which is designed to enable a popular role in governance and to peacefully manage competing interests. In a democratic system, civil society increasingly has influence over the state, rather than being controlled by the state.

Civil society and social capital

Civil society can be defined with emphasis on the principle of free association, as any entities formed volitionally by their members to pursue a common objective, serve a cause, or express collective sentiments. These entities, which occupy the public space, can be found on a continuum between the family and the state. The organs of civil society are non-primordial associations. That is to say, they are neither inherited nor compulsory. While individuals cannot choose their family and rarely change their ties to a nation-state, they often change their volitional associations. Organizations which constitute civil society may have membership restrictions, but that membership always depends upon the wilful contractual engagement of a free individual. Civility, i.e. peaceful transaction, is known to be associated with civil society.

Social capital can be viewed as an output of civil society or civic associationalism: the norms of trust, reciprocity, and networks which enable sustainable development to take place (Putnam 1993). It is now recognized that social capital is a key ingredient for development. The extent to which trust exists within a society has a clear influence on the transaction cost of dealing with anyone outside the immediate family or clan. Therefore the existence of a strong civil society or its potential to be fostered will have a positive effect on development.

Civil society in its institutional form ranges from associations which provide welfare services at the community level to political parties which seek to influence decision-making, and to share or assume power at the national level.[1] The spectrum of civil society thus includes groups near one end point having functions similar to that of the nuclear family, and organizations at the other which approach the role of the state. The demarcation between civil society and state is commonly blurred, but should be recognizable to the extent that civil society is a highly diverse gamut of associations and institutions operating in accordance with the laws set by the state. Between the two end points on this continuum there lies a diversity of associative life which can be categorized for the purpose of closer examination.

The spectrum of civil society

We intend to trace the way in which voluntary formations of civil society can evolve from undertaking basic functions like the provision of welfare, through more sophisticated advocacy roles, and often into political life. Faith-based organizations have proven to be among the most effective at both undertaking this evolution and developing broad grassroots networks which cut across socio-economic formations in Arab society.

Proceeding from the family towards the state, we first observe organizations dedicated to providing for the welfare of a broader community of individuals, but doing so with the care and sensitivity found in familial relationships. This first category includes small clubs fostering basic solidarity and companionship, but also larger charity organizations. Next are development associations or non-governmental organizations (NGOs) which are not engaged in direct aid, but rather seek to enable groups or communities to take care of themselves through projects such as micro-finance, job training, educational assistance, cooperatives, and environmental groups. The third category consists of advocacy organizations engaged in protecting or promoting common interests from human rights, to the concerns of professional associations or organized labour, and the promotion of greater democracy. Finally, and abutting the boundaries of the state, are organizations such as protest movements which seek to influence the behaviour of the state, and political parties which desire an active role in sharing power. It follows, that once a political party gains a plurality of that power, they cease to be a part of civil society, and can be considered integrated to the functions of the state – at least for the duration of its electoral mandate.

The conception of a civil society organization occurs at a given point on the continuum in accordance with the articulated goals and interests of that entity. Some formations within civil society, however, exhibit greater consciousness of their interests and have thus been quicker than others in organizing their ranks to move along the continuum in a steady progression towards influencing, sharing, or exercising political power. Less conscious and less organized formations learn over time by emulation. While this evolution from left to right is not necessarily undergone by all civil society organizations, it is an observable trend which is central to the process of democratization.

Comparative advantage of civil society in development

Civil society is a training ground in problem solving and a leadership school for participatory and democratic governance. If human capacity is not first developed in civil society, then no amount of money thrown at a developing country is worthwhile without the capacity to make use of it.

First and foremost, civil society asserts the free will of individuals to organize collectively. Normatively, civil society implies values and behavioural codes of toleration, acceptance, and peaceful management of differences among competing or conflicting groups which share the same public space. Those norms, thus, overlap with the norms of democracy. As these organizations evolve, the members learn the art of compromise and skills essential to democratic governance. Individuals who establish their capacity at the community level often rise to greater prominence from the grassroots.

The members of civil society learn to assess and solve the problems of their community in a way which promotes decentralization. As communities become more capable of addressing their own needs, there is less reliance on the centralized state. This is the basis of substantial democracy where citizens participate as stakeholders in their future, rather than waiting for far-off elites to solve problems. Civil society can often act more quickly in response to the needs of communities and, while operating on a smaller scale, can readjust its mode of operation more quickly than a cumbersome bureaucracy. Moreover, though civil society organizations are not profit-driven, they still contribute to the economy through income and employment generating activities.

Civil society is not a substitute for state or market driven development, but helps to ensure a socially valued outcome that does not rely heavily on state interventionism. Alternative methods of achieving economic prosperity or equality can be explored by the organs of civil society. Indeed, at the grassroots level, civil society has often proven more effective in providing basic services than the private sector or the bureaucratic state. Civil society will be the realm in which social justice, equality, and the concerns of communities are vocalized, and faith-based organizations are often the first to raise concerns of social justice.

The organizations comprising civil society affect development from the ground up and learn to demand a greater role in participatory governance as they move through the continuum. Eventually, a critical mass of civil society, often in the form of a coalition among socio-economic formations, arrives at the threshold of the state with the capacity to articulate and defend its rights and interests. Thus, democratization is extracted from the state as civil society learns and grows.

Civil society-state relations

In theory, the state apparatus in a democracy is neutral and preserves a level playing field for all units of civil society. It must establish stability and an environment in which civil society can flourish. While this may be true to a greater extent in western democracies where civil society emerged simultaneously with the nation-state and the two have established symbiotic relationship, it is true to a lesser degree in the Arab world where authoritarian regimes have often exhibited hostility towards civil society. Likewise, in the absence of a robust civil society, the state can easily slip into a despotic entity and remain there. It should not be assumed, however, that the state and civil society in the Arab world are two monolithic entities engaged in a zero-sum game. This would be misleading and imply autonomy when the reality is one of far more complex interaction and interdependence.

Civil society must maintain a reasonably good relationship with the state – even under an authoritarian regime – in order that civil society functions properly. If the relationship with the state is too close, organizations from within civil society eventually become co-opted. If they distance themselves too far from the state or define themselves in opposition to it, then very little can be accomplished. To sustain the optimum balance is a continuous struggle, even in the most mature of democracies.

When the state, especially an autocratic regime, has a preponderance of power in all aspects of politics and life, civil society can be stifled. In the Arab world, myriad laws and decrees restrict free association, the formation of voluntary organizations, and large public gatherings. State interference in the realm of civil society is a detrimental reality. When the organs of civil society, whose existence is tolerated, are restricted to their respective premises and not allowed to work or exercise so to speak, they atrophy. In many cases, it is the tampering of the state which impedes the evolution of civil society organizations along the continuum. If the formations of civil society are restricted as they democratically attempt to take on a more participatory role, they may be forced to operate covertly, sidetracked from the continuum, or at worst, steered toward less civil and more undesirable means of having their voice heard. Organizations, deprived of a participatory role in governance, have at times branched off of the continuum and adopted violence as a means of expression or method of attempting to recalibrate the balance of power with the state. This will be witnessed in the evolution of the Muslim Brotherhood.

It does not follow, however, that a weak state is beneficial to the growth of civil society. In fact, a strong civil society rarely flourishes in the presence of a weak state, nor does a strong state flourish in the presence of a weak civil society. While no Arab country, with the possible exception of Morocco, presently has both a strong civil society and a strong state, most can be described as having both a weak civil society and a weak state. This is a potentially dangerous predicament as illustrated by the case of Somalia in the early 1990s. When the weak state collapsed, no civil society existed capable of helping society cope, and thus primordial clan or tribal relations dominated in the ensuing period of unrest. When a stronger civil society has existed in the event of a crisis in which the state breaks down – such as the Lebanese civil war or the invasion of Kuwait – civil society continued to function through the crisis, offering partial alleviation and helping the society to recover in the aftermath.

Moreover, comprehensive development requires a state which is sufficiently strong to enforce the rule of law, competent and transparent enough in the formation of policy, and in possession of the legitimacy needed to make and enforce economic decisions (Fukuyama 2002). If development is to progress apace, especially economic aspects thereof, the dedication of political elites is a requirement. The private sector and civil society are necessary complements which ideally work in tandem with the state, but lack the capacity to bear the burden alone.

Faith-based organizations

The notion of faith-based development has recently come to prominence with the Bush administration in the United States, which has funded faith-based organizations as a way to compete with liberal and secular civil society organizations. American donor agencies have begun to apportion a substantial sum to faith-based organizations which used to lie outside the development literature and the practice of development work, at least in the last few decades. The development field has begun to acknowledge the role which faith-based organizations can play at the community level. Indeed, organizations bound by the glue of common faith and endowed with an innate stock of social capital, may have a comparative advantage over secular formations within civil society.

Arab civil society's resurgence since the 1970s has coincided with the withering credibility and scope of the region's post-populist authoritarian regimes, large-scale globalization, and a resurgence of religiosity. As secular regimes have failed to deliver development, or have exacerbated income inequality through practices which are perceived as part of a western 'neo-liberal' agenda, Islamic movements, often with a nationalist agenda, have experienced a surge in popular support. Indeed, organs of civil society which are anchored in religious faith have grown exponentially and most possess a staggering grassroots network that dwarfs its secular counterparts. Some organizations, which are in fact far older, have in the period since the 1970s been able to take on a more significant role as the financially strapped state has retreated from the provision of welfare and other services. In Egypt, as in much of the Arab world, the Muslim Brotherhood is the example par excellence. A more thorough survey of the Brotherhood and other faith-based organizations will be undertaken below.

The continuum of civil society resolves the dilemma of where to fit religious groups. Hamas, Hizbollah, and the Muslim Brotherhood among others, are certainly all part of civil society. Though they are the basis of a common faith and in some cases a specific sect, their membership is still voluntary. They are neither family, nor primordial. Membership requirements having been met, these organizations are joined by people of their own free will. Civil society can be empowered by faith-based organizations as long as they pursue development goals and refrain from promoting or engaging in sectarian conflict. Faith-based organizations have an innate endowment of social capital because they speak the language of a common faith within the community and thus benefit from the trust of those for whom they are attempting to provide aid.

When they work through existing mosques and churches, faith-based organizations have a natural place and an established constituency within a community. Faith-based organizations are instinctively in tune with the needs, values, and mores of a community. A clear advantage of organizations bound by the glue of a common faith is that they have an easier time in recruiting those who would volunteer their time and money to a cause in which they have faith and trust. A doctor or lawyer, for instance, might feel more compelled to volunteer pro-bono assistance with the conviction that they are donating their work to a trustworthy and worthwhile cause. Religion not only supplies the motives – love, compassion, charity – but also defines the content of their work (Thomas 2004). Organizations thus find religious reasons to provide for greater social justice and wrap their assistance in the discourse of their faith.

Furthermore, zeal can compensate for lack of resources. When people feel that they are contributing to a good cause, or in some cases to God, they bring with them a level of passion and determination which might be lacking in secular organizations. An hour of their time becomes more productive and they are often more creative. Many organizations, whether in the private, public, or civic sector, fail due to a poor incentive structure. If the incentive is eternal life or salvation in the hereafter, the incentive becomes inexhaustible.

Faith-based organizations in a local civil society also have an inherent connection to international organizations which can offer vital transmission of experience, techniques, information and funding. For example, Catholic organizations might find this link in the international humanitarian network Caritas. Muslim organizations benefit from Islamic Relief, among others.

Civil society in the Arab world

An historical tradition of civil society: Its pre-modern forms

Some have argued that civil society is a western notion, implying that the Arab world has not known civil society in the past. This is not entirely true, as the Arab and greater Muslim world has indeed known these types of voluntary organizations. Even in Medieval times, civil society was present in Islam as evidenced by Sufi orders, apprentice occupational groups, brotherhoods, and endowments. Endowments, or *al qaf,* were created by wealthy Muslims to provide services which the pre-modern state apparatus of the time was unable to provide its people. The *sabil* is an example.

Pre-modern society in what is now called the Arab world was fairly closely ordered around a political authority whose legitimacy was derived from a combination of conquest and religious sources. The public space was immediately shared by the *ulama* (learned men of religion), merchants, guilds, Sufi orders, and *millat* (sects). Outside this first concentric zone, the public space was populated by peasants and tribes, where political authority asserted itself most clearly. Outside the first zone, its assertion varied markedly – in most cases it was hardly felt. Other collectives, especially the tribes, were quite autonomous from, if not outright defiant of, the central authority. Then in the first concentric zone, often within city walls, various groups coexisted and interacted with a great deal of autonomy. Guilds, religious sects, and ethnic groups ran most of their own internal affairs through elders, elected or appointed leaders. The latter were accountable to both the political authority and their own communities. Tension, no doubt, existed within each category but was of low intensity. Equally, tension may have existed between or among two or more of these communities, but was often resolved inter-communally. Only occasionally did it warrant the direct intervention of the political authority.

This traditional equilibrium of governance was maintained by a multitude of mechanisms such as clear hierarchies, occupational and residential segregation, and autonomous resources (mostly from *awkaf* or *hubus* religious endowments). Social solidarities existed along occupational, religious, and ethnic lines. Central authority collected taxes, administered justice through the *shari'a,* maintained public order and defence, and occasionally patronized the arts and sciences. Social services and direct economic functions were not expected obligations of the 'state', but were mostly left to local communities. In this sense,

traditional Arab society not only knew the equivalent of civil formations but also depended on them for survival. Individuals relied on
these formations for their identity and most of their basic needs. In this
manner they were insulated from direct dealing with the political
authority. In the traditional equilibrium, the public space in which civil
formations interacted coincided with the physical space in which they
lived and worked.

This traditional equilibrium of governance was occasionally disrupted
by seditions (*fitan*, singular *fitna*) or calamities (*nakbat*, singular *nakba*).
The Arabic political vocabulary referred to *fitna* as a sharp internal
strife, usually accompanied by armed conflict. A *nakba*, meanwhile,
referred to an invasion by an alien (non-Muslim) power, often accompanied by mass looting, destruction, and dislocation. Both *fitan* and
nakbat would lead to disintegration of this traditional equilibrium for a
shorter or longer time. Often, however, the equilibrium would be pieced
together and would reassert itself. At least this seemed to be the case for
much of the first 12 centuries of Arab-Islamic history.

The last two centuries have witnessed what seems to be an irreversible
disintegration of the traditional equilibrium of governance and its
accompanying socio-economic symbiosis, a direct function of western
penetration of Arab-Muslim societies and those societies' coercive integration in the budding world-system. Most of the traditional civil formations were to wither away, and new ones were born through the
hardest of labour. Among the latter was the new Arab 'state' itself. With
the advent of the modern state, many of these traditional organizations
dwindled in influence or became obsolete and disappeared.

The birth of modern civil society

As the Arab state was born, albeit painfully and under the forced guidance of western powers, new forms of economic and political governance made the traditional formations of civil society obsolete. The Arab
world shared some, but not all, of the processes that had accompanied
the emergence of the modern state and civil society in the West – such
as the withering away of traditional equilibriums, rapid population
growth, and urbanization. But the processes of capitalization and industrialization lagged far behind and new socio-economic formations,
which are the backbone of the modern state and civil society, have not
grown progressively or evenly. Nonetheless, modern forms of civil society emerged on the basis of these socio-economic formations such as
classes, occupational categories, and interest groups during capitalization and industrialization.

The inception phase for modern forms occurred during the nineteenth century, not long after Napoleon's arrival in Egypt. The first modern civil society organization was established in Egypt in 1821, an expatriate community of Greeks called the Hellenic Welfare Association. The Association was formed, not based on kinship, but on common interest among those facing common challenges in a foreign country. We use that as the original date for the start of modern civil society organizations in Egypt and the Arab world.

Despite the authoritarian nature of governance in many Arab states for much of their post-independence history, the seeds of modern civil society have sprouted in nearly all of them. Some of these new civil organizations, especially in the northern tier of the Arab world, date back to the second half of the nineteenth century, but they increased in number and thrived in the interwar period (1918–1939). Civil society flourished in this period as universities, theatres, museums, hospitals, and medical centres were all established by civil society. Under colonial rule, many of them took on the explicitly political role of liberating their respective countries. From the ranks of these organizations emerged the leaders of independence.

A few years after independence, several Arab states witnessed a wave of radical politics, mostly through populist military coups. These radical regimes ended the liberal experiments that some of their societies had engaged in briefly before and immediately after independence. One-party rule, or rule by junta, became the dominant pattern of governance. The new populist regimes gave the state an expansionist socioeconomic role. An explicit or implicit social contract was forged under the terms of which the state was to affect development, ensure social justice, satisfy the basic needs of its citizens, consolidate political independence, and achieve other national aspirations like Arab unity or the liberation of Palestine. In return, citizens would forgo, at least for the time being, participatory politics. This social contract was popularized in pan-Arab nationalism and socialist ideologies.

The populist social contract had, among other things, a detrimental impact, not only on existing political parties, but also on other organizations of civil society. The latter were either prohibited or severely restricted by an arsenal of laws and decrees or were annexed outright to the single party in power. Under populist rule, civil society lost part or all of its autonomy.

The defeat of populist regimes at the hands of Israel in 1967 and successive reversals, culminating in the 1990–1991 Persian Gulf crisis, led to the discrediting of the populist social contract and the steady erosion of the legitimacy of most Arab regimes. Clinging to power, many populist regimes escalated their oppression, others engaged in external adventures, while some did both.

The expansionist role of the Arab state seems to have reached its zenith in the 1970s, in rich and poor countries alike. As state budgets declined and social spending was cut back, largely due to neo-liberal prescriptions for economic growth, state services have largely been reduced to protecting the regime's base in middle class and elite urban areas. The social contract of the populist era was abandoned. In most cases, that retreat has been disordered, leaving in its aftermath structural and situational misery that could have been avoided or reduced had civil society been in better shape. In many cases, the public space vacated by the state has been filled by often extremist Islamist movements that had been covertly active in spite of state oppression. Islamist organizations stepped in to provide social services that states were no longer providing, and in fact benefited from the economic stabilization and structural adjustment programmes of the IMF and the World Bank which created a growing income inequality and popular disenchantment with what to many appeared as foreign domination.

The Muslim Brotherhood's evolution in Egypt

Though the word brotherhood implies a family bond which might appear to be primordial, the Muslim Brotherhood is in all respects a voluntary formation of civil society. Founded in 1928 by Hassan Al Banna, the Muslim Brotherhood arose as a modern organization for religious solidarity which filled a spiritual vacuum vacated with the fall of the Ottoman Empire, the last traditional pan-Islamic empire. The Muslim Brotherhood, at first providing welfare at the village or community level, has evolved through the entire continuum of civil society, never giving up a single function along the way and recently winning 88 out of 454 seats in the 2005 Egyptian parliamentary elections. The organization's development from welfare provision to political representation has not always progressed smoothly, having been sidetracked from the continuum and engaging in violence at times. Nonetheless, the Brotherhood has survived attempts at containment, domination, intimidation, and destruction to emerge as the most powerful faith-based organization of civil society in the Arab world. The Muslim Brotherhood's evolution and its history are illustrative of the evolution undergone by civil society formations as well as of the role played by faith-based organizations in development.

Hassan Al Banna, a simple man of conviction and charisma, created the Muslim Brotherhood by travelling from village to village. He would stay for roughly ten days in each community, preaching the message of Islam and establishing a sustainable infrastructure which would continue to do the core work (*al dawa*) of preserving Islamic values, educating, and socializing young Muslims with pride in their faith, heritage, and future. The inherent religiosity of Egyptian villages was fertile ground where the content of his message, that if one follows the path of Islam, corruption and injustice will be eliminated, resonated among Muslims of all ages and continues to do so today. The Muslim Brotherhood was founded as a simple movement calling people to Islam, and was never intended to become a political movement.

The collapse of the Ottoman Empire coincided with a rising tide of nationalist sentiments in Arab countries. A year after acquiring nominal independence, Egypt created its first constitution in 1923, still under the auspices of the British. By 1930, the Muslim Brotherhood already possessed an astounding grassroots network throughout Egypt and became an integral part of the push for British withdrawal, to an even greater degree after a 1936 treaty in which the British agreed to move its presence in the country to the Suez Canal region. Political power was in the hands of three competing actors: the British, the Egyptian monarchy, and the nationalist Wafd Party, which led the drive for independence. The Wafd Party was popular and tolerated by the monarchy, though on multiple occasions when it won parliamentary power in democratic elections, the king dissolved the parliament. In spite of winning a majority several times between 1923 and 1952, Wafd only governed for a total of seven and a half years. During this period, the popularity of the Muslim Brotherhood grew progressively.

By the late 1940s, the Brotherhood already had a desire for political participation and took part in the planning of the 1952 Free officers' coup which overthrew King Faruq and brought Colonel Gamal Abdel Nasser to power. Nasser, however, reneged on any previous agreement and, viewing the Muslim Brotherhood as a threat to his consolidation of power, outlawed the organization in 1954. The Brotherhood was forced underground and a failed assassination attempt on Nasser in 1954 landed thousands of the organization's activists in prison.

One of these activists was Sayyid Qutb, a writer and former government official whose writings, largely those completed in prison, formed the foundation of Islamic radicalism and several offshoots of the Muslim Brotherhood in Egypt which espoused violence in the next half century (Benjamin and Simon 1966). Qutb was released in 1964, plotted another coup attempt in 1965, and was promptly executed in 1966. Thousands of Brothers were again arrested. Egypt's defeat at the hands of Israel in the 1967 war was a crushing blow to Nasser's pan-Arab ideology and gave way to much contemplation. The Egyptian population, in a large part, concluded that Nasser's Arab socialism had turned the country away from Islam and the result was a dramatic rise in religiosity, as well as growing sympathy with the Muslim Brotherhood.

The Muslim Brothers who were imprisoned at this time, still in shock that the Egyptian people had not risen behind them to overthrow what they perceived as an atheist dictator, also re-evaluated their approach. They concluded that it was imprudent to confront an authoritarian regime head-on, that the time was not yet right for a rise to political power, and redesigned the organization again to building support gradually through their civil society roots at the community level. This period can be considered the NGO phase of the Muslim Brotherhood's evolution along the civil society continuum as they continued to provide food and medical care for the needy, and to run youth education and vocational training programmes in Mosques. During the oppression of the Nasser era, several prominent businessmen with ties to the Muslim Brotherhood sought refuge in Saudi Arabia where they grew wealthy and awaited an opportunity to return to Egypt.

This opportunity came in 1970 when Anwar Sadat assumed power upon Nasser's death. Sadat reversed Nasser's populist social contract, sought political support among the middle and elite classes, aligned Egypt with the West, instituted the *infitah* (open door) policy in 1974 upon regaining the Sinai in the 1973 Arab-Israel war, and began to tolerate the Muslim Brotherhood, releasing those who were jailed and allowing others to return to Egypt. Many of those who had left for Saudi Arabia during the Nasser era repression returned and amassed significant wealth, often in collaboration with Sadat's regime. The *infitah* economic policy was the demise of state-led development in the Middle East, but formed a new upper middle class of entrepreneurs, and by 1980, eight of the 18 families who dominated Egypt's economy were affiliated with the Muslim Brothers. The leadership of the Muslim Brotherhood in the 1970s and 1980s largely came from this new landed bourgeoisie (Benin 2005). The *infitah* policy incorporated cuts in the state budget and subsidies as per the IMF prescription, and the public sector was no longer able to provide the former level of social services, creating a windfall of Brotherhood support as they picked up the slack. A simultaneously increasing number of university graduates from 1975 to 1985 created an aggrieved class of educated young men unable to find employment and amass the necessary wealth for marriage. They formed the new social base of the Muslim Brotherhood.

Many of the students who became activist leaders on university campuses during the 1970s were Muslim Brothers who came from Egypt's rural areas and graduated in the elite fields of medicine, pharmacy, law, and engineering. President Hosni Mubarak came to power in 1981 after Sadat was assassinated by violent offshoots of the Muslim Brotherhood, Jamaah Islamiya (Islamic Group) and Al Jihad, but initially established an open posture toward political reform. In spite of reinstated emergency law in 1981, he did not initially crack down on the Muslim Brotherhood, and the organization was allowed to form an electoral alliance with the Wafd Party in the 1984 parliamentary elections and some of the most prominent former student leaders were elected. The Brotherhood also conceived a plan to contest the leadership of professional associations, enrolling over one million of these newly graduated young men in medical, dental, pharmaceutical, legal, and engineering syndicates. By 1992, nearly all professional associations, including the traditionally leftist Journalists' Association, were in the hands of the Muslim Brotherhood. The Mubarak regime's response was to tamper significantly in the associations and to change the electoral regulations of professional associations by instituting new and undemocratic rules, which prevented elections from being decided without a majority turnout of eligible voters.

Nonetheless, the success of the Muslim Brotherhood in assuming control of the professional associations marked yet another phase in the organization's evolution and provided significant training in electioneering and politics. Had the professional associations remained a democratic environment, it would have been the ideal time for the Brotherhood to gain further experience in the art of democratic compromise before rising to greater prominence in national politics.

The Muslim Brotherhood has benefited in many ways from globalization and learned to harness its force. Globalization largely aided resurgent religiosity among Egypt's population with the perception that it was a vehicle of the West in an attempt to economically and culturally invade Arab-Muslim countries. This perceived threat to cultural identity and civilization authenticity has lent greater popular support to the Brotherhood as it decried the income inequality created by state-led development policies and continuously raised the flag of Islamic nationalism. Meanwhile, the new middle class intelligentsia of the Muslim Brotherhood has adapted to the globalized economy. The organization now holds bank accounts and offshore investment companies in the

Isle of Man, Switzerland, and the Bahamas. It has forged connections with the World Islamic Council and Islamic relief, helped establish satellite television channels, continued to permeate radio airwaves, and developed a mastery of electronic networking which aids them in organizing large-scale demonstrations.

The Muslim Brotherhood takes its place on the national stage

The recent electoral success of the Muslim Brotherhood in the 2005 parliamentary elections has given rise to many questions regarding their upsurge in popularity and commitment to democracy, especially in light of the dismal performance of secular opposition forces. Western attention to the promotion of democracy in the Middle East and the pressure which has accompanied it in recent years can largely claim responsibility for the Mubarak regime's narrow democratic overture in Egypt. A multi-candidate presidential election was contested for the first time in September 2005. While the Muslim Brotherhood, still denied legal party status, did not field a candidate, they did explicitly encourage their supporters to vote for the candidate of their choosing, so long as he 'was not a despot or a tyrant'. This encouragement was, in fact, a very sophisticated voter education effort. Knowing that the parliamentary elections of November were coming close on the heels of the presidential election and nearly 160 Muslim Brothers would be running as independent candidates, it was important for voters to become familiar with voting lists, regulations, and local polling places. Using openly for the first time the traditional Brotherhood slogan, 'Islam is the Solution', the organization won 88 of 454 seats in the new parliament. Fewer than 20 candidates of the legally recognized secular opposition parties won seats. The Muslim Brotherhood's gradual evolution left it as the only opposition force poised to benefit from marginally freer elections.

After the long tenure of authoritarianism and emergency law, secular opposition has remained weak and insignificant, while the Muslim Brotherhood has progressively developed its capacity from the grassroots up, emerging as Egypt's strongest oppositional force. Rarely granted permits are required for secular organizations and political parties to operate in the public space, which means that as long as they have been relegated to their campaign headquarters, unable to use their platform and develop a constituency, their popularity has withered away. The Muslim Brotherhood and other Islamist groups are an exception because of their work at the grassroots level and the ability to access their constituency on Fridays and five times every day in the thousands of mosques. Hardly able to close down mosques, the Mubarak regime has resorted to mass arrests and disenfranchisement in an attempt to curb the Brotherhood's gradual march into electoral politics.

Many analysts, secular Egyptians and especially the 10 million Coptic Christians, have reacted with fear to the Brotherhood's recent success. It remains unclear to many whether the Muslim Brotherhood will respect the rules of the democratic game. It seems clear that the organization ran fewer candidates than would have been needed to gain one third of the Egyptian parliament, the fraction necessary to block legislation put forth by the ruling National Democratic Party, in order to preclude a massive reactionary crackdown from the regime, or worse a situation like that which occurred in Algeria in 1991. In spite of having sworn off violence in the early 1990s, some still fear that the Muslim Brotherhood desires little more of liberal democracy than free and fair elections.

What does this success mean for the future of democratic development and civil society in Egypt, especially if the Brotherhood continues to amass greater political power? It can be claimed with relative certainty that it is better for Islamists, those who incorporate the teachings of the Quran, the hadith, and shari'a in their political agenda, to gain power by elections rather than by civil war or revolution as was the case in Afghanistan, Sudan, and Iran. All empirical evidence from countries in which Islamists have entered the political arena – Turkey, Jordan, Yemen, and Morocco – substantiates the claim of politics as a moderating norm for Islamists. In none of these latter countries have Islamists reneged on the rules of democracy. Their success may in fact revitalize the liberal and secular elements of Egyptian civil society, but that largely depends on the degree to which the regime keeps narrow the public space for these other non-state players.

The Muslim Brotherhood's rise to political prominence on the national level represents the completion of their evolution through the continuum of civil society. From its beginnings in 1928, the Muslim Brothers have benefited from the training ground offered by civil society. They have learned grassroots development providing services at the community level, the articulation of advocacy, political entrepreneurship in professional syndicates, and outlasted the repression and fatigue of authoritarian regimes. Though they were indeed sidetracked from the continuum and fell into a period of violent opposition, the norms of civil society seem to have prevailed. At present, the Muslim Brotherhood's middle class leadership and its grassroots base may provide the sort of class alliance necessary to push for further democratic reforms. It is evident that on the national stage, the organization will continue to fight against corruption and for greater social justice. For now, one must accept, even if sceptically, the Muslim Brotherhood's professed commitment to democratic values, and hope that the norms of civil society prevail.

Hamas' reluctant evolution from protest to politics

Hamas, whose name is an acronym for the Islamic liberation movement that also means 'zeal' in Arabic, came into existence during the first intifada in 1988. It was rumoured at the time that it was encouraged by the Israeli authorities as a rival of the Palestine Liberation Organization (PLO) and its main faction, the Fatah movement headed by Yasser Arafat, as a way of creating dissention and weakening all Palestinian parties. True or not, it took Hamas several years before it gained prominence and credibility. However, it was not until the second intifada in the year 2000, known as the al-Aqsa uprising, that Hamas would have significantly expanded its following and attracted worldwide attention. This was particularly done through its newly innovated suicide tactics. Though losing sympathy and respect worldwide, those tactics enhanced its standing with the Palestinians, especially in the refugee camps. Its approval rate inched up steadily from less than ten per cent before the al-Aqsa intifada to as high as 20 per cent by 2005.

Thanks to the failure of the Oslo Accord, signed in 1993, to deliver the promise of an independent Palestinian state and a better life for the people, Hamas had rejected the Oslo process and as time passed they reminded the Palestinian people of how prophetic they had been and reiterated that the only way to liberate all of Palestine is a continuous *jihad* (Islamic holy war).

Most observers, however, failed to take note that, apart from the suicide operations inside Israel by the Hamas fighters (referred to as martyrs), there was steady provision of basic services to the needy Palestinians in the refugee camps and employment for young Palestinians newly graduated from college. Although the Palestinian Authority has never been quite a state, as a quasi-state it was an embodiment of what many social scientists had called 'failed' states even in embryonic form, i.e. it failed to develop the economy, provide basic services, mobilize its population behind a national project, and it failed to project good governance. Tales of corruption in high places were circulating among middle class Palestinians as well as in refugee camps, and some of the manifestations of that were the ebullient private homes that some leaders of the

PLO built along the Mediterranean coast of Gaza and Rafah, or in the heart of the West Bank. In pointed contrast, the leaders of Hamas, many of whom grew up in the refugee camps, have maintained modest life-styles and projected an image of personal piety and incorruptibility. This, of course, has added to their popularity at a time of deteriorating living conditions in the West Bank and Gaza.

Hamas, however, remained cool if not outright sceptical about 'democracy'. Not only did it refrain from participating in the 1996 elections, but it also called for a boycott of the January 2005 presidential and following parliamentary elections after the death of Yasser Arafat. However, as the majority of Palestinians did not heed the boycott call and turned out in record numbers to participate in the elections, despite some 800 Israeli roadblocks, Hamas leaders seemed to have got the message. Coupled with other regional events like an Iraqi election later in the same month, a burgeoning 'Kefaya' movement against Mubarak in Egypt, and a Lebanese uprising calling for democracy and a withdrawal of Syrian forces following the assassination of former Prime Minister Rafiq al-Hariri, Hamas leaders revised their stand on the issue of democracy, recognizing what people all over the Middle East seem to want. This was further reinforced by similar enthusiasm about municipal elections in Saudi Arabia, the presidential and parliamentary elections in Pakistan, the amendment of the Kuwaiti constitution to allow for women to participate in politics on a more equal basis, and the issuance of a draft Qatari constitution.

Hamas first dipped its toe into democratic waters in the end of 2005 during the municipal elections, when they took control of a number of municipal councils. Following their success there, Hamas decided to jump in the pool in the 2006 parliamentary contests. To their surprise as well as that of the world, they won a plurality, putting them on top and guaranteeing them the formation of the new Palestinian government. The elections were internationally monitored, and former US President Carter testified as head of the monitoring team that the voting was largely free and fair. Equally impressive were the absence of violence and the smooth transition of power from Fatah to the newly elected Hamas.

Instead of welcoming these developments, shocked western observers argued for pressure to be applied in order to force Hamas to change its position. This writer, having met and spoken with the new Hamas parliamentarians and top officials, found a new spirit of willingness to move gradually from their former strategy of armed resistance to peaceful participation in ordinary politics. They were asking for time to effect the transition and reminded that the ultimatum to recognize Israel by the United States and the European Union fails to recognize that it took Egypt 30 years – from 1948 to 1978 – before it made the transition from belligerency to peace, and yet Hamas was not even allowed three months to make its move. Its leaders fear that their more radical members, raised as fervent believers in the *jihad* against the Zionist enemy, are not yet ready for such a significant departure from the movement's ideology.

Based on other liberation movements from South Africa (the African National Congress) to the Irish Republican Army (IRA) to Fatah in Palestine, they all evolve from their militant radicalism into politics as a norm. We saw signs of that within Hamas, and the Brotherhood in Egypt seems to be moving in that direction as well. Therefore, it behoves pro-democracy circles in the Arab world as well as in the West to encourage and bless this tendency, especially as any other alternative would be more costly, at least for the time being.

For our general thesis, however, both the Muslim Brothers and Hamas, and before them the Justice and Development Party in Turkey (AKP) and the Partie de Justice et Democratie in Morocco have travelled similar routes. They nearly all started as faith-based organizations as a vertical take-off point of departure, and now that they end up in power it looks as if this gradual transition will be the prevailing wave in the next decade at least.

Note

1. Political parties, though not universally considered part of civil society by all scholars, fit within this conceptual framework because free will to join the party is the essential element of their composition.

References

Benin, J. (2005) 'Political Islam and the New Global Economy: The Political Economy of an Egyptian Social Movement', *The New Centennial Review*, 5(1): 111–139.

Benjamin, D. and Simon, S. (1966) *The Age of Sacred Terror*, New York: Random House.

Brumberg, D. (2005) 'Liberalization versus Democracy: Understanding Arab Political Reform', in Carothers, T. and Ottaway, M. (eds) (2005) *Uncharted Journey: Promoting Democracy in the Middle East*, Washington, DC: Carnegie Endowment for International Peace.

Carothers, T. and Ottaway, M. (eds) (2005) *Uncharted Journey: Promoting Democracy in the Middle East*, Washington, DC: Carnegie Endowment for International Peace.

Fukuyama, F. (2002) 'Social Capital and Development: The Coming Agenda', *SAIS Review,* 22(1): 23–37.

Putnam, R. D. (1993) *Making Democracy Work: Civic Traditions in Modern Italy,* Princeton: Princeton University Press.

Sen, A. K. (1999) *Development as Freedom,* New York: Knopf.

Thomas, S. M. (2004) 'Building Communities of Character: Foreign Aid Policy and Faith-Based Organizations', *SAIS Review,* 24(2): 133–148.

UNDP (2004) *Arab Human Development Report,* New York: UNDP.

10
The Cultural Dimension of Gender in Education

Penina Mlama

Gender and development

Vigorous analysis has been done related to the gender dimension of development, and many theories have been advanced on the need to integrate this dimension in development processes. Approaches have moved from that of 'Women in Development' to 'Gender and Development' and to 'Women and Empowerment'. The main focus has been on how to ensure that women and men have equal opportunities and get equal returns from development processes, and on providing equal protection of the human rights of both genders.

Many gender-based hindrances to development have been exposed in the process of trying to position women's and men's welfare on equal footing. Foremost among the hindrances are the deeply entrenched patriarchal economic and social structures that have for centuries relegated women to an inferior and disadvantaged position to men. In many societies women have no right to ownership of the means of production or the products of their labour. Legal and governance structures also deny women many rights, while cultural values and attitudes as well as socialization processes condition the society to believe and enforce the superiority of man over woman.

The attainment of gender equality in development therefore calls for the elimination of such structural forms of gender inequality that permeate all spheres of life.

Numerous steps have been taken at all levels to fight various forms of gender discrimination. Globally, the United Nations has been at the forefront of efforts to make gender equality a basic human right. This is manifested in various UN declarations and conventions and other documents, including the UN Declaration on the Elimination of

Discrimination against Women (1967), the UN Convention on the Elimination of All Forms of Discrimination against Women (1981), the World Plan of Action for the Implementation of the Objectives of the International Women's Year (Mexico City, 1975), the Nairobi Forward-Looking Strategies for the Advancement of Women Towards 2000 (1985), the Beijing Declaration and Platform of Action (Beijing, 1995,) and the Millennium Development Goals (2000).

The UN world conferences from which these declarations and conventions emerged helped to put the limelight on gender in relation to development. Numerous regional, sub-regional, and national fora have also been organized as a means of keeping the gender issue on the development agenda. In addition, gender has featured prominently in most sector development fora to such an extent that today it is not politically correct not to address gender in any serious discussion on development.

At the national level, governments have given the gender dimension of development increasing attention. Action has included creation of ministries in charge of gender issues, legal reforms to provide equal rights to women and men, elimination of gender discriminatory laws, especially those relating to property ownership, inheritance and marriage, setting up of gender desks in sector ministries, provision of equal access to education for girls and boys, and reducing the gender gap in governance structures, especially through the promotion of women in senior decision-making positions.

Civil society has been at the forefront fighting for gender equality. Indeed, most of the gains in favour of women's rights have been won through the relentless efforts of civil society. Civil society interventions have involved all sectors, including economic, political, legal, educational, health, and other social sectors. Of major significance is the continuous advocacy for gender equality at all levels and in all spheres, in which civil society movements have excelled.

The success of civil society is largely attributed to the fact that it operates at the grass root level and, in most cases, with the marginalized and disadvantaged. This has plunged civil society into the realities of the impact of gender inequality and forced it to come up with practical solutions. It is therefore not by coincidence that today, as compared to, say, ten years ago, most governments are working in collaboration with civil society to incorporate their best practices into mainstream processes for change.

Such efforts have borne fruit in the sense that many significant changes have taken place towards reducing the gender gap in various sectors. The last decade has seen an increased number of women on decision-making positions in for example cabinets, parliaments, ministries, institutions, and governmental and non-governmental organizations. In many countries, legislation now enables women to own property. Sub-Sahara Africa, which has lagged behind in the education of girls in particular, has recorded a significant increase in school enrolment for girls between 1990 and 2000 (UNESCO 2003/2004).

Numerous studies and documents have analysed and recorded the above processes, their achievements, and challenges. It is clear, however, that, despite significant achievements, much remains to be done before any claim of success in attaining gender equality can be made.

It is the contention of this paper that the cultural factor of gender equality and development remains the most elusive. Development strategies continue to ignore the cultural impediments to development and instead concentrate mostly on economic and political factors. For example, economic empowerment of women is concentrated in providing economic opportunities, such as credit facilities or acquisition of entrepreneurial skills, without attention to the culturally determined factors that prevent women from controlling resources at the household level.

It is important to recognize the fact that the culturally determined male superiority in Africa, for example, leading to male control of property and family income, can easily lead to misuse of the benefits of economic ventures, and thus keep a family in perpetual poverty. Examples abound of how income generated by women cooperatives in rural Africa has forcefully been taken by husbands as heads of families, and ended up in misuse such as excessive beer-drinking. The wives, who according to cultural traditions are expected to be subservient to their husbands, have not been able to challenge this male control, and where they have tried to do so, they have received no support from the family or the community.

It is sad to note that, even though there have been many programmes to improve women's welfare in Africa through credit facilities, setting up of cooperatives or entrepreneurial training, since the cultural framework at the household level has been ignored, there has been little improvement in the welfare of women and their families. Indeed, in many cases cooperative economic ventures have caused much distress in families, sometimes leading to divorce. The main problem is the cultural framework which makes a man refuse to accept a situation where his wife can independently earn money and be in control. This is because cultural values and attitudes dictate that the husband must be in control of property and family income. In fact, even contemporary highly educated women, employed in the formal sector in urban areas, are grappling with culturally determined negative reactions of husbands who cannot accept economic superiority or independence of a woman.

Similarly, legal provisions in many African countries make it difficult for women to own or inherit property. This reinforces customary laws that recognize only men as rightful inheritors of property, regardless of a woman's contribution or birthright. This situation often throws women and their children into abject poverty, especially on the death of a husband or father. It is difficult to imagine the pain a bereaved woman goes through in losing the benefits of all the labour she has put into the acquisition of the family property when her husband dies. The HIV/AIDS pandemic in Africa has accentuated the viciousness of this culturally determined injustice, whereby wives or daughters on a daily basis lose all their property to male inheritors. Considering that HIV/AIDS is claiming millions of lives, leaving millions of orphans behind, it is shuddering to imagine the many lives that are destroyed and will continue to be destroyed by these cultural practices. Unfortunately, women are very often not in a position to redress the injustices due to the complexity and people-unfriendly nature of the legal systems and the predominant values and attitudes that condone such practices. Their families and the society at large, normally do not support women's action to redress injustices, and can even ostracize the bereaved for infringing upon accepted norms.

A lot of emphasis has also been placed on political empowerment, through giving women more opportunities to participating in decision-making bodies and democratic processes such as voting or taking up political positions in parliaments and cabinets. Little attention, however, is paid to the male dominance of the political structures, which often makes it almost impossible for women who join the political ranks to be effective. For example, whereas there has been a significant increase of female parliamentarians in many African countries, with Rwanda's 49 per cent being the highest number in the world, many of them have not been effective in bringing about gender equality through legislation. Many bills that are not gender responsive at all are passed through parliament without resistance from female parliamentarians. Female parliamentarians often get drawn into supporting male-led political power plays and factions, losing sight of the interests of women on whose ticket they entered the parliament. In most cases, they simply sit quietly through their parliamentary terms.

It is indeed unrealistic to expect a woman to have the skills of political participation, including speaking in public, debating, lobbying, or even manipulating, because in the traditional cultural set up and social-ization processes these are male domains and women are therefore not equipped with such skills. Many political development strategies, including the much publicized introduction of western-style demo-cratic rule, pay little or no attention to the cultural factors that seriously impede gender equality in political participation.

From these few examples, it is clear that, unless development strat-egies include steps to address the cultural factor, there will be little change at the household or national level to improve the welfare of women and communities as a whole.

The cultural factor of gender equality

The need to address the cultural dimension of development has been extensively discussed, and the debate in favour of including cultural considerations in the processes of developmental change long concluded.

Attention has been drawn to the linkage between the economic struc-ture and the socio-cultural superstructure that supports it. Analyses of societies have shown how the major means of production determine the organization of social and cultural settings of a society. This explains the differences in the socio-cultural framework between, for example, pastoralist, agricultural, and fishing communities. One sees, for example, how the social organization of a pastoral society is centred on the cattle. The value of a person in society is determined by the size of the herd, the value of a wife by the number of cows given as bride price, and the value of one's labour skills by how well she or he can take care of the cattle. The importance of the cow to the welfare of the community is also reflected in the community's arts, religion, language, beliefs, values, attitudes, and overall ways of life. The community will also formulate and enforce laws, regulations, and norms of practice and behaviour, which foster the pastoral way of life and ensure that both the economic structure and the socio-cultural superstructure that supports it are regenerated and sustained from generation to generation.

The same kind of analyses applies to agricultural and fishing com-munities, as well as to more complex socialist or capitalist structures, all of which develop their own ideological superstructure to support their economic base. The spirit of free market, competition, entrepreneur-ship, and the success of the individual are some of the tenets of capital-ism, while socialism espouses egalitarianism, the common good, and the welfare of the society before that of the individual.

As discussed earlier, the numerous development strategies targeted at the developing world have tended to de-link culture from development and instead focussed on economic change. Health and education have become part of the development equation due to the realization that without them, people will not be healthy enough to take part in economic processes or have the skills to execute the production processes. It is obvious that if people die of diseases, the labour force will be reduced, and if the labour force is not adequately skilled, the quality of production and consequently the profits will be negatively affected.

Somehow, the economic theorists and strategies have failed to recognize the link between culture and development. In a way, it is difficult to understand why this is so, because the 1960s and 1970s witnessed many sociological studies showing clearly how the neglect of a community's cultural values and practices could lead to the failure of externally designed development projects. Examples have been given of how the design of a water pump determined whether women used or rejected it, regardless of the fact that the water pump was a source of clean water or was closer to their homes than their traditional water sources. In some parts of Tanzania, for example, women found it indecent to use a water pump whose design forced them to lift their legs to a level that was considered unfit for women, taking into account their traditional attire. Therefore they had to take young boys to pump water for them, an inconvenience that pushed them back to using the traditional water sources of rivers and unprotected wells, which were often long distances away from their homes. Consequently, water-borne diseases continued to inflict people, and women continued to suffer walking long distances to fetch water.

Health outreach officers have also been regularly confronted with cultural beliefs and practices detrimental to the health of mothers and children. Most common in many African countries has been the belief that it is taboo for pregnant women to eat eggs. Of course there was a logical explanation to the taboo, linked to the underdeveloped midwifery that made it safer to deliver a small baby rather than a big baby, and thus the necessity to frighten off pregnant women from eating foods that could result in a big baby. However, such taboos often led to the ill health and death of mothers.

Similarly, the introduction of western-style modern agriculture has suffered in areas where farmers would not adopt new seeds supplied by agricultural research institutions simply because it was culturally shameful for a man to be given seeds by another person, signifying that he is too lazy to produce enough crop to have his own seeds for the next planting season.

Such incidents have compelled health and agricultural extension workers to address the cultural forces at play and to sensitize communities before introducing new practices or technologies.

The World Decade for Cultural Development, 1988–1997, affirmed the position that balanced development can only be ensured by making cultural factors an integral part of the strategies designed to achieve it (World Commission on Culture and Development 1995). Concerted effort has also been directed at convincing governments and development agents to acknowledge the cultural dimension of development. The Intergovernmental Conference on Cultural Policies for Development, in Stockholm 1998, for example, recommended UNESCO to include cultural policy objectives in all development programmes and activities, to integrate a cultural perspective into the next International Development Strategy, and invite the specialized agencies to evaluate their development practices and policies in this perspective, and to suggest to the Secretary- General that one year of the Decade for the Eradication of Poverty (1997–2006) be devoted to the connection between culture and development, and the elimination of poverty.

It has also been agreed for governments to review their national cultural policies with a view to linking culture to the development process and making cultural policy one of the key components of development strategies. Significant activity has been directed towards achieving this goal. Quite a number of countries have reviewed their cultural policies or developed new ones. Cultural policy perspectives have been expanded beyond the limitations to arts, museums, and sports to include the broader and multidimensional fabric of what constitutes a people. The debate of the World Decade for Cultural Development also brought to the fore the need to seriously consider affirmation and enrichment of cultural identities, broadening participation in cultural life, promoting cultural diversity, promoting creativity in all spheres, and promoting international cultural cooperation.

The world has, to some extent, responded positively to the arguments put forward on the link between culture and development. There is evidence to show that development strategies are giving the cultural factor more attention. For example, programmes on combating the HIV/AIDS pandemic, on sustaining the environment, and on food security and poverty reduction increasingly recognize the cultural factor as important in enhancing or impeding the programmes (Mlama 2003).

In the process of addressing the overall cultural dimension of development, the gender factor in development has become even more glaring. It has become clear that deeply entrenched cultural values, attitudes, and practices make it extremely difficult to bring about meaningful change, because the gender construction works against the welfare of women in many spheres of life.

However, even though much has been done towards achieving gender equality in general, the cultural dimension of gender and development still calls for more concerted effort. The cultural construction mind set is still deeply rooted in complex forms of gender inequality. Values, attitudes, and practices that foster gender inequality in all spheres of life abound, and people of all levels, even those with significant levels of education, are not sufficiently responsive to gender equality in their day-to-day lives and undertakings.

This situation is explained by the fact that both women and men are socialized into systems that stress the superiority of man over woman and the inferiority and subservience of the woman to man. This leads to a serious state of disempowerment of women, acquired from an early age. Socialization processes raise the girl child to be subservient to men, not to challenge them, to leave them to make the decisions, not to speak out or challenge the status quo. This is reinforced at the home, in school, by religious institutions, and by society at large. Brought up in structures, systems, values, attitudes, and practices in which they are always the underdogs, many women internalize their inferiority and accept it as given, even if they may be suffering gravely. Many women thus display characteristics of disempowerment, including lack of self-confidence, assertiveness, and self-esteem, inability or reluctance to make decisions, fear to challenge injustices, helplessness in fighting the injustices meted out to them, and the lack of courage to speak out or to fight for their rights. And, accordingly, many efforts to eliminate gender inequalities have been hindered by this status of disempowerment of women.

The next section looks at the gender factor in the formal education system, illustrating how cultural values, attitudes, and practices can stand in the way of meaningful development.

Gender equality in the formal education system

There is an agreement that education is a key factor to the development of any society. Indeed, those countries that have invested heavily in the education of its citizens are the ones that have attained high levels of development. Studies have also shown that there is correlation between levels of education and societal welfare economically and socially. With particular reference to women, it has been shown that six years of education of a mother significantly decreases infant mortality, and improves the health of the family, the economic status, and the possibility for the children to go to school.

This realization has been the driving force behind the various steps taken globally and nationally towards gender equality in education. Realizing that, due to historically determined gender-biased structures, there was a big gender gap in education in favour of boys and men, various steps have been taken towards improving access, retention, and performance of girls and women in education. Gender equity and equality are specific goals of the 1990 Education for All (EFA) Declaration, the 2000 Dakar Framework for Education for All, and the 2000 Millennium Development Goals (MDGs), aiming to 'ensure that, by 2015, children everywhere, boys and girls alike, will be able to complete a full course of primary schooling' (MDG 2), and to 'eliminate gender disparity in primary and secondary education preferably by 2005 and in all levels of education no later than 2015' (MDG 3).

In line with the EFA and MDGs, governments have instituted various measures towards reducing the gender gap in education. These have included free and compulsory basic education, forcing parents who do not believe in sending girls to school to do so, provision of scholarships to needy girls including HIV/AIDS orphans, provision of boarding facilities where there are long distances to schools, introduction of re-entry policies, allowing schoolgirls who get pregnant to go back to school after delivery, increase of female teachers in rural school to act as role models for girls, institution of affirmative action in favour of girls in transition to higher levels of education especially at secondary and university levels, and mainstreaming of gender and best practices in girls' education in sector policies and plans.

All these efforts have shown positive results in improving the participation of girls and women in education. The UNESCO Education for All Monitoring Report, for example, acknowledges a significant increase in the enrolment of girls over the last ten years (UNESCO 2003/2004).

All these achievements not withstanding, gender inequalities in the provision of formal education still abound in most countries. One proof is the fact that most countries in Sub-Sahara Africa failed to reach the 2005 Education for All and Millenium Development Goal to attain gender parity at primary and secondary school level. Caution has also been given that, unless the governments and the international community seriously step up their efforts in this area, most countries will miss the 2015 target for gender equality in education.

This is a very serious situation indeed. There are many reasons to this failure, one of which is lukewarm political commitment. Despite the wide agreement on the equality and education goals, not enough action has been forthcoming in translating commitments into concrete action. This is manifested in the reluctance to allocate the required human and financial resources to undertake programmes to improve gender equality in education. The overall deterioration of education systems in many countries in Africa has not helped the situation.

A major reason for the persistence of gender inequality in education, which is not receiving the required attention, is the context of cultural gender construction.

The cultural context of gender inequality in education

The school is a key socialization agent considering that children spend a large part of their growing years in school. The school shapes the character of a child at the same time as the family and the community outside the school do.

The important point is that the socialization processes both at home and at school are fed by the cultural values, attitudes, and practices that form the basis of gender relations in the community where the school is located.

In the face of the gender transformation taking place globally and nationally in the economic or political spheres, one would expect that similar gender transformation processes take place in the formal education systems. Experience, however, shows that this is not the case.

The education of girls in Africa, on the whole, is faced with persistent challenges in terms of access, retention, and performance.

A first major challenge is the cultural values and attitudes which place little worth on formal school education for girls, especially in rural areas and places where parents do not have sufficient levels of formal education. Such parents carry cultural values and attitudes that see a woman's most important role and status in society as getting married. A person does not see her or his role as a parent fulfilled if a daughter is not married. There is also fear that too much formal education may lead to non-marriage of the daughter or, worse still, pregnancy out of wedlock, both of which are viewed as very shameful to the family. Such attitudes often lead to girls' non-enrolment or withdrawal from school for early marriage. Girls are also withdrawn from school to undergo initiation ceremonies, in some cases including genital mutilation. Again, cultural values put great value on these practices and parents feel obliged to take their children through these initiations, without which a girl is considered unfit for marriage and thus never accorded the social status of being an adult.

In a situation where parents are too poor to afford formal education, as is common in most countries in Sub-Sahara Africa, such cultural values and attitudes again work against girls because parents normally use the little resources they have to send boys rather than the girls to school. Indeed, sending a girl who is expected to get married anyway, to school, is seen as a bad investment.

Such cultural values and attitudes have indeed contributed towards the failure of education systems to enrol or retain girls in school, accounting for the fact that, despite efforts to send all children to school, two thirds of children out of school are girls, a rate that has remained constant since 1990 even though gross enrolment for girls has been improving.

Surprisingly, however, not enough evidence is available that national education development programmes are according this cultural challenge due weight. There are no clear strategies on how Ministries of Education and other education providers can change these cultural values and attitudes so as to enable parents to enrol and retain both girls and boys in school. Even where governments have instituted such legal provisions as compulsory primary education or sanctions against early marriage, there are no structures or mechanisms on the ground to facilitate or ensure the enforcement of such legal provisions. In 2004, for example, a study by the Forum for African Women Educationalists (FAWE) found that most heads of schools in Kenya were not aware of the existence of a government policy that allows school girls who get pregnant to be readmitted after delivery. As a result, many girls continued to be expelled from school due to teenage pregnancy, thus keeping the drop-out rates for girls high (FAWE 2004a).

The second major challenge is that negative cultural values and attitudes manifest themselves in various ways within the formal education system, contributing to difficulties in retaining girls who have had the fortune to enrol in school, as well as negatively affecting their academic performance.

In most African countries, school environments are characterized by a culturally conditioned lack of gender responsiveness, academically, physically, and socially.

The lack of respect for gender equality in the school environment is reinforced by male dominated values and attitudes, which are prevalent in school among students and teachers. The boys and male teachers are not empowered to recognize and accept gender equality. This in turn leads to sexual harassment, bullying, and disregard for girls' academic capabilities.

Observations of classroom practices show teaching and learning processes that are largely gender-biased. Many teachers apply teaching methodologies which do not give girls and boys equal opportunities to participate. They also use teaching and learning materials that perpetuate gender stereotypes. Of more concern is the fact that the gender dimension of education is not part of the curricula of teacher training. As such, teachers, both women and men, carry whatever gender constructs they have picked up from their own socialization into the classroom.

Classroom dynamics show a tendency for boys to dominate learning processes, especially in practical scientific experiments. Many teachers are seen to favour boys in class participation, especially in asking questions. There is also much gender-biased language in the classroom, which makes girls feel academically inadequate and inferior to boys. A survey conducted in a secondary school in Tanzania in 2006, where students were asked to write down language directed at girls by teachers in the classroom, which they thought undermined their academic confidence, revealed statements such as

'Even you, a girl, you want to take Mathematics! Mathematics has its owners.'

'Stop rolling your eyes at me, you are so ugly I could never think of seducing you.'

'Girls are only good enough for marriage, you are wasting your time here.'

'Girls are just goal keepers' (a term used to refer to wives who are not employed and therefore just waiting to be fed).

Such language use, bullying, and sexual harassment of girls by boys and teachers negatively affect girls' academic performance. The same review showed, however, that there was no mechanism to discourage or sanction such practices in schools and that girls were left to fend for themselves (FAWE 2005a, 2006).

Since girls are already socialized to accept their inferiority to men, they passively tolerate this situation and do little to challenge it. Female teachers, who are also products of the gender-biased socialization processes, also do little to eliminate the gender constraints to girls' education. Indeed, many female teachers are as disempowered as the girls, and subjected to the same gender discrimination practices by their male colleagues. In some cases, female teachers even use their position as teachers to reinforce gender discrimination practices. For example, some female teachers have been found using the same language as male teachers to discourage girls from taking science subjects with the argument that the sciences are subjects for boys.

An informal survey in schools participating in a programme by FAWE to transform school environments to be gender responsive showed that female teachers often also abuse girls with particular reference to their physical attributes, especially their beauty or lack of it. This situation makes it difficult for girls to participate effectively in academic processes leading to inability to continue to higher levels of education, thus accounting for the less than 30 per cent female enrolment at university level for most countries in Sub-Sahara Africa (FAWE 2005b).

The third challenge relates to lack of empowerment of women to combat and eliminate the gender inequalities directed against them. Socialization processes, including traditional education, religion, practices, behavioural norms, social sanctions, and reward systems place women in an inferior position to men. By the time a girl is in her teens, she has already been conditioned to accept that boys and men are superior to girls and women, and that it is the bound duty of women to be subservient to men. Women are forced to accept that men should be served and have the prerogative of making family decisions, of owning and controlling family property and income, and of determining what is good for the family and the community as a whole. Strict sanction mechanisms are in place to enforce this gender power relation, which women can only challenge at the risk of severe consequences. Indeed, social systems are such that girls grow up to believe that such gender relations are the norm, despite the injustices and the suffering that they cause.

This all forces women to suffer in silence from the various forms of injustices meted against them, such as forced and/or early marriage, non-enrolment or withdrawal from school by parents, female genital mutilation, wife inheritance, and other forms of sexual abuse.

The same disempowerment is brought into the classroom and school environment, whereby girls and female teachers silently accept male superiority and the accompanying oppression and sexual mistreatment of both girls and female teachers.

The fourth challenge is the socialization of men that makes them accept unequal gender relations as their birthright. From the time they are very small, they are socialized to believe that they are superior to women, even those who are older than them. They assume attitudes seeing women as under the mercy of men, with the duty to obey and serve men without questioning. Initiation rites and other socialization processes in many traditional societies enforce this superiority of men over women with an iron hand. As they grow up, boys are frequently punished for any show of weakness in dealing or interacting with women. They are jeered at for displaying any tendencies to be soft to women or to behave like them. Songs are composed to tease men with tendencies of what is deemed as female behaviour, such as crying, or for spending too much time in the company of women, staying in the kitchen or carrying out chores expected to be done by women, such as cooking, fetching water or carrying babies on the back. Ironically these songs are often sung by women when they see a man entering the female domain. Among the Kaguru of Kilosa district in Tanzania, for example, there is a song which women sing when a man enters the kitchen or comes to sit with women which goes *msebwege kenda ku wafele; ku wagosi nghondo nghondo* (the foolish man likes to sit with women; because he is very scared of the company of his fellow men).

The result of such social control is a strong mindset among both women and men, which makes them adhere strictly to the laid down norms of behaviour and gender relations. It becomes very difficult for the individual to depart from the norms without risking appearing as a misfit and losing face or status in society.

This gender construction makes it possible for members of society to trample upon the human rights of women through such practices as forced marriage, female genital mutilation, wife beating, disinheriting women and girls of family property in the event of death of a husband or father, preventing women from owning property or having control over the products of their labour, and preventing women from having a voice in determining their welfare or that of their children and family.

Boys and men also carry these cultural values and attitudes of their superiority over women into the classroom and school compound. During gender sensitization workshops in schools, conducted by FAWE, it has become very obvious that boys and male teachers take their superiority over women for granted, admitting that they have never realized that the way they behave affect girls and women negatively, simply because nobody has ever challenged them.

Indeed, due to these socialization processes, many women and men accept the unequal gender relations as normal, justify them as part of the culture, and are often surprised that anybody would want to challenge this status quo.

Serious attention must therefore be paid to transforming this gender construction in ways that allow women and men equal access to the means of production, ownership and control of property, as well as protection of their human rights. Without resolving these inequalities, it will not be possible to claim any level of development because women will continue to be marginalized.

Unfortunately, however, despite the many arguments, most development programmes do not sufficiently address the cultural factor of development, and there is little to show in terms of confronting the culturally determined gender constraints to development.

Addressing the cultural factors of gender inequality in education

The above discussion makes it clear that serious intervention is required to address the cultural factors of gender inequality in education with a view to eliminating rampant gender disparities. Aiming to reach the 'Education for All' goals, the last ten years have witnessed increased efforts by governments to attain gender equality in education by addressing some of the cultural factors impeding enrolment, transition, and performance of girls. Most efforts to eliminate gender disparities in education, however, are done by civil society, with many NGOs relentlessly attacking the problem through numerous interventions.

One example is the Forum for African Women Educationalists (FAWE), a leading Pan-African NGO on the promotion of girls' education. FAWE has worked to sensitize teachers, students, parents, and community leaders and members, in order to raise their understanding of the need to support girls' education; to train teachers in order to make teaching and learning processes respond to the specific needs of girls and boys; to empower girls to increase their self-confidence, assertiveness, and ability to speak out, make decisions, and negotiate in order to overcome gender-based constraints to their education; and to empower boys for them to de-link from gender oppressive attitudes and practices, such as machoism, bullying, and sexual affronts, and to develop sufficient self-confidence to appreciate gender equality.

Teachers' handbooks have also been developed, and teachers trained to use them, in order to make schools gender responsive academically, socially, and physically, focussing on gender sensitization, societal gender constructions, and gender responsive teaching and learning processes (FAWE/University of Dar es Salaam/Miali Training Centre 2005; FAWE 2005a, 2005b).

Furthermore, teachers and students have been trained in guidance and counselling skills, and guidance and counselling desks have been established to provide services for the social and psychological development of girls and boys. There has been training in reproductive health and protection against sexually transmitted diseases, particularly HIV/AIDS, in order to manage sexual maturation issues of girls and boys. Gender responsive infrastructure has been provided, including boarding facilities, separate and adequate toilets for girls and boys, adequate water and sanitation, especially to enhance menstruation management. To decrease drop-out rates, scholarships have been provided to needy girls and boys, and to improve girls' enrolment, attendance, and performance, their participation in science, mathematics, and technology has been promoted. To ensure gender equality in the governance and operations of schools, gender responsive school management systems have been established, as well as databases to track students' performance and the gender responsiveness of different aspects of the school. Throughout, local communities and other stakeholders have been involved in monitoring and taking action for gender equality (FAWE 2005b).

Schools at different stages in the transformation to gender responsiveness have been involved in FAWE activities, and all of them show reduced negative impact of culturally based gender factors in education. Girls' enrolment to secondary school has increased and, as parents have been convinced of the importance of education for their daughters, they have also found ways to raise the school fees.

In a school in Kenya, where traditional cultural practices tolerate early marriage, the community leaders have played a big role in eliminating that practice. Local chiefs have been involved in sensitizing parents against early marriage, prosecuting those who marry off schoolgirls, and taking girls back to school. There has also been a drastic reduction of teenage pregnancies in the schools involved in FAWE activities.

Teachers have become more responsive to the specific needs of girls and boys. They use more participatory methods, giving girls and boys equal chances to ask and answer questions, and encouraging them to participate as equals. Teachers also pay more attention to gender stereotypes in textbooks and even produce their own teaching and learning materials in order to achieve a better gender balance. Moreover, teachers have changed their attitude towards girls' abilities, especially in the sciences, encouraging them and using a more gender-friendly language, thus creating better rapport and enabling girls to communicate with teachers and seek academic help without fear.

Girls also display higher levels of empowerment. According to teachers, they participate more actively in class than before, answering questions, speaking out, contributing to discussions, and taking leading roles in group work. They seem more self-confident and assertive, interacting more with boys as equals and standing up for their rights when they perceive gender discrimination.

Students have also influenced the school management systems to ensure equal numbers of girls and boys in student leadership. A system has been established which gives girls and boys equal opportunities to be school prefects, and thus develop leadership skills and confidence. Girls are engaged in various steps to solve gender related problems in their academic and social development. Through peer educators, they get guidance and counselling, form study circles to assist each other academically, support needy colleagues, and institute networks through which they support each other to succeed academically and socially.

Overall, high levels of gender awareness has been reported among teachers, students, and surrounding communities, with community members being supportive of girls' education, actively assisting in ensuring that girls are enrolled and monitoring their retention in school (FAWE 2006).

The FAWE experiences thus shows that the gender dimension in education can be addressed and existing gender inequalities reduced. A number of challenges have been faced, however. One challenge has been that, due to deeply rooted values and attitudes, teachers, students, and community members initially often do not even realize that gender inequality is a problem and a constraint to girls' education. A second challenge has been that the teacher education does not include training on cultural values and gender dimensions that have a negative impact on education, and that teachers thus lack awareness and skills to handle gender-based constraints to teaching and learning. As a third challenge, school management systems are largely blind to gender issues and lack mechanisms to foster a gender responsive environment for students and teachers.

The fourth challenge has been the gender inequalities that exist in society as a whole. Whereas schools are recognized as key agents for change academically, they have not played that role when it comes to cultivating cultural values and attitudes for development, but rather perpetuated and fostered existing gender inequalities. A last, and related, challenge has been the lack of gender responsiveness in national education policies, education systems, and overall culture, implying that a change in schools calls for a major gender transformation of over-all education systems and gender constructions.

Conclusion

The chapter has shown how complex the cultural factor is in the provision of education in Africa. It is well known that education is key to any process of development and that, unless both women and men receive sufficient levels of education, there can be no meaningful development.

The challenge facing Africa today is therefore how to transform the formal education system into an effective tool for eliminating cultural impediments to development, emerging from deeply entrenched gender-biased socialization processes. Accordingly, transformation of the education system has to go hand-in-hand with addressing the broader gender constructions in society. This calls for wider interventions, addressing the cultural dimension of gender and development, including research with particular attention to the grassroots level, community sensitization to foster human rights and gender equality, individual and group empowerment of women to combat gender impediments, and of men to accept and support gender equality, systems to support gender equality practices, legal enforcement to eliminate detrimental values, attitudes, and practices, and a review of socio-economic structures and cultural superstructures.

There is no doubt that the cultural dimension of gender and development in Africa requires serious attention. Without addressing the cultural factor, and its negative impact on gender equality in development, there cannot be any meaningful development. With enough commitment, however, the cultural factor can be effectively addressed by action such as described in this chapter.

References

FAWE (2000) In search of an ideal school for girls, Nairobi: FAWE.

FAWE (2002) Annual Report, Nairobi: FAWE.

FAWE (2002) The ABC of Gender Responsive Education Policies; Guidelines for developing a gender responsive plan, Nairobi: FAWE.

FAWE (2002) Promoting girls' education through Re-entry policy for adolescent mothers, Nairobi: FAWE.

FAWE (2003) Annual Report, Nairobi: FAWE.

FAWE (2003) Quest for Quality in girls' education, FAWE Centres of Excellence, AIC Girls' Kajiado, Kenya, Nairobi: FAWE.

FAWE (2003) Quest for Quality in girls' education, FAWE Centres of Excellence, Diourbel, Senegal, Nairobi: FAWE.

FAWE (2003) Quest for Quality in girls' education, Mgugu, Tanzania, Nairobi: FAWE.

FAWE (2003) Improving girls' education through Re-entry policy for adolescent mothers, Nairobi: FAWE.

FAWE (2003) Study for Quality in girls' education; FAWE Centre of Excellence, Rwanda, Nairobi: FAWE.

FAWE (2004a) Study on the implementation of the Re-entry for pregnant school-girls policy in five countries, Nairobi: FAWE.

FAWE (2004b) Tuseme 'Speak Out' – Tanzania: Best Practices in Girls' Education in Africa Series, Nairobi: FAWE.

FAWE and Midlands State University, Zimbabwe (2004) Introduction to Gender Studies: A Training Module for Student Teachers, Nairobi: FAWE.

FAWE/University of Dar es Salaam/Miali Training Centre (2005) Empowering the youth trough TUSEME, Let Us Speak Out, A Teachers' Handbook, Nairobi: FAWE.

FAWE (2005a) The Gender Responsive Pedagogy, handbook for teachers, Nairobi: FAWE.

FAWE (2005b) The Gender Responsive School: The FAWE Centres of Excellence model, A Handbook for Education Practitioners, Nairobi: FAWE.

FAWE (2006) Peer review on the status of the transformation of Centre of excellence schools into gender responsive environments, Nairobi: FAWE.

Mlama, P. (2003) Cultural policies and EFA, Stockholm: UNESCO conference.

Mlama (2004) Building capacity for scaling up what works in girls' education in sub Sahara Africa. The perspective of the graduated Working Group for female participation, (FAWE), Geneva: ADEA Steering Committee Meeting.

Mlama (2004) Creating Gender Responsive Learning Environment For Girls In Marginalized Communities, The FAWE Experience, Conference on Multiple Marginalities, Helsinki, Finland.

Mlama (2004) Positioning the performing arts in the efforts towards social change, EATI Conference, Mombasa, Kenya.

Mlama (2005) Challenges for teacher training in instituting gender responsive pedagogy in schools in Africa, Seminar, Bergen, Norway.

Mlama (2005) Empowering girls out of the gender trap: The TUSEME experience in Africa, Uppsala: The Nordic Africa Institute.

Mlama (2005) Equity issues, gender and education in rural areas, ADEA/FAO seminar 7–9 September 2005, Addis Ababa.

Mlama (2005) FAWE's experience in Africa in changing teaching for gender equity, Dfid/Oxfam Seminar on Education, Nairobi.

Mlama (2005) Education and empowerment of women, Beijing + 10, New York.

Republic of Kenya, Ministry of Education, Science, and Technology (2005) Education Sessional Paper, Nairobi.

Republic of Kenya (2005) Kenya Education Sector Support Programme 2005–2010, Ministry of Education, Science, and Technology.

UNESCO (1998) The Power of Culture, Intergovernmental Conference on Cultural Policies for Development, Stockholm: UNESCO.

UNESCO (2003/2004) Gender and Education for All. The Leap to Quality; EFA Global Monitoring Report, Paris: UNESCO.

UNESCO (2003) Guidelines for implementing, monitoring and evaluating gender responsive EFA plans, Bangkok: UNESCO.

UNICEF (2004) Accelerating Progress on Girls' Education, Operational Strategy, Eastern and Southern Africa, Nairobi.

UNICEF (2005) The State of the World's Children 2005, Childhood under threat, New York: UNICEF.

University of Dar es salaam, Department of Fine and Performing Arts (2004) Tuseme Project Guide Kit, Dar es Salaam.

United Nations (2000a) The Dakar EFA Framework for Action, New York: United Nations.

United Nations (2000b) United Nations Millennium Development, New York: United Nations.

United Republic of Tanzania (1999) The Education Sector, Reform and Development Programme, Ministry of Education and Culture, Dar es Salaam.

World Commission on Culture and Development (1995) Our Creative Diversity, Paris: UNESCO.

11
Islam and Cosmopolitanism

Jan Nederveen Pieterse

> The effort to 'understand Islam', to locate it, describe it, and reduce it to intelligible summary, is caught up in the excitements of the present moment. It is a thing of responses and reactions – of warnings, reassurances, advices, attacks.
>
> (Geertz 2003: 27)

One association that cosmopolitanism brings to mind is its western legacy, but what about non-western cosmopolitanisms? We can view cosmopolitanism, broadly, as perspectives and sensibilities that stress human bonds and interconnectedness across cultural and political boundaries. These can be found also in Buddhism, Hinduism, Confucianism, and so forth (cf. Camilleri and Muzaffar 1998). This discussion focusses on Islamic cosmopolitanism and the historical role and self-perception of the Islamic world as a 'middle nation', a bridging civilization. A further question is whether and how this applies to contemporary radical political Islam, which is often viewed as an anti-modern and anti-western bunker mentality.

It was not so long ago that political Islam was acknowledged – though not necessarily welcomed – as a major alternative to western modernity. Khomeini's revolution in Iran, Hezbollah, Islamic Jihad, and a host of Islamist movements were part of this momentum. But after the end of the Cold War and once the Afghan freedom fighters became the Taliban and the mujahideen turned into 'Arab Afghans' who challenged governments in Algeria and Egypt, political Islam slipped off the map of emancipatory struggle. Still many of today's conflicts concern the Middle East, Palestine, Iraq, Afghanistan, and the sprawling war on terrorism. It is as if there are parallel universes: one in which 'global civil society', such as the World Social Forum, takes on the Washington consensus, and an entirely different one in which militant Islam confronts American hegemony. The two universes of global civil society and 'Muslim defiance' do not seem to intersect. Militant Islam seems to be a rare instance where hegemonic policy, mainstream views, and majority progressive views converge.

Cosmopolitanism is a theme with a considerable lineage and resonance. Unlike globalization, it carries a normative charge and cultural and intellectual depth. Cosmopolitanism used to come with elite and urban overtones, but in recent times it has been revisited in wider contexts, in discussions of modernity, international relations, migration, and multiculturalism. Ulrich Beck advocates 'methodological cosmopolitanism' (Beck 2006; see also Ulrich Beck's contribution in this volume). We may choose to bracket cosmopolitanism, we may prefer global solidarity, or resignify cosmopolitanism as globalization in the affirmative. Whatever our views on cosmopolitanism, it enables us to discuss globalization in a normative way and with some historical perspective.

Cosmopolitanism is at a dramatic cusp. Technological developments enable unprecedented worldwide interconnections across all dimensions of social life. But complex high-density interdependence also brings major conflagrations, a configuration that James Rosenau refers to as 'fragmegration' (fragmentation-and-integration) (Rosenau 1990). As the capabilities for transnational rapport are growing, also at an institutional level, as in the International Criminal Court and the Kyoto Protocol, so are conflicts and claims for global justice.

How should cosmopolitanism be rethought in twenty-first century conditions of crisis-prone neo-liberalism and belligerent American hegemony? Are the typical legacies of cosmopolitanism and internationalism, such as European humanism and labour internationalism, still adequate or too Eurocentric? What is the contribution of cosmopolitanism in view of notions such as Huntington's clash of civilizations and 'the age of Muslim wars' (Huntington 2003)? Should we view political Islam as part of contemporary cosmopolitanism or place political Islam and Islamism beyond the pale of modernity and globalization? Cosmopolitan horizons of global solidarity are sidelined by grim narratives of global divide such as the clash of civilizations and assessments of global threats.

'Islamo-fascism' has become a new ideological target. Slavoj Zizek counsels that we should not distinguish between Islamic fundamentalism and Islam. 'Instead, one should gather the courage to recognize the obvious fact that there is a deep strain of violence and intolerance in

Islam – that, to put it bluntly, something in Islam resists the liberal-capitalist world order.' After dismissing Muslim civilization, he wonders whether Islamic resentment could perhaps be redirected towards socialism (Zizek 2004: 3). American neo-conservatives and their counterparts in Europe such as Bernard-Henri Lévi and Oriana Fallaci offer similar views (Fallaci 2002). Etzioni uses a term from pathology by speaking of 'virulent Islam' (Etzioni 2002). Conservatives and liberals alike urge strong American intervention in the Middle East because radical Islam presents a threat to the West. Real as the risks of transnational terrorism and crime may be, threat inflation may become a habit and since threat inflation produces force inflation, the remedy may be worse than the disease. Neo-liberal policies wreak economic havoc on many societies. The war on terrorism is destabilizing and also produces a dangerous world. What perspectives point beyond planetary perplexity? There is no cosmopolitanism without access to collective history and collective memory as the threshold to a collective future. A cosmopolitanism that is informed from one part of the world only, that monopolizes the world by a single language and a single cultural style, such as liberal pluralism, is not cosmopolitanism but hegemony and a 'standardization of dissent' of the kind that Ashis Nandy cautioned against (Nandy 1989).

The first section in this treatment discusses the cosmopolitan scope of Islamic culture. How does this fare when the Islamic world loses its intercontinental middleman position during the era of European dominance? This is taken up in the second section. The third section focusses on contemporary political Islam and its relationship to American hegemony and the closing section reflects on how clichés of 'Islamic fundamentalism' translate into American national security perspectives on the Islamic world.

Recentring Islam

In social science the relationship between theory and history is often uneven, and it is also the case in Islamic studies. Theoretical work in the tradition of anti-foundationalism (e.g. Al-Azmeh 1993; Sayyid 2003) offers important critiques of essentialist treatments of Islam à la 'fundamentalism', but sometimes sophisticated theory is premised on conventional history. Al-Azmeh repeatedly refers to universalism as a western legacy and thus short-changes the Islamic contributions to universalism.[1] Many authors note how globalization enables Islamism (Baker 1999; Lubeck 1999; Sayyid 2003), but few recognize how Islam enables globalization. It is important to step back and combine what Anouar

Abdel Malek calls the depth of the historical field with the breadth of the historical field. Part of this record is well known, but for a complete picture it is worth recontextualizing recent historical assessments of Islam alongside recent historical perspectives on Asia and then to revisit theory.

In discussing Islamic cosmopolitanism I propose a triple movement of recentring, decentring and again recentring the Islamic world – in a broad geopolitical, geo-economic and cultural sense. In each round, Islam makes different contributions to cosmopolitanism.

Recentring the Islamic world by acknowledging the central place of the Orient and Islam in early globalization and early modernity. During this phase the Islamic world makes foundational contributions to cosmopolitanism.

Decentring Islam in view of its loss of status during the centuries of European dominance. During this period Islam spreads widely beyond the Arab world and reform movements reshape Islam, so the Muslim world becomes more cosmopolitan and Muslim cosmopolitanism becomes more diverse and less Arab-centric.

Recentring the Islamic world from the twentieth century onward because of the strategic significance of fossil fuels and the Middle East. This involves accounting for the co-dependence of American hegemony and the rise of Islamism. In this phase the Muslim diaspora spreads to the West and Islam takes the form of an alternative and rival globalization project.

Recentring Islam involves a twofold logic, historical and theoretical. Historically it means viewing the Middle East and Asia as an early modernity in terms of trade, merchant capital, productivity, population densities, and urbanization. Janet Abu-Lughod pushes the time line of early capitalism back to the thirteenth century, locates it in the Middle East, and notes that 'the fall of the East precedes the rise of the West' (Abu-Lughod 1989). Andre Gunder Frank views the early world economy as centred, not in northern Europe, but in East and South Asia as part of an Afro-Eurasian world economy (Frank 1998). Recent global history studies go further back in time. John Hobson dates the central role of the Middle East in the emerging world economy from about 500 AD, lasting till about 1000 AD when China and India play a propelling role in the world economy (Hobson 2004). A strong version of this view is the thesis of oriental globalization that overturns Eurocentrism and views the Middle East and Asia as the first globalizing forces.[2] The economic dynamism centred in the Middle East and then in China and India, travelling via Silk Routes by land and sea via Hormuz and the

Persian Gulf to Mesopotamia and the Mediterranean, is then the infra-structure of early globalization. The Middle Eastern and Asian bazaars are the world's oldest.

According to Sheldon Pollock, the Latin cosmopolis and the Sanskrit cosmopolis coincided in time, the former initially clustered around the Roman Empire and the latter existing as a civilizational framework. Both went into decline around the same time and gave way to the increasing use of vernacular languages (Pollock 2000). The Muslim cosmopolis – in part centred on Arabic but extending far beyond the Arab world – was the major successor to these cosmopolitan worlds, arose geographically and culturally in between them, touched many more cultures, and lasted far longer and into the present.

Marshall Hodgson's 'The Venture of Islam' took Islamic history beyond its conventional focus on the Middle East to cover the entire region from Morocco to China and could thus appreciate Islam's global expanse. Richard Eaton, following Hodgson and William McNeill, treats Islamic history as global history and the Islamic world as 'history's first truly global civilization':

> For the Arab conquests inaugurated a thousand-year era, lasting from the seventh till the seventeenth century, when all the major civiliza-tions of the Old World – Greco-Roman, Irano-Semitic, Sanskritic, Malay-Javanese, and Chinese – were for the first time brought into contact with one another by and within a single overarching civil-ization. What is more, Muslims synthesized elements from those other civilizations – especially the Greek, Persian, and Indian – with those of their Arab heritage to evolve a distinctive civilization that proved one of the most vital and durable the world has ever seen. (Eaton 1993: 12; cf. McNeill 1979; Burke 1979)

Eaton compares the travels of Marco Polo, who was a stranger every-where he went, with those of his near-contemporary Ibn Battuta who travelled much farther, from Andalusia to China.

> In contrast, Ibn Battuta, in his intercontinental wanderings, moved through a single cultural universe in which he was utterly at home. Most of his travels took place in what Muslims have always called *Dâr al-Islâm*, the 'abode of Islam' [...] If Ibn Battuta intuitively under-stood that the Muslim world of his day constituted a truly global civilization [...] it has taken Western historians some considerable time to understand it as such. (Eaton 1993: 32)

By comparison, the lineages of European cosmopolitanism – such as the transnational networks of nobles and clergy during the Middle Ages and of humanists and Nietzsche's *freie Denker* – appear provincial for they are largely confined to the European peninsula and Christendom. How, for instance, to accommodate information such as this in a Eurocentric framework?

> Around 900 C.E. Ibn Khordãdbeh, postmaster of the Arab province of al-Jibãl in Persia, compiled his eight-volume *Book of the Roads and Countries* as a guide for the postal system. He described roads and sea routes as far as Korea, giving detailed directions, distances, weather conditions, and road security. (Hoerder 2002: 31)

This is echoed in Korean records of Arab traders in the ninth century (Cohen 2000).

Islam may be the most cosmopolitan of the world religions, if only for geographical reasons: no other major religion has been geographically adjacent to so many different continents and cultures and mingled with them over so long a time. Historical considerations are that Islam emerged when Mecca and Baghdad were major long-distance trade hubs, peaked during the high tide of Asian economic dynamism and as a 'middle civilization' relayed Asian dynamism to the Mediterranean world and Europe. The world of Islam is crisscrossed by long distance trade networks and diasporas, caravan trails and Silk Routes, and dotted by caravanserais, trading ports, and emporia. It encompasses many languages and cultures such as Persian, Turkic, and Uyghurs in Central Asia.

Islam's role as 'middle civilization' is a major part of Islamic self-awareness. Osman Bakar notes,

> The idea of Islam as the *middle nation* is not an after-thought or a later invention made after it had established itself as an empire, a world religion and world civilization.' The idea is to be found in the Quran where the new faith and its followers are described as *'ummatan wasatan,* meaning the middle nation': 'Thus have we made you a middle nation that you might be witnesses over the whole human family or the world community. (Quran 2: 143). (Bakar 1996: 1)

As a religion and a culture Islam is and seeks to be 'a bridge between East and West'.

In Islam, civilization-consciousness is deeply rooted in such Quranic ideas as common human ancestry, common humanity, universal goodness of the human being, universality of divine favours to the human race, the wisdom of ethnic and cultural pluralism [...] Islam is very much interested in the idea of a *universal civilization*. (Bakar 1996: 2)

This is one of the reasons why Huntington's thesis of a clash of civilizations is so fundamentally misplaced, and alien to Muslim thinkers (e.g. Rashid 1997).

The deep tradition of tolerance in Islam is scripted in the Quran.[3] Emerging *after* Judaism and Christianity as the other Abrahamic religions, Islam acknowledges their legacies, a gesture that has not generally been reciprocated. This is not merely an abstract or theological point. In the system of *dhimmis* or protected peoples, the rights of adherents of other religions were recognized under Muslim law and payment of a poll tax entitled non-Muslims to the protection of the Muslim state (Weeramantry 1988: 90). The Muslim record of centuries of peaceful coexistence of peoples of the book contrasts with the European pogroms of Jews, and the Crusades against Muslims. There is no record of genocide, pogroms or Inquisition in Islamic culture or under Islamic rule.[4] The florescence of al Andalus hinged on the creative cohabitation of Muslims, Jews, and Christians and inspired Europe's Renaissance. The Ottoman millet system is an early instance of what we now call multiculturalism. Europe, ensconced in a more bigoted culture, lagged behind: 'In the Turko-Arab-Islamic World, the Ottoman state codified coexistence at a time when the Latin Church exorcized peaceful ethno-religious relations from its realm'. (Hoerder 2002: 109). Centuries of Muslim rule from Andalusia to the Mughal Empire extended this cosmopolitan history and gave depth to Islamic jurisprudence. Law was 'the master science of the Islamic world'. The Sri Lankan Supreme Court judge and scholar Weeramantry's study of Islamic jurisprudence provides a painstaking account of Islamic legal schools, legal ideas and perspectives on tolerance, human rights, and international law (Weeramantry 1988).

These cosmopolitan episodes enabled and shaped European modernity, which would be unthinkable without it. Acknowledging the scope of Islam, then, means provincializing and decentring Europe and its precedence as the pioneer and exemplar of modernity and capitalism. European modernity is layered and includes, as Edward Tiryakian argues, strata of chthonic Greek legacies and Gnostic Christianity

(Tiryakian 1996). Islamic legacies are among these strands. The steps in this line of thinking are to some extent familiar and can be briefly reiterated.

Hellenism in the Mediterranean world was a mélange culture of oriental and occidental elements (Bernal 1987). To the more advanced civilizations, Europe until 1100 appeared backward. 'Muslim Iberia was an "urban" society in 1000 AD compared not only to Christian Iberia, with the single city of León, but also to the rest of Europe.'(Hoerder 2002: 51). In the middle ages the Mediterranean was a 'Muslim lake' and the Renaissance, especially the twelfth century Renaissance, built on the efflorescence in the Muslim world. Many features that are held to be characteristic of European civilization are of external origin: 'The central element of the Gothic style, the pointed arch, was Arabic in origin and was probably introduced by men returning from crusades'. (Hoerder 2002: 85). The medieval European division of the world into three parts according to the three sons of Noah derives from medieval Arab-Islamic culture (Al-Azmeh 2003: 15). Influences from the Orient shaped European technology, philosophy, and aesthetics, as in the application of geometry in architecture and the design of gardens, in notions of luxury and sensuousness, the tradition of the troubadours, and understandings of love (Boase 1977, 1978; Nederveen Pieterse 1989, 1994b).

European capitalism was propelled by the Levant trade. Oriental influence also indirectly concerns another cornerstone of modernity: the modern state system established by the 1648 Treaty of Munster. The victory of the Protestant powers over the Catholic-Habsburg axis was enabled by the political and military cooperation between the Ottomans and the Protestant powers united against their common enemy, the Catholics (Atasoy 1999). This influence extends to international law. For Victoria in Spain and Grotius in the United Provinces, Muslim international law was the only sophisticated literature that was available to build on, and was far advanced in the treatment of prisoners of war and civilians, the right to asylum and safe conduct, and the prohibition of killing non-combatants.

The first encyclopedia was published in Basra in 980 AD in 52 volumes, brought to Spain before 1066 and translated in English by Abelard of Bath, Europe's first Arabist (Weeramantry 1988). The model of Islamic institutions of learning inspired the formation of European universities (Alatas 2006; Makdisi 1981), and Islamic scholarship influenced the *philosophes* and their *Encyclopédie*. Rousseau held Muslim thinking in high regard (unlike Voltaire) and some argue that his theory of general will may have been influenced by the Islamic notion of *Ijma* or consensus.

Table 11.1   Early globalization and Islam

Regional dynamics	Islamic world	Islamic cosmopolitanism
Middle East: centre of first globalization 500–1000 AD	Central to world economy, conquests	A bridging civilization passing on legacies of Egypt, Mesopotamia and Hellenism
East to South Asia: early globalization 1000–1850	Middleman and go-between civilizations	Middling between Asia, Africa, Europe
Africa: gold trade; later slave trade	Andalusia, Maghreb	Enabling European reconnaissance (navigation); Islamic jurisprudence
Rise of Europe	Ottoman Empire	Links with Jews and Protestants, support for Reformation; Islam spreads to Africa and Asia; Islamic reform movements

Montesquieu referred, in passing, to the Quran, biographies of Muhammad and reports by travellers in Muslim lands (in the *Lettres Persanes* and *De l'Esprit des lois*). His observations on the relationship between climate and culture echo those of Ibn Khaldun centuries earlier. Ibn Khaldun's comparative historical method has been seminal in sociology (Alatas 1993).

This re-orientation of history suggests that we must decentre Eurocentric social theory and instead develop a historicist theory of modernities. As the emphasis shifts to examining how Asia and the Islamic world shape and inform European development and modernity, Eurocentric perspectives on modernity increasingly come across as ethnocentric. Marx's Asian mode of production is a myth, Weber's view of Islam is biased, and the Protestant ethic is *not* a general requirement of modernity (Turner 1992). In this light, European cosmopolitanism emerges as a late, derivative, and reluctant cosmopolitanism. Table 11.1 gives a simplified, incomplete sketch of Islamic contributions to cosmopolitanism during early phases of globalization.

Decentring Islam

The Islamic world was shaken by the attack of the Mongols that destroyed the Abbasid caliphate of Baghdad in 1258. From the sixteenth century onward it gradually lost its middling position as intercontinental go-between to the Portuguese, the Dutch, and other European entrants in the Indian Ocean and Asian and African trade. During the Crusades the European objective was to break through the Muslim encirclement and establish direct links with the fabled world of the Orient and the Spice Islands. What the Crusades did not accomplish, Vasco da Gama and other voyagers did. European infiltration into the Arab trading networks in Asia and Africa gradually undermined the middleman role of the Middle East. Precious metals from the Americas gave Europeans an edge that outflanked Muslim traders.

For the Arab world, geopolitical trauma due to the rise of the Mongols in the East and geo-economic trauma due to the expansion of the Europeans merged in a growing marginalization. Nevertheless, this period also saw the rise and expansion of the Ottoman Empire. Marshall Hodgson does not treat the history of Islam after 1258 as one of protracted decline, but recognizes

> the coincidence of and relationship between political fragmentation and cultural florescence in Islamic history [...] it was only in the centuries after 1258 that the Islamic religion, as a belief system *and* as a world civilization, grew among the peoples of Asia and Africa. (Eaton 1993: 24)

Studies of Islamization have come to view it not as a process of expansion or imposition but rather in terms of assimilation (Levtzion 1979) or what we would now call hybridization. Besides, these were times of active reform. As Mortimer notes, 'alterations in patterns of trade helped to disrupt Muslim and partly Muslim societies, and this may in turn account for the rapid spread of the reform movements' (Mortimer 1982: 71).

A related question is how Islamic is Islam? This question is as appropriate in relation to the Islamic world as it is in relation to Europe.[5] Islam is not merely a religion but a civilization with a legacy of pre-Islamic cultural resources from Mesopotamia, Egypt, Persia, Greece, etc. William McNeill described the expansion of the charioteers and the early Middle Eastern empires under the heading 'Cosmopolitanism in the Middle East 1700–500 BC', which illustrates that cross-civilizational linkages had a vast scope already early on (McNeill 1979: chapter 3; cf. Veenhof 1997).

Sufism in particular serves as a link to older civilizational strata (Ernst 1992), a sensibility that has found wide resonance in Rumi's poetry.

Local pre-Islamic cultures and non-Islamic contributions, such as Hellenism and Persian and Turkic culture, shaped the Arab world (Amin 1978). These lineages inform the layered texture and sprawling diversity of Islamic culture and generate many Islams. 'Like other religions, Islam is not a generic essence, but a nominal entity that conjoins, by means of a name, a variety of societies, cultures, histories and polities' (Al-Azmeh 1993: 60). Islam is multi-textured and includes folk Islam, urban and clerical Islam, Sunni and Shia, and Sufism (Geertz 1968).

Nineteenth century modernization in the Islamic world took multiple forms such as the Tanzimat reforms in the Ottoman Empire and efforts at industrialization in Egypt and Persia. The latter were sabotaged by the British for the same reason as the Indian manufacturing sector was sabotaged (Stavrianos 1981). The Nahda in the Arab world ushered in nationalism and Pan movements such as Pan-Islam, Pan-Arabism, and Pan-Turkism. Reform movements of Young Turks and Young Persians led to secular parties and modernizing regimes such as that of Mustafa Kemal Ataturk and new combinations of Islam and nationalism (as in al Afghani), Marxism (as in Ali Shariati and Sukarno) and philosophy (as in Muhammad Iqbal).

Recentring Islam: McJihad

In the course of the twentieth century the Middle East returned to the centre of geopolitics through its petroleum resources. This peaked in 1973 with the OPEC oil boycott. At the same time, the region incurred what economists refer to as the resource curse: rent seeking, oligarchies, and unbalanced development. This pattern of uneven and dependent development produced a social condition that has been characterized as neo-patriarchy. Its lasting imprint is documented in the Arab Human Development Reports (Sharabi 1988; UNDP 2002, 2003). The growing role played by militant political Islam is part of this equation.

While Benjamin Barber contrasts *Jihad versus McWorld*, Timothy Mitchell offers a radically different view under the heading *McJihad*.

If conservative religious reform movements such as the *muwahhidan* in Saudi Arabia or the Muslim Brotherhood in Egypt have been essential to maintaining the power and authority of these states and if, as we are often told, the stability of the governments of Egypt and Saudi Arabia, perhaps more than that of any other governments in the global South, are vital to the protection of US strategic and economic interests, in particular the control of oil, it would seem to follow that political Islam plays an unacknowledged role in the making of global capitalism. (Mitchell 2002: 3)

The warlord Ibn Saud came to power in what later became Saudi Arabia with the help of British oil companies and military forces and the Ikhwan, a local conservative Islamic movement. In 1930 he defeated the Ikhwan, switched from British to American protection and developed a new compromise, in which the religious establishment tolerated the role of the foreign oil company, and in return received funding for their programme of converting Arabia to puritanical Islam from the proceeds from oil. Several forces came together in this ensemble: the Arabian American Oil Company (Aramco) provided funds and technical and material assistance; the US government provided security support and training through its military base in Dhahran, established in 1945; and the religious establishment created the moral and legal order of the state and suppressed political dissent. In the late 1950s, in response to denunciations of corruption and misuse of 'Arab oil' from nationalist governments in Egypt and Iraq, 'the government of Saudi Arabia used oil money to enable the religious establishment to promote its programme of moral authority and social conservatism abroad' (Mitchell 2002: 11). They funded the revival of an Islamic political movement in Egypt, Pakistan and beyond, and supported a US military coup in Iraq that brought the Baath, the party of Saddam Hussein, to power in 1963. Mitchell concludes,

Given the features of the political economy of oil – the enormous rents available, the difficulty in securing these rents due to the over-abundance of supply, the pivotal role of Saudi Arabia in maintaining scarcity, and the collapse of older colonial methods of imposing anti-market corporate control of the Saudi oil fields – oil profits depended on working with those forces that could guarantee the political control of Arabia, the House of Saud in alliance with the *muwahiddun*. [...] 'Jihad' was not simply a local force antithetical to the development of 'McWorld'. McWorld, it turns out, was really McJihad, a necessary combination of a variety of social logics and forces. (Mitchell 2002: 11)

Fatema Mernissi refers to this constellation as 'palace fundamentalism' (Mernissi 2003). Over time this dynamic unfolded to affect developments in Iran, Afghanistan, Sudan, and other elements came into play: the role of Israel, international banks recycling petrodollars (which later precipitate the debt crisis in the global South), arms exporters, the IMF, and structural adjustment. According to Mitchell,

> We live in an age of 'McJihad' [...] an age in which the mechanisms of capitalism appear to operate, in certain critical instances, only by adopting the social force and moral authority of Islamic conservative movements. [...] It follows that such religious movements have played a small but pivotal part in the global political economy. (Mitchell 2002: 3)

McJihad exemplifies the deficiency of capitalism:

> Seen as a process of McJihad, capitalism no longer appears self-sufficient. Its success depends on other forces, which are both essential to the process we call capitalist development and disjunctive with it. (Mitchell 2002: 12)

The Cold War is a specific episode within this process. The Cold War 'Green Belt' strategy sponsored Muslim allies as counterweights against leftwing forces and local popular dissent and thus nourished Islamism. To outflank leftwing forces, western and pro-western governments forged alliances with conservative religious movements such as Moral Rearmament, evangelical Christians, and Islamic movements (Nederveen Pieterse 1992a). Gandhi and Gramsci, as contemporaries, were aware of the importance of popular religion (Pantham 1995). Teaming up with popular religion has been a strategy of insurgency and counter-insurgency all along, notably in the decolonization struggles. In Egypt president Sadat legalized the Muslim Brotherhood; Moroccan and Algerian governments leaned over to the mosques; Israel sponsored Hamas as a counterpoint to Fatah and the PLO; and the US together with Pakistan, Saudi Arabia, and Israel funded, supplied, and trained the mujahideen in the Afghan war. The Soviets were aligned with the northerners in Afghanistan, while the US supported the mujahideen in the South who were mostly Pashtuns. The ensuing 'Talibanization' is a variant of McJihad (Rashid 2001; Ahmed 2003). The CIA term is blowback: blowback from the Afghan war and 'Arab Afghans' returning to Egypt, Algeria, and later Bosnia with new military skills further nourished Islamic radicalism (Johnson 2000; Rashid 2001; Cooley 1999).

Mahmood Mamdani views this episode as part of the wider American effort to enlist proxy forces against communism and militant nationalist regimes, such as Unita in Angola, Renamo in Mozambique, the

Contras in Nicaragua, rightwing paramilitaries in Colombia, and the Afghan mujahideen (Mamdani 2004). Towards the end of the Cold War the Reagan administration relied on low-intensity conflict and in the process created a privatized and ideologically stateless resistance force and transnational cadres of uprooted individuals across the Middle East. State terrorism has a long lineage, but this period is significant in the evolution of political terrorism also because it coincides with lethal arms becoming cheaper and more widely available. The 'Green Belt' of the Cold War era has returned as the contemporary 'arc of extremism'.

This is not to suggest a reductionist interpretation. Conservative trends in Islam are several and have diverse sources. They have been nourished by Wahhabism and its puritanical influence, and by madrassas in Muslim countries and the Muslim diaspora. State Islam (such as Al-Azhar in Egypt, Dyanet in Turkey) plays a conservative role of a different hue (Barraclough 1998). The early Muslim labour migration to Europe often consisted of immigrants of rural background led by imams with little education. Information technology enables the spread of alternatives from the Zapatistas to the World Social Forum and Islamism. Trendy Muslim websites in the West, for all their techno savvy, often disseminate orthodox Islam because of their disconnection from the dynamics of Islamic renewal (Khatib 2006).

Several of these trends are co-dependent with western developments, typically clustered around fossil fuels, geopolitics, and the Cold War. As the Cold War came to a close, western attitudes towards Islam changed. Liberal democracy seemed to be the sole victor; proxy forces had to be brought back under control and yesterday's freedom fighters became the new enemy. In this u-turn, Huntington's 1993 article on the clash of civilizations was a signal moment. According to Huntington, 'Islam has bloody borders' (Huntington 1996).[6]

Globalization involves projects on the part of many diverse players (corporations, feminists, human rights campaigners, etc.). The umma is one among several globalizations, and contemporary Islam is both co-dependent with western modernity and deeply wired to the career of global capitalism and neo-liberalism *and* an alternative cosmopolitanism that is interspersed with many cultures. In Bryan Turner's words,

> Islam is now able to self-thematize Islamic religion as a self-reflective global system of cultural identity over and against the diversity and pluralism involved in the new consumer culture. (Turner 1994: 90)

Table 11.2   Contemporary globalization and Islamism

Dimensions	Episodes	Outcomes
Fossil fuels	US-Saudi-Wahhabi complex, palace fundamentalism	McJihad, petrodollars
Coercive modernization	Kemalism, Nasser, Iran (Shah), Baath parties, Tunisia	Backlash: Muslim Brotherhood, Iranian revolution, Alevis
Cold War anti-communism	Support Islam against the left: Egypt, Morocco, Algeria, Israel, US	Blowback: Cold War dialectics
Low-intensity conflict	US recruiting proxies (mujahideen)	Blowback: transnational resistance
Neo-liberalism	Infitah in Egypt, Turkey, Lebanon, Jordan	Rise of Islamist social services
Postmodernism	Muslim diaspora	Decentring of the West, multiculturalism
Information technology	Virtual umma	Virtual Mecca, websites
	Virtual caliphate	Al Qaeda

In Turkey this involves Islamic consumerism and entrepreneurialism that, though it has a history of its own, assimilates a neo-liberal ethos (Göle 2000; Adas 2003).

The umma suggests greater unity than exists and is fragmented along many lines. In this setting, Islamism of various kinds has become not merely an alternative globalization (Beeley 1992), but a rival project. Al Qaeda and September 11th are part of this equation. Al Qaeda's sources go back to the Saudi connection, Wahhabism, the Egyptian Ikhwan, the Afghan war, and the Arab Afghans, and the United States is involved in each of these junctures. Table 11.2 gives a simplified overview of ways in which contemporary globalization and Islamism are interrelated.[7]

In this light, let us revisit the usual accounts of 'Islamic fundamentalism'. Islamism is interpreted as a reaction or backlash against modernity, a bastion outside the modern, and a backwater of globalization, as argued by Bernard Lewis, Fouad Ajami, Daniel Pipes, Samuel Huntington, Martin Kramer, Bassam Tibi, Thomas Meyer, and others. This view is shared by Enlightenment rationalists, western feminists, terrorism experts, and others who find a foe in 'Islamic fundamentalism'. This outlook generally shares the following features:

- It focusses on ideas, values and politics that are divorced from political economy.
- These ideas are seen as arising from internal conditions that are divorced from the role of external forces (oil companies, western powers, arms exporters, etc.).
- Western modernity is viewed in its postcard image divorced from its dark side (such as colonialism and racism) and dialectics.

This representation glosses over the interrelations between modernity and Islam past and present. While the alleged foe of modernity is 'fundamentalism', in the United States, conservative Christianity is a major electoral base of the Republican Party.[8] In this outlook Muslim societies are deemed less capable of development and democracy. According to Etzioni, 'it is an elementary fact that Islamic cultures are less amenable to fast-paced development than East Asian societies' (Etzioni 2002: 34) which apparently overlooks Malaysia, Turkey, and the United Arab Emirates.

The present discussion yields fundamentally different claims. The Islamic world has been a hub and driving force of early globalization and has made fundamental contributions to cosmopolitanism. Transnational networks such as *hawal* banking build on old infrastructures of Muslim globalization. When the Islamic world lost its intercontinental middling position, Islam spread beyond the Middle East and mixed with cultures in Asia, Africa, and eventually the Americas, giving Islamic cosmopolitanism a more diverse profile. This is what Malcolm X encountered on his hajj in Mecca. Contemporary radical Islamism is, as many have argued, a political rather than a religious phenomenon. Radical Islam, in contrast to the cliché view of fundamentalism, is an essentially modern Islamic Jacobinism (Esposito 1992; Ray 1993; Nederveen Pieterse 1994a, Achcar 2003; Simons 2003). The traditionalist account of fundamentalism ignores the ongoing reforms and internal modernization within Islamism, such as the 'new Islamism' and the 'renewal of renewal' in Egypt (Baker 2004; Hamzawy 2003). Militant Islam is co-dependent with global capitalism and American hegemony, a relationship that may be summed up as McJihad. Part of this is blowback of the Cold War, including the role of American proxies. Networks such as Al Qaeda build on these far flung links. Militant Islamic movements primarily concern struggles within Muslim countries. The turn against the United States, which culminated in September 11th, has come since the American u-turn after the end of the Cold War. The United States abandoned its former allies (as in Afghanistan) and in the next round, declared them the new enemy.

The polemical account of 'Islamic fundamentalism' for general consumption is at odds with US national security accounts of Islamic threats. The former presents Islamism as an irrelevant anti-modernity, while the latter treats it as a major threat and views Bin Laden as the CEO of Al Qaeda as a modern transnational enterprise (Nederveen Pieterse 2004: 48).

Assimilating the new enemy with the old under the heading of total-itarianism has been a long-term concern of Bernard Lewis. 'Islamic fascism', a theme that emerged in 2006 and in the US elections, makes a similar case. The aim is to equate the war against 'Islamo-fascism' with the wars against Hitler, Fascism and Leninism, as a war for civilization and as 'the ideological war of the twenty-first century'.

Islam and American national security

The point of departure of a brief study of the Rand Corporation is that 'the outside world should try to encourage a moderate, democratic inter-pretation and representation of Islam' and this has 'gained great urgency after September 11th 2001' (Benard 2003: 1). The exercise carries some weight because Rand is a research subcontractor of the CIA and the Pentagon and because it generally matches the Washington approach in the 'war for civilization' (e.g. Satloff 2004). Let us examine this approach as a summing up of emerging core tenets of American national security policy vis-à-vis Islam. Cheryl Benard distinguishes four essen-tial positions in Islam as overlapping segments on a continuum:

1. *Fundamentalists* who put forth an aggressive, expansionist version of Islam. This includes scriptural fundamentalists (Iranian Shia and Sunni Wahhabis) and radical fundamentalists (such as Al Qaeda and the Taliban).
2. *Traditionalists*, including conservative (resisting change) and reform-ist varieties (cautious adaptation to change).
3. *Modernists* who believe in the historicity of Islam and seek far-reaching changes in orthodoxy.
4. *Secularists* who believe in the separation of state and religion.

(Benard 2003: 8f)

In addition, she mentions Sufism ('Sufism represents and open, intellectual interpretation of Islam'). Of the modernists she says, 'The modernist vision matches our own. Of all the groups, this one is most congenial to the values and the spirit of modern democratic society' (Benard 2003: 36f). The modernists however face two handicaps: financial (fundamentalists receive far more funding) and political. After setting forth the positions of these groups on a wide range of issues, Benard proposes a strategy along the following lines:

> Support the modernists first, enhancing their vision of Islam over that of the traditionalists by providing them with a broad platform to articulate and disseminate their views.
>   Back the traditionalists enough to keep them viable against the fundamentalists [...] and to prevent a closer alliance between these two groups. Encourage disagreements between traditionalists and fundamentalists. Encourage the popularity and acceptance of Sufism, etc.
>   Confront and oppose the fundamentalists. Encourage divisions among fundamentalists.
>   Selectively support secularists.
>
> (Benard 2003: 47, xif)

Let us unpack this approach. First, it is a variation on the New Policy Agenda that USAID and OECD agencies adopted in the 1990s throughout the developing world: 'building democracy by fostering civil society' (Bernard et al. 1998). This report echoes this premise in practically identical wording: 'This approach seeks to strengthen and foster the development of civil, democratic Islam and of modernization and development' (Benard 2003: 47). In a speech to the Heritage Foundation in December 2002, Colin Powell announced a new 'US-Middle East Partnership Initiative' that will 'provide American support and $29 million of initial funding for a variety of programmes to promote civil society, political participation, and democracy in the Arab world' (Gordon 2003: 161). This Rand study is a policy study of how best to allocate such funds.

The report is ahistorical – understandable in a brief study, yet even so historical memory is strikingly absent. Erasing history comes with the modernizing, engineering approach to Islamic societies in which history does not count or counts only as an obstacle – replicating the modernization approach in development, which is long bankrupt (Nederveen Pieterse 2001).

The unproblematic perspective on modernity reveals a deeper binary structure. The fundamental matrix of American perspectives on Islam is a binary view in which the West is modern and democratic, and Islam, especially militant political Islam, is pre-modern or anti-modern. A differentiated view that allows for nuances and subdivisions within the Islamic world does not belie this matrix, as this passage suggests: 'The modernist vision matches our own. Of all the groups, this one is most congenial to the values and the spirit of modern democratic society' (Benard 2003: 37). The implication is that *we* are modern and *they* are not (but some of them are like us). The casual binarism in US American perceptions also comes across in views on occupied Iraq, as in this headline: 'Iraq navigates between Islam and democracy' (Sachs 2004). This approach echoes a US attitude to development: the search for their mirror image, the middle class and the entrepreneur as culture hero; another trend that goes back to early post-war development policy.

The weaknesses of the modernists, according to Benard, are financial and political. Absent in this account is class analysis and political economy. Modernists are viewed as key allies, but there is no analysis of the political economy of modernism and no recognition of the way in which policies such as structural adjustment (in the Middle East known as infitah or opening) and OECD trade barriers *impede* the development of a middle class in Muslim societies (cf. Kuran 2002). National security perspectives and political economy do not interact; the paradigms do not meet. The institutional foundation of policy incoherence is the compartmentalization of knowledge.

Strengthening the modernists is taken as a matter of outside ideological intervention, and the imagined US American capability for intervening in the Islamic world and engineering ideological change is large and taken to great lengths, such as 'Publish and distribute their works at subsidized cost. Encourage them to write for mass audiences and for youth. Introduce their views into the curriculum of Islamic education', etc. This approach does not reflect on the political and ethical implications of this kind of engineering and the blowback it may produce, such as growing domestic suspicion of modernist positions. The time frame is immediate, now, so there is no developmental perspective to this strategy. A remarkable passage notes:

> While U.S. officialdom appears to be seeking *a symbolic rapprochement* with Islam on the level of outward lifestyle issues, European leaders seem more inclined to try for *a rapprochement on political issues*

they believe to be important to Muslims. The split between the United States and Europe over Iraq is in part attributable to this difference. (Benard 2003: 35; emphasis added)

This reveals the true blue American approach: it is essentially a matter of ideological repackaging. There is not a single mention of the obvious, common sense way to strengthen moderates in Muslim societies: simply by adopting more even-handed policies in the Middle East.

Viewed in this light, this edifice of modernists, traditionalists etc. is contrived and circumvents the real issue: the United States wants the Middle East to change on its terms and does not want to change itself. Hence there is no real dialogue. There cannot be because the United States does not even contemplate changing its policies on Israel or its alliance with Saudi Arabia and other regimes according to the Friendly Tyrant principle. Ideological engineering and propaganda will have no effect as long as the real issues – Israel, Palestine, and American hegemony itself – are no-go zones of US policy. This is another policy study that is studiously devoid of self-reflection or reflection on US policies and does not acknowledge blowback. The attitudes of Muslim fundamentalists and traditionalists are described but not explained; they are presented as ideological dispositions (read: Muslim rage) rather than as reactions to policies, including US policies. Instead the emphasis is on ideas (democracy, civil society, modernity) which are taken in the abstract and decontextualized from Middle East realities.

'Islam's current crisis', according to Benard, 'has two main components: a failure to thrive and a loss of connection to the global mainstream' (Benard 2003: ix). Richard Falk refers to the geopolitics of exclusion (Falk 1996). But exclusion is not entirely accurate. The instances of exclusion that Falk mentions – double standards, a discriminatory non-proliferation regime for nuclear weapons, policies in the world economy, responses to terrorist incidents, the stigmatization of 'rogue states' – are, rather, instances of asymmetric inclusion or *integration* in a world order on unequal terms. Indeed, exclusion does not sync with decades of global economic integration via the oil industry and political integration under the tutelage of US hegemony.

The Rand approach is not entirely without self-criticism; it criticizes the 'official Muslim Life in America Web site' of the US State Department for being 'exclusively dedicated to traditionalist content'. And it cautions, 'Accommodating traditionalists to an excessive degree can weaken our credibility and moral persuasiveness. An uncritical alliance with traditionalists can be misunderstood as appeasement and fear' (Benard

2003: 36). In other words, it counsels against 'going soft'. This intervention is a one-dimensional approach of Americanizing the Middle East,
ideological, Machiavellian, and unreflexive.

Awareness of Islam's long cosmopolitan lineage should inspire a sense
of historical modesty. For over a millennium the Muslim world has mixed
and mingled with many cultures from Africa to Asia and Europe. This
gives it a unique depth, sprawl, and resilience. Awareness of this background should lead to a dialogue with the worlds of Islam and Islamism.
This dialogue should be civilizational, political, and reflexive. It should
be civilizational in recognizing Islamic cosmopolitanism past and
present, political in taking seriously the concrete grievances of Muslims,
in particular the question of Palestine, and reflexive in considering one's
own role in the process and in recognizing global dynamics.

This should also include reflexivity and willingness to come to terms
with the past in the Muslim world. Nostalgia for the caliphate and for
past Muslim cultural splendour and accomplishment is no substitute
for coming to terms with the geopolitical, geo-economic, and geo-
cultural trauma that the Muslim world suffered by losing its intercontinental middleman role. The second trauma that afflicted the Muslim
world is the resource curse of fossil fuels and its conservative ramifica-
tions, including McJihad. The third trauma that afflicts Islam is that
since the end of the Cold War, targeting Islam and 'fundamentalism'
has become an ideological and cultural successor to attacking communism. They have a polarizing effect within Islam, strengthen hardliners,
and crowd out precisely the humanistic and cosmopolitan strains of
Islam (Qureshi 2006; cf. Qureshi and Sells 2003). It requires profound
sophistication on the part of Muslims to address these three traumas,
but it is the only way to recover Islamic cosmopolitanism.

Notes

1. Huntington makes the ethnocentric claim that 'the very notion that there
   could be a "universal civilization" is a Western idea' (1993: 41).
2. This literature is too large to reference here; note Subrahmanyam 1997, 1998;
   Pomeranz 2000; Hobson 2004; and references in Nederveen Pieterse 2006.
3. 'Let there be no compulsion in religion' (Quran 2: 256), quoted in
   Weeramantry (1988: 85).
4. According to Mazrui, this reflects the 'relatively nonracial nature' of Islam.
   He also notes, 'While Islam may generate more political violence than
   Western culture, Western culture generates more street violence than Islam'
   (1997: 129f).
5. Elsewhere I ask, 'how European is Europe?' (Nederveen Pieterse 1994b).

6. An early treatment is Said 1981; recent discussions are Qureshi and Sells 2003.
7. Besides those mentioned in previous notes, sources include Sayeed 1997, Johnson 2000, Abdo 2000, Ahmed 1992, Lubeck 1999, Simons 2003, Noor 2000.
8. On Christianity and capitalism, see Frank (2000).

References

Abdo, G. (2000) *No God but God: Egypt and the triumph of Islam*, New York: Oxford University Press.

Abu-Lughod, J. L. (1989) *Before European Hegemony: the world-system A.D. 1250–1350*, New York: Oxford University Press.

Achcar, G. (2003) *The Clash of Barbarisms: September 11 and the making of the new world disorder*, New York: Monthly Review Press.

Adas, M. (ed) (1993) *Islamic and European expansion: the forging of a global order*, Philadelphia: Temple University Press.

Adas, E. (2003) *The prophet and profit: the rise of Islamist entrepreneurs and new interpretations of Islam in Turkey*, University of Illinois at Urbana-Champaign, Dissertation.

Ahmed, A. S. (1992) *Postmodernism and Islam*, London: Routledge.

Ahmed, D. S. (ed) (2003) *Gendering the spirit: women, religion and the post-colonial response*, London: Zed Books.

Alatas, S. F. (1993) 'A Khaldunian perspective on the dynamics of Asiatic societies', *Comparative Civilizations Review*, 29.

Alatas, S. F. (2006) 'From Jāmi`ah to University: multiculturalism and Christian-Muslim dialogue', *Current Sociology*, 54(1): 112–32.

Al-Azmeh, A. (1993) *Islams and modernities*, London: Verso.

Al-Azmeh, A. (2003) *Ibn Khaldun: an essay in reinterpretation*, Budapest: Central European University Press.

Amin, S. (1978) *The Arab nation*, London: Zed Books.

Archibugi, D. and D. Held (eds) (1995) *Cosmopolitan democracy: agenda for a new world order*, Cambridge: Polity Press.

Armstrong, K. (2001) Islam through history, pp. 53–70 in Hoge Jr, J. F. and Rose, G. (eds) (2001) *How did this happen? Terrorism and the new war*, New York: Public Affairs.

Atasoy, S. (1999) 'Globalization and Turkey: from capitulations to contemporary civilization', pp. 257–70 in Ismael, S. T. (ed) (1999) *Globalization: policies, challenges and responses*, Calgary: Detselig.

Bakar, O. (1996) 'Islam's destiny: a bridge between East and West', *JUST Commentary*, 33: 1–5.

Baker, R. W. (1999) 'Egypt in the space and time of globalism', pp. 243–56 in Ismael, S. T. (ed) (1999) *Globalization: policies, challenges, and responses*, Calgary: Detselig.

Baker, R. W. (2004) *Islam without fear: Egypt and the new Islamists*, Cambridge, MA: Harvard University Press.

Barber, B. R. (1995) *Jihad vs. McWorld: how the planet is both falling apart and coming together and what this means for democracy*, New York: Times Books.

Barraclough, S. (1998) 'Al-Azhar: between the government and the Islamists', *Middle East Journal*, 52(2): 236–49.

Beck, U. (2006) *Cosmopolitan vision*, Cambridge: Polity Press.

Beeley, B. (1992) 'Islam as a global political force', pp. 293–311 in McGrew, A. G. and Lewis, P. G. (eds) (1992) *Global Politics*, Cambridge: Polity Press.

Benard, C. (2003) *Civil democratic Islam: Partners, resources, and strategies*, Santa Monica, CA: Rand Corporation.

Bernal, M. (1987) *Black Athena: Afroasiatic roots of classical civilization: the fabrication of Ancient Greece 1785–1985*, London: Free Association Press.

Bernard, A., Helmich, H. and Lehning, P. B. (eds) (1998) *Civil society and international cooperation*, Paris: OECD.

Boase, R. (1977) *The origin and meaning of courtly love*, Manchester: Manchester University Press.

Boase, R. (1978) *The troubadour revival*, London: Routledge and Kegan Paul.

Burke III, E. (1979) 'Islamic history as world history: Marshall Hodgson, "The Venture of Islam"', *International Journal of Middle East Studies*, 10(2): 241–64.

Calhoun, C., Price, P. and Timmer, A. (eds) (2002) *Understanding September 11*, New York: New Press.

Camilleri, J. A. and C. Muzaffar (eds) (1998) *Globalization: the perspectives and experiences of the religious traditions of Asia Pacific*, Petaling Jaya: International Movement for a Just World.

Cohen, R. and Rai, S. (eds) (1999) *Global social movements*, London: Routledge.

Cohen, W. I. (2000) *East Asia at the Center: Four thousand years of engagement with the world*, New York: Columbia University Press.

Cooley, J. (1999) *Unholy Wars: Afghanistan, America, and International Terrorism*, London: Pluto Press.

Dean, J., Anderson, J. W. and Lovink, G. (eds) (2006) *Reformatting politics: information technology and global civil society*, London: Routledge.

Delanty, G. (ed) (2006) *Europe and Asia beyond East and West: towards a new cosmopolitanism*, London: Routledge.

Eaton, R. M. (1993) 'Islamic history as global history', pp. 1–36 in Adas, M. (ed) (1993) *Islamic and European expansion: the forging of a global order*, Philadelphia: Temple University Press.

Ernst, C. W. (1992) *Eternal Garden: Mysticism, History, and Politics at a South Asian Sufi Center*, Albany: State University of New York Press.

Esposito, J. L. (1992) *The Islamic threat: myth or reality?* New York: Oxford University Press.

Etzioni, A. (2002) 'Opening Islam', *Society*, 39(5): 29–35.

Falk, R. (1996) *False universalism and the geopolitics of exclusion: the case of Islam*, Princeton University Center of International Studies, unpublished paper.

Fallaci, O. (2002) *The rage and the pride*, Milan: Rizzoli.

Ferguson, N. (2001) 'Clashing civilizations or mad mullahs: the United States between informal and formal empire', pp. 115–41 in Talbott, S. and Chanda, N. (eds) (2001) *The age of terror: America and the world after September 11*, New York: Basic Books.

Frank, A. G. (1998) *ReOrient: global economy in the Asian age*, Berkeley: University of California Press.

Frank, T. (2000) *One market under god: extreme capitalism, market populism and the end of economic democracy*, New York: Doubleday.

Geertz, C. (1968) *Islam observed: religious development in Morocco and Indonesia*, Chicago: Chicago University Press.

Geertz, C. (2003) 'Which way to Mecca?', *New York Review of Books*, June 12: 27–30.

Goldstone, J. A. (2002) 'States, terrorists, and the clash of civilizations', pp. 139–58 in Calhoun et al. (eds) (2002) *Understanding September 11*, New York: New Press.

Göle, N. (2000) 'Snapshots of Islamic modernities', *Daedalus*, 129(1): 91–117.

Gordon, P. H. (2003) 'Bush's Middle East vision', *Survival*, 45(1): 155–65.

Gunn, G. C. (2003) *First globalization: the Eurasian exchange, 1500–1800*, Lanham, MD: Rowman & Littlefield.

Halabi, Y. (1999) 'Orientalism and US Democratization Policy in the Middle East', *International Studies*, 36: 375–92.

Hamzawy, A. (2003) 'Exploring theoretical and programmatic changes in contemporary Islamist discourse: the journal *Al-Manar al-Jadid*', pp. 120–46 in Karam, A. (ed) (2003) *Transnational political Islam*, London: Pluto Press.

Hobson, J. M. (2004) *The Eastern Origins of Western Civilization*, Cambridge: Cambridge University Press.

Hodgson, M. G. S. (1974) *The venture of Islam: Conscience and history in a world civilization*, 3 vols, Chicago: University of Chicago Press.

Hoerder, D. (2002) *Cultures in contact: world migrations in the Second Millennium*, Durham: Duke University Press.

Hoge Jr, J. F. and Rose, G. (eds) (2001) *How did this happen? Terrorism and the new war*, New York: Public Affairs.

Huntington, S. P. (1993) 'The clash of civilizations', *Foreign Affairs* 72(3): 22–49.

Huntington, S. P. (1996) *The clash of civilizations and the remaking of world order*, New York: Simon and Schuster.

Huntington, S. P. (2003) 'America in the world', *Hedgehog Review*, 5(1): 7–18.

Iqbal, A. M. (1996) *The reconstruction of religious thought in Islam*, Lahore: Sang-e-Meel.

Ismael, S. T. (ed) (1999) *Globalization: policies, challenges and responses*, Calgary: Detselig.

Johnson, C. (2000) *Blowback: the costs and consequences of American empire*, New York: Henry Holt.

Karam, A. (ed) (2003) *Transnational political Islam*, London: Pluto Press.

Keohane, R. O. (2002) 'The globalization of informal violence, theories of world politics and the "liberalism of fear"', pp. 77–91 in Calhoun et al, (eds) (2002) *Understanding September 11*, New York: New Press.

Kathib, L. (2006) 'Communicating Islamic fundamentalism as global citizenship', pp. 69–84 in Dean, J., Anderson, J. W. and Lovink, G. (eds) (2006) *Reformatting politics: information technology and global civil society*, London: Routledge.

Kuran, T. (2002) The religious undertow of Muslim economic grievances, pp. 67–74 in Calhoun et al. (eds) (2002) *Understanding September 11*, New York: New Press.

Kuran, T. (2004) *The Islamic commercial crisis: institutional roots of the delay in the Middle East's economic modernization*, papers.ssrn.com/abstract_id=276377.

Levtzion, N. (ed) (1979) *Conversion to Islam*, New York: Holmes & Meier.

Lewis, B. (2002) *What went wrong? The clash between Islam and modernity in the Middle East*, New York: Perennial.

Lewis, B. (2003) *The crisis of Islam: holy war and unholy terror*, New York: Modern Library.

Lubeck, P. (1999) 'The antinomies of Islamic revival: why do Islamic movements thrive under globalization?', in Cohen, R. and Rai, S. (eds) (1999) *Global social movements*, London: Routledge.

Makdisi, G. (1981) *The rise of colleges: institutions of learning in Islam and the West*, Edinburgh: Edinburgh University Press.

Mamdani, M. (2004) *Good Muslim, bad Muslim: America, the Cold War and the roots of terror*, New York: Pantheon.

Mazrui, A. A. (1997) 'Islamic and Western values', *Foreign Affairs*, 76(5): 118–32.

McGrew, A. G. and Lewis, P. G. (eds) (1992) *Global Politics*, Cambridge: Polity Press.

McNeill, W. H. (1979) *A world history*, third edition, Oxford: Oxford University Press.

Mernissi, F. (2003) 'Palace fundamentalism and liberal democracy', pp. 58–67 in Qureshi, E. and Sells, M. A. (eds) 2003) *The new Crusades: constructing the Muslim enemy*, New York: Columbia University Press.

Mitchell, T. (2002) 'McJihad: Islam in the US Global Order', *Social Text*, 20(4): 1–18.

Mortimer, E. (1982) *Faith and power: the politics of Islam*, New York: Vintage.

Nandy, A. (1989) 'Shamans, savages and the wilderness: on the audibility of dissent and the future of civilizations', *Alternatives*, 14(3): 263–277.

Nederveen Pieterse, J. (1989) *Empire and emancipation: power and liberation on a world scale*, New York: Praeger.

Nederveen Pieterse, J. (1992a) 'Christianity, politics and Gramscism of the right', pp. 1–31 in Nederveen Pieterse, J. (ed) (1992b) *Christianity and hegemony. Religion and politics on the frontiers of social change*, Oxford: Berg.

Nederveen Pieterse, J. (ed) (1992b) *Christianity and hegemony. Religion and politics on the frontiers of social change*, Oxford: Berg.

Nederveen Pieterse, J. (1994a) '"Fundamentalism" discourses: enemy images', *Women against Fundamentalism*, 1(5): 2–6.

Nederveen Pieterse, J. (1994b) 'Unpacking the West: how European is Europe?' pp. 129–49 in Rattansi, A. and Westwood, S. (eds) (1994) *Racism, modernity, identity: on the Western front*, Cambridge: Polity.

Nederveen Pieterse, J. (2001) *Development theory: deconstructions/ reconstructions*, London: Sage.

Nederveen Pieterse, J. (2004) *Globalization or empire?*, New York: Routledge.

Nederveen Pieterse, J. (2006) 'Oriental globalization: past and present', pp. 61–73 in Delanty, G. (ed) (2006) *Europe and Asia beyond East and West: towards a new cosmopolitanism*, London: Routledge.

Noor, F. A. (2000) *The caliphate: coming soon to a country near you?*, Berlin, unpublished paper.

Pantham, T. (1995) Proletarian pedagogy, Satyagraha and charisma: Gramsci and Gandhi, pp. 165–189 in Roy, R. (ed) (1995) *Contemporary crisis and Gandhi*, New Delhi: Discovery.

Pollock, S. (2000) 'Cosmopolitan and vernacular in history', *Public Culture*, 12(3): 591–626.

Pomeranz, K. (2000) *The great divergence: China, Europe and the making of the modern world economy*, Princeton, NJ: Princeton University Press.

Quran 2: 256

Qureshi, E. and Sells, M. A. (eds) (2003) *The new Crusades: constructing the Muslim enemy*, New York: Columbia University Press.

Qureshi, E. (2006) 'The Islam the riots drowned out', *New York Times*, 12 February 2006: WK 15.

Rashid, A. (2001) *Taliban: the story of the Afghan warlords*, London: Pan Macmillan.

Rashid, S. (ed) (1997) *'The clash of civilizations'? Asian responses*, Karachi: Oxford University Press.

Rattansi, A. and Westwood, S. (eds) (1994) *Racism, modernity, identity: on the Western front*, Cambridge: Polity.

Ray, L. J. (1993) *Rethinking social theory: emancipation in the age of global social movements*, London: Sage.

Rosenau, J. N. (1990) *Turbulence in world politics*, Brighton: Harvester.

Roy, R. (ed) (1995) *Contemporary crisis and Gandhi*, New Delhi: Discovery.

Sachs, S. (2004) 'Iraq navigates between Islam and democracy', *New York Times*, 7 March : WK 3.

Said, E. W. (1981) *Covering Islam*, New York: Pantheon.

Satloff, R. (2004) *The battle of ideas in the war on terror*, Washington, DC: The Washington Institute for Near East Policy.

Sayeed, K. B. (1997) *Western dominance and political Islam: challenge and response*, Karachi: Oxford University Press.

Sayyid, S. (2003) *A fundamental fear: Eurocentrism and the emergence of Islamism*, (second edition) London: Zed Books.

Sharabi, H. (1988) *Neopatriarchy: a theory of distorted change in Arab society*, New York: Oxford University Press.

Simons Jr, T. W. (2003) *Islam in a globalizing world*, Stanford Law and Politics.

Stavrianos, L. S. (1981) *Global rift: the Third World comes of age*, New York: Morrow.

Subrahmanyam, S. (1997) 'Connected histories: notes towards a reconfiguration of early modern Eurasia', *Modern Asian Studies*, 31(3): 735–62.

Subrahmanyam, S. (1998) 'Hearing voices: vignettes of early modernity in South Asia, 1400–1750', *Daedalus*, 127(3).

Talbott, S. and Chanda, N. (eds) (2001) *The age of terror: America and the world after September 11*, New York: Basic Books.

Tiryakian, E. (1996) 'Three metacultures of modernity: Christian, Gnostic, Chthonic', *Theory Culture & Society*, 13(1): 99–118.

Toulmin, S. (1990) *Cosmopolis: the hidden agenda of modernity*, Chicago, University of Chicago Press.

Turner, B. S. (1992) *Max Weber: from history to modernity*, London: Routledge.

Turner, B. S. (1994) *Orientalism, postmodernism, and globalism*, London: Routledge.

UNDP (2002) *Arab Human Development Report*, New York: Oxford University and Arab Fund for Economic and Social Development.

UNDP (2003) *Arab Human Development Report*, New York: UNDP.

Veenhof, K. (1997) 'Modern' features in old Assyrian trade', *JESHO*, 40(4): 336–66.

Wallerstein, I. (2003) *The decline of American power*, New York: New Press.

Weeramantry, C. G. (1988) *Islamic jurisprudence: an international perspective*, New York: St Martin's Press.

Zizek, S. (2004) 'Passion: regular or decaf?', *In These Times*, 27 February.

12
Place and Voice in the Global Age: A View from Latin America

Enrique Rodriguez Larreta

The relation between the local and its representation in the context of various macrosocial interrelations is a subject directly related to Professor Karl Eric Knutsson's intellectual trajectory. In the inaugural lecture of his chair in social anthropology 'Reflections on the identity of a discipline' (1970; author's translation from Swedish), anthropological knowledge is studied, departing from the analysis of participant observation, the characteristic method of the discipline. Knutsson examines the relation between the researcher and the human group which she/he studies. He argues that the work of the anthropologist is due to fail if the anthropologist does not establish confidence or does not sympathize with the essential qualities of the culture that she/he is studying (ibid.: 74).

Inspired by Håkan Thörnebohm's epistemological notion of perspective, Knutsson considers that the peculiarity of the 'anthropological perspective' is that it is built up from below and from the interior of the human group under study. The human groups studied by anthropology are in general situated in a subordinated and dominated place (ibid.: 79). In Professor Knutsson's conception which he shares with other anthropologists (Otavio Velho and Renato Rosaldo for example), anthropology in some sense may be considered as a moral community. In this way, it keeps the relationship with the Rousseaunian romantic roots of the discipline, in the sense that Immanuel Kant considered Rousseau the 'Newton of the moral world'. But another aspect of the anthropological perspective is the modernist dimension of the discipline, to study the variations of society and culture at global scale from a scientific point of view, empirically informed.

Karl Eric Knutsson's intellectual biography is essentially contained in that inaugural lecture. He was the Africanist who did extended field work in East Africa, and was later involved in the building of aid to the Third World institutions in the best Nordic tradition of engagement with social equality, and, at the same time, the social scientist who studied ritual forms of local cultures at the African Horn, and had a permanent theoretical interest in the new problems posed to social sciences.

Which is the relation between the local and the global? Which is the ontological status of these categories? How is the resistance of sub-altern groups expressed in the context of globalization? *Can the subaltern speak*, to refer to the question posed by Gayatri Chakravorty Spivak, and if not, who may speak in their place? What is the place of global institutions like the United Nations in the definition of world agendas?

These are some of the questions suggested by the reading, more than 30 years later, of the perspective presented by Professor Knutsson in his inaugural lecture. In this essay I will explore very briefly some of the key concepts of the discussion: locality and globalization. In the second part I will present in brief some of the examples about the interrelation between locality, globalization and voice in the South cone of Latin America.

The local as a problem

An archaeology of the local in human sciences undoubtedly has anthropology as a privileged protagonist in the wide spectrum of its central tradition, from Malinowski to Claude Levi Strauss and Clifford Geertz. The methodology of investigation in anthropological research has centred around the local, understood as a natural *container* of the social relationships. The local perspective adapts exactly to the fieldwork techniques concentrated in the study of social relations and institutions at a small scale. Urban anthropology and the study of populations on the move challenged this methodology, but during most of its history the local worked as a non problematic entity in the anthropological tradition.

One of the uses of the local in anthropology was the search for certain universals in the multiple repertories of cultures studied by anthropologists. The comparison between rituals, social institutions, technologies, and cognitive structures would be incorporated into the archive of anthropological knowledge. Thus the *Others*, from the point of view of the West, would be added to the common ground of a human nature postulated as an axiom. But at the same time, local knowledge allowed the discovery of exceptions from supposed universals. From the exchange systems to the Oedipal complex, the anthropological archive contributed to relativise the European reason, bringing forward material potentially critical of western civilization.

In the framework of the studies of the colonial encounter and the early investigations on acculturation and internal colonialism, the local is a threatened field gradually absorbed or destroyed in the imperial encounter. In some tendencies of contemporary anthropology, the local is being thought of as a construction. From this perspective, it has been said that locality

> is primarily relational and contextual rather than scalar or spatial. I see it as a complex phenomenological quality, constituted by a series of links between the sense of social immediacy, the true technologies of interactivity and the relativity of contexts. This phenomenological quality which expresses itself in certain kinds of agency, sociality, and reproductivity is the main predicate of locality as a category (or subject) that I seek to explore. In contrast, I use the term neighbourhood to refer to the actual existing social forms in which locality, as a dimension or value is variably realized. Neighbourhoods, in this usage, are situated communities characterized by their actuality whether spatial or virtual and their potential for social reproduction. (Appadurai 1996: 179)

The Anthropology of Globalization (Inda and Rosaldo 2002) has focussed on the processes of global production of locality. This production exists in conflictive form due to the participation of various agents: national states which have specific logics of incorporation and affiliation, social movements that circulate through different territorial spaces and are producers of meaning, and technologies of production and communication of increasingly complex and powerful images and meanings that facilitate the formation of diasporas and translocal communities. What the increasing body of literature suggests is that the local, far from being a natural given space, is the result of complex practices of localization and identification.

Thus, to fully understand the local, it is necessary to analyse the global processes that contribute to its formation, especially since the local refers mainly to the formation of a sense of belonging and community. It is not explained isolated in the contemporary world, but in the interrelation between different contexts of production of meaning.

Anyway, though the reflection on space and locality, as well as the analysis of the dissociations between culture, territory, and identity, is increasing in the mainstream of social sciences, and mainly in the public sphere, 'locality', 'culture', and 'identity' are understood as self-evident categories. Local resistance, the struggle of certain populations for cultural rights, is often considered an internal process of the human group in question, as a reaction from below. The global is considered the problematic, artificial, transitory pole vis-à-vis the ancestral solidity of the local. In a phenomenological description we would say that the local is associated to the values of home and intimacy, the warm and immediate, and the organic against the mechanic. Local culture is often perceived in the metaphor of family and blood ties. In order to try to better understand the nature of this phenomenon, it is necessary to examine the other pole of the apparent opposition and try to present a general description of the genealogy of the global.

The global as a problem

The periodization of globalization is a common chapter in the literature on this subject. In effect, if one considers globalization mainly as a process of interdependence between areas and human groups, it can be said that its origin may be traced back to the origins of mankind. Although this is a plausible argument, the exaggeration of continuities may erase certain singularities of the present. Thus, it obscures the fact that the planetary interconnection and the compression of space and time produce deep alterations in the mode of *being in the world* of all the populations of the planet. What we today call human population is a semiotic pluriverse which has more than five thousand languages and uncountable interconnected dialects.

In the age of fast transportation and communication at real time, we experience collectively the disenchantment of old self-contained local structures. In its intensification, the globalization erodes the imaginary communities, referred to ancestral territories and oriented towards themselves. The communities lose the privilege of the ethnocentrism, which places them symbolically as the centre of the world, and for all future become part of a wider intercontextual semiotic network.

Possibilities are thus open for the formation of new collective solidarities, but also for identity closings, struggles for recognition, and intensification of local and national conflicts. The present crisis and conflicts of globalization partly reflects the fact that the national state, one of the most successful central inventions of mankind as a collective unity of meaning and internal political order, turns out to be insufficient to face the increasing complexity of ecological and economic phenomena that limit its autonomy. At the same time, from below and inside its frontiers it is challenged by diasporic imaginary communities, centred on their territory and many polyethnic conflicts.

In short, globalization, due to its own extension and scale, is an inexorable process that does not need to justify itself. It has been observed that, 500 years after Columbus's travels, earth has been discovered, represented, occupied, and utilized intensively as a body covered by a dense net of circulatory movements and regular telecommunication systems. By means of electronic transmission systems, the suppression of distances has been solved technically in the big centres of power and consumption. From an aeronautical point of view earth has been reduced to a 50 hours jet trajectory, while in the case of satellites, time units of less than 90 minutes have been obtained. For radio and light transmission, earth has been reduced to a single point.

Facing an historical transformation of such magnitude and scale, the categories of individual psychology, optimism, and pessimism, are obviously insufficient. Risk and uncertainty are the main components of the new global condition. In any case, according to the description by Blaise Pascal: nature is an infinite sphere which has its centre everywhere and the circumference nowhere. Not by chance, in a later manuscript, Pascal used the word dreadful (*effroyable*) about the sphere: nature is a dreadful sphere. The inventor of modern mathematics of probabilities was at the same time one of the first thinkers of modem subjectivity. The interiorized dramatic theatre of transcendental consciousness is the necessary counterpart in a world that is no longer a cosmos or a community of problems (an *oikoumene* in Eric Voegelin's sense), but multiple universes of meaning hardly interconnected. A world, barely integrated by processes of colonial expansion, economic mechanisms, diffusion of images and meanings, cultural simulacra, international police interventions, and processes of extension of global political norms.

Latin America as a problem

Back then to our local perspective after this short tour: the region that we call 'Latin America'. It is a territory that is living the results of the processes of globalization. We experience a relevant redefinition of identities and culture followed by new ethnical and political emergencies. The subjects of national identity, the situation of cultural minorities, and conflicts with central countries, mainly the United States, are present in the entire region.

In a generic sense, the names of all continents have a cultural character. However, 'Latin America', as the name of a continent, is the only one that hears the name in a special sense. In an imperial way, Spain, Portugal, and France introduced Latinity in South America from the beginning of the modern ages. Regarding the chronology, in the mid-nineteenth century the name Latin America appeared written in Spanish by Hispano-American writers, before the French versions of the 1860s. Regarding the conceptualization, the origin of the concept Latin America was the Hispano-American resistance to the expansionism of the United States. The incursions of the pirate Walker in Central America, the annexation of Texas, and the imperial expansions on Mexican soil were the background to the Latin identification of America in contrast to the Anglo-Saxon North America (Ardao 1986: 44).

Those historical episodes, at the origin of the historic and cultural identification of Latin America, are relevant today since an important diaspora from Latin America in North America has provoked agitated academic debates about the North American cultural identity (Huntington 2004). The Latin immigration in the United States has had important cultural and economic consequences, initiating processes of transculturation and hybridization.

But at the same time, the increasing interregional economic interdependency has generated tension and conflict areas within national states in Latin America: growth of regionalism and development of ethnic-political movements in countries like Bolivia and Ecuador, tensions between national states due to economic interests and conflicts like the present controversy between Uruguay and Argentina caused by the installation of Finnish and Spanish cellulose factories by the Uruguay river, controversies between Brazil and Argentina due to the economy and the political leadership, and potential economic conflicts between Brazil and Bolivia regarding the natural gas and Petrobras investments in the neighbouring country. This is not an exhaustive list, but examples of factors of uncertainty and of a growing risk threshold, produced by the complex interrelations between the global and the local that were presented in the first part of this essay.

References

Appadurai, A. (1996) *Modernity at Large. Cultural Dimensions of Globalization*, Minneapolis: University of Minnesota Press.

Ardao, A. (1986) *Nuestra America Latina*, Montevideo: Ediciones de la Banda Oriental.

Huntington, S. (2004) *Who Are We?: The Challenges to America's National Identity*, New York: Simon & Schuster.

Inda, J. and Rosaldo, R. (ed) (2002) *The Anthropology of Globalization: A Reader*, Malden, MA: Blackwell Publishers.

Knutson, K. E. (1970) *Det Antropologiska Perspektivet: Reflexioner kring ett Ämnes Identitet*, Vetenskapliga Perspektiv, Stockholm: Stockholm Universitet.

Conclusion

Björn Hettne

This book, focussing on *sustainable development in a globalized world* is, together with a companion volume on *human values and global govern-ance*, the final outcome of six years' work of the 'Sector Committee on Culture, Security and Sustainable Social Development' within Riksbankens Jubileumsfond. A conceptual framework for the project has been given in the editor's preface. The project, described in the preface, is reported in two volumes which are complementary but also possible to read as separate books: *Sustainable Development in a Globalized World* and *Human Values and Global Governance*. The first deals with the development problem on different societal levels in the era of globaliza-tion. The second deals with relations between social formations on dif-ferent levels. Both can be said to belong to the genre of 'global studies' and the theoretical approach to this field should be 'global social the-ory'. Global social theory does not yet exist as such, it will be created by the theoretical discourse focussing on the causes and consequences, as well as improvement, of the globalized condition in all parts – more or less and differently globalized – of the world. Thus the discourse on global development is not concluded, it has just begun. It is my hope that this book (as well as he companion volume focussing on global relations), can serve as illustrations of the field.

What does 'development' mean in the globalized condition? The idea of development is rooted in the nation-state, both because development was considered to take place in a national space, that is to say the terri-tory that the sovereign state controlled, and also because the state was seen as the main player behind the national development strategy. This perception has become an anachronism because of globalization. Globalization, or more precisely the adaptation to the globalized condi-tion, seems to have become the current word for development. There was never any great agreement on the meaning of the development concept, and nowadays some speak of an era of 'post-development'. Development is in this view supposed to be over, together with the so called modern project, that is to say the belief that society, even the 'backward society', is continually improved by social reforms immanent in history.

Development can only be global development, and to the extent that national development strategies are to be meaningful they have to take the global context into consideration. Regarding globalization, there are already too many definitions for this concept to be a useful research tool in global studies. This is not to say that the definitions, distinctions, and elaborations of this phenomenon, proposed in the growing literature, do not make good sense. We live in a globalized condition, but this condition cannot be understood by simply applying the concept of globalization, which merely is an expression of this condition; in fact a measure of ignorance. We would need global social theory to explore the global condition further, in a more systematic way beyond methodological nationalism. The globalization debate signifies a crisis in social theorizing; and in development theory as the favourite child of modernity in particular. This theoretical crisis in turn derives from the crisis of the nation-state as the social science universe (methodological nationalism). A crisis of the nation-state does not imply its disappearance, but rather a change of its functions; for instance a reorientation from (inward-oriented) welfare states to (outward-oriented) competition states, a change which is perceived as a crisis by many of those who experience it, as well as by some (but far from all) of those who analyse it. We may also witness an 'unbundling' of state functions through the emergence of supranational protective and interventionist structures strengthening the societal dimension of world order and increasing the quality of international relations, that is what above was called global development, necessitating multilevel global governance with a strong role for the region but combined with a non-territorial network society.

The regional perspective dominated the first chapters of this book. Regions constitute an intermediate level between the global and the national and tend to become players in their own right. An 'imagined community' (Benedict Anderson's description of nation-states) can in principle be greater than the nation; it could be a region. However, we have so far seen little of such an identity on the regional level except in the case of the European Union, but even in this case many would argue that the existence of the EU has strengthened national as well as sub-national (micro-regional) identities. The historical role of Europe in shaping the world is obvious. What is Europe's role in the globalized condition? Ulrich Beck gives a challenging answer: 'Without Europe there is no answer to globalization'. In other words, Europe is not to be sought in the past (e.g. the Empire of Charlemagne), but must take shape as a political response to questions of the future – and particularly to the challenges of globalization. If that is right, and Beck undeniably has a point, European studies must be seen as a variant of *regional studies*, which in turn must be linked to *global studies* and *global social theory* to create a meaningful research context.

Regional players may also create institutional links between themselves – which constitutes some kind of foreign policy traditionally pursued by the EU. The emphasis on interregionalism by the European Union may in the longer run prove to be important in the reconstruction of a multi-lateral world order in a regionalized form, here called multiregionalism, meaning a horizontalized structure formed by organized regions, linked to each other through multidimensional partnership agreements. The EU ambition is to formalize the relations (now called 'partnerships') as being between two regional bodies rather than bilateral contacts bet-ween countries, but for pragmatic reasons, the forms of agreement show a bewildering variety. Nevertheless we can talk about a post-national, post-sovereign, post-Westphalian tendency. The states system would be replaced or complemented by a regionalized world order, and by a strengthened global civil society supported by a 'normative architecture' of world order values: regional multilateralism and multiculturalism.

A multipolar world order structure will most probably be based on regions, a 'new' formation closely linked to the process of globalization. The globalized condition is manifest in two very different and intri-guing concepts: civilization and world order (one from cultural and one from political studies). The first concept is a crucial part of the western heritage, the second is a more recent conceptualization, but also with a western bias.

The oldest pre-Westphalian civilizations, normally contained within regional imperial structures, were more or less insular, at least introvert (except for occasional contacts with peoples regarded as 'barbarians'). 'Civilization' (in the singular) forms part of 'the modern project' and has a clear western bias. By civilization (in its plural meaning) one can quite simply mean the supreme level of aggregation for a complex but on one plane nonetheless uniform cultural identity. Because of the high level of aggregation, essentialist interpretations should be excluded.

It contains thus both unity and diversity and is often described in religious terms (but should not be confused with religion). In Europe it was possible to combine this macro-cultural complex centred on Christianity with a decentralized political order, but elsewhere it was normally an integrated part of empire-building. It lost importance during the nation-state era (Westphalia) when the nation became the most important identity-carrier and together with other states shaped international order or what today most often is called world order. World order shapes the pattern of the global development process and may be structured differently. Thus there are different definitions.

After the First World War, Europe believed in the power of collective security through the League of Nations. After its collapse, the United Nations constituted mankind's new hope for a stable and just world order based on multilateralism and international law (and the fiction of an international community of equal states). Later, in the 1970s, there was discussion of a New International Economic Order (NIEO) and thus the issue of order *and* justice was raised on a global plane. More recently, after the first Gulf war in 1991, President George H. W. Bush coined the concept 'a new world order', based on multilateralism and international law and upheld via US hegemony. The multilateral world order, based on US hegemony, is being transformed. The question is: in what direction? The definition of world order suggested here is constituted by three dimensions: structure, mode of governance, and forms of legitimization. On the structural dimension a distinction is made between unipolar, bipolar, and multipolar, and in the area of governance between unilateral, plurilateral, and multilateral. In terms of legitimacy, finally, there is a declining scale from the rule of international law, over hegemony (which means acceptable dominance) to dominance based on coercion. Multilateralism is associated with the UN system, basically an inter-state or Westphalian system. The current world order situation can be described as a tension between multipolarity/plurilateralism/ international law (the EU approach) and unipolarity/unilateralism/ coercion (the current US approach). The tension between these two orders defines the post-September 11th era, and the way this conflict is resolved will have great implications for the future world order – unipolar or multipolar. Theoretically, there are various options of world order The liberal view of globalization (globalism), which still enjoys a hegemonic position, stresses the homogenizing impact of market forces on the creation of an open society. Liberals take a minimalist view on political authority and are sceptical of regionalism.

To interventionist thinkers on the left, who want to politicize the global differently, the liberal project is not realistic. These critics tend to see the unregulated market system as analogous to political anarchy and demand control of the market. The return of the 'political' may appear in various forms of governance. One possible form, assuming a continuous role for state authority, is a reformed 'neo-Westphalian order', governed either by a reconstituted UN system that can be called 'assertive multilateralism', or by a more loosely organized 'concert' of dominant powers, assuming the exclusive privilege of governance (including intervention) by reference to a shared value system grounded in stability and order rather than justice. This we can call 'militant plurilateralism'. The first is preferable in terms of legitimacy, but, judging from several unsuccessful attempts at reform, hard to achieve; the second is more realistic but dangerously similar to old balance-of-power politics (the Concert of Europe of the nineteenth century). The multilateral model in a more 'assertive' form would be based on radical reforms in order to upgrade the UN into a world order model. Instead, the UN has lately entered its worst crisis ever.

A more appropriate form for the return of 'the political' in today's globalized world would be a post-Westphalian order, where the locus of power moves up the ladder to the transnational level by means of the voluntary pooling of state sovereignties. The state can be replaced or complemented by a regionalized order, or by a strengthened global civil society supported by a new 'normative architecture' of world order values. 'Global cosmopolitanism' thus emphasizes the role of community at the global level, as well as the formation of global norms. There is also the possibility of moving down the ladder, which implies a decentralized, 'neo-mediaeval', world, whether constituted by self-reliant communities ('stable chaos') suggested by 'green' political theory or something more Hobbesian ('durable disorder'), which at present seems more likely. Transnational forms of government on the regional and global level are meant to prevent such a 'decline of world order' and 'pathological anarchy'.

Of course, there was never such a thing as fully fledged multilateralism. By 'false multilateralism' is meant political and military actions that take place in the guise of multilateralism, but which in reality are expressions of more limited interests: plurilateralism, if it is a matter of a group of major powers; regionalism, if it is a geographically united bloc; or unilateralism, if a superpower or regional major power is, to all intents and purposes, acting alone. Unilateralism globally obviously encourages unilateralism at the regional level. A certain kind of regionalism (interregionalism) may, however, be supportive of multilateral principles (regional multilateralism, or multiregionalism). But this is a long-term perspective and will depend on the strength of the political project of taking regionalism as the crucial element in reorganizing world order.

Index